Networks and Trans-Cultural Exchange

Atlantic World

EUROPE, AFRICA AND THE AMERICAS, 1500–1830

Edited by

Benjamin Schmidt (*University of Washington*)
Wim Klooster (*Clark University*)

VOLUME 30

The titles published in this series are listed at *brill.com/aw*

Networks and Trans-Cultural Exchange

Slave Trading in the South Atlantic, 1590–1867

Edited by

David Richardson and Filipa Ribeiro da Silva

BRILL

LEIDEN | BOSTON

Cover illustration: Photograph of Giclee print of 'Disembarkation' by Johann Moritz Rugendas (1835), by permission of the Wilberforce Institute for the study of Slavery and Emancipation, University of Hull, UK.

Library of Congress Cataloging-in-Publication Data

Networks and trans-cultural exchange : slave trading in the South Atlantic, 1590-1867 / edited by David Richardson and Filipa Ribeiro da Silva.
      pages cm. -- (Atlantic world : Europe, Africa and the Americas, 1500-1830, ISSN 1570-0542 ; volume 30)
   Includes bibliographical references and index.
   ISBN 978-90-04-28057-1 (hardback : acid-free paper) -- ISBN 978-90-04-28058-8 (e-book)
1. Slave trade--Portugal--History. 2. Slave trade--Brazil--History. 3. Slave trade--South Atlantic Ocean--History. 4. Slave trade--Africa, Sub-Saharan--History. 5. Portugal--Commerce--History. 6. Brazil--Commerce--History. 7. South Atlantic Ocean--Commerce--History. 8. Africa, Sub-Saharan--Commerce--History. 9. Business networks--South Atlantic Ocean--History. 10. Social networks--South Atlantic Ocean--History. I. Richardson, David, 1946- II. Silva, Filipa Ribeiro da, 1974-

   HT1222.N48 2014
   306.3'6209469--dc23

                              2014032338

This publication has been typeset in the multilingual "Brill" typeface. With over 5,100 characters covering Latin, IPA, Greek, and Cyrillic, this typeface is especially suitable for use in the humanities. For more information, please see www.brill.com/brill-typeface.

ISSN 1570-0542
ISBN 978-90-04-28057-1 (hardback)
ISBN 978-90-04-28058-8 (e-book)

Printed by Printforce, the Netherlands

In memory of José Capela (1932–2014), who did so much to enlighten us about the history of Lusophone Africa

∴

Contents

Acknowledgements

This volume of essays forms part of the published output of the four-year European Union, Framework Seven project entitled *Slave Trade, Slavery, Abolitions and their Legacies in European Histories and Identities* (www .EURESCL.eu), which began in 2008 and ended in 2012. Coordinated by Professor Myriam Cottias (CNRS, Paris), EURESCL brought together academics based in universities in Europe, the Americas and Africa with the goals of improving our knowledge of the history and legacies of European involvement in slavery and of making that knowledge more publicly available. These were goals shared by the University of Hull's Wilberforce Institute for the study of Slavery and Emancipation (WISE), which was one of the partners in EURESCL and which, through Professor David Richardson, then Director of WISE, assumed responsibility for the work package of which this book of essays was a part. The appointment of Dr Filipa Ribeiro da Silva, funded by EURESCL, to a two-year post-doctoral research fellowship at WISE in 2009–2011 was critical to delivery of the objectives of the work package, including this collection of essays, the publication of which she has continued actively to support during her subsequent academic appointments, first in Amsterdam and more recently in Macau. While Richardson and da Silva have been architects of the book and responsible for its completion, it could not have reached publication without the timely support and patience of the colleagues who contributed essays to it, without the unfailing encouragement of Myriam Cottias and her colleague and EURESCL manager, Nathalie Collain, and without the very positive response to our initial manuscript of our publisher and its academic readers, who made helpful suggestions for its improvement. We are especially grateful to Nozomi Goto, our managing editor at Brill, for helping to keep us on track in the publication process. Organizing what we hope is considered a coherent collection of essays on the South Atlantic world in the era of transatlantic slavery would be a challenging task in any circumstances, but the fact that some of the essays were initially written in Portuguese and had to be translated, that the various authors of the essays were scattered around the Atlantic Basin, and that in the last two years the editors were based at institutions thousands of miles apart only added to the complexity of the task. We trust that all those who have contributed to the book, but especially those authors who had to deal with our efforts to translate their work into English, will think that the final product lived up to their expectations. As editors, we remain profoundly grateful to the European Union Framework Seven Programme for the financial support and to our fellow contributors for the academic and moral support that made this book possible. The editors note with sadness that José Capela died while the book was in production and thus did not live to see his contribution in print.

We thank the Afriterra Foundation (www.afriterra.org) for permission to reproduce the image "Regna Congo et Angola, 1700," reference 419 used in Chapter 7 by Stacey Sommerdyk.

List of Graphs, Maps and Tables

List of Abbreviations

AGM	Arquivo Geral da Marinha (Lisbon, Portugal)
AHI	Archivio Storico Italiano (Florence, Italy)
AHM	Arquivo Histórico de Moçambique (Maputo, Mozambique)
AHNA	Arquivo Histórico Nacional de Angola (Luanda, Angola)
AHU	Arquivo Histórico Ultramarino (Lisbon, Portugal)
ANRJ	Arquivo Nacional do Rio de Janeiro (Rio de Janeiro, Brazil)
BML	Biblioteca Municipal de Luanda (Luanda, Angola)
BNP	Biblioteca Nacional de Portugal (former Biblioteca Nacional de Lisboa) (Lisbon, Portugal)
BNRJ	Biblioteca Nacional do Rio de Janeiro (Rio de Janeiro, Brazil)
BOGGPA	*Boletim Oficial do Governo Geral da Província de Angola*
BSGL	Biblioteca da Sociedade de Geografia de Lisboa (Lisbon, Portugal)
cx.	caixa
doc.	document
FF	*Feitos Findos*
FO	*Foreign Office*
fl(s).	folio/folios
IAN/TT	Instituto dos Arquivos Nacionais/Torre do Tombo (Lisbon, Portugal)
IHGB	Instituto Histórico Geográfico Brasileiro (Rio de Janeiro, Brazil)
JIM	*Juízo das Índias e Mina*
JU	*Justificacões Ultramarinas*
lv.	livro/book
mç.	maço
MCC	*Middelburgsche Commercie Compagnie*
MME	*Ministério dos Negócios Estrangeiros*
PRO	Public Record Office (or National Archives, Kew, UK)
SAA	Stadsarchief van Amsterdam (Amsterdam, The Netherlands)
SGL	Sociedade de Geografia de Lisboa (Lisbon, Portugal)
ZRA	Zeeland Rijksarchief (Middelburg, The Netherlands)

List of Contributors

Arlindo Manuel Caldeira
holds a degree in History (University of Lisbon) and is currently researcher at
the CHAM (Portuguese Centre for Global History) at the New University of
Lisbon, in Portugal. His main area of specialization is African history, in particular, the social and economic history of Angola and the islands of the Gulf
of Guinea, as well as the slave trade in the South Atlantic. He has published
dozens of articles and book chapters in national and international academic
journals. He is also author of three monographs on the Archipelago of São
Tomé and Príncipe. His book *Mulheres, sexualidade e casamento em São Tomé
e Príncipe (séculos XV–XVIII)*, published in 1998, was awarded the Dom João de
Castro prize, one of the most distinguished recognitions for historical research
in Portugal. His latest book is entitled *Escravos e traficantes no Império
Português. O comércio negreiro português no Atlântico durante os séculos XV
a XIX* (Lisbon, 2013).

Mariana P. Candido
teaches at the History Department at the University of Kansas. She is the
author of *An African Slaving Port and the Atlantic World. Benguela and its
Hinterland* (New York, NY: Cambridge University Press, 2013); *Fronteras de
Esclavización: Esclavitud, Comercio e Identidad en Benguela, 1780–1850* (Mexico:
Colegio de Mexico Press, 2011); and co-editor of *Crossing Memories: Slavery and
African Diaspora,* with Ana Lucia Araujo and Paul Lovejoy (Africa World Press,
2011). She has also published in *Slavery and Abolition, African Economic History,
Journal for Eighteenth-Century Studies, Portuguese Studies Review, Afro-Ásia,
Cahiers des Anneaux de la Mémoire, Luso-Brazilian Review,* and *Brésil(s):
Sciences Humaines et Sociales.*

José Capela
was a Research Fellow at the Centre of African Studies of the University of
Porto (Portugal). Between 1956 and 1968, he was chief-editor of the newspapers
Diário de Moçambique and *Voz Africana*, in Mozambique; and between 1970
and 1976 editor of the *Voz Portucalense*, published in Porto. Capela was also
cultural attaché to the Portuguese Embassy in Maputo between 1978 and 1996.
He published extensively on Portugal-Mozambique colonial relations, including: *Moçambique Pelo Seu Povo* (Porto: Edições Afrontamento, 1971);
A Burguesia Mercantil do Porto e as Colónias 1834–1900 (Porto: Edições Afrontamento, 1979); *Donas Senhores e Escravos* (Porto: Edições Afrontamento, 1997);

and more recently *O Tráfico de Escravos nos Portos de Moçambique* (Porto: Edições Afrontamento, 2002).

Roquinaldo Ferreira

is Vasco da Gama Associate Professor in the History Department and the Portuguese and Brazilian Studies Department at Brown University. He is the author of *Cross-Cultural Exchange in the Atlantic World: Angola and Brazil during the Era of the Slave Trade* (New York, NY: Cambridge University Press, 2012). He is doing research towards a Global Microhistory of the Indian textile trade (*Carreira da India*) in the Portuguese Empire.

Gustavo Acioli Lopes

(PhD University of São Paulo) is Associate Professor of Economic History at the Universidade Federal Rural de Pernambuco (UFRPE) in Brazil. Before joining the UFRPE, Gustavo also held lectureships in economic history in two other Brazilian federal universities. Acioli Lopes has published multiple articles and chapters on the Luso-Brazilian slave trade, the historiography of Brazil's colonial economy and the Atlantic economy, in both Portuguese and English languages, including several entries in *The Encyclopedia of the Middle Passage* and an article on the slave trade between Brazil and the Slave Coast. Recently, he has edited a special number on economic history for the Brazilian history journal *Saeculum*, together with Maximiliano M. Menz, with whom he has cooperated in several publications and research projects.

David Richardson

graduated from Manchester University and is Professor Emeritus in Economic History at the University of Hull, where he was founder and first Director of the Wilberforce Institute for the study of Slavery and Emancipation (2004–12). He was co-author with David Eltis of the multiple award-winning *Atlas of the Transatlantic Slave Trade* (New Haven, CT: Yale University Press, 2010) and of www.slavevoyages.com (2008) on which it was based.

Filipa Ribeiro da Silva

is Assistant Professor of History at the University of Macau (China). She is also a member of the Global Collaboratory on the History of Labour Relations at the International Institute of Social History of the Netherlands Royal Academy of Arts and Sciences and an Honorary Fellow of the Wilberforce Institute for the study of Slavery and Emancipation of the University of Hull (UK). Filipa obtained her PhD at Leiden University in 2009, after reading History and the History of Portuguese Oceanic Expansion at the New University of Lisbon, where she received her BA honours and Masters degree in 1996 and 2002, respectively. *Dutch and Portuguese in Western Africa: Empires, Merchants and the Atlantic System, 1580–1674* (Leiden: Brill, 2011) is her latest book.

Stacey Sommerdvk

is a Post-Doctoral Fellow at the Department of History at the University of the Witwatersrand. Before moving to South Africa, she obtained her doctorate at the Wilberforce Institute for the study of Slavery and Emancipation, University of Hull, UK and her Masters degree at the Tubman Institute, York University, Canada. Stacey is currently working on a book manuscript entitled "Negotiating Atlantic Spaces: The Middelburg Commercial Company on the Loango Coast, 1732–1796." She has recently published an article "Reexamining the Geography and Merchants of the West Central African Slave trade: Looking behind the Numbers" (with Filipa Ribeiro da Silva) in a special issue of *African Economic History*. Stacey's broader fields of interest are African history, merchant communities, the Dutch trading empire, the transatlantic slave trade, Atlantic history, and diaspora histories.

CHAPTER 1

Introduction

The South Atlantic Slave Trade in Historical Perspective

David Richardson and Filipa Ribeiro da Silva

Cultural encounters have been defining characteristics of the modern world. They involve the mixing of ideas, institutions and people across cultural boundaries and have produced a variety of humanly destructive as well as positive or beneficial outcomes historically. At the heart of these processes has been a millennium-long re-mixing through various forms of migration of peoples of different cultural backgrounds, a process which the European-led 'Age of Discoveries' and the associated colonization of the Americas by Portugal, Spain and other Western European powers accelerated dramatically. In tandem with colonization by Europeans there occurred a widespread collapse of the American indigenous populations through exposure to diseases to which they had no natural immunity. Faced with one on-going catastrophe, European colonial powers keen to maximum returns from the rich land and other resources of their new-established colonies sowed, according to some historians, the seeds of another by seeking to overcome insufficiency of local American supplies of manageable labour by recruiting new workers from overseas. Some came from Europe, often under some form of indenture, but the vast majority came from Africa as European ships carried across the Atlantic a rising tide of chattel slaves from the continent to work in mines and commercial agricultural activities run by Europeans. Overall, at least 12.5 million enslaved Africans boarded ship bound for the Americas in 1500–1867; some 10.7 million survived the Atlantic crossing.[1] It was the largest ocean-borne forced migration in human history, outstripping threefold or more the migration of all Europeans to the Americas before 1820.[2]

---

1   For figures on slave shipments see: www.slavevoyages.com and David Eltis and David Richardson, *Atlas of the Transatlantic Slave Trade* (New Haven, CT: Yale University Press, 2010).

2   For comparisons between transatlantic flows of Europeans and Africans and between them and coerced migrations within the Old World, see: David Eltis, "Europeans and the Rise and Fall of African Slavery in the Americas: an Interpretation," *American Historical Review* 98:5 (1993): 1399–1423; David Richardson, "Involuntary Migration in the Early Modern World, 1500–1800," in David Eltis and Stanley L. Engerman, eds., *The Cambridge World History of Slavery, Volume 3, AD1420–AD1804* (Cambridge: Cambridge University Press, 2011), 563–593.

© KONINKLIJKE BRILL NV, LEIDEN, 2015 | DOI 10.1163/9789004280588_002

According to some historians, the transatlantic slave trade had a regressive impact on African short- and long-term economic development while simultaneously 'unjustly' enriching those who profited from slave trafficking and from the production, marketing and consumption of slave-produced commodities.[3] Whatever the merits of such lines of argument are – and both remain highly contentious – it is evident that, together with Southeast Africa which became a regular supplier of African captives to the Americas from the 1780s onwards, Atlantic Africa became one of the world's major arenas of cross-cultural exchange in the three and a half centuries after Columbus' landfall in the Americas. A key goal of this collection of essays, largely written by scholars whose native language is Portuguese, is to shed new light on the workings of such exchange and thus on our overall understanding of the Atlantic slave trade as a cultural encounter.

The term 'triangular trade' has often been used to describe the Atlantic slave trade. At one level, this conceptualization may be seen to identify the linking of European capital and management skills with the labour of Africans to exploit the natural resources of the Americas. At another, it reflects the journey of ships from Europe to Africa for slaves, who were then carried across the Atlantic for sale in the Americas, with the proceeds being returned to Europe in the form of slave-grown produce, precious metals (or specie), or bills of exchange. The latter scenario reminds us of the sheer complexity of slaving voyages at a time when, in the age of sail, communications between those with vested interests in slaving voyages were often slow and erratic. It also provides in the second leg of the triangular voyage – commonly known as the 'middle passage' – a metaphor of the inhumanity and brutality of the Atlantic slave trade, as enslaved Africans, packed sardine-like on board ship for two to three months or more, struggled to survive the horrors of the Atlantic crossing or to escape their captivity through suicide or rebellion.[4] When, from the late

---

3   The classic statement of the harmful impact on Africa is to be found in Walter Rodney, *How Europe Underdeveloped Africa* (Washington, DC.: Howard University Press, 1974), while a similar and more recent assessment is to be found in Nathan Nunn, "Historical Legacies: A Model Linking Africa's Past to its Current Underdevelopment," *Journal of Development Studies* 83:1 (2007): 157–175; idem, "The Long Term Effects of Africa's Slave Trades," *Quarterly Journal of Economics* 123:1 (2008): 139–176. The classic statement of how Europe, specifically Britain, gained from transatlantic slavery is Eric Williams, *Capitalism and Slavery* (Chapel Hill, NC: University of North Carolina Press, 1944, 1994 edition) while a more recent statement is to be found in Joseph E. Inikori, *Africans and the Industrial Revolution in England: A Study in International Trade and Development* (Cambridge: Cambridge University Press, 2002).

4   For images of the packing of slaves on board ship produced by abolitionists and for data on rebellions, see: Eltis and Richardson, *Atlas*, 74, 77, 164, 189–191.

eighteenth century onwards, abolitionists attacked the slave trade, it is perhaps unsurprising that they often chose to focus attention on the middle passage and the high incidence of slave mortality on the voyage from Africa to the
Americas.

Recent research, however, has qualified the image of the Atlantic slave trade
as essentially a triangular trade. In doing so, it has suggested that in practice
there were two separate and maybe even increasingly geographically distinct
Atlantic slave-trading circuits, the patterns of which were largely dictated by
the prevailing winds and ocean currents of the north and south Atlantic. The
accompanying map 1.1, based on a recently published atlas of the transatlantic
slave trade, underlines the distinction. In the north, voyages originating in
Europe and mainland North America tended to follow a classic triangular pattern, with traders on this circuit taking advantage of the eastward-flowing
Guinea current to sail as far south as the Loango Coast, north of the River
Congo, in search of slaves before heading out across the Atlantic towards the
Americas. By contrast, voyages in which slaves were taken from south of the
Congo tended increasingly to originate not in Europe but in Brazil and, to a
much lesser extent, the Rio de la Plata. From there they pursued a bilateral
trading pattern to Africa, sailing out on the southern westerlies towards the
Cape before heading north along the African coast south of the Congo to
acquire slaves and then sailing home with the help of the Southeast trade
winds. The distinction between these two trading circuits was never wholly
absolute, as some of the essays in this volume as well as other evidence from
the online dataset of 35,000 slaving voyages attest.[5] Some voyages originating
in Europe, especially Portugal, went to places south of the Congo, while a significant proportion of those from Brazil traded bilaterally with West Africa,
particularly the Bight of Benin or Slave Coast, commonly known to Portuguese-
Brazilians as the *Costa da Mina*. But, in the age of sail, the influence of Atlantic
winds and currents on trading patterns was strong, helping to determine
'which Africans arrived in which parts of the Americas, as well as which slave-
trading nations would dominate' the different circuits.[6] This book focuses on
the South Atlantic trading circuit, which commonly tends to be neglected in

---

5   www.slavevoyages.com. There is evidence to suggest that up to 15 percent of ships docking at
    Luanda in 1736–1770 came from Lisbon, though what proportion, if any, of these were slave
    ships is unclear. The remainder came from ports in Brazil. Luiz Felipe de Alencastro, "The
    Economic Network of Portugal's Atlantic World," in Francisco Bethencourt and Diogo
    Ramada Curto, eds., *Portuguese Oceanic Expansion, 1400–1800* (Cambridge: Cambridge
    University Press, 2007), 122.
6   Eltis and Richardson, *Atlas*, 8.

the English-language literature on the Atlantic slave trade, in part because it was dominated by Portuguese-Brazilian traders.[7] The South Atlantic trading systems, however, lasted almost four centuries, as this introduction will show, and in doing so provides vital insights into the workings of the Atlantic slave trade as a whole.

The bifurcation of the Atlantic slave trading world into north and south, largely depending on the ports of origin of slaving voyages, has also been reflected in the distinction that historians typically make between West and West-Central Africa as sources of captives. In this scenario, West Africa is commonly defined as the stretch of coast between the River Senegal in the north and Cape Lopez in the south, while West-Central Africa is seen to embrace the coast between Cape Lopez and the Orange River to the south. For purposes of analysis historians have commonly sub-divided West Africa into sub-regions – from Senegambia in the north through Sierra Leone, the Windward Coast, the Gold Coast, and the Bight of Benin (or Slave Coast) to the Bight of Biafra in the south – whereas, with few exceptions, West-Central Africa has traditionally been seen as one single region.[8] This format of analysis had begun to change, however, as historians have discerned differences in trading patterns in West-Central Africa north and south of the Congo River and, even more importantly, have come to appreciate the levels of concentration of slaving activity throughout Atlantic Africa and beyond that occurred at a relatively small number – maybe ten – of trading venues located in both West and West-Central Africa traditionally defined.[9] It is now clear that the connections of these leading African slave ports with their counterparts in Europe and the Americas came to be the axes around which the operation and outcomes of the transatlantic slave trade as a form of cross-cultural exchange as well as the more general commercial integration of Africa into the Atlantic world primarily revolved.

In bringing together this collection of essays we have broadened our definition of the South Atlantic to go beyond the commercial world shaped by Atlantic winds and currents. The South Atlantic was, as other historians have shown and the essays in this volume confirm, a world largely dominated by Portuguese-Brazilian traders and other agents working in tandem with local African and mulatto (or Luso-African) groups. The core of that commercial world was the region known to contemporaries as Angola, the area of

---

7   During the whole course of the Atlantic slave trade, over one in three (or 35 percent) of voyages were outfitted in Brazilian ports (Ibid., 13).
8   This coastal classification was the one first adopted by Philip Curtin in 1969. Philip D. Curtin, *The Atlantic Slave Trade: A Census* (Madison, WI: University of Wisconsin Press, 1969).
9   Eltis and Richardson, *Atlas*, 90.

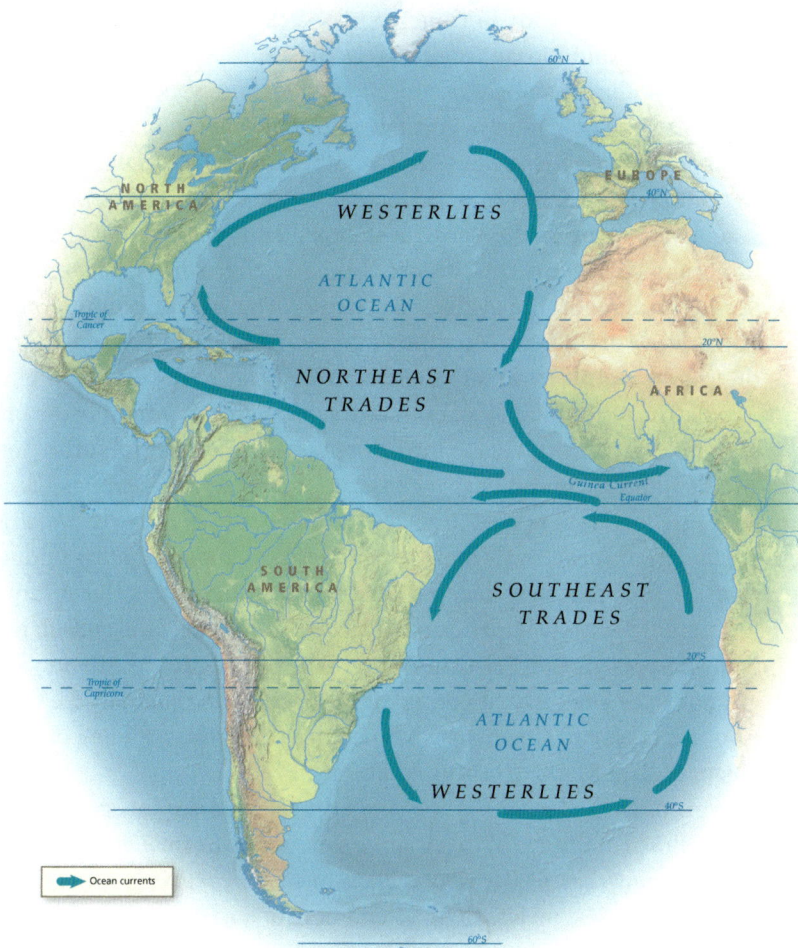

Winds – trade winds and westerlies – and ocean currents determined which Africans arrived in which parts of the Americas, as well as which slave-trading nations would dominate. The winds and currents effectively created two slave-trading systems – one in the north with voyages originating in Europe and North America, and the other in the south with voyages originating in Brazil and the Río de la Plata. For slave traders using the northern circuit, the Guinea Current that carried vessels to West Africa was also important (see Daniel Domingues da Silva, "The Atlantic Slave Trade to Maranhão, 1680–1846: Volume, Routes and Organisation," *Slavery and Abolition* 29 [2008]: 477–501).

MAP 1.1   *Atlantic winds and currents*
             Yale University Press, 2010

West-Central Africa south of the River Congo, with the Portuguese settlement at Luanda at its centre but with, in time, important independent settlements at other places, notably Benguela.[10] The commercial links that these two key

---

10   Luanda is the focal point of Joseph C. Miller's *Way of Death: Merchant Capitalism and the Angolan Slave Trade, 1730–1830* (Madison, WI: University of Wisconsin Press, 1988) and of

'Angolan' ports forged with Brazilian ports, such as Recife (Pernambuco), Salvador da Bahia and Rio de Janeiro, were pivotal to the workings of South Atlantic slave trading circuits. Appropriately, therefore, several essays in this book focus on these twin hubs of Portuguese trading operations in its Angolan core. The book also includes, however, two other essays that highlight aspects of slave trading in the South Atlantic that lay outside the Angolan-Brazil axes that were at the heart of the Portuguese-Brazilian dominance of the South Atlantic commercial world. One, by José Capela, explores the Portuguese presence at Mozambique in the eighteenth century. This was of no little importance to our study of the South Atlantic slave trade as Southeast Africa emerged from the 1780s onwards as an important source of slaves for voyages originating in Brazil. The other, by Stacey Sommerdyk, brings to our attention the presence of non-Portuguese traders in the sub-region of West-Central Africa north of the Congo known as the Loango Coast. In doing so, she reminds us that Portuguese traders were unable to sustain in the face of growing competition from northern European rivals the powerful position in slave trading throughout Atlantic Africa that they had first established in the sixteenth century. In short, Sommerdyk's essay underlines the fact that ultimately the considerable and enduring presence of Portuguese-Brazilian traders in the Atlantic slave trade primarily hinged on their control of slave trafficking south of the Congo River, though, as we note later, they did sustain a major slave-trading presence in the Bight of Benin for two centuries after 1650.

Online records of slaving voyages underline the close linkages between Angola and Brazil in the age of the Atlantic slave trade. Estimates derived from such records show that, of the 12.52 million or so slaves leaving Africa for the Americas in 1500–1867, no less than 5.85 million, or 46.7 percent, probably left in ships with Portuguese-Brazilian owners. Their closest rivals were the British, who carried an estimated 3.26 million slaves from Africa. Among all the places in Africa where slaves boarded ship, West-Central Africa, traditionally defined, accounted for almost 5.7 million captives, with the Angolan ports of Luanda and Benguela together supplying no less than an estimated 3.5 million people. Luanda and Benguela ranked first and third, respectively, among the leading African ports of slave embarkation for the Americas.[11] Although some slave

---

José Curto's *Enslaving Spirits: The Portuguese-Brazilian Alcohol Trade at Luanda and its Hinterland, c.1550–1830* (Leiden: Brill, 2004), while Benguela is the focus of Mariana P. Candido's *An African Slaving Port and the Atlantic World: Benguela and its Hinterland* (Cambridge: Cambridge University Press, 2013).

11   The second most important was Ouidah (Whydah) in the Bight of Benin, from where the Portuguese-Brazilians also carried large numbers of slaves (Eltis and Richardson, *Atlas*, 121–122).

ships trading at Luanda departed from Lisbon and other ports in Europe, as Filipa Ribeiro da Silva has shown,[12] the vast majority would ultimately originate in Brazil. In most cases, they were destined to return directly to their homeport with their human cargo. Principle among outfitting ports for slave ships in Brazil were Rio de Janeiro and Salvador da Bahia, which in terms of slaves carried from Africa individually outstripped Liverpool, Europe's premier slaving port, and collectively accounted for close to 2.9 million (or almost a third) of the 9 million slaves taken from Africa in ships with a known outfitting port.[13] Whichever way one seeks to analyze available slave voyage data, the Brazilian-Angolan South Atlantic commercial axes and, within them, linkages between Recife, Bahia, and Rio de Janeiro, on the one side, and Luanda and Benguela, on the other, were critical to understanding the growth and sustainability of the Atlantic slave trade as a whole.

The historical literature written in Portuguese has long recognized the importance of the bilateral connections across the South Atlantic to the Atlantic slave trade, but their importance has only gradually become recognized in the literature written in other languages. Publications by David Birmingham on Angola and the Portuguese, by Charles Boxer on the history of the Portuguese empire and by Philip Curtin on the Atlantic slave trade began this process in the 1960s.[14] It continued with English-language publications by, among others, Phyllis Martin, Joseph Miller, Robert Harms, John Thornton, Linda Heywood, José Curto, Mariana Candido, and Roquinaldo Ferreira on slaving and the history of West-Central Africa and by Robert Conrad, Stuart Schwartz, Mary Karasch, Herbert Klein, Francisco Vidal Luna, João Reis, Laird Bergad, and James Sweet on slavery and the African diaspora in Brazil.[15] More recently still, the publication in English of an international slave voyages

---

12   Filipa Ribeiro da Silva, "Crossing Empires: Portuguese, Sephardic, and Dutch Business
      Networks in the Atlantic Slave Trade, 1580–1674," *The Americas* 68:1 (2011): 7–32; idem,
      *Dutch and Portuguese in Western Africa: Empires, Merchants and the Atlantic System, 1580–
      1674* (Leiden: Brill, 2011).

13   On the numbers of enslaved Africans estimated to have been carried by slaving ships
      outfitted at specific ports in Brazil and Europe, see: Eltis and Richardson, *Atlas*, 39.

14   David Birmingham, *Trade and Conflict in Angola: The Mbundu and their Neighbours under
      the Influence of the Portuguese, 1483–1790* (Oxford: Clarendon Press, 1966); Charles R.
      Boxer, *The Portuguese Seaborne Empire, 1415–1825* (New York, NY: Alfred A. Knopf, 1969);
      Curtin, *Census*.

15   Phyllis M. Martin, *The External Trade of the Loango Coast, 1576–1870: The Effects of
      Changing Commercial Relations on the Vili Kingdom of Loango* (Oxford: Oxford University
      Press, 1972); Joseph C. Miller, *Kings and Kinsmen: Early Mbundu States in Angola* (Oxford:
      Clarendon Press, 1976); idem, *Way of Death*; Robert W. Harms, *River of Wealth, River of
      Sorrow: The Central Zaire Basin in the Era of the Slave and Ivory Trades, 1500–1891* (New

database, first in CD-Rom format in 1999 and then in a revised and enlarged format online in 2008 (www.slavevoyages.com), has further enhanced the process, underpinning, among other things, an atlas of the transatlantic slave trade that has thrown into even sharper historical perspective the scale, trends, and longevity of the South Atlantic slave trading world.[16] The slave voyages database provides an important evidential foundation for several of the essays in this volume, including this introduction, thereby underlining the centrality of electronic resources to ongoing research into the multi-national history of transatlantic slavery.

The atlas and other publications based on the slave voyages database show that ships owned by Portuguese and Spanish speakers dominated the Atlantic slave trade in the sixteenth and early seventeenth centuries, with Portuguese-Brazilian ships accounting for perhaps three out of four of all Africans shipped to the Americas as slaves before 1641.[17] The Portuguese-Brazilians continued to be major shippers of slaves over the following two centuries, as the essays by

---

Haven, CT: Yale University Press, 1981); John K. Thornton, *The Kingdom of Kongo: Civil War and Transition, 1641–1718* (Madison, WI: Wisconsin University Press, 1983); idem, *Africa and Africans in the Making of the Atlantic World, 1400–1680* (Cambridge: Cambridge University Press, 1992, second revised and enlarged edition, 1998); Curto, *Enslaving Spirits*; Linda Heywood and John Thornton, *Central Africans, Atlantic Creoles, and the Foundation of the Americas, 1585–1660* (Cambridge: Cambridge University Press, 2007); Bethencourt and Curto, eds., *Portuguese Oceanic Expansion*; Roquinaldo Ferreira, *Cross-Cultural Exchange in the Atlantic World: Angola and Brazil during the Era of the Slave Trade* (New York, NY: Cambridge University Press, 2012); Candido, *African Slaving Port*; Stuart B. Schwartz, *Sugar Plantations in the Formation of Brazilian Society: Bahia 1550–1835* (Cambridge: Cambridge University Press, 1985); Robert E. Conrad, *World of Sorrow: The African Slave Trade to Brazil* (Baton Rouge, LA: Louisiana University Press, 1986); Mary C. Karasch, *Slave Life in Rio de Janeiro, 1808–1850* (Princeton, NJ: Princeton University Press, 1987); João José Reis, *Slave Rebellion in Brazil: The Muslim Uprising of 1835 in Bahia* (Baltimore, MD: Johns Hopkins University Press, 1995); Laird W. Bergad, *Slavery and the Demographic and Economic History of Minas Gerais, Brazil, 1720–1888* (Cambridge: Cambridge University Press, 1999); James Sweet, *Recreating Africa: Culture, Kinship, and Religion in the African-Portuguese World, 1441–1770* (Chapel Hill, NC: University of North Carolina Press, 2003); Francisco Vidal Luna and Herbert S. Klein, *Slavery and the Economy of São Paulo, 1750–1850* (Stanford, CA: Stanford University Press, 2003); Herbert S. Klein and Francisco Vidal Luna, *Slavery in Brazil* (New York, NY: Cambridge University Press, 2009).

16 David Eltis, Stephen D. Behrendt, David Richardson and Herbert S. Klein, *The Transatlantic Slave Trade 1527–1867: A Database on CD-Rom* (Cambridge: Cambridge University Press, 1999).

17 In addition to the atlas, published by Eltis and Richardson, the slave voyages website was fundamental to *Extending the Frontiers: Essays on the New Transatlantic Slave Trade*

Arlindo Manuel Caldeira and Gustavo Acioli Lopes in this volume and other data attest. Critical to such continuing buoyancy in this branch of slave trafficking was the demand for slaves in Brazil, which, as Acioli Lopes notes, was closely related to shifts through time in the relative importance of international, especially Portuguese, markets for slave-produced goods such as tobacco, gold, coffee and sugar. In the sixteenth century, the slaves taken from Africa by Portuguese-Brazilian carriers came from Upper Guinea, notably Senegambia and Guinea-Bissau, as well as from localities around and south of the Congo estuary. Large proportions of enslaved Africans from both areas were carried in ships originating in Lisbon and Seville, the latter reflecting, among other things, the then Portuguese dominance of the *asiento*, or contract to supply Spanish America with slaves. By the 1570s, however, Portuguese-based slave ships outfitted in Iberian ports were beginning to face competition at African ports from slave ships outfitted in Brazil. This was especially so in West-Central Africa, where Lisbon ships seeking slaves to carry to Spanish America encountered Brazilian-based ships intent on acquiring slaves for the Portuguese colony. Over the following century the latter increasingly overshadowed the former, reflecting a shift in the organizational centre of the Portuguese-Brazilian slave trade from Europe to Brazil. The principal factors determining this trend were economic, linked in part at least to patterns of Atlantic winds and currents and the resulting geographical proximity of Angola to Brazilian slave ports. But political factors cannot be totally ignored as tensions and trade embargoes between the Iberian powers at the time of the separation of the Portuguese and Spanish crowns in 1640 discouraged continuing Portuguese participation in the *asiento* and would ultimately create opportunities for competitors from the Netherlands and later from England to challenge for and gain the contract.[18] The upshot of these developments was that Lisbon's status as a slave trading port declined over the seventeenth century and never fully recovered thereafter. At the same time burgeoning demand for slaves in Brazil helped to ensure continuing growth in slaving activities out of and into Recife,

---

Database (New Haven, CT: Yale University Press, 2008), edited by David Eltis and David Richardson, which, with the *Atlas*, informs the following paragraph.

18   For background to the slave trade to Spanish America and the *asiento*, see: António de Almeida Mendes, "The Foundations of the System: A Reassessment of the Slave Trade to the Spanish Americas in the Sixteenth and Seventeenth Centuries," in Eltis and Richardson, eds., *Extending the Frontiers*, 63–95; Georges Scelle, "The Slave-Trade in the Spanish Colonies of America: the *Asiento*," *American Journal of International Law* 4:3 (1910): 612–661.

Salvador da Bahia, and Rio de Janeiro. It was to be competition between the latter rather than between metropolitan and colonial ports that would largely dictate the size and direction of the Portuguese-Brazilian slave trade from the mid-seventeenth century onwards. In total, ships from each of the three major Brazilian slave ports typically carried many more slaves from Africa than ships from Lisbon. Moreover, the gap tended to grow through time. For each of the three leading Brazilian slave ports, Luanda and Benguela were consistently among the leading embarkation points for slaves in Africa throughout the time of their association with transatlantic slave trafficking.[19]

It is widely agreed that growth of slave shipments in both North and South Atlantic trading circuits was largely dictated by demand for imported slaves in American markets. Recent research on the slave trade to the Caribbean, which, together with Brazil, accounted for the great majority of slave imports into the Americas in 1520–1867, has underlined the centrality of American demand in driving growth of transatlantic slaving. Slave imports into the Caribbean rose in tandem with rising slave prices and slave labour productivity in the region.[20] Patterns of imports shifted through time from the eastern Caribbean, which led the way in terms of the sugar revolution that underpinned demand for African captives from the 1640s onwards, to the western Caribbean islands of Jamaica, Saint-Domingue, and ultimately Cuba, which, as colonies of Britain, France and Spain, respectively, tended to dominate sugar and other cash crop production in the region in the century after 1750. In effect, slave imports followed the changing geography of cash crop, especially sugar, production. Moreover, the scale of slave imports reflected not just the rising value of crop outputs, but also the 'consumption' of slaves themselves in producing crops for sale in Europe. The absorption of slaves in plantation agriculture was a chronic feature of Caribbean slavery, and while it varied between colonies, between colonial jurisdictions, between crop types, and even through time, it ensured that in many cases slave populations in the Caribbean failed to sustain

19   Lisbon ships supplied some slaves to Brazil after 1642, including the north-eastern and south-central areas served by the three principal slaving ports of Brazil, but in the second half of the eighteenth century a major destination for slaves shipped by Lisbon vessels was Amazonia, which absorbed over 150,000 enslaved Africans in that period. These slaves, however, came principally from Senegambia, not West-Central Africa. Eltis and Richardson, eds., *Extending the Frontiers*, 268.

20   David Eltis, Frank D. Lewis and David Richardson, "Slave Prices, the African Slave Trade and Productivity in the Caribbean, 1674–1807," *Economic History Review* 58:4 (2005): 673–700.

themselves through natural reproduction.[21] Though various factors were involved, sugar production seems to have had a decisive influence on this outcome. Satisfying Europe's growing addiction to sugar had major implications for the scale and intensity of slave trafficking into the Caribbean between the 1640s and the early nineteenth century.[22]

Like the Caribbean, Brazil's history during colonization was largely dominated by large-scale capitalist production of sugar and other cash crops. In some cases, in fact, it preceded the Caribbean in such activities, with evidence of investment in sugar plantations dating from the mid-sixteenth century and of expansion of both sugar production and other slave-based activities continuing at varying rates even as cash crop production spread through the West Indies from the 1640s onwards.[23] Evidence of long-run trends of slave prices in Brazil is less robust than for the Caribbean, but there are indications that prices tended to fall as Portuguese-Brazilian producers faced competition in international sugar markets from rival and possibly more efficient producers in the Caribbean.[24] Moreover, there is strong evidence that self-sustained growth of slave populations was achieved in Brazil in Minas Gerais where slave-based economies diversified production towards local rather than primarily export markets.[25] In these and other respects, therefore, Brazil's evolution as a slave-owning society may have diverged from the Caribbean model.

Nevertheless, similarities between the Caribbean model and the situation in Brazil are discernible. As Acioli Lopes notes in his essay in this volume, variations in flows of slave arrivals in Brazil were closely linked to changes in rates of growth of the colony's export-orientated products such as sugar, tobacco, coffee, and gold and precious stones. Furthermore, periods of most rapid expansion in output of such exports were commonly identified with uplifts in slave prices, as, for example, during the gold boom in the first half of the eighteenth century

---

21   David Eltis and Paul Lachance, "The Demographic Decline of Caribbean Slave Populations: New Evidence from the Transatlantic and Intra-American Slave Trades," in Eltis and Richardson, eds., *Extending the Frontiers*, 335–365.

22   Michael Tadman, "The Demographic Cost of Sugar: Debates on Slave Societies and Natural Increase in the Americas," *American Historical Review* 105:5 (2000): 1534–1575.

23   Schwartz, *Sugar Plantations*.

24   For price data and their limitations, see: Joseph C. Miller, "Slave Prices in the Portuguese Southern Atlantic, 1600–1830," in Paul E. Lovejoy, ed., *Africans in Bondage: Studies in Slavery and the Slave Trade* (Madison, WI: University of Wisconsin Press, 1986), 43–77; Bergad, *Slavery and the Demographic and Economic History of Minas Gerais*, 160–215.

25   Bergad, *Slavery and the Demographic and Economic History of Minas Gerais*, 144, 171–172, 185.

and during the so-called 'renaissance' of the sugar sector and the rise of coffee exports from the 1790s linked, among other things, with improving labour productivity in both sectors.[26] Such changes were, in turn, associated with geographical shifts in the long-term centre of gravity of commercial activity in Brazil from Pernambuco in the north, which pioneered sixteenth-century Brazilian commercial sugar production, towards Salvador da Bahia and ultimately São Paulo in the south. These shifts were mirrored in the long run in first Bahia's eclipse of Recife and then Rio de Janeiro's eclipse of both as the leading Brazilian slave port, whether for outfitting slaving voyages or for importing enslaved Africans.[27] Moreover, while some areas of Brazil may have attained natural growth of slave populations in time, surges in and continuing commitment to export-orientated commercial activity seem to have been commonly identified with heavy reliance on imports of slaves from elsewhere, including slave arrivals from Africa, the male dominance of which typically proved inimical to slave reproduction in the principal localities affected. This applied to sugar cultivation in rural Bahia, to mining activities in eighteenth-century Minas Gerais, and to those parts of São Paulo which embraced first sugar and then coffee production from the late eighteenth century onward.[28]

---

26 See: Miller, "Slave Prices." See also: Bergad, *Slavery and the Demographic and Economic History of Minas Gerais*, 163–167, who relates changes in slave prices in Minas Gerais in 1715–1780 to cycles in gold production for export. He also argues that while there was little evidence of upward movement in slaves prices in Minas Gerais in the early decades of the agricultural renaissance after 1790, prices moved sharply upward in the 1820s (and thereafter) in tandem with coffee's "spread dynamically throughout Rio de Janeiro, São Paulo, and in southeastern Minas in districts to the north of the Paraíba River," attributing these movements to "the general expansion of Brazil's coffee export economy [that] had a marked impact on the economic structures of the province" (167). On the growth of coffee production, see: the essay by Acioli Lopes in this volume and Luna and Klein, *Slavery and the economy of São Paulo*, which identifies some improvement in both sugar and coffee outputs per slave in that province between 1817 and 1854 (51, 73).

27 On shifts in patterns of slave arrivals between Brazilian regions after 1776–1800, see: Eltis and Richardson, *Atlas*, 203.

28 In the absence of direct information on slave arrivals in specific commercial export crop-growing localities in Brazil, the strongest indicators of reliance on imported captives to sustain enslaved populations may be found in ratios of African-born to Creole slave numbers and of enslaved children to women. These suggest that in some parts of Minas Gerais slave populations were self-sustaining by the end of the eighteenth century, but this may not have happened in the Diamantina region until around 1820 (Bergad, *Slavery and the Demographic and Economic History of Minas Gerais*, 130–144) and not until probably even later in the sugar-growing areas of Bahia and sugar- and coffee-growing areas of São Paulo (Schwartz, *Sugar Plantations*, 359; Luna and Klein, *Slavery and the economy of São Paulo*, 51, 156).

As in the Caribbean, therefore, Brazil's demand for imported slaves rested on both expanding production for export markets and the demographic deficits among slave populations often associated with it.

Almost a quarter of the 4.86 million Africans estimated to have disembarked in Brazil as slaves are thought to have boarded ship in Atlantic Africa north of the Congo River.[29] As noted earlier, Senegambia and the Bight of Benin were among the principal embarkation points of such slaves. Links with Senegambia first developed in the sixteenth century, largely as a result of activities by Lisbon-based traders, who continued to dispatch slave ships to Africa in the following centuries, both to Senegambia and to venues further south in Atlantic Africa and beyond. Estimates suggest that between 1642 and 1863 ships outfitted in Lisbon carried over 410,000 captives from Africa, almost one third of whom boarded ship between Senegambia and the Congo River.[30] Many of these, including high proportions of those boarded at Senegambia, were destined for Amazonia, notably from the 1760s onwards, the rest being largely shipped to Recife, Bahia, and Rio de Janeiro. Overall, however, the principal source of slaves taken from West Africa to Brazil was the Bight of Benin, commonly known to Portuguese-Brazilian traders as the 'Mina Coast'. Initiated by Lisbon-based traders, Portuguese-Brazilian slaving activity in this region was increasingly dominated from the mid-seventeenth century onwards by Brazilian-based traders, especially those resident in Bahia, who forged commercial ties with Ouidah and other ports at Mina or the 'Slave Coast', bartering Brazilian-produced tobacco and gold, among other things, for slaves.[31] Later, from the last third of eighteenth century, Porto Novo and then Lagos also became important slave ports in the Bight of Benin for Bahian and other Portuguese-Brazilian ships. Relative to other Brazilian regions, therefore, Amazonia and Bahia obtained large proportions of their slaves from Africa

---

29   For figures on the embarkation points in Africa of slaves carried by ships leaving Lisbon, Recife, Salvador da Bahia and Rio de Janeiro, see: David Eltis and David Richardson, *Atlas*, 43, 46, 61, 66–69, 76, 80–83.
30   For figures on slaves carried by ships from Lisbon, see: Ibid., 61, 76.
31   On tobacco, see: Pierre Verger, *Flux et Reflux de lu Traite des Negres entre le Golfe de Benin et Bahia de Todos os Santos du XVIIe au XIXe Siècle* (Paris: Mouton & Co, 1968) and Jean-Baptista Nardi, *O Fumo Brasileiro no Período Colonial: Lavoura, Comércio e Administração* (São Paulo: Editoria Brasiliense, 1996). On gold in slave transactions, see: E.W. Evans and David Richardson, "Empire and Accumulation in Eighteenth-Century Britain," in Terry Brotherstone and Geoffrey Pilling, eds., *History, Economic History, and the Future of Marxism: Essays in Memory of Tom Kemp (1921–1993)* (London: Porcupine Press, 1996), 79–103; Judith M. Spicksley, "Pawns on the Gold Coast: the Rise of Asante and Shifts in Security for Debt, 1680–1750," *Journal of African History* 54:2 (2013): 147–175.

north of the equator. Of these flows, the larger was plainly towards Bahia. This had important consequences for the ethnic identity of diasporic Africans in these areas of Brazil as well as its links with the history of slave resistance, notably in the 1835 Male slave revolt in Bahia.[32]

Overall, however, the number of slaves entering Brazil through South Atlantic trade circuits greatly exceeded that from West Africa north of the equator. Detailed estimates of the movement of slaves to Brazil through the South Atlantic are presented in Table 1.1. The figures are based on total shipments of slaves from five key ports in Atlantic Africa south of Cape Lopez – Luanda, Benguela, Cabinda, Malemba, and Ambriz – and shipments from two ports – Mozambique Island and Quelimane – in Southeast Africa. These include slaves carried by ships outfitted in Lisbon as well as in Brazilian ports. The figures in column 2 of the table show the total estimated number of all slaves shipped from these seven ports; those in column 3 are estimates of the numbers arriving in Brazil from the same seven African ports. In aggregate, some 5.55 million African captives are estimated to have boarded ship at them; of those who survived the Atlantic crossing, almost 3.8 million disembarked in

TABLE 1.1   *Slave departures from selected ports in West-Central and Southeast Africa and arrivals in Brazil, 1582–1864*

(1) Ports and Period	(2) Departures (in thousands)	(3) Arrivals (in thousands)	(4) (3)/(2) (in percent)
Luanda 1582–1850	2826	2262	80.1
Malemba 1660–1861	549	84	15.3
Mozambique Island 1664–1859	293	157	53.4
Cabinda 1681–1863	753	359	47.7
Benguela 1688–1864	764	663	86.8
Ambriz 1786–1863	206	141	68.4
Quelimane 1797–1852	159	132	83.0
Totals	5550	3798	68.4

Source: Eltis and Richardson, *Atlas*

---

32   Reis, *Slave Rebellion*.

Brazil. Of these totals, 5.1 million (or almost 92 percent) boarded ship on the Atlantic coast of Africa and 452,000 (8 percent) in Southeast Africa, while 3.5 million (or 92.1 percent) of those landing in Brazil came from Atlantic Africa and 288,000 (7.9 percent) from Southeast Africa. Allowing for variations in slave mortality at sea, which partially explains the differences in the totals of columns 1 and 2, the Brazilian market for slaves clearly constituted the dominant market for slaves from Luanda, Benguela, Ambriz and Quelimane throughout their history as slave ports. It was also, as we shall see, the leading market for other ports covered in Table 1.1 at certain times in their history.

Disaggregating the data in Table 1.1 and focusing on patterns across individual ports, two important features of the South Atlantic slave trading circuits supplying Brazil are evident. One is the centrality of Luanda throughout the history of Brazil's slave import trade. The first major slave port to emerge in Atlantic Africa south of the Congo, Luanda is estimated to have dispatched over 2.8 million African captives into transatlantic slavery between 1582 and 1850. This amounted to some 22 percent of all slaves entering the Atlantic slave trade as a whole and more than half of those entering the South Atlantic system as defined by Table 1.1. It accounted, in turn, for some 61 percent of slave arrivals into Brazil from the seven ports included in the table. The other feature is that despite Luanda's continuing leading position as a slave supplier to Brazil before 1850, other ports emerged in time as suppliers too. The first was Mozambique Island in Southeast Africa, which Brazilian-based ships, especially from Bahia, occasionally visited in the century after 1664. Mozambique Island, however, only became a regular source of slaves for Brazil from the last third of the eighteenth century. By then, Benguela, south of Luanda, had also emerged as an important source of slaves for the Brazilian market. Ships from Brazil occasionally stopped at Benguela for slaves from the late seventeenth century onward, and possibly even earlier, but a more regular and increasingly extensive trade in slaves developed there after 1730, with slave shipments averaging around 6,000 a year in 1740–1850 and in the nineteenth century challenging in some years the totals dispatched from Luanda.[33] No other African port in the South Atlantic trading circuits threatened to challenge Luanda's position to the extent that Benguela did in the second quarter of the nineteenth

---

33   On the possibility that Benguela was a source of slaves before 1690, the first recorded date of slave ships visiting the port, see: Candido, *African Slaving Port*, 150–152. Some, if not most, of those early 'Benguela' slaves may have been shipped coastwise to Luanda, whence they were dispatched to the Americas. In that respect, they would be included among captives leaving Luanda. The firmest early evidence of direct shipments to Brazil from Benguela dates, as Candido notes (p. 161), from around 1725.

century, but the four others noted in Table 1.1 certainly followed it in developing sizeable slave-trading links with Brazil. Quelimane, like Mozambique Island, in Southeast Africa, began dispatching slaves to Brazil from the late 1790s and remained thereafter a regular source of slaves for it through 1850. It was joined after 1807 by Ambriz, Cabinda and Malemba, all of them in Atlantic Africa but, unlike Benguela, located to the north of Luanda.

The patterns of slave trading evinced by Table 1.1 raise four questions. First, why was Luanda so pivotal to the South Atlantic trade circuits on which Brazilian-based producers of commercial crops and other goods relied for slave supplies? Second, why did Portuguese-Brazilian shippers look more regularly to other ports in southern Africa as sources of slaves from the early eighteenth century onward? Third, what explains the chronology of entry of those other ports into the South Atlantic slave trade to Brazil? And, fourth, what are the implications, if any, of the factors underlying that chronology for our understanding of the Portuguese-Brazilian role in the Atlantic slave trade? The existing historiography throws some light on these questions. So, too, do the other essays in this volume.

To explain Luanda's dominance of the South Atlantic we need briefly to review Portugal's early history in Atlantic Africa. The Portuguese were the first Europeans to make contact by sea with local peoples along Africa's Atlantic coast and, through their base in Luanda, were from the 1570s onward the only ones to establish a major colonial presence in Africa before the nineteenth century.[34] Portugal's exploration of Africa during the fifteenth century was prompted by a mix of commercial, political and religious motives, which, in turn, encouraged from the 1480s diplomatic exchanges between African states and Portugal; the founding of forts at Elmina and other places on the Gold Coast in 1482–1523; and, importantly, alliances with West Central African states from 1483 onward. Pivotal to the earliest of these alliances was the Kingdom of Kongo, which ruled some 300,000 people in a core territory of some 100,000 square kilometres. From the beginning Luso-Kongolese relations involved both violent and spiritual (or ideological) interventions by the Portuguese. They included military and other aid to Kongo in conflicts with rivals such as Ndongo, Teke, and Matamba and efforts to convert Kongo elites to Christianity. The former anticipated the bloodshed later to be associated with commercial exchanges based on slave trafficking; the latter, the social capital

---

34   The rest of this paragraph draws on Joel Quirk and David Richardson, "Europeans, Africans and the Atlantic World, 1450–1850," in Shogo Suzuki, Yongjin Zhang and Joel Quirk, eds., *International Orders in the Early Modern World: Before the Rise of the West* (London: Routledge, 2013), 147–152.

and networking that would prove critical in promoting efficiency in such exchanges at the coast. The historians Linda Heywood and John Thornton have suggested that the introduction of Christianity encouraged the emergence within Kongo of local groups with Afro-European identities.[35] Though the extent to which these 'Atlantic Creoles' abandoned their traditional local cosmologies is open to debate, as James Sweet has observed, their emergence was, nevertheless, an important factor in creating the social and institutional foundations upon which later Luso-African exchanges would develop.[36] By the early sixteenth century such exchanges already included slaves, in this case bound for Portuguese-owned sugar plantations in São Tomé.[37] In retrospect we now know that this was just the prelude to the much larger South Atlantic slave trade that from the mid-sixteenth century would dominate Luso-African relations for the next three centuries. Luanda was central to that story.

Portuguese efforts to build a settlement at Luanda began in the 1570s nearly a century after their first contact with Kongo. They may have originated with problems in Kongo itself, which was largely overrun in the late 1560s by Imbangala invaders. The invaders were repelled with the help of troops sent from Lisbon, but the episode exposed Kongo's weakness and its reliance on Portuguese support. It also served to expose the vulnerability of Portuguese traders and settlers in the region at the very time when external demand for slaves was growing.[38] This perhaps helps to explain why in 1571 King Sebastião of Portugal issued a charter to Paulo Dias de Novais, granting him extensive economic privileges in exchange for his efforts to 'subjugate and conquer the Kingdom of Angola' and to establish a new colony south of the River Congo.[39] Novais chose to locate his base at Luanda, where a slave trade had already begun to emerge. The chief obstacle to this plan was the state of Ndongo inland, which was less centralized than Kongo, and had many relatively autonomous sobas (local vassals) who paid tribute to it. Novais' efforts to build alliances with Ndongo proved unstable, precipitating armed conflict at times. Moreover, sickness and warfare ensured that of the several thousand Portuguese immigrants into Luanda after 1575, only a few hundred still survived in 1594.[40] But with support from migrants who relocated from Kongo and its governors' skills in allying with local sobas and other groups, Luanda began

---

35   Heywood and Thornton, *Central Africans*, 67.
36   Sweet, *Recreating Africa*, 113.
37   Eltis and Richardson, *Atlas*, 7.
38   Birmingham, *Trade and Conflict in Angola*, 42–48.
39   Heywood and Thornton, *Central Africans*, 82.
40   Curto, *Enslaving Spirits*, 56.

to prosper as a Portuguese-Brazilian slave-trading base. Its position was further enhanced when the Portuguese crown assumed responsibility for it after Novais died.[41] From Luanda the Portuguese expanded their territorial rule as well as their larger sphere of influence from the late sixteenth century onward. In doing so, they encountered setbacks, including a disastrous invasion of Kongo in 1622–1623 and the Dutch occupation of Luanda in 1641–1648 in alliance with Kongo. These, however, did not prevent the long-term consolidation of Portuguese power at Luanda and in its immediate hinterland through continuing financial and other support from the Portuguese crown and internal divisions among the other regional powers. Such divisions were to be a major source, sometimes in conjunction with regional famines, which they helped to exacerbate, of many of the captives shipped from Luanda.[42] They also provided opportunities for the Luanda authorities to establish new settlements and forts in the interior as they sought, in tandem with local allies, to develop their capacity to satisfy long-term growth in Brazilian demand for enslaved labour.[43]

Though a community with a constantly changing mix of African and Portuguese-Brazilian people that probably never exceeded 10,000 in number before 1850, Luanda, as the political hub of Portugal's embryonic empire in West-Central Africa, exercised a centripetal influence over the South Atlantic sector of the Atlantic slave trade unmatched in the trade's long history.[44] The reasons are not difficult to uncover. Luanda offered a safe anchorage and place of trade for slave ships. It came to develop a commercial infrastructure, range of services, and a knowledge base of markets unrivalled in the South Atlantic trading world. And the consolidation of its trading hinterland and the networks of agents that underlay it provided security for the dispersal inland of the

---

41   Miller, *Kings and Kinsmen*, 176–223.

42   On the significance of famine, see: Joseph C. Miler, "The Significance of Drought, Disease and Famine in the Agriculturally-Marginal Zones of West-Central Africa," *Journal of African History* 23:1 (1982): 17–61.

43   Miller, *Kings and Kinsmen*, 196; Miller, *Way of Death*, 230–231; Silva, *Dutch and Portuguese*, 188–190.

44   The fullest and possibly most reliable population figures exist for the period after 1780 and suggest a peak population of just under 10,000 in 1781, subsiding to less than 5,000 in the 1810s and then recovering modestly through 1844 (José C. Curto and Raymond R. Gervais, "The Population History of Luanda during the late Atlantic Slave Trade, 1781–1844," *African Economic History* 29 (2001): 1–59, especially 52). By way of comparison, Benguela's population was said in 1796 to number just under 1,500 people, over 1,100 of them reported as being slaves. This excluded people, free and enslaved, living in neighbouring residential areas (Candido, *African Slaving Port*, 107).

textiles, liquor and other imported goods used to barter slaves, for the credit embodied in such goods, and for the reciprocal movement of large numbers of enslaved Africans to the coast. Arguably, however, none of these things would have mattered without the identification of African polities as trading partners and military allies of Luanda-based merchants and agents and the incentive mechanisms that induced them to form such alliances. Large proportions of the slaves passing through Luanda to overseas markets were acquired through wars and raids, some of them initiated by the Portuguese but almost always primarily fought by their African allies. The process is vividly and succinctly portrayed by historian Joseph Miller in his monumental study of Luanda's involvement in the South Atlantic slave trade. Miller writes that in the seventeenth century slave trading caravans 'accompanied marauding armies...waiting in the rear to exchange textiles and wines for people'.[45] By the following century, he goes on to argue, 'African political institutions specialized in conducting most of the warfare associated with slaving, while the European-financed caravans of that period limited themselves to the more purely commercial ties between central markets, in which flowed the captives seized in battle between African armies'.[46] A separation of enslavement and slave marketing activities thus became discernible in time, perhaps encouraged by extensions of enslavement frontiers inland as Portuguese-Brazilian demand for captive Africans mounted. We shall return to that issue later. For the moment it is evident African demand for imported trade goods channelled through Luanda proved a powerful motivator of the violent seizures of people for trade while the extensive credit-based trading networks radiating out from Luanda created systems of dependency and security to ensure their victims' passage to the sea.

One of ten African slaving ports that would eventually control some two-thirds of all shipments of Africans as slaves to the Americas through 1867, Luanda was by a considerable margin the leader among such ports. Moreover, it continued to dominate slave shipments south of the equator well into the nineteenth century. But despite its geographical, political, and other advantages, Luanda failed to sustain the near monopoly of slave shipments to Brazil from Africa south of the equator that it established in the seventeenth century. Six other African ports in the southern hemisphere would eventually join Luanda in supplying slaves to Brazil. Benguela, south of Luanda, which is the subject of Mariana Candido's contribution to this volume as well as her recent book, was the first to do so on a regular basis from around 1730.[47] Sixty years

---

45   Miller, *Way of Death*, 196.
46   Ibid., 197.
47   Candido, *African Slaving Port*.

later, around 1790, Mozambique Island and Quelimane in Southeast Africa began regularly to ship slaves to Brazil. José Capela's essay in this volume examines their early connections with the Portuguese-speaking world. Finally, in the early nineteenth century, the ports of Ambriz south of the River Congo, and Cabinda and Malemba north of it on the Loango Coast emerged as important sources of slaves for Brazil. Stacey Sommerdyk's essay in this volume offers insights into the eighteenth-century history of Malemba, which drew slaves from Kongo among other places, before it became a source of African captives for Brazil. The chronological order in which these six ports began supplying slaves to Brazil is an important focal point of the rest of this introductory essay.

The motives encouraging slave carriers to Brazil to search for new sources of captives from the late seventeenth century onward probably originate in slave price trends at Luanda itself. These, as Miller has shown, increasingly shadowed those in Brazil.[48] Evidence relating to Luanda prices is patchy before the mid-seventeenth century but is more abundant, if still sometimes problematical to interpret, for the following two centuries. From these data three long upswings are discernible in real slave prices at Luanda (measured in terms of the goods exchanged for slaves) from the late sixteenth century through the 1840s. The first occurred before 1640, after which prices levelled out or even fell back at times through 1690. The second upswing then began in the 1690s and continued through the 1730s, when prices came close to matching those of the pre-1640 peak, before prices then flattened out again for the next fifty years. This second era of price stability ended around 1790 as Luanda prices again began to climb in the 1790s and continued to do so through the 1830s and beyond, reaching unprecedented levels in the process and easily eclipsing previous peaks.

The key long-run drivers of these Luanda price trends largely lay in Brazil and specifically its capacity to compete internationally for consumers of its slave-produced goods. The early near monopoly of New World sugar supplies to Europe largely explains slave price rises in Brazil and thus in Luanda before 1640. The loss of that monopoly in the face of increasingly competitive and expansive sugar production in the Caribbean from the 1640s also largely explains the low level of slave prices in the South Atlantic for much of the following century and a half, as Acioli Lopes' essay in this volume reminds us. A boom in gold and precious stone exports from Minas Gerais, however, helped to stem and even reverse that trend for several decades after 1690 and then an 'agricultural renaissance' in Brazil after 1790, linked in large part to problems in sugar

---

48   Miller, "Slave Prices," 43–77.

and coffee production in the contemporary Caribbean, triggered the renewed rise in slave prices in both Brazil and Luanda that would last more or less through the mid-nineteenth century. It was in the two main periods of slave prices rises after 1640 – 1690–1740 and 1790–1850 – that other ports in southern Africa joined Luanda as suppliers of slaves to Brazil. Between these two periods of price upswings, slave arrivals in Brazil from Africa quadrupled from about 10,000 to 40,000 a year, with the vast majority travelling through South Atlantic trade routes. Luanda contributed substantially to this increase, but its share diminished in time as, in succession, Benguela, then Southeast Africa and, finally, ports north of Luanda entered the trade. As Miller noted, after 1810 Brazil 'had to receive a growing percentage of its slaves from the Loango Coast and Mozambique'.[49]

Underlying the diversification in slave-supply routes were various factors. One was the increasing role of Rio de Janeiro in Brazilian-based slave trafficking, which itself reflected the southward shift of the centre of gravity of the Brazilian slave economy from the seventeenth century onward that was noted earlier. Except for Malemba, where Bahia traders congregated by the 1820s, Rio-based shippers typically took much higher shares of slaves from other South Atlantic African ports than they did from Luanda. Thus, whereas ships from Bahia and Recife together accounted for almost as many slaves leaving Luanda in 1582–1850 as ships from Rio de Janeiro, ships from Rio accounted for three times as many slaves leaving Benguela in 1688–1864 as those from Recife and Bahia combined. Moreover, with the exception of Malemba mentioned above, this pattern was replicated, sometimes with even greater disparities in ratios, at other ports in southern Africa frequented by Brazilian-based slave ships from the late eighteenth century onward.[50] At one level, this might be seen as no more than a reflection of the timing of Rio de Janeiro's growing importance in the South Atlantic slave trade. But it might equally suggest that as relatively late entrants into slave trafficking compared to their rivals at Recife and Bahia, merchants from Rio de Janeiro were more prepared to look outside established commercial channels in order to develop their competitive edge and grow their slaving business. However one interprets it, Rio de Janeiro's rise to dominance of the Portuguese-Brazilian slave trade from the late eighteenth century matched that of Liverpool in the north Atlantic slave trade by 1790 and like their British counterparts, who traded for slaves in West Africa, the success of merchants based in Rio de Janeiro owed much to their

---

49   Ibid., 59.
50   For the data underlying this argument, see: Eltis and Richardson, *Atlas*, 143, 147, 149, 151, 153, 156, 158.

willingness to exploit new trading opportunities at African locations south of the equator.[51]

Two other factors perhaps underlay the role of merchants from Rio de Janeiro in reconfiguring patterns of slave supply in the South Atlantic between 1700 and 1850. The first was a decline through time in the capacity of slave suppliers at Luanda to respond to changes in external slave price incentives. The second was changing perceptions of the costs of or barriers to opening up additional sources of slaves at South Atlantic ports other than Luanda. Such costs or barriers varied among the ports concerned and probably helped to determine the sequence in which they emerged as sources of slaves for Brazilian markets. The two factors were in some ways inter-related but merit separate attention as determinants of the changing geographical and ethnic diversity of sources of slaves reaching Brazil through Southern Atlantic trade circuits by 1800.

Because Luanda was for so long the dominant source of slaves for the South Atlantic, it is tempting to neglect possible constraints on its traders' responsiveness to external demand for slaves. Yet it is precisely because of its dominance that constraints on slave supply at Luanda could have been associated with changes in the geography of slave embarkations across the South Atlantic. Whether or not historians have explored that connection, they have produced evidence consistent with the emergence of long-term barriers to slave supply responsiveness at Luanda. Candido has argued that, as the centre of Portuguese administration in Angola, it became difficult for traders visiting Luanda, unlike those visiting Benguela, 'to avoid fiscal control over their business by the Crown'.[52] In addition, Miller has shown that trading margins on shipping slaves between Angola (effectively Luanda) and Brazil were much narrower from the 1760s onwards than before.[53] This remained the case even during the agricultural renaissance in Brazil when slave prices reached unprecedented levels. The causes of this decline in estimated trading margins are not wholly clear but since Miller's own calculations suggest a fall in the burden of oceanic shipping costs between the 'early' and 'late' slave trade from Angola to Brazil, it appears that they are most likely to be found in Angola, where, on the evidence adduced by Miller, coastal prices of slaves may have risen relative to those in Brazil over the eighteenth century. As Miller himself has noted, declines in the

---

51   On the strength of Liverpool's presence in the eighteenth-century slave export trade, for example, at Sierra Leone, the Windward Coast, and the Bight of Biafra, see: Ibid., 100, 108, 129, 131–132, 134.

52   Candido, *African Trading Port*, 162.

53   Miller, "Slave Prices," 63.

mid-eighteenth century Brazilian *réis* price for slaves produced no comparable decline in the value of the prime *peça* slave in Africa.[54] The most likely cause of such tendencies, Miller argues, were higher slave purchase and delivery costs in the interior, linked in turn to the increasing reliance by Luanda slave dealers on supplies of captives from more remote regions inland and to higher transit costs, including slave mortality, associated with them. Exacerbating such problems were other factors, including growing competition for slaves within Angola itself as near coast areas sought to rebuild populations lost through earlier violent raids by acquiring some captives bound for Luanda and as African slave suppliers to Loango Coast ports, eager to accommodate slave traders from Europe, began to draw on 'the same hinterland that Portuguese and Brazilian merchants tapped through Luanda'.[55] It is highly likely, therefore, that the slave supply curve to Luanda dealers moved upwards over the course of the eighteenth century, thereby reducing their historic advantages as a source of slaves relative to potential rivals and providing an incentive for Portuguese-Brazilian carriers to seek African captives at other ports.

Seen from the perspective of Brazilian-based traders, innovations in slave procurement, of which diversification in places of embarkation of captives was clearly one, might be considered as exercises in risk management. Historians have widely acknowledge that slaving voyages were risk-filled ventures, whether in relation to slave transactions at the African coast, to the survival rate of captives in transit, to the sale of survivors in the Americas, or to the recovery of payment for them. But pursuing new trade opportunities in Africa, even when slave price incentives in Brazil were strong, may well be thought to have compounded for Brazilian-based traders the risks commonly identified with coastal slaving activities even at established ports such as Luanda. Such initiatives required the negotiation of protocols for governing the conduct of transactions (and for the resolution of disputes that inevitably arose in relation to them) if trade was to be established and to grow.[56] These were not risk-free, but took time to develop and typically required investment in iterative exchange, social capital and networking, key issues for the essays included in

---

54   Ibid., 57.

55   Ibid., 56, 66 (quotation). Candido notes that as early as 1727–1734 Luanda traders were complaining that while they advanced goods on credit to *pombeiros* intent on visiting inland markets for slaves, those same *pombeiros* delivered the slaves they acquired to Benguela 'where slavers were offering better prices' (Candido, *African Slaving Port*, 162).

56   For background to such issues, see: Alencastro, "Economic Network," 109–137; David Richardson, "Cultures of Exchange: Atlantic Africa during the Era of the Slave Trade," *Transactions of the Royal Historical Society*, sixth series, 19 (2009): 151–179.

this book. This also applied to the establishment of specific local practices relating to barter arrangements for the purchase of slaves, to the credit needed to lubricate transactions, and to the turnaround times of ships in port.[57] All these had potential implications for rates of slave survival in transit, the market price of captives in Brazil, and ultimately the financial outcome of voyages.

The growing contribution of southern African ports outside Luanda to slave supplies to Brazil suggests that, on balance, Brazilian-based carriers successful managed the risks associated with that transition. Reflecting on its chronology offers two insights into how it occurred. One draws on claims made by historian Philip Curtin some forty years ago (and subsequently endorsed by other scholars) that pre-existing forms of commercial diasporas were often vital in supporting subsequent growth of slaving activities.[58] Our analysis offers confirmation of that claim. The other draws attention to the wider Atlantic political context in which expansion of Portuguese-Brazilian slaving across the South Atlantic occurred. In doing so, it leads us also to reflect on how international politics helped to determine the ending of the South Atlantic slave trade, a subject to which Roquinaldo Ferreira's essay in this volume refers. We explore each of these issues in turn.

In widening geographically their slave purchasing in the South Atlantic, Brazilian-based traders did not initiate *ab initio* commercial exchange with the ports concerned. To the contrary, each port had pre-existing forms of Afro-European commercial exchange before Brazilian-based slave traders arrived. There were, as both Candido and Capela remind us, resident Portuguese and Afro-Portuguese at Benguela, Mozambique Island and Quelimane years before Portuguese-Brazilians began regularly to acquire slaves there. Transcending race and, at Benguela, even gender, as Candido notes, these groups were commonly integrated into the local and regional socio-economic networks that supported cross-cultural exchange in various commodities, including slaves. As a result, they offered a commercial platform from which transatlantic slave trafficking with fellow Portuguese-speaking Brazilian-based traders might develop. In this respect, the pre-existing commercial infrastructures of Benguela, Mozambique Island, and Quelimane and their 'creative adaptation'

---

57   On the importance of credit in Angola, see: Miller, *Way of Death*, 187.

58   Philip D. Curtin, *Economic Change in Pre-Colonial Africa; Senegambia in the Era of the Slave Trade* (Madison, WI: University of Wisconsin Press, 1975); idem, *Cross-Cultural Trade in World History* (Cambridge: Cambridge University Press, 1984); Michael N. Pearson, "Markets and Merchant Communities in the Indian Ocean: Locating the Portuguese," in Bethencourt and Curto, eds., *Portuguese Oceanic Expansion*, 88–108.

to support growth of transatlantic slave trafficking were reminiscent of developments at Luanda up to two centuries earlier.[59] This, in turn, may account for why Brazilian-based traders who were probably already familiar with commercial processes at Luanda turned first to Benguela when seeking additional supplies of African captives from around 1730 onward.[60] Longer voyages and a higher incidence of shipboard slave mortality in the crossing to Brazil may also largely explain why such traders were generally slower in venturing to Southeast Africa for slaves, despite the presence of resident Portuguese there.[61] Only when slave prices in Brazil rose to unprecedented heights after 1790 did Brazilian-based traders regularly seek slaves in Southeast Africa.[62]

At Ambriz, Cabinda, and Malemba, there were no resident Portuguese or other European or Afro-European agents, a point that Sommerdyk specifically notes in relation to eighteenth-century Malemba, where Europeans conducted trade with local indigenous merchants essentially on a ship-to-shore basis. In that respect the commercial infrastructure of Malemba as well as of the other two ports in question was not unlike that found at ports such as Bonny and Old Calabar in the Bight of Biafra but it differed from that of Benguela and Luanda.[63] A mix of British, Dutch, French and US traders had, nevertheless, established close commercial ties with indigenous merchants at Ambriz, Cabinda and Malemba over the course of the eighteenth century.[64] Moreover, such ties had proved more than sufficient to sustain substantial levels of

---

59   For the concept of 'creative adaptation' and its use in the context of African coastal slave transactions, see: Paul E. Lovejoy and David Richardson, "Trust, Pawnship and Atlantic History: the Institutional Foundations of the Old Calabar Slave Trade," *American Historical Review* 104: 2 (1999): 333–355 and the sources cited therein.

60   For a more extended interpretation of the pre-existing structures at Benguela, see: Candido, *African Slaving Port*, 31–87.

61   On voyage times and slave mortality on ships departing from Southeast Africa for Brazil, see: Eltis and Richardson, *Atlas*, 184. Capela, in this volume, proposes another factor deterring Portuguese-Brazilians in seeking slaves in Southeast Africa before 1793 was French competition, a suggestion consistent with our own argument below about trade at the Loango Coast.

62   The fact that children apparently constituted a high proportion of the captives leaving Southeast Africa from the earliest stages of its involvement in transatlantic slavery underscores the importance of high slave prices in Brazil to the growth of slave supplies from that part of Africa to Brazil. On the ages of slaves leaving Southeast Africa before 1808, see: Ibid., 165.

63   On Old Calabar, see: Lovejoy and Richardson, "Trust," and Stephen D. Behrendt, A.J.H. Latham and David Northrup, *The Diary of Antera Duke: An Eighteenth-Century African Slave Trader* (Oxford: Oxford University Press, 2009). On Bonny, see: Paul E. Lovejoy and David Richardson, ""This Horrid Hole": Royal Authority, Commerce, and Credit at Bonny, 1690–1840," *Journal of African History* 45 (2004): 363–392.

64   Martin, *Loango Coast*.

cross-cultural trade across a range of commodities, including slaves destined for Caribbean markets.[65] Though Brazilian-based traders venturing to purchase slaves at the Loango Coast after 1808 were clearly entering unfamiliar waters commercially-speaking, nonetheless they found there, as they did earlier at Benguela, Mozambique Island and Quelimane, functioning commercial structures, which, on the evidence of subsequent slave exports, they proved more than adept at exploiting to their own gain.

For Brazilian-based traders, however, the upsurge of their slave exports from the Loango Coast after 1808 was as much a testament to their opportunism as to their commercial flexibility. Until 1808, competition from other carriers, notably the Dutch and French through 1793 and American and British thereafter, had effectively deterred Brazilian-Portuguese traders from pushing north of Luanda. The latters' inability or refusal to challenge their North Atlantic rivals at the Loango Coast before 1808 remains a puzzle, not least because traders from Bahia regularly and successfully competed for slaves against the British, the Dutch and French in the Bight of Benin from the late seventeenth century onward.[66] The absence of Brazilian-based traders from the Loango Coast before the nineteenth century cannot be properly explained here, but probably was related, among other things, to their lack of competitiveness in accessing the trade goods commonly exchanged for slaves at the Loango Coast.[67] Whatever the obstacles were that inhibited Brazilian-based traders from acquiring slaves there before 1808, moves by the British Parliament in 1807 and by the Federal government in the USA in 1808 to outlaw slave-trading by their nationals created an opportunity for them on the Loango Coast that had previously been unavailable. Moreover Britain's proscription of its own slaving coincided with moves by British merchants to expand exports to Brazil as part of the nation's efforts to maintain its overseas earnings in the face of Napoleon's wartime continental blockade against its trade.[68] Such exports included

---

65   Eltis and Richardson, *Atlas*, 145, 148.

66   On Portuguese-Brazilian shares of slave shipments from Ouidah and Porto Novo after 1726, for example, see: Ibid., 122, 124.

67   The goods in demand on the eighteenth-century Loango Coast commonly included large proportions of East Indian textiles (which by the end of the century were being supplemented by cheaper British-produced cotton piece goods) as well as firearms and gunpowder, items in which Dutch, English and French traders may have had a comparative advantage (Martin, *Loango Coast*).

68   The classic study is Alan K. Manchester, *British Pre-eminence in Brazil: its Rise and Decline* (Chapel Hill, NC: University of North Carolina Press, 1933; reprinted New York, NY: Octagon Books, 1964). One study suggests that British exports to Central and South America,

domestically produced cotton piece goods and other commodities, often on liberal credit terms, which before 1807 British slave traders themselves had typically taken to the Loango Coast and other parts of Africa to barter for slaves.[69] Within a few years British manufacturers would thus become major suppliers of the trade goods bartered for slaves by Portuguese-Brazilian traffickers, a point reinforced by Roquinaldo Ferreira's essay in this volume.[70] A combination of law, war, and industrial change in Europe, therefore, proved pivotal in allowing Brazilian-based slave trading at the Loango Coast to develop at a time of unprecedented expansion of the South Atlantic economy between 1790 and 1850.

If the Haitian Revolution and British abolition of its slave trade were instrumental in re-invigorating and re-shaping the centuries-old Angolan-Brazilian commercial nexus from the 1790s, the international anti-slavery movement of which those two events were critical early manifestations was to have profound implications for its ending in the second half of the nineteenth century. The late eighteenth century origins of anti-slavery and its subsequent political articulation internationally have been subjects of much debate.[71] It is now recognized, however, that they embodied a profound shift in values that ultimately made chattel slavery socially unacceptable regardless of the costs of outlawing it. It is also evident that while Britain was by 1815 the principal architect of an emerging international anti-slave trade policy and, as the first industrial nation, was prepared to invest diplomatic, financial, and military resources to implement it, other nations as much associated historically with transatlantic slavery such as Portugal and, after 1822, an independent Brazil, were for

including Brazil, underwent a 'fairly steady' upward trend in 1817–1848, and dominated by cotton piece goods, which were falling in price in real terms, were already worth around £43 million a year by the 1820s. Arthur D. Gayer, Walter W. Rostow and Anna J. Schwartz, *The Growth and Fluctuation of the British Economy, 1790–1850*, 2 vols. (Oxford: Clarendon Press, 1953), 1: 182, 215, 251, 282, 314; 2: 783.

69 According to one source, exports of UK cotton piece goods to America (other than the USA) amounted to 56 million yards by 1820 and then grew to 141 million and 279 million yards by 1830 and 1840, respectively, by which time the 'uninterrupted increase' in exports to the region ensured that it was the largest single export market for such British goods, accounting for 35 percent of the total by 1840. Brazil was part of that market. Thomas Ellison, *The Cotton Trade of Great Britain* (London: Effingham Wilson, 1886), 63–64.

70 David Eltis, "The British Contribution to the Nineteenth–Century Transatlantic Slave Trade," *Economic History Review*, second series, 32 (1979): 211–227; Joseph C. Miller, "Imports at Luanda, 1785–1823," in Gerhard Liesegang, Helma Pasch, and Adam Jones, eds., *Figuring African Trade* (Berlin: Dietrich Reimer Verlag, 1986), 165–246.

71 Seymour Drescher, *Abolition: A History of Slavery and Antislavery* (Cambridge: Cambridge University Press, 2009) places British abolitionism in a wider global perspective.

several decades more reluctant to embrace the British-led cause.[72] It is true that under pressure from Britain Portugal signed a treaty in 1818, effective in 1819, to end slaving in Africans north of the equator. This applied to both Brazilian-based as well as Portuguese-based traders since Brazil was then still under Portuguese rule. It would continue, moreover, to do so even after Brazilian independence. Under the treaty, some seizures of Brazilian-based slavers and the liberation of their captives occurred, but overall it had little perceptible impact on growth of the South Atlantic slave trade. Indeed, if anything, it may have increased the South Atlantic's share of total Luso-Brazilian slave trafficking by encouraging traders who traditionally procured slaves in the Bight of Benin to redirect some of their activities further south, thereby contributing to the 1820s surge in slave shipments to Brazil from Malemba and perhaps other places north of Luanda.[73]

Of potentially more potent significance for the scale and continuance of the South Atlantic slave trade were treaties signed by Britain with Brazil in 1826, effective in principle only from 1831, and then with Portugal in 1842, following a formal Portuguese ban on slaving in 1836. These aimed to extend proscription of Luso-Brazilian slaving to territories south of the equator. As with the earlier 1818 treaty, these new measures prompted some Royal Navy seizures of offending slave ships, including in this case ships off the Loango and Angolan coastlines. Moreover, the perceived risks posed by naval patrols and the costs incurred by slave ship operators seeking to evade them may have caused some decline in investment in slave voyages by Brazilians below what it might otherwise have been. But the immediate effect of the 1826 treaty, with its five-year delay in effective application, was to encourage a surge in Brazilian-based slave ship departures to Africa and thus African arrivals in Brazil in the late 1820s in anticipation of the closure of the slave trade.[74] Furthermore, following actual implementation, both the treaty of 1826 and the measures of 1836–1842 proved impossible fully to enforce in practice, even when, as Ferreira's essay in this volume shows, some Portuguese government officials at Luanda, conscious of their nation's fears about British intentions in Africa, were by the 1840s still sympathetic to the ending of the slave trade. Various factors conspired to thwart such officials. They included the limited capacity of

---

72   David Eltis, *Economic Growth and the Ending of the Transatlantic Slave Trade* (Oxford: Oxford University Press, 1987).

73   Eltis and Richardson, *Atlas*, 147.

74   www.slavevoyages.com/estimates/flag/disembarked/five years period, which suggests that disembarkations in Brazil rose from about 223,000 in 1821–1825 to 313,000 in 1826–1830, before falling back to about 85,000 in 1831–1835 and then rising again to 273,000 in 1836–1840.

naval patrols to police African waters, the continuing buoyancy of Brazilian demand for slaves, and the lure of the profits to be made by ship owners and merchants in Brazil as well slave dealers and officials in Angolan ports in meeting that demand.[75] This did not mean that Portuguese moves to suppress slaving in West-Central Africa were wholly ineffective, as Ferreira notes. But, ultimately, only action in Brazil itself, notably a British blockade of Brazilian ports in 1850 and then later separate local measures by the Brazilian authorities would end slave imports into the country in the mid-1850s. Pending such interventions, nearly 0.75 million African captives would be embarked illegally for Brazil in 1837–1856, the great majority of them via South Atlantic trade circuits.[76]

Though more protracted and confused, the final closure of Brazil's Atlantic slave trade in the 1850s through internal political action ultimately followed a pattern not dissimilar to that established by Denmark, Britain and the United States some fifty years or so earlier. But whereas additional measures from 1815 onward by North Atlantic nations, notably Britain, to outlaw slave trafficking at sea only marginally affected the dimensions of the Atlantic slave trade during subsequent decades, Brazil's own proscription of its oceanic slave trafficking would deal it a near-terminal blow. After 1856, only Cuba remained a significant importer of enslaved Africans and its slave trade closed in 1867. In tandem with the changing political context of slaving in Africa, the actions by the Brazilian authorities in the early 1850s proved particularly devastating for South Atlantic trading networks, which had been the most enduring and arguably the most resilient among those underpinning the whole transatlantic slave trade. At their heart were commercial axes linking ports in West-Central Africa, notably Luanda and Benguela, with Salvador da Bahia, Recife and Rio de Janeiro. It is a measure of the commercial sophistication and adaptability of those networks that they were able to evolve and sustain a large-scale traffic in enslaved Africans in 1815–1850 even in the face of growing international opposition. It is a measure, too, of their ultimate dependence on the continuing political acceptability of slave trafficking in Africans on both sides of the Atlantic that state action against the slave trade in Brazil effectively undermined them and, with them, the South Atlantic slave trade they had done so much to sustain.

---

75   Eltis, *Economic Growth*; Leslie Bethell, *The Abolition of the Brazilian Slave Trade: Britain, Brazil, and the Slave Trade Question, 1807–1869* (Cambridge: Cambridge University Press, 1970, 2009 edition).

76   Eltis and Richardson, *Atlas*, 274.

CHAPTER 2

Brazil's Colonial Economy and the Atlantic Slave Trade

Supply and Demand[1]

Gustavo Acioli Lopes

Several decades ago the historian Gilberto Freyre identified three key features at the heart of colonial Brazilian society: large-scale landownership, monoculture and slavery. Huge rural estates producing sugar cane with the use of forced African labour were, for Freyre, at the core of the new society, determining its prevailing features.[2] Since then, historical research in and on Brazil has continued to advance in both quantity and quality. It is fair to say that advances in historiography have deepened and amplified the picture that Freyre sketched, emphasizing new features and characteristics. These developments have not contradicted the weight that Freyre attached to forced labor nor to sugar's role in colonial Brazil's economy, but they have enriched our understanding of this epoch in Brazil's history.[3]

Developments in public understanding in the last 20 years or so of Brazil's colonial history have not passed completely unnoticed by historians of the classical school. But analysis of colonial Brazil has become more diversified in terms of overall approach and in respect to new issues previously largely unaddressed by researchers. Among the last, while not ignoring sugar, historians have focused particularly on tobacco growing and gold mining.[4]

---

1 I would like to thank Maximiliano M. Menz for reading and commenting on an earlier draft of this chapter. His suggestions were very valuable. I also acknowledge Gwen Midlo Hall for answering many questions and providing me with useful material on the debate concerning the Atlantic slave trade. Finally, I would like to extend my thanks to Chris Ebert for his generosity.

2 Gilberto Freyre, *Casa Grande e Senzala* (São Paulo: Círculo do Livro, 1980), 60, 70–71.

3 Drawing on a long-standing methodological approach followed by Brazilian historians, we will be using here the concept of 'colonial economy' to refer to Brazil's linkage to the slave trade up to 1850 regardless of the political independence of Brazil from Portugal and its empire. On this definition of "colonial economy," see: Caio Prado Júnior, *Formação do Brasil Contemporâneo* (São Paulo: Brasiliense, 1961), 19–32; Jacob Gorender, *O Escravismo Colonial* (São Paulo: Ática, 1978), 170.

4 The first studies on the Brazilian colonial economy have not hitherto ignored the relevance of those branches for the colonial economy, especially in eighteenth century, since the widely

© KONINKLIJKE BRILL NV, LEIDEN, 2015 | DOI 10.1163/9789004280588_003

It has taken time for the significance of tobacco growing and gold mining to attract due attention in clarifying not only their quantitative importance in terms of Brazilian output and exports but also in assessing their impact on work and ownership relationships in these economic occtois as well as their broader repercussions for neighbouring regions and the colonial, metropolitan, and Atlantic economies as a whole. Today, however, a deeper understanding is now possible about the role of each of colonial Brazil's economic sectors in demanding African slaves and in shaping the chronological and geographic patterns of the transatlantic slave trade to Brazil, even though quantitative data on the slave traffic before the latter half of seventeenth century are still limited.

The issue of the number of African slaves disembarked in Brazil throughout the era of the transatlantic slave trade has been tackled by Portuguese-speaking scholars and other researchers since the nineteenth century. We may distinguish at least two phases in the historiography of the Luso-Brazilian slave trade. The first one is characterized by a broad approach to the slave trade, which seeks to comprehend its overall duration but does not distinguish slave flows to each captaincy or the African regions whence the slaves came. The authors of such studies barely resorted to original sources. Among the estimates they produced, the one elaborated by Pandiá Calógeras was very influential. Calógeras suggested that 8,000,000 to 9,000,000 enslaved Africans were imported into Brazil in the years 1650–1850.[5]

The second phase of the debate on the Luso-Brazilian slave trade started when more sophisticated approaches were adopted concerning existing hypotheses, as well as the geography of slaves' African origins and Brazilian ports of disembarkation. The second phase was also marked by greater use of original sources in deriving estimates of patterns of trade. In short, scholars have increasingly worked with primary records and more refined analytical tools.

However, the main feature of this second phase in the historiography, which started in the 1930s, is the fact that the pioneers of new methodologies defined the guiding hypotheses for subsequent researchers, as we note below. Reacting

---

known work by Antonil mentioned both as well as cattle breeding in the early eighteenth century. See, for instance, Prado Junior's classical work, Prado Junior, *Formação do Brasil Contemporâneo*.

5   João Pandiá Calógeras, *A Política Externa do Império* (Rio de Janeiro: Imprensa Nacional, 1927), 1: 301–302. The author's figures were not based on primary sources, but rather on "row estimates," calculated using the size and the (negative) natural increase of Brazil's slave population on the eve of Abolition (1888). To offset for slave smuggling which he judged equal to the official disembarkation figures, the author used a multiplier.

against what they considered as exaggerated claims, researchers started more closely to relate the Portuguese slave trade to trends in Brazil's colonial economy in order to track its quantitative features. Using a variety of procedures, these new researchers put forward figures which clearly differed from those previously accepted as reflecting the scale of the Luso-Brazilian slave trade. Roberto Simonsen – who was the founder of this second phase in research – took as his main assumption that imports of slave labour should conform to the level of colonial production, or to put it another way, that slave labour imports were a function of commodity trade exports.[6] This assumption has since guided other researchers in their attempts to create better estimates of the Luso-Brazilian slave trade. However, later scholars have challenged the assumption of Simonsen and his followers, as we shall see.

In what follows, we focus on estimates of Brazil's slave imports during the Atlantic slave trade era calculated by several researchers. We also present an outline of current knowledge on the colonial economy with which that human traffic was interlinked, seeking to comprehend its distinct fields and productive sectors. Each period is viewed against secular trends, even though we try to make clear the distinct conjunctures in which the colonial economy was entangled.

Sugar: the Cradle of Colonization

We should start with sugar, since this commodity was the pivotal crop of the New World Portuguese colony for almost one and a half century, being the cornerstone of Brazil's economy in the sixteenth and seventeenth centuries. One may assert that the transatlantic slave trade grew in tandem with sugar production in the eastern Atlantic Islands and its ultimate migration to the Americas. There were failed projects that aimed to turn Angola into a sugar-producing and exporting captaincy.[7] Eventually, however, large-scale sugar production migrated during the sixteenth century from the eastern Atlantic islands off Africa to Portuguese American coastal territories.[8] As Luiz Felipe de

---

6   Roberto C. Simonsen, *História Econômica do Brasil* (São Paulo: Companhia Editora Nacional, 1962), 133–135.

7   David Birmingham, *Trade and conflict in Angola: the Mbundu and their neighbours under the influence of the Portuguese, 1483–1790* (Oxford: Claredon Press, 1966), 45–47; David Eltis, *The Rise of African Slavery in the Americas* (Cambridge: Cambridge University Press, 2000), 142–144.

8   Stuart B. Schwartz, *Segredos Internos: Engenhos e escravos na sociedade colonial* (São Paulo: Companhia das Letras, 1999), 24–39.

MAP 2.1   *Brazil*
          Author: Gustavo Acioli Lopes, 2013

Alencastro asserted, São Tomé was the "tropical laboratory," where the pattern of colonization that was eventually developed in Brazil was established: a seasonal crop, produced with techniques and slave labour from abroad, that is, the plantation model, the output of which was destined for overseas markets.[9]

---

9 Even though Madeira had been very important as a pathway for sugar's transfer from the Mediterranean shores to the New World, the pattern of slave-based production was not established there. See: Alberto Vieira, "Sugar Islands: The Sugar Economy of Madeira and the Canaries, 1450–1650," in Stuart B. Schwartz, ed., *Tropical Babylons: Sugar and the Making of the Atlantic World, 1450–1680* (Chapel Hill, NC: University of North Carolina Press, 2004), 56–61.

The American lands under formal Portuguese jurisdiction were actually settled in the early 1530s, when the Portuguese crown established the hereditary captaincies system.[10] Map 2.1 charts that system. Only a couple of *donatários* (recipients of captaincies) initially conquered parts of the land they were granted. Pernambuco (or New Lusitania) was the most successful, thanks to the sugar cane crop, by the mid-1530s. Bahia began to match Pernambuco only after Salvador Town (in the northeast of the Recôncavo) became the General Governor's headquarters in 1548, with sugar production thereafter being sponsored by the Portuguese monarchy. Thus, Brazil began to demand African slave labour only from the middle of sixteenth century.[11] By the turn of the century, it had become the leading sugar producer and exporter in the world.[12] The number of sugar mills is a good guide to the increasing sugar production: between 1570 and 1629, the number of mills leapt from 60 to 349. Almost half were in Pernambuco (150) and in the other northern captaincies of Alagoas, Paraíba and Rio Grande do Norte. Map 2.2 notes Portuguese settlements in Pernambuco.

It has been a hard task for scholars to ascertain the number of slaves carried from Africa to Brazil before 1600. On the one hand, the sources available for this period are scanty; on the other, most slaves recorded as taken from Africa in Portuguese slave ships in the second half of the sixteenth century were

---

10   For a careful analysis of the system and its specificities in Brazil, see: António Saldanha, *As capitanias do Brasil: antecedentes, desenvolvimento e extinção de um fenómeno atlântico* (Lisboa: Comissão Nacional para as Comemorações dos Descobrimentos Portugueses, 2001).

11   A comprehensive survey of Brazil's sugar society in the sixteenth century can be found in Schwartz, *Segredos Internos*, 21–72. The grantee of Pernambuco, Duarte Coelho, wrote to the king in the 1540s, requiring a licence to import African slaves. See: J.A. Gonsalves de Mello and Cleonir X. Albuquerque, eds., *Cartas de Duarte Coelho a El Rei* (Recife: Imprensa Universitária, 1967), 29–33.

12   Frédéric Mauro, *Portugal, o Brasil e o Atlântico, 1570–1670* (Lisboa: Estampa, 1997), 244–253; Philip D. Curtin, *The Rise and Fall of the Plantation Complex: Essays in Atlantic History* (Cambridge: Cambridge University Press, 1990), 26. The origin of sugar traded in Antwerp, the main port for the re-export of overseas commodities in the sixteenth century, clearly shows the rise of Brazil's sugar in the European market: in 1570 São Tomé island supplied 70 percent of the sugar disembarked in that port, whereas Brazil's sugar made up only 15 percent; however, in the years 1590–1599, Brazil's sugar represented 86 percent and imports from São Tomé only two percent. Eddy Stols, "The expansion of the sugar market in Western Europe," in Schwartz, ed., *Tropical Babylons*, 260. In the major Northwestern European sugar importing ports of Antwerp, Amsterdam and Hamburg, Brazilian sugar outstripped Atlantic Island supplies by 1610. Christopher Ebert, *Between Empires: Brazilian Sugar in the Early Atlantic Economy, 1550–1630* (Leiden: Brill, 2008), 7, 12.

MAP 2.2　　*Pernambuco*
　　　　　　Author: Gustavo Acioli Lopes, 2013

destined for Spanish America, particularly what is today Peru and Mexico, rather than for Brazil. Relying on contemporary observers who reported the number of slaves alive in Pernambuco and Bahia (the only captaincies with sizeable African slave populations at the time) scholars have nevertheless speculated that some 50,000 slaves disembarked in Brazil between 1550 and 1600. This has become a commonly accepted figure.[13] For the settlement of Bahia in the colonial era, see Map 2.3.

13　　Maurício Goulart, *A Escravidão Africana no Brasil: Das origens à extinção do tráfico* (São Paulo: Martins Fontes, 1950); Mauro, *Portugal, o Brasil e o Atlântico*, 241; Philip D. Curtin, *The Atlantic Slave Trade: a Census* (Madison, WI: University of Wisconsin Press, 1969), 206–207. Mauro put forward this figure as relating only to 1575–1600, while Goulart assigns it to the entire second half of the sixteenth century.

As regards the African regional origin of those slaves, most scholars have pointed to West Africa as the overwhelming source of Brazil's slave labour until late sixteenth century. The Portuguese referred to that region as *Guiné* (Guinea).[14] It comprised Senegambia (between Senegal and the Sierra Leone Rivers), in which Bissau and Cacheu, two "Portuguese" ports, were located and the offshore Cape Verde Islands. The share of Bantu people from West-Central Africa tended to grow, but only in the late sixteenth century. Originating largely from Congo and Angola, the slaves were embarked at Mpinda and Luanda harbours, or in some cases, through São Tomé.[15]

Information from the *Transatlantic Slave Trade Dataset 2* (hereafter TSTD2) depicts, however, a different picture of the coastal origins of enslaved Africans entering Brazil before 1600.[16] It suggests that 80 percent of the slaves carried away from Africa in the period 1519–1600 came from West-Central Africa.[17] Given that the Portuguese overwhelmingly controlled the Atlantic slave trade at this time, Brazil would thus seem to have got as many slaves from Angola as Spanish America, which was then the main point of disembarkation of enslaved Africans.[18] The evidence in TSTD2 has, nevertheless, been questioned, notably by Gwendolyn M. Hall, who argues that it underestimates the share of Africans from Senegambia embarked as slaves between 1540 and 1640. She claims that underestimate stems from mis-identification of the geographical origin of the slaves, mainly due to the fact that, because *Guiné and Rios da Guiné* were not seen as precise regions of supply, slaves coming from such places were classified as having an *unknown origin*.[19] Hall's argument was

---

14   Between the mid-fifteenth and the late sixteenth century, the term *Guiné* was synony-
      mous of Africa for the Portuguese.

15   Curtin, *The Atlantic Slave Trade*, 110–112; Gwendolyn Midlo Hall, *Slavery and African
      Ethnicities in the Americas: Restoring the Links* (Chapel Hill, NC: University of North
      Carolina Press, 2005), 80–88.

16   An updated version of the same database can be accessed on www.slavevoyages.org. The
      new data added since 1999 concerned mainly the Luso-Brazilian slave trade; David Eltis
      and David Richardson, "A New Assessment of the Transatlantic Slave Trade," in David Eltis
      and David Richardson, eds., *Extending the Frontiers: Essays in the New Transatlantic Slave
      Trade Database* (New Haven, CT.: Yale University Press, 2008), 6–7.

17   Eltis, *The Rise of African Slavery in the Americas*, 33, 44, table 2.

18   Daniel D.B. Silva and David Eltis, "The Slave Trade to Pernambuco, 1561–1851," in Eltis and
      Richardson, eds., *Extending the Frontiers*, 114.

19   Hall, *Slavery and African Ethnicities*, 85–88. Hall resorts to data on the origin of slaves in
      Peru and Mexico (1560–1650) and to data regarding the Portuguese *asiento*, in addition to
      contemporary reports. For the former data, her basis is Frederic P. Bowser, *The African
      Slave in Colonial Peru, 1524–1650* (Stanford, CA: Stanford University Press, 1974).

anticipated by Curtin some years ago.[20] But if the suggestions of TSTD2 are accepted, consensus on the ethnicity of Africans entering Brazil in the second half of the sixteenth century evidently breaks down.[21]

In this period, however, it is evident that Native Americans made up most of coerced workers in the sugar mills of Brazil.[22] The transition in this branch of colonial industry from Indian captives to African slaves came about between 1590 and 1620.[23] At the same time, West-Central Africa, namely Congo and Angola, increasingly became the major source of slaves for the Portuguese traders, particularly between 1560 and 1620.[24]

Throughout the seventeenth century, sugar was still Brazil's major export crop. Moreover, Rio de Janeiro joined Pernambuco and Bahia among the sugar exporting captaincies, holding the third position by volume of exports. However, Brazil's sugar economy underwent several hardships at this time. In the first half of the seventeenth century, issues concerning the marketing of sugar and European politics combined to hit hard Portugal's American economy. Underpinning them were trends in sugar prices, which in the 1620s began to reverse the long upward trend since the late fifteenth century, a process that marked the closing of "the

---

20   Curtin, *The Atlantic Slave Trade*, 103–112.

21   In the two Spanish American ports which imported slaves legally in the sixteenth and seventeenth centuries, Upper Guinea slaves were the largest group of slaves disembarked (accounting for more than 90 percent) in the years 1585 and 1590, while, at 48.4 percent, they slightly outnumbered the share of slaves from Angola landed between 1626 and 1633. In New Spain, Angolan slaves made up two thirds of slaves intended to be landed in the years 1612 and 1622, according to slave licences issued by the Spanish crown. These conclusions are supported by figures concerning the activities of the major slave merchant supplying Spanish America in the early seventeenth century, Manuel Bautista Pérez. Relying upon this information and other slave trading data, two scholars recently claimed that the transition from Upper Guinea slaves to slaves from West-Central Africa (mainly from Angola) in Spanish America was still ongoing in the second decade of seventeenth century. Linda A. Newson and Susie Minchin, *From Capture to Sale: The Portuguese Slave Trade to Spanish South America in the Early Seventeenth Century* (Leiden: Brill, 2007), 47, 61–63, 66–67, table 2.4.

22   On the transition from barter to slavery as the way the Portuguese settlers came by Indian labour, see: Alexander Marchant, *Do Escambo à Escravidão. As relações econômicas dos portugueses e índios na colonização do Brasil, 1500–1580* (São Paulo: Nacional, 1943); John Hemming, *Ouro Vermelho. A Conquista dos Índios Brasileiros* (São Paulo: Edusp, 1995).

23   Schwartz, *Segredos Internos*, 51–72. This conclusion relies upon Bahian data; likely, the same was true regarding Pernambuco, but not Rio de Janeiro.

24   Birmingham, *Trade and conflict in Angola*, 42–43, 79–81; Joseph C. Miller, *Way of Death: Merchant Capitalism and the Angolan Slave Trade, 1730–1830* (Madison, WI: University of Wisconsin Press, 1988), 141.

long sixteenth century"[25] and for some historians represented the starting point
of the general crisis of the seventeenth century.[26] The consequences of that crisis
were to be strongly felt in Brazil only in the latter half of the century, in part
because troubles within the main sugar producing captaincies of Brazil earlier in
the century initially overshadowed the effects of the more general crisis on the
colony. We can now survey the earlier half of the century, including the slave
trade to Brazil at that time, taking 1654 as our end point.

MAP 2.3   *Bahia*
           Author: Gustavo Acioli Lopes, 2013

---

25   Fernand Braudel, *The Wheels of Commerce* (Berkeley, CA: University of California Press,
      1989), 79.

26   The debate on the nature and scope of the crisis is very wide; besides Ruggiero Romano,
      Conjuncturas Opuestas (Mexico: Fondo de Cultura, 1993), see also: the insightful survey by
      Immanuel Wallerstein, *The Modern World System* (New York, NY: Academic Press, 1974).

In the sixteenth century, the Dutch were the main distributors and refiners of Brazilian sugar in Europe.[27] Owing to the struggles between the United Provinces and the Spanish Habsburgs, who took over the Portuguese crown in 1580, the Dutch were deprived of direct access to Brazilian sugar at the beginning of the seventeenth century.[28] In addition to piracy and privateering against Iberian shipping, the Dutch West India Company (hereafter WIC) tried to encroach on the colonial territories in Brazil. After conquering and then losing Bahia in 1624–1625, the WIC was more successful in Pernambuco in 1630–1637, extending its sovereignty from Sergipe to Maranhão.[29] These events had significant short-term effects on sugar prices, delaying what otherwise would have been potentially the onset of a prolonged fall in prices. This was largely due to damage to Brazilian sugar mills caused by Dutch conquest and hence restraints on the level of sugar supply.[30] Prices for Brazilian sugar in Lisbon and Antwerp showed the same trend from 1577 through 1630: increasing up to 1613–1615, turning downward from then to 1624, but then recovering again in the ensuing years.[31]

Throughout the years of war in 1630–1637 and 1647–1654, Pernambuco continued exporting sugar, though its volume was reduced. Simultaneously, Bahia and Rio de Janeiro profited from rising sugar prices linked to problems facing Pernambuco's sugar supply.[32] This is not to say that Brazil was completely isolated from the emerging economic turnaround in Europe, because the fall in

---

27 Stols, "The Expansion of the Sugar Market in Western Europe," 259, 271–272. On the growing importance of Lisbon's re-exports to Amsterdam's external trade, see: Christopher Ebert, "Dutch trade with Brazil before the Dutch West India Company, 1587–1621," in Johannes Postma and Victor Enthoven, eds., *Riches from Atlantic Commerce: Dutch Transatlantic Trade and Shipping, 1585–1817* (Leiden: Brill, 2003), 57–58, 68–69, table 3.2; see also: Ebert, *Between Empires*, 36–37, 173–174.

28 On the impact of the Habsburg's trade embargoes imposed on the United Provinces in 1585–1590, 1598–1603 and 1604–1609, see: Ebert, "Dutch Trade with Brazil," 60–63.

29 The historiography on this theme is large; for a good introduction, see: Charles Boxer, *O Império Marítimo Português* (São Paulo: Companhia das Letras, 2002), 115–130. For recent approaches, see: José Manuel Santos Pérez and George F. Cabral de Souza, eds., *El Desafio Holandés al Dominico Ibérico en Brasil en el Siglo XVII* (Salamanca: Ediciones Universidad de Salamanca, 2006).

30 Leonor Freire Costa, O *Transporte no Atlântico e a Companhia Geral do Comércio do Brasil (1580–1663)* (Lisboa: Comissão Nacional para as Comemorações dos Descobrimentos Portugueses, 2002).

31 Ebert, *Between Empires*, 159–162, tables 8.5 and 8.6.

32 Evaldo Cabral de Mello, *Olinda Restaurada: Guerra e açúcar no Nordeste, 1650–1654* (Rio de Janeiro: Topbooks, 1998), Chapter 3.

sugar prices in European markets in 1615–1624 was the root of the conflict between the Portuguese and the WIC in Pernambuco, and which continued until the ultimate expulsion of the Dutch from Brazil in 1654.[33]

Patterns of slave imports into Brazil during the first half of the seventeenth century reflected these wider political changes. During the period of Dutch control, slaves were primarily supplied by the WIC.[34] Overall estimates of imports vary for the first half of the century. Goulart estimated that slave imports ranged from 300,000 to 350,000 slaves, primarily to meet sugar production. As a result, he assumed slave imports corresponded to the colony's export trends.[35] Mauro, however, estimated that no more than 200,000 slaves were imported in the same period.[36]

The best known and most reliable figures concerning this period come from the WIC's slave trade to Brazil from 1630. Ernest van den Boogaart and Pieter Emmer revised existing data.[37] In doing so, they presented an upward revision, which has since been corroborated by newer data, though with a slight increase in the grand total.[38] Regarding the period before 1630, Dutch sources report Pernambuco's slave imports only for 1620–1623.[39] Nevertheless, when figures relating to the whole of Brazil were reviewed, drawing analogies between slave imports into the British Caribbean during its sugar revolution later in the century and Brazil before 1650, it seems unlikely that the number of slaves

33 According to Mello, the downturn of sugar prices in the European market undermined the policy of Nassau, the Governor of Dutch Brazil between 1638 to 1646, of granting generous loans to Portuguese sugar growers. Mello, *Olinda Restaurada*, 344–347.

34 Ernest van den Boogaart and Pieter C. Emmer, "The Dutch Participation in Atlantic Slave Trade, 1596–1650," in Henry A. Gemery and Jan S. Hogendorn, eds., *The Uncommon Market: Essays in the Economic History of Atlantic Slave Trade* (New York, NY: Academic Press, 1979), 353–375; Johannes Postma, *The Dutch in the Atlantic Slave Trade* (Cambridge: Cambridge University Press, 1990), 97–99; Silva and Eltis, "The Slave Trade to Pernambuco," 98–99. In this same period, the Dutch conquered the Portuguese fortress of São Jorge da Mina (present-day Elmina, Ghana) and Angola, holding the former until the nineteenth century, but losing the latter in 1648.

35 Goulart, *A Escravidão Africana no Brasil*, 122; the author estimates this figure as the upper limit, and maybe an overestimation.

36 Mauro, *Portugal, o Brasil e o Atlântico*, 240.

37 Hermman Wätjen, *O Domínio Colonial Holandês no Brasil: Um capítulo da história colonial no século XVII* (São Paulo: Companhia Editora Nacional, 1938), 485–487. According to this author, 23,163 slaves were imported in Brazil between 1636 and 1645.

38 Boogaart and Emmer, "The Dutch Participation in Atlantic Slave Trade," 369; Silva and Eltis, "The Slave Trade to Pernambuco," 98–99, based on the TSTD2.

39 David Eltis, Stephen Behrendt and David Richardson, "A participação dos países da Europa e das Américas no tráfico transatlântico de escravos: novas evidências," *Afro-Ásia* 24 (2000): 27–28.

disembarked in Brazil in 1601–1650 was greater than in the British Caribbean in the second half of the century. On this basis, it is likely that 150,000 slaves were imported in Brazil in 1601–1650.[40]

In the second half of seventeenth century, Brazil's sugar production was hit by rival and growing British and French Caribbean supply from the "sugar islands"[41] to the European market. This started in 1640s, but gathered momentum during the following decades.[42] This depressed sugar and other colonial commodity prices in Portugal and Europe, and in Brazil itself, brought about the first major sugar economy crisis.[43]

The price of tithes in the major captaincies reveals the hardships associated with sugar exports in this period.[44] Bahia, Pernambuco and Rio de Janeiro tithe contract prices varied between bad and good years for sugar, but generally underwent a downward trend or at best stagnation in value after the mid-1650s. In Pernambuco, there was some recovery from about 1680, with tithe values exceeding those of mid-century but being lower than the early century.[45] At Rio de Janeiro, where tithes stagnated between 1660 and 1680 (largely due most likely to Pernambuco's resurgence in sugar production), there seems to have been some recovery in tithe values in late century. At Bahia, the major sugar producing region after the Dutch invasion in Northeast Brazil, stagnation in tithe values occurred after mid-century.[46]

---

40   Ibid., 28.

41   Richard Dunn, *Sugar and Slaves: The Rise of the Planter Class in the English West Indies, 1624–1713* (New York, NY: Norton, 1973), 204–205, 230; Robin Blackburn, *A Construção do Escravismo no Novo Mundo, 1492–1800* (Rio de Janeiro: Civilização Brasileira, 2003), 403.

42   Dunn, *Sugar and Slaves*, 19–20, 59–64; Blackburn, *A Construção do Escravismo*, 282, 383; John J. Mccuscker and Russell R. Menard, "The Sugar Industry in the Seventeenth Century. A new perspective on the Barbadian "Sugar Revolution," in Schwartz, ed., *Tropical Babylons*, 291–292.

43   Vitorino de Magalhães Godinho, "Portugal, as frotas do açúcar e as frotas do ouro (1670–1770)," *Revista de História da Universidade de São Paulo* 15 (1953): 69–88; Schwartz, *Segredos Internos*, 147, 151.

44   The collection of tithes used to be leased out to private collectors in public auction. Usually, leases were granted to the highest bidders.

45   Gustavo Acioli Lopes, "Negócio da Costa da Mina e Comércio Atlântico. Tabaco, Açúcar, Ouro e Tráfico de Escravos: Capitania de Pernambuco (1654–1760)" (unpublished PhD thesis, Universidade de São Paulo, 2007), 23–26; Angelo Carrara, *Receitas e despesas da Real Fazenda no Brasil* (Juiz de Fora, MG: Editora da Universidade Federal de Juiz de Fora, 2009), 1: 81.

46   In nominal values, Bahia's tithes showed a rising trend in 1650–1686, but in real values (measured in coined gold) there was a stagnant trend; Carrara, *Receitas e despesas da Real Fazenda*, 1:80–81, 85, graphs 2-A and 4.

When one looks at the unstable and troublesome state of Brazil's sugar economy, with weaknesses in production and exports, the estimates by Mauro and Goulart of slave imports in the colony in second half of the seventeenth century seem high. In place of the 325,000 slave arrivals they project between 1651 and 1700,[47] a figure around 177,000 slaves has been proposed.[48] Luiz Felipe de Alencastro, however, has raised questions about this revision and thus of the Luso-Angolan slave trade. He challenges revisionists' assumptions about the extent to which the seventeenth-century crisis entangled the Luso-Atlantic economy and thus helped to diminish the Atlantic slave trade to Brazil. For Alencastro, the export of Brazilian tobacco and sugar cane rum (*jeribita* or *cachaça*) and their exchange for African slaves in Angola allowed Portuguese merchants to sustain slave trafficking at former levels, with the result that some 245,000 Angolan slaves were unloaded in Brazil from 1651 to 1700. The purchasing power of colonial products in Angola and the interference of colonial governors from Brazil in the slavery channels in Angola's interior fostered in effect a growing "brazilianization" of the Brazil-bound slave trade.[49]

Hard data covering the years 1651–1700 are scanty. Alencastro introduced some new figures, notably for 1666 to 1672, into the debate. However, the author on whom he relied for data for these specific years misread the sources.[50] According to Alencastro's source, 73,461 captives were deported from Angola in the seven years noted above, averaging 10,494 per year, but according to a file

---

47   Goulart, *A Escravidão Africana no Brasil*, 116.

48   Eltis, Behrendt and Richardson, "A participação dos países da Europa e das Américas no tráfico transatlântico," 29.

49   Luiz Felipe de Alencastro, *O trato dos viventes: a formação do Brasil no Atlântico Sul* (São Paulo: Companhia das Letras, 2000), 43, 69, 378–380. For critics on this approach, see: José Curto, *Álcool e Escravos. O comércio luso-brasileiro de álcool em Mpinda, Luanda e Benguela durante o tráfico atlântico de escravos (c. 1480–1830) e o seu impacto nas sociedades da África Central Ocidental* (Lisboa: Vulgata, 2002), 155–199; Gustavo Acioli Lopes and Maximiliano M. Menz, "Resgate e Mercadorias: uma análise comparada do Tráfico Luso-Brasileiro de Escravos em Angola e na Costa Da Mina (século XVIII)," *Afro-Ásia* 36 (2008): 43–73. The role of Luso-Brazilian governors in Angola is argued in Miller, *Way of Death*, 256.

50   António Luís Alves Ferronha, "Angola: 10 anos de história: 1666–1676" (Unpublished PhD Thesis, Faculdade de Letras da Universidade de Lisboa, 1989), 1: 119–120. The source was AHU, *Angola*, cx. 10, doc. 64: 1672-03-14: 'Relação por maior das contas que o Desembargador Sebastião Cardoso de Sam Payo [...] Sindicante Geral neste Reino de Angolla, e Estado do Brasil tomou [...] aos Procuradores do Senado da Camara desta cidade de Sam Paulo de Assumpção de todo o tempo que administrarão os direitos novos [...]'.

written in Angola,[51] and originating from an official checking the collection of "gifts" for "The Britain Queen and the Dutch Peace,"[52] rather lower numbers were on average exported. Indeed, according to this source, from 1667 to 1671, Luanda exported 30,380 slaves of all ages and gender, or some 6,076 a year. The figures are shown in Table 2.1.

How do we explain this discrepancy? It is likely that in reading the documents, Alencastro's source conflated "new taxes" levied on slave exports, for which Luanda's town council rendered account, with the tax of 1$000 (one thousand *réis*) per slave head tax attached to the "gift." Two observations help to underline the mistake. First, in 1688, the "new taxes" yielded 12:956$618 (twelve *contos*, 956,618 *réis*), from which figure it might be assumed that 12,956 slaves were exported, using a "gift" tax rate of 1$000 reis per slave. This assumption is clearly wrong, however, for it leaves a fraction of the total tax yield unex-

TABLE 2.1   *Slaves exports from Angola, 1667–1670*

	(1)	(2)	
Years	Slaves	Ships	(1)/(2)
1667	5,109	13[a]	408
1668	6,908	15	461
1669	5,293	14	378
1670	6,461	17	380
1671	6,609	16	413
Total	30,380	75	405

Sources: AHU, *CU, Angola*, cx. 10, doc. 40: 1672-05-24: 'Papeis pertencentes as contas q se tomarão do donativo, com que estes moradores servem a Vossa Alteza, pera o dote da Senhora. Rainha da Grã Bretanha e pax de Holanda. São Paulo de Assunção [Luanda]'. AHU, *CU*, Angola, cx. 10, doc. 64: 'Relação por maior das contas que o Desembargador Sebastião Cardoso de Sam Payo [...]'.
Note:
a. According to one source, eleven slave ships departed from Luanda between September 2 and December 31, 1667, and 1,048 slaves were exported before the duty (*subsídio*) has been enforced, that is, from January to August, 1667; while another source certifies that 19 slave vessels cleared from Luanda in the same year.

---

51   AHU, *Angola*, cx. 10, doc. 40: 1672-05-24: 'Papeis pertencentes as contas que se tomarão do donativo, com que estes moradores servem a Vossa Alteza que Deus guarde, pera o dote da Senhora Rainha da Gra Bretanha e pax de Holanda. São Paulo de Assunção'.
52   Duties had been levied on the Portuguese colonies to finance the royal wedding of Catarina de Bragança (Princess of Portugal) and the English king, and to pay reparations to the Dutch Republic for losses and damages to the WIC in Brazil, as agreed in the 1662 Peace Treaty.

plained.[53] Nevertheless, if this value was the same concerning the $1000 tax, the collected sum would be round, as one may observe regarding the collected tax on slaves exported from 1667 to 1671.[54]

Secondly, if the number of slaves exported from Luanda in the five years from 1667 to 1671 was as Alencastro assumes, then the average number loaded per ship (covering 62 ships) would be 670, and reached a peak of 849 per ship in 1667. Such mean loadings of slaves on Portuguese slave ships seem exceptional and were not subsequently reached until the late eighteenth century.[55] Projections based on such mean loadings of ships would moreover yield estimates for the second half of the seventeenth century that some 520,561 *Angolan* slaves were shipped to Brazil. Bearing in mind that slaves reached Brazil from other sources, as we shall see, such figures are difficult to reconcile with the problems evidently encountered in the sugar sector of the colony. Unfortunately, hard evidence on Angolan exports in this period is confined to 1667–1671, but at just over 6,000 slaves per year, was substantially lower than Alencastro assumed and suggests that upward revisions of slave imports into Brazil in 1651–1700 based on his calculations need to be reassessed.[56]

During the second half of the seventeenth century, Brazil began to import slaves from the Slave Coast of West Africa. This was particularly evident at Bahia and Pernambuco. Slave trading between these Atlantic regions likely

<hr/>

53 That is, 12:956$618 divided by 1$000. If this sum was derived from slaves exported, we would exactly have 12:956$000. Actually, the "new duties" (*novos direitos*) of 3$000 were levied on Angola's slave exports; Joseph C. Miller, "Capitalism and Slaving: The Financial and Commercial Organization of the Angolan Slave Trade, according to the Accounts of António Coelho Guerreiro (1684–1692)," *International Journal of African Historical Studies* 17:1 (1984): 44; however, the tax collection, according to Goulart, was not a fixed value per slave, but varied in accordance with the slave ship's destination in its homeward voyage; Goulart, *A Escravidão Africana no Brasil*, 194. The document quoted in footnote 50 seems to support Goulart's assertion.

54 AHU, *Angola*, cx. 10, doc. 40: 1672-05-24: 'Papeis pertencentes as contas q se tomarão do donativo […] pera o dote da Senhora Rainha da Gra Bretanha'. The same can be checked for Bahia and Pernambuco regarding the 10 *tostões* tax (that is, *mil réis*) per slave from *Costa da Mina*, collected to support the Portuguese fortress of Ajudá (Portuguese spelling for Whydah) from 1724. See also: Pierre F. Verger, *Fluxo e Refluxo do Tráfico de Escravos entre o Golfo de Benin e a Bahia de Todos os Santos: dos séculos XVII a XIX* (Salvador: Corrupio, 1987), 161, 163.

55 Herbert S. Klein, *The Middle Passage. Comparative Studies in the Atlantic Slave Trade* (Princeton, NJ: Princeton University Press, 1978), 27–31.

56 Eltis and Richardson, "A new assessment," 16–17, table 1.3 and 18; Silva and Eltis, "The slave trade to Pernambuco," 110. If that average of just over 6,000 for 1667–1671 is extended over the latter half of the century, we get closer to Goulart's figures.

grew in tandem with growing tobacco cultivation in both Brazilian captaincies, given that at that time Brazilian tobacco became the main item of trade among Portuguese traders to the Slave Coast. In that respect it matched tobacco's importance as an export good to Europe from Brazil in the later seventeenth century.[57] Although no Portuguese or any other European source reports Portuguese slave ships trading at the Slave Coast prior to 1678, it is likely that such trade did exist before that date, though at modest levels.[58] The Portuguese king acknowledged it as a lawful trade in 1677, and a letter from Pernambuco in the same year reported that the main trade taking place in the Slave Coast was the trade "of negroes for Brazil, because without them one cannot raise the sugar mills nor cultivate the crops."[59] This was certainly true regarding Bahia.

We do not have direct evidences of "Mina" (or West African) slaves disembarking in Brazil in the years 1651–1700. Drawing on shipping data, historians initially suggested that 60,800 slaves from the Slave Coast were shipped to Brazil in the last decade of the century.[60] More recent estimates for Bahia by Alexandre Ribeiro have raised that number to 78,484.[61] Both calculations assumed 400 slaves per ship sailing on that route. Data on slave ship voyages as well as tobacco exports from Bahia to the Slave Coast are the source for yet another calculation by Nardi which suggests that only 12,000 slaves may have been imported into Bahia in 1676–1700.[62] This implies that other calculations were gross overestimates. Accordingly to Nardi, each ship carried some 65 slaves on average on this route during the years 1691–1700.[63]

---

57   Jean-Batiste Nardi, *O fumo brasileiro no período colonial. Lavoura, Comércio e Administração* (São Paulo: Brasiliense, 1996), 89, 115.

58   Eltis and Richardson, "A new assessment," 18.

59   AHU, *Pernambuco*, cx. 11, doc. 1084: 1677-07-26: 'Carta de João Fernandes Vieira ao príncipe regente [Dom. Pedro] sobre as dificuldades enfrentadas pelos armadores que efetuam o transporte dos escravos da Costa da Mina para Pernambuco'.

60   Verger, *Fluxo e Refluxo*, 692–707; Patrick Manning, "The Slave Trade in the Bight of Benin, 1640–1890," in Henry A. Gemery and Jan S. Hogendorn, eds., *The Uncommon Market: Essays in the Economic History of Atlantic Slave Trade* (New York, NY: Academic Press, 1979), 137–138.

61   Alexandre Ribeiro, "The Atlantic Slave Trade to Bahia, 1582–1851," in Eltis and Richardson, eds., *Extending the Frontiers*, 135, table 4.3; table 4.4, 153–154, Appendix 4.1. Although 1,617 slaves are assigned to the years 1581–1680, we may assume that they were disembarked from 1640s onward. The author also estimates that 24,565 slaves, mainly from West-Central Africa, were disembarked in Bahia in 1651–1700.

62   The author gauged 13,555 slaves exported, from which I have deducted 11 percent to account for mortality in the Atlantic crossing.

63   Nardi, *O fumo brasileiro no período colonial*, 224, table VII.I, 383–394, Appendix 2.1.

However, both recent sets of revisions of Bahian slave imports from West Africa before 1700 call for some reappraisal. For one thing, the mean shipload of slaves entering Bahia before 1710 assumed by Ribeiro may have been high.[64] For another, though Bahia's tobacco export licences as used by Verger and others may provide a reliable proxy to measure the trend of this branch of the slave trade, they are not enough to measure its actual scale. Moreover, for Bahia and Pernambuco slave traders, gold also had a key role in procuring slaves from Slave Coast in the last five years of the seventeenth century. Against such evidence, Nardi's assumption of mean slave loadings per ship was likely too low.

Outside of Bahia and Pernambuco, two other Brazilian regions continued to receive African slaves during the second half of the seventeenth century: Rio de Janeiro and Maranhão and Grão-Pará.[65] Rio de Janeiro had engaged in sugar production since late sixteenth century, but, as in Bahia and Pernambuco, the first sugar mills used forced Indian labour and only belatedly – and following the Northern captaincies – was it replaced by African slaves.[66] Rio de Janeiro's sugar output, however, was small relative to Bahia's and, usually, Pernambuco's before 1700. Thus, although slave imports equal to 70 percent of Bahia's have been imputed to Rio de Janeiro for the years 1620–1709 in the face of scanty data, that ratio seems implausible, if one compares, as an indirect measure, the average value of the southeast captaincy's tithe farm with that of the major sugar-producing captaincies in 1655–1691. The relevant figures are presented in Table 2.2.[67]

---

64 Verger calculated this average from data for the years 1727–1728 (425 slaves per ship) and 1743–1756 (475 slaves per ship). In those years, the volume of this branch of the Atlantic slave trade was higher than in the last quarter of the seventeenth century. Verger, *Fluxo e Refluxo*, 702.

65 During the sixteenth century Maranhão and Grão-Pará were under the authority of Brazil's central government, but in 1621 they acquired autonomous political jurisdiction.

66 João Fragoso, "A formação da economia colonial no Rio de Janeiro e de sua elite senhorial (séculos XVI e XVII)," in João Fragoso, Maria de Fátima Gouvêa and Maria Fernanda Bicalho, eds., *Antigo Regime nos Trópicos: A dinâmica imperial portuguesa (séculos XVI a XVIII)* (Rio de Janeiro: Civilização Brasileira, 2000), 34, 38–39.

67 One may reckon the tithes as a flawed measure of projecing trends, as Ruggiero Romano does; R. Romano, *Mecanismo y elementos del sistema económico colonial americano. Siglos XVI–XVIII* (México: Colegio de México, Fideicomisso Historia de Las Américas, FCE, 2004), 353. Other scholars, however, consider it as a feasible index. See: J.H. Galloway, "Nordeste do Brasil, 1700–1750: Reexame de uma crise," *Revista Brasileira de Geografia* 36:2 (1974): 85–102; Schwartz, *Segredos Internos*, 154, 174; who with reservations suggests that tithes are "a fairly good guide to the health of the economy."

TABLE 2.2   *Values of tithes farmed out in three major sugar-producing captaincies (average in cruzados), 1655–1691*

	(1)	(2)	(3)	(3)/(1)	(3)/(2)
	Bahia	Pernambuco	Rio de Janeiro	(in percent)	(in percent)
1655–1658	92.550[a]	28.000[a]	45.000	49	161
1658–1661	84.500[a]	28.167	23.416[a]	28	83
1661–1664	73.000[a]	20.000[b]	23.472	32	117
1664–1667	82.500[b]	29.163[a]	22.500	27	77
1667–1670	99.250[a]	22.100[b]	22.067	22	100
1670–1673	94.013[a]	41.350[a]	22.033	23	53
1673–1676	85.000[b]	39.000[b]	22.000	26	56
1676–1679	108.000[a]	38.800[a]	25.000	23	64
1679–1682	95.333	44.100[b]	29.277	31	66
1682–1685	–	–	30.666[a]	–	–
1685–1688	110.000[a]	46.700	43.333	39	93
1688–1691	88.000[a]	20.000[b]	43.333[b]	49	217
Grand average				32	99

Source: Based on Carrara, *Receitas e despesas da Real Fazenda*, I: 126–127
Notes:
a. Two years only
b. One year only
The first and last years of each time period overlap because contracts lasted from August 1 to July 31

Although there are gaps in the series of figures, a perusal of the data shows that seldom did Rio de Janeiro's tithes exceed one third of Bahia's tithe contract values between 1655 and 1685, and in most years were closer to a quarter or less. Compared to Pernambuco, tithe values relating to Rio de Janeiro were much closer but only in the mid 1650s, when Pernambuco was recovering from seven years of Dutch warfare did they exceed those of Pernambuco. In most years before 1685 they were between a half and two-thirds of Pernambuco's tithe assessment. If one concedes that "the slave trade reflects commodity trade patterns"[68] and that the latter are reflected in tithe assessments, then it seems likely that calculations that assume Rio de Janeiro slave imports before 1709 were equal to 70 percent of Bahia's will over-estimate slave landings in the southern captaincy during the second half of the seventeenth century. It was not by chance

68   Eltis and Richardson, "A new assessment," 19.

that Rio's settlers complained to the King of Portugal of shortages in slave supply in the late 1670s.[69] Together with projections on slave exports from Angola based on 1660s data, this reassessment of Rio de Janeiro's slave imports suggests that some recent calculations that some 865,000 slaves were imported into Brazil over the whole seventeenth century may require downward revision.

Up to the middle eighteenth century, the Grão-Pará e Maranhão region lagged behind export development of other coastal regions of Portuguese America.[70] Transitions from Indian labour to African slave labour in both settlement and production failed to take place here. Projects simultaneously to lighten forced labour burdens on Indians by importing African slaves were centred on two monopolist trade companies, which operated in 1676–1684 and 1686–1696, but their results proved modest. In the ensuing decades, the slave trade was free before it was halted in 1755. But the region lacked a steady and sizeable commodity trade: Maranhão's main export was cacao, while Pará's was "drogas do sertão" – drugs of the wilderness – goods for which demand was inelastic in European market.[71] As a result, the scale of the Africa slave trade to this region remained very low before 1755, being estimated at some 2,613 slaves.[72]

The Eighteenth Century Through 1770: the Rise of Mining and the Crisis of Agricultural Exports

Brazil's pattern of slave labour demand in the eighteenth century was shaped by gold discoveries in 1695, the effects of which continued through the mid-eighteenth century, when gold mining began to decrease.[73] From then on, demand for slave imports fell, with the effects of shrinking gold exports being

---

69   Alencastro, *O Trato dos Viventes*, 377–378. See also: "Sobre os navios que despacharem de Angolla para o Rio de Janeiro não tomarem este porto. Lisboa, 6 de novembro de 1679," in "Informação Geral da Capitania de Pernambuco. [1749]," *Annaes da Bibliotheca Nacional do Rio de Janeiro* 28 (1906): 211–212. According to this source Rio de Janeiro slave ships sailing to Angola did not return to this captaincy; instead, they went to Pernambuco and Bahia where they preferred to sell their slave cargoes.

70   The same was true regarding São Paulo captaincy up to the early eighteenth century.

71   Alencastro, *O Trato dos Viventes*, 139–140.

72   Daniel Domingues da Silva, "The Atlantic Slave Trade to Maranhão, 1680–1846: Volume, Routes and Organization," *Slavery and Abolition* 29:4 (2008): 478–481.

73   It is not by chance that during this same period and after years of prohibition and lively debates, the Portuguese crown legalized the exports of *jeribita* (sugarcane rum) from Brazil to Angola, in order to facilitate slave imports from Angola by Brazil-based merchants, particularly in Rio de Janeiro. Curto, *Álcool e Escravos*, 123–149.

compounded by downturn or stagnation in other major export branches of the colonial economy, which entered crisis even as gold exports rose.

In the first half of the eighteenth century, gold exports drove the demand for slave imports in Brazil, with sugar exports and to a lesser extent tobacco exports playing more subordinate roles. In the areas surrounding mining, demand for slaves was reinforced by development of foodstuff production tied to local markets. By the late century, this branch of slave production came to be one of the most important in slave labour demand.

At the very moment when sugar exports showed signs of recovery in the late seventeenth century,[74] mining activity reinforced sugar in promoting demand for slaves. Gold was discovered in the region neighbouring the São Paulo, Rio de Janeiro and Espírito Santo captaincies, on the River São Francisco tributaries, becoming known as Minas Gerais. Brazilian gold exports grew steadily from around 1695 until about 1750, reaching a peak from the 1730s to the 1740s. In addition to Minas Gerais,[75] Goiás, where production peaked in the 1740s, and Mato Grosso, where it peaked in 1750–54, were both important gold-producing areas from the third decade of the 'gold' century. Minas' gold output, however, was greater than the two other captaincies combined. It peaked in the 1740s, declining from the following decade on.[76]

A similar chronology to gold output can be observed in collections of *quintos* (one fifth), in the tax collected on imported goods at customs posts at entry routes (*entradas*) and in the contract prices for farming out tithes. These three variables point out to a decline of Minas' mercantile activity from the 1750s and 1760s onward.[77] Diamond digging, another mining sector, offset some of the decline in gold as it began to expand, notably from the 1740s, but it too fell away in the 1770s.[78]

Coincidental with rising southwestern mining activity through 1750, in the surrounding areas, estates developed a combination of cattle raising and arable crop production to satisfy local markets. The estates included *fazendas* (farms) and

---

74 Carrara, *Receitas e despesas da Real Fazenda*, 1: 107, graph 5; Lopes, "Negócio da Costa da Mina," 31–51.
75 The captaincy was set up in 1720, after almost three decades of gold mining.
76 Virgílio Noya Pinto, *O Ouro Brasileiro e o Comércio Anglo-Português* (São Paulo: Companhia Editora Nacional, 1979), 51–81, 85–115.
77 Laird W. Bergad, *Escravidão e história econômica: demografia de Minas Gerais, 1720–1888* (Bauru, SP: Editora da Universidade do Sagrado Coração, 2004), 46–50; Angelo Alves Carrara, *Minas e Currais: produção rural e mercado interno em Minas Gerais, 1674–1807* (Juiz de Fora, MG: Universidade Federal de Juiz de Fora, 2007), 36, 110–111.
78 Bergad, *Escravidão e história econômica*, 48–49, graph 1.2.

sítios (lesser estates) – both near gold mines and main access routes – and *currais* (or cattle ranches in the back-lands or *sertão*). Those activities were also founded on African forced labour, supplying most of the foodstuff traded in the local markets during the peak years of gold output.[79] Map 2.4 describes Minas Gerais during the gold boom.

From the earliest gold discoveries until about 1730, the slave trade through Bahia and Pernambuco supplied most of the slaves engaged in the southwestern gold mining. Those two captaincies held the major share of slave imports into Brazil from the late sixteenth century onward and up to about 1730 some of their imported Africans were re-exported to the mining regions, through São Francisco road, or reshipped to the port of Rio de Janeiro.[80] From the 1720s,

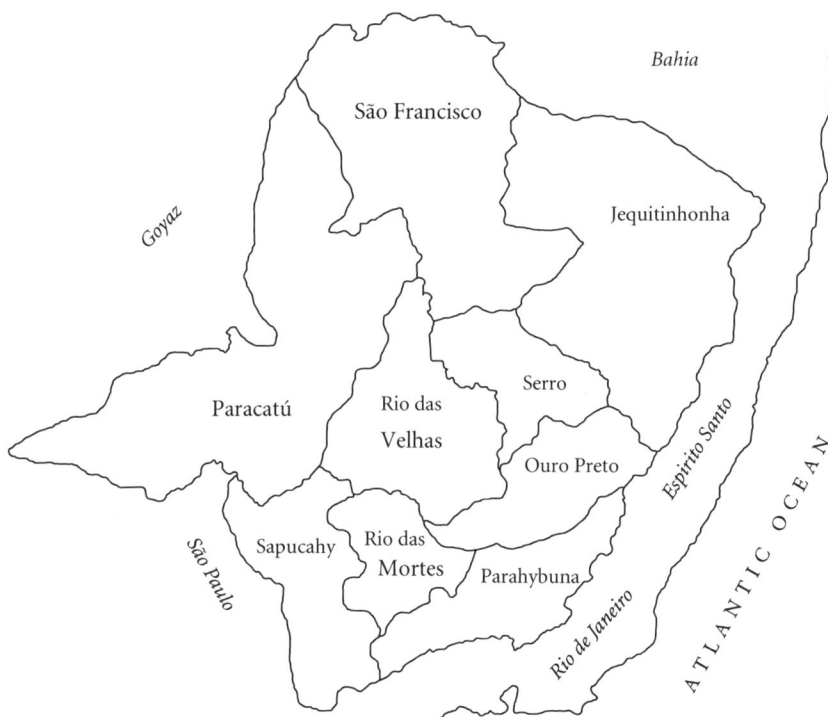

MAP 2.4   *Minas Gerais*
Author: Gustavo Acioli Lopes, 2013

79   Carrara, *Minas e Currais*, 144–145, 187–188, 199–206.
80   Up to the first quarter of the seventeenth century, Pernambuco, as the major sugar producing captaincy, received most of African slaves disembarked in Brazil. From the middle of the century onwards, Bahia took over the first position in imports and exports. Schwartz, *Segredos Internos*, 150, 158; Silva and Eltis, "The slave trade to Pernambuco," 108.

however, Rio itself became the main gateway from Africa for slaves bound to Minas.[81] Through Rio de Janeiro also entered the African slaves destined for São Paulo, where they would become engaged in foodstuff cash crops to meet growing demand in Minas Gerais and later in Rio de Janeiro itself.[82]

As long as most mining slaves come through Bahia and Pernambuco, both of which had ties with the Bight of Benin in the first third of eighteenth century,[83] "minas" slaves were a large component of slaves entering the mining regions of Brazil through 1730. *Mina* was the name that the Portuguese assigned to several West African ethnic groups[84] shipped from the Slave Coast.[85] The growing share of slaves from the lower Guinea Coast among the captives imported in Brazil in the golden age is also explained by the emergence of the Slave Coast as one of the major sources of forced labour through the transatlantic slave trade.[86]

---

81   From the 1730s, Rio became the main destination for the slaves exported from Luanda. Joseph C. Miller. "The Numbers, Origins, and Destinations of Slaves in the Eighteenth-Century Angolan Slave-Trade," in Joseph E. Inikori and Stanley L. Engerman, eds., *The Atlantic Slave Trade: Effects on Economies, Societies and Peoples in Africa, the Americas and Europe* (Durham, NC: Duke University Press, 1992), 90–95, tables 1 and 2.

82   In 1728, the contract for the collection of duties on slave imports inland through the "caminho novo" (new pathway) and the "caminho velho" (old pathway), both starting in Rio de Janeiro, superseded the contract for collecting duties on slave imports via the "caminho do sertão," starting in Bahia. However, this does not necessarily mean that Rio de Janeiro was already importing more slaves straight from Africa than indirectly through Bahia. In the years 1728–1731, the contract for slaves re-exports from Bahia to Minas Gerais had still a higher value than the contract for duty collection on slave imports from Rio to Minas. In those years most slaves departing from Pernambuco and Bahia to Minas Gerais were likely to be carried by the sea, in lieu of being carried along the São Francisco river shore, since the duties levied on slaves transported in this route doubled the taxes on slaves carried by sea to Rio de Janeiro. See: Carrara, *Minas e Currais*, 119–120; Lopes, "Negócio da Costa da Mina," 77, table 13.

83   In the case of Pernambuco, Angola was also its main source of slaves in the 1740s.

84   *Mina* slaves were mainly Kwa speakers from the Gold and Slave Coasts. See: Hall, *Slavery and African Ethnicities*, 47, 101–102.

85   Ibid., 111–114, 120, 124.

86   The slave trade was both cause and consequence for many wars in West Africa involving local states, as it was the case in the Bight of Benin, with the war between the *obá* (king) of Benin and the *egaevbo* (the officer in charge of foreign trade) in 1690. In this specific case, both Portuguese and Dutch intervened in support of the king, resulting in an increasing and steady supply of slaves. Identical results were achieved through European intervention in the wars between Dahomé kingdom and the kingdoms of Ardra (or Allada), Uidá (Whydah) and Oió (Oyo) in the years 1720–1740. See: Alberto da Costa e Silva, *A Manilha e o Libambo. A África e a escravidão, de 1500 a 1700* (Rio de Janeiro: Nova Fronteira, Fundação Biblioteca Nacional, 2002), 343–344; Robin Law, "Royal

Despite an alleged preference among mining entrepreneurs in Brazil for *minas* slaves,[87] as soon as Rio de Janeiro superseded Bahia and Pernambuco as the major entry point of African slaves entering Brazil, Angola became the main source of forced labour toiling in Brazilian gold mines. Luanda was the primary port of call for Portuguese-Brazilian slave ships arriving in Angola. From the 1720s it was joined by the southern port of Benguela, the trade in slaves from which had strong ties with Rio's slavers.[88]

Monopoly and Private Enterprise in the Atlantic Trade: The Case of Dahomey," *Journal of African History* 18 (1977): 558–559.

87   According to eighteenth-Brazilian mining entrepreneurs "mina" slaves were the fittest for mining work; slaves from the Bight of Benin, in particular, were regarded as more resistant and skilled for gold mining than Angolan slaves, who were deemed as more friendly, although less resilient and thus more appropriate for agricultural work. Luis Viana Filho, *O Negro na Bahia* (Rio de Janeiro: Nova Fronteira, 1988), 87–92; Verger, *Fluxo e Refluxo*, 94. Nevertheless, as three leading scholars point out: "Buyers of slaves in the Americas wanted a cheap supply of undifferentiated labor for field work [...]. Buyer preferences for peoples from particular regions in Africa could be exercised only in the largest markets of the Caribbean, such as Barbados, Jamaica, and Saint Domingue, where vessels from all parts of Africa arrived in large numbers. Even in these places, planter preferences were not central." David Eltis, Philip Morgan and David Richardson, "Agency and Diaspora in Atlantic History: Reassessing the African Contribution to Rice Cultivation in the Americas," *American Historical Review* 112:5 (2007), 1339. This seems to have been the case regarding slaves' regional origins, but buyers' preference probably determined the gender pattern of the Atlantic (and Indian Ocean) slave trades, although this claim has been recently challenged; see: Herbert S. Klein, *The Atlantic Slave Trade* (New York, NY: Cambridge University Press, 1999), 165. For a counter-argument, see: Joseph. E. Inikori, "Review of Herbert S. Klein, *The Atlantic Slave Trade* (New York, NY: Cambridge University Press, 1999)," *Hispanic American Historical Review* 82:1 (2002): 130–135. Information on the British slave trade provided by other scholars underpins Inikori's argument. See again: Eltis, Morgan and Richardson, "Agency and Diaspora in Atlantic History," 1350–1351, where references to slave merchants' letters testifying their preference for male slaves can be found.

88   Miller, *Way of Death*, 232–233; Curto, *Álcool e Escravos*, 275–276, 340, table 4. Mina Gerais' inventories of slave owners, baptismal registers, obituaries and tax rolls for the eighteenth and nineteenth centuries confirm that *mina* slaves predominated up to 1730, while *angolas* were the majority between then and the 1780s. Bergad, *Escravidão e história econômica*, 229, graph 4.10; Francisco Vidal Luna and Iraci del Nero Costa, "Algumas características do contingente de cativos em Minas Gerais," in F.V. Luna, I. del N. Costa and Herbert S. Klein, *Escravismo em São Paulo e Minas Gerais* (São Paulo: Imprensa Oficial, Editora da Universidade de São Paulo, 2009), 25–29, tables 5–8.

   Although gold mining increased demand for slaves in Brazil and helped to
reinvigorate the slave trade of its northeastern ports, it is also brought about
higher slave prices, thereby increasing the costs of sugar production, which
depended on slave imports too. This posed problems for northeastern sugar
growers when sugar prices declined or stagnated during and after 1720–1730.[89]
In this context, it is worth noting that sugar exports from Bahia and
Pernambuco waxed and waned, with 5–15 year cycles of expansion alternating
with cycles of decline. Thus they increased in 1701–1710; declined in the following five years; recovered and increased in 1716–1730; and then turned steeply
downward from the 1730s.[90] Such trends were not, however, uniform across all
cash crop exports, including tobacco. Tobacco, as we have seen, was produced
in Brazil from the early seventeenth century onwards, but it became a regular
export commodity only from the middle of the century and by the 1670s taxation on Brazilian tobacco was one of the chief sources of Portugal's state revenues. In Portugal, sales of tobacco to the home market were subject to a
monopoly contract sold at auction. Brazilian tobacco was also re-exported to
other European markets, including France, Spain, Italy and Northern Europe.
In these markets, however, Brazilian tobacco faced strong competition from
increasing tobacco production in British mainland America.[91] Such tobacco
dominated the British market and increasingly challenged Brazilian tobacco
in other ones, particularly France.[92] Although never a major employer of
slave labour – it was usually a kind of small-scale cash crop feasible for household production without slaves – nevertheless tobacco exports from Brazil

---

89   Schwartz, *Segredos Internos*, 147, 151, 166–167.
90   It is worth mentioning, though, that historians disagree on the time spam of the Bahia's
      export crisis. For Schwartz the crisis was already a reality in the early 1720s. Galloway, "Nordeste
      do Brasil, 1700–1750. Reexame de uma crise," 92–93, 95; Schwartz, *Segredos Internos*, 165–169.
      Tithe auction values showed a similar trend: the value for the captaincy of Pernambuco felt
      continuously from 1706–1711, with only a slight increase between 1712 and 1721, followed by
      stagnation and decline between mid-1720 and the late 1750s. As for the tithes of Bahia, the
      contract value grew until the 1710s but remained below average in the following decades.
      Therefore, in the first half of the eighteenth century, while demand for slaves in mining areas
      grew, in sugar areas it tended to decline steadily. Galloway, "Nordeste do Brasil, 1700–1750.
      Reexame de uma crise," 93, 97; Carrara, *Receitas e despesas da Real Fazenda*, 2: 72, 107.
91   Alan Kulikoff, *Tobacco and Slaves* (Chapel Hill, NC: University of North Carolina Press,
      1986), 31–32.
92   France tried even to support tobacco growing in their own Caribbean colonies and cre-
      ated a market for the product by overtaxing the import and consumption of Brazilian
      tobacco. Jacob Price, *France and the Chesapeake: A history of the French tobacco monopoly,
      1674–1791* (Ann Arbor, MI: University of Michigan Press, 1973), 4–5, 21, 42.

TABLE 2.3 *Brazilian tobacco exports to Portugal, 1671–1750*

Years	Tons	Index
1671–1675	1,470	
1676–1680	1,275	87
1681–1685	1,829	124
1686–1690	1,183	80
1691–1695	1,496	102
1696–1700	2,112	144
1701–1705	2,540	173
1706–1710	2,310	157
1711–1715	1,763	120
1716–1720	2,110	144
1721–1725	2,290	156
1726–1730	2,477	168
1731–1735	1,471	100
1736–1740	2,196	149
1741–1745	2,330	159
1746–1750	2,506	170

Source: Based on Nardi, *O Fumo Brasileiro*, 115, table 3.5
Note: Nardi gives the amounts in *arrobas*
(where one *arroba*=14.7 kilograms)

rose in the first half of the eighteenth century. This reflected shipments to Portugal which increased somewhat unevenly at that time, as Table 2.3 shows.[93] It also reflected exports through Bahia and, to a lesser extent, through Pernambuco to the Slave Coast, where, together with gold, tobacco became through 1740 one of the two chief colonial commodities by which Portuguese traders procured European trade goods from the other traders in order to make up the bundles of goods required to buy slaves there.[94] We shall return to this later.

93 Catherine Lugar, "The Portuguese Tobacco Trade and Tobacco Growers of Bahia in the Late Colonial Period," in Dauril Alden and Warren Dean, eds., *Essays Concerning the Socioeconomic History of Brazil and Portuguese India* (Gainesville, FL: University Press of Florida, 1977), 28–29, 33; Nardi, *O fumo brasileiro no período colonial*, 111–115, 336–342.
94 Lopes, "Negócio da Costa da Mina," 25, 129, *et passim*; Lopes and Menz, "Resgate e Mercadorias," 58–60.

In sum, growing demand for slaves to produce precious metals and other minerals, to produce cash crops to satisfy local markets for foodstuffs in mining areas, and to meet growing markets for Brazilian tobacco in Portugal and Africa offset weakening demand for newly imported African in the sugar sector, helping to explain Brazil's import of almost one million slaves direct from Africa in the first half of the eighteenth century.[95]

From Crisis to Agricultural Renaissance: the Late Colonial Economy and the Peak of Slave Trade to Brazil

In the decade 1760–1770, Brazil's colonial economy underwent a serious crisis, stemming from the decline of gold mining as well as weak performance among other Brazilian commodity exports. The measures devised by the Portuguese crown to try to solve the economic troubles of its pivotal colony are well known and have been widely debated.[96] As regards sugar, still the most important of Brazil's commodity exports at the time, exports dwindled from the mid-1750s down to 1780, though they occasionally recovered at times when warfare in Europe hindered exports of sugar from the colonies of other powers. Overall, the number of sugar mills in the northeastern captaincies (Bahia, Pernambuco, and the ancillary captaincies Sergipe and Alagoas) clearly fell up to the early 1770s.[97] Likewise, the number of slaves disembarked in the two major captaincies fell between 10 and 20 percent between 1720–1740 and 1760–1780.[98]

Between the 1780s and the beginning of the following century, and in tandem with continuing decline in gold mining, a decrease occurred absolutely and proportionally in Minas Gerais' slave population: the proportion of slaves in the captaincy's population fell from almost 50 percent to just under 35 percent. During these years, the captaincy's demographic and socio-economic

---

95   Slave imports totalled some 976, 268 slaves, including disembarkations in the "Amazon," which accounted for less than one percent of the total. Eltis and Richardson, "A new assessment," 16–17, table 1.3.

96   One of the best surveys can be found in Kenneth R. Maxwell, "Pombal and the Nationalization of the Luso-Brazilian Economy," *Hispanic American Historical Review* 48:4 (1968): 608–631.

97   Schwartz, *Segredos Internos*, 339–343; see also: Dauril Alden, *Royal Government in Colonial Brazil* (Berkeley, CA.: University of California Press, 1968), 557.

98   Silva and Eltis, "The slave trade to Pernambuco," 102–103; Ribeiro, "The Atlantic Slave Trade to Bahia, 1582–185," 134.

structures were redrawn. A major part of the population moved towards the southern and southwestern frontier, away from the mining areas; at the same time, farming, cattle breeding and dairy-farming became Minas Gerais' chief economic sectors. This transition was only possible because of rising demand for foodstuffs in the local markets, particularly Rio de Janeiro after 1808.[99]

From the last quarter of the eighteenth century, political and economic factors in the Western Hemisphere encouraged rising Brazilian commodity exports other than gold and, in conjunction with this, rising imports of enslaved Africans. More specifically, the War of American Independence (1776–1783), the French Revolution and subsequent Revolutionary and Napoleonic Wars (1793–1815), and the Haitian Revolution (1791) pushed up commodity prices generally and re-opened opportunities for Brazilian goods in European markets.

Sugar and coffee exports increased for more or less four decades, bringing back prosperity to more traditional regions and stimulating production in regions more recently developed, especially in São Paulo and in particular areas of Rio de Janeiro. We have already observed how Minas Gerais turned to food-stuff production for local markets and for coastal exporting regions. The same occurred also in the most southerly region of Portuguese settlement, Rio Grande do Sul, which supplied *charque* (jerked beef) and wheat to Rio de Janeiro and to the northeastern captaincies, receiving in exchange European merchandize, tropical goods, and African slaves.[100] Earlier this region had been the gateway for African slave smuggling from Brazil through Buenos Aires and toward Potosí's silver mines (in present-day Bolivia), whence silver found its way into Portuguese hands. Portuguese settlement had been initiated there in 1680, but had been only properly established from the mid-eighteenth century.[101]

In the lands of northern Rio de Janeiro, sugar mills multiplied, increasing sugar's share among the captaincy's exports.[102] The number of sugar mills in

---

99   Bergad, *Escravidão e história econômica*, 56, 160–165. The author challenges Martins and Martins' argument that after the mining crisis Minas Gerais' economy became auto-sufficient depending mainly on internal captaincy markets, and abandoning its connections with Brazilian external trade. A.V. Martins Filho and R.B. Martins, "Slavery in a no export economy: nineteenth-century Minas Gerais revisited," *Hispanic American Historical Review* 63:3 (1983): 537–568.

100 Maximiliano M. Menz, *Entre Impérios: Formação do Rio Grande na crise do sistema colonial português* (São Paulo: Alameda, 2009), 120–121.

101 Alden, *Royal Government*, 67–68, 117. In 1680, the Portuguese Crown set up a fortified settlement in the eastern margin of Rio de la Plata, named Sacramento. Despite lasting over a century, the fort remained a stronghold used for smuggling, and never evolved into a settlement colony.

102 After 1756, the headquarters of the Royal Government of Brazil were based in Rio.

Campos dos Goitacazes grew from 56 in 1759 to 378 in 1798–1799, while the overall total in the captaincy reached 616 by the latter date.[103] In São Paulo (shown
in Map 2.5), sugar became the main economic activity in the late eighteenth
century, and was sponsored by the Portuguese state. It was produced on the
northern shore and in the areas to the west of São Paulo itself. Although the
captaincy of São Paulo had a diversified farming economy, producing cash crops
for sale in Rio de Janeiro and Minas Gerais from the early eighteenth century,
sugar was the first principal export crop of the *Paulista* captaincy. In the years
before sugar emerged as a major cash crop, the share of slaves in São Paulo's
population was modest, reaching 27 percent in 1760. As sugar production developed, that percentage grew together with the average number of slaves per
owner, with as many in sugar production as in producing other foodstuffs.[104]

MAP 2.5   *São Paulo*
            Author: Gustavo Acioli Lopes, 2013

103   Dauril Alden, "O período final do Brasil colônia: 1750–1808," in Leslie Bethell, ed., *História
      da América Latina* (São Paulo; Brasília, DF: Editora da Universidade de São Paulo; FUNAG,
      2004), 2: 559–560.
104   Francisco V. Luna and Herbert S. Klein, *Evolução da sociedade e economia escravista de São
      Paulo, de 1750 a 1850* (São Paulo: Editora da Universidade de São Paulo, 2006), 39, 41, 55, 62,
      70–75. In Jundiaí, the main sugar producing town in the captaincy of São Paulo, the slave

In Pernambuco and Bahia, too, the revival of the sugar economy saw an increase in the number of sugar mills. In Pernambuco, there were 268 in 1761 and 390 in 1777 (including the neighbouring Paraíba). Sugar exports rose on average by close to 32 percent between the late 1760s and the end of the following decade. From 1800 down to 1810, in nominal figures, sugar exports rose almost 90 percent.[105] In real prices, the value of Pernambuco's sugar exports doubled between the years 1836–1840 and 1846–1850.[106]

In Bahia (including Sergipe), the number of sugar mills rose from 166 in 1759, to 400 in 1798, to 500 in 1820, and to 603 in 1834.[107] Sugar exports reached 30,000 boxes (ca. 17,640 tons) in 1817; four decades earlier, in the 1770s, Bahia had exported only 10,000 boxes on average.[108]

To buoyancy in sugar exports, one might also add growth in tobacco and cotton exports, too, from the late eighteenth century. After decades of stagnation in 1728–1774, Bahia's tobacco exports increased once again: the average Lisbon import in 1801–1805 was double that of 1771–1775. Some decline occurred after 1815 and lasted until the 1830s, before recovery began again in the middle of the following decade.[109] At the same time, tobacco exports to the Slave Coast almost doubled between the years 1791–1795 and 1801–1805; and they continued to rise thereafter, by 1826–1830 reaching triple the level of 1791–95.[110] One factor driving such exports was rising slave prices in Africa above the Equator, consequent upon continuing high demand for slaves after 1815 and efforts to suppress the slave trade in West Africa.[111] The result of these trends was a further cementing of the use of slave labour in tobacco cultivation that had begun during the eighteenth century. In places where tobacco, together with foodstuffs, was the main crop, slaves comprised from one fifth to one third of local population, according to data for the period

---

population trebled between 1778 and 1836. Moreover, whereas in 1778 two thirds of the slave population lived in plantations with 10 or fewer slaves, by 1836 that proportion had fallen to 28 percent.

105   Alden, *Royal Government*, 557–559, table 6; José Jobson de A. Arruda, *O Brasil no Comércio Colonial* (São Paulo: Ática 1980), 224, table 26.

106   Peter Eisenberg, *Modernização sem mudança* (Campinas: UNICAMP, 1977), 42, graph 3.

107   Schwartz, *Segredos Internos*, 343–344.

108   Ibid., 344. Each sugar crate (or box) contained 40 thousand *arrobas* or 588 kilograms.

109   Nardi, *O fumo brasileiro no período colonial*, 151, table 4.3, 163, table 5.1; Bert J. Barickman. *Um Contraponto Baiano: açúcar, fumo, mandioca e escravidão no Recôncavo, 1780–1860* (Rio de Janeiro: Civilização Brasileira, 2003), 65–67.

110   Nardi, *O fumo brasileiro no período colonial*, 263, table 8.1.

111   After 1811, the number of slaves from the *Costa da Mina* disembarked in Bahia in fact declined. Ribeiro, "The Atlantic Slave Trade to Bahia, 1582–1851," 140, table 4.4.

1780–1860.[112] Average slave ownership in tobacco operations was 6.5 slaves, though units with 5 or fewer slaves were in the majority.[113]

Cotton was a late cash crop in colonial Brazilian history. Its farming was sponsored by two monopoly companies chartered in Portugal – the *Companhia Geral de Pernambuco e Paraíba* (hereafter CGPP) (1755–1777) and the *Companhia do Grão-Pará e Maranhão* (hereafter CGPM) (1756–1777) – but it boomed in part in response to British demand for cotton from the last quarter of eighteenth century. Table 2.4 provides information on Brazilian cotton exports through 1811. In the captaincies from Sergipe to Paraíba, most cotton production was household based from the 1770s, and developed after the worst years of the sugar economy in 1760–1770. Following a drought in 1790, which harmed the region's commodity output, cotton production inland in the *Zona da Mata* – Atlantic forest region – and *Agreste* – semi-arid region – was adopted on both household units of production as well as on slave estates.[114] In Maranhão, the CGPM sowed the seeds of cotton and rice cash crops, the success of which in the following decade prompted rising slave imports into the captaincy: only 34 slaves on average disembarked in the years 1680–1755 but the average rose to 472 in 1756–1777, to more than 1,500 in the 1780s and 1790s, and to 2,149 in the first decade of the following century.[115] Cotton's share in Brazil's exports remained important up to 1830, but thereafter diminished in the face of North American and Asian competition in cotton supply to western markets. In the years 1801–1810, however, its share in Bahia's exports stood at 14.5 percent; in Pernambuco's 48.3 percent; and in Maranhão's 70.3 percent.[116]

Among the newer crops introduced into Brazilian exports after the 1770s, it was coffee that had the greatest importance in the long run. First introduced in Pará in eighteenth century and subsequently commercially produced in Maranhão and Bahia, it was to be in Rio de Janeiro where it would become the main export crop from the second decade of nineteenth century. Within

---

112   This proportion is inferior to parishes in sugar growing areas. There, between half and two third of the population was enslaved. Barickman also points out that between three quarters and 90 percent of the tobacco and sugar planters were owners of slaves. These figures might have been, however, slightly distorted by the use of inventories as the main primary source, as the author also highlights. Barickman, *Um Contraponto Baiano*, 214–215, 217, footnote 4.

113   Ibid., 237–241.

114   Guillermo Palacios, *Cultivadores libres: Estado y crisis de la esclavitud en la época de la Revolución Industrial* (México, DF: Colegio de México, Fondo de Cultura, 1998), 122–124, 143–149.

115   Silva, "The Atlantic Slave Trade to Maranhão," 484, 497, appendix A.

116   Calculations based on Arruda, *O Brasil no Comércio Colonial*, 206, 226, 246, tables 23, 27, 41.

TABLE 2.4   *Brazil's cotton exports, 1796–1811*

Year	Tons	Cruzados (1=1X1.000)
1796	5,447	2.986.746
1797	2,005	1.309.632
1798	3,400	2.678.639
1799	4,801	4.441.910
1800	6,015	5.302.701
1801	6,439	5.270.485
1802	8,278	5.766.615
1803	8,725	6.267.730
1804	7,380	5.912.353
1805	8,310	5.992.212
1806	7,525	5.733.280
1807	9,302	7.289.994
1808[a]	121	94.568
1809	3,296	2.296.289
1810	1,510	1.051.576
1811	711	325.228

Source: Arruda, *O Brasil no Comércio Colonial*, 368–369, table 52
Note:
a. In 1808, Brazil's exports plummeted due to the Napoleonic Wars and the
Continental Blockade. After the Portuguese royal family moved to Brazil under
British protection and, then, opening Brazil's ports to all friendly nations,
exports tended to normalize.

another decade, it had become the most important of all Brazil's exports.
Accounting for 18.4 percent of Brazil's exports by value in the 1820s, coffee
accounted for 40 percent from the 1830s through the 1850s, when it was the
chief Brazilian export commodity.[117] Coffee growing was concentrated overwhelmingly in the Paraíba Valley, particularly on the Rio de Janeiro side, but
was also centred around São Paulo's northeastern cities as well as Minas Gerais'
Zona da Mata, as noted earlier. By the 1840s Brazil had 40 percent of world coffee output, and its output has been second to none since then.[118]

---

117   Leslie Bethell and J.M. de Carvalho, "1822–1870," in Leslie Bethell, ed., *Brazil: Empire and
Republic (1822–1930)* (Cambridge: Cambridge University Press, 1989), 86–87, tables 1, 3.
118   Ibid., 85.

Renewed export growth in more traditional crops allied to the emergence of new export crops such as cotton and above all coffee triggered an unprecedented rise in the import of forced African labourers in Brazil. According to the newest estimates, average annual slave disembarkations in Brazil were just above 20,000 between 1740 and 1780. They then rose to close to 30,000 in the last decade of the eighteenth century, to more than 36,000 in the following decade, to 48,000 in the 1810s, and to just over 55,000 in the 1820s.[119] It is estimated that in the first half of nineteenth century, Brazil imported more slaves than in the whole former century.[120] Growth of imports was matched by changes in their control, with the port of Rio de Janeiro accounting for 42 percent of slaves disembarked in 1791–1820 and 60 percent in 1821–1830.[121] From Rio, slaves were dispersed to coffee, sugar and foodstuff-producing areas in the Paraíba Valley, São Paulo and Minas Gerais.[122]

Though Minas Gerais was entangled in the "agricultural revival" in late eighteenth century Brazil through supplying foodstuffs to areas producing export crops as well as to smaller local markets, Bergad has argued that, with the exception of a few areas and years, Minas no longer depended on African slave imports after 1780 to replenish the captaincy's slave labour force. He supports his argument by reference to changes in the sex balance of the population, a rising share of slaves reported under 20 years old in the population, and a rise in the child/woman ratio within the slave population not dissimilar to that found in the British North American mainland colonies before 1776 as well as the southern United States before 1860, where the slave population generally grew through natural reproduction.[123]

---

119 Eltis and Richardson, "A new assessment," 16–17, table 1.3.

120 Actually, six percent greater.

121 These figures are based on Eltis and Richardson, "A new assessment," 16–17, table 1.3 and data for Rio de Janeiro provided by Manolo Florentino, "The slave trade, colonial markets, and slave families in Rio de Janeiro, ca. 1790-ca. 1830," in Eltis and Richardson, *Extending the frontiers*, 280, table 10.2. Manolo Florentino, *Em costas negras. Uma história do tráfico entre a África e o Rio de Janeiro* (São Paulo: Companhia das Letras, 1997), 66, table 4, calculated Rio de Janeiro's share at 42 percent in the 1790s, and rising to 70 percent in the 1820s, using data from David Eltis, *Economic Growth and the Ending of the Transatlantic Slave Trade* (Oxford: Oxford University Press, 1987), which were updated in TSTD 2.

122 Crops were not necessarily separated, for instance coffee production was frequently linked foodstuff crops, as was the case in São Paulo. Luna and Klein, *Evolução da sociedade e economia escravista*, 83–86.

123 Bergad drew on the population censuses for the eighteenth and nineteenth centuries, as well on inventories for the four counties, which counted 10,000 slaves. Bergad, *Escravidão e história econômica*, 176–184, graphs 3.2 to 3.3; 206–220, graphs 4.2 to 4.6 and table 4.1.

Nevertheless, the available data on African slave re-exports from Rio to Minas Gerais in the first decades of nineteenth century cast doubt on the possibility that Minas' slave population growth was due only to natural increase. From 1810 to 1812, 41 percent of African slaves traded in Rio de Janeiro had as their final destination Minas Gerais.[124] Moreover, this pattern did not change markedly in later years. In 1825–30, for example, 43 percent of the slaves traded in Rio de Janeiro were bound for Minas Gerais.[125] This represented a sizeable number of slaves given the scale of Rio's slave imports in 1810–30.

The remaining gold-mining areas of Minas as well as the thriving areas of coffee production were importing slaves. In Serro Frio and Vila Rica, both mining centres, as well as in the coffee producing southeastern *Zona da Mata* counties, masculinity ratios were still around 60 percent in the 1830s, a pattern strongly indicative of continuing slave imports from Africa.[126] In the last region, coffee production had been set up in the early nineteenth century and provided almost one quarter of its exports in the 1840s.[127] As Bergad himself concedes, slave imports into Minas Gerais increased in the years 1790–1795, 1805–1815 and 1820–1830; in the first period, they reflected a steep rise in commodity exports, which boosted local demand for foodstuffs from the hinterland's slave-based activity. That in the second resulted from the rise in food production in response to the arrival of the Portuguese Court in Rio de Janeiro. The third was attributed to renewed and increased levels of gold mining.[128]

After decades of declining returns from alluvial gold extraction, gold mining partially regained its former importance in Minas Gerais' economy in the same places where it had thrived one hundred years earlier. On this occasion, however, the entrepreneurs were foreign groups authorized after 1808 to carry out new searches in Brazil. The resulting scale of gold mining exceeded previous levels, thus absorbing a sizeable proportion of the province's slave labour force in the 1830s (though not as big as its share in the earlier peak years of mining)[129] and contributing about 20 percent of Minas' exports in the years between 1818–19 and 1854.[130]

124   Florentino, "The slave trade," 296–297, table 10.2.

125   João L. Fragoso, *Homens de Grossa Aventura: Acumulação e hierarquia na praça mercantil do Rio de Janeiro (1790–1830)* (Rio de Janeiro: Civilização Brasileira, 1998), 177, table 12.9.

126   Douglas C. Libby, *Transformação e trabalho em uma economia escravista: Minas Gerais no século XIX* (São Paulo: Brasiliense, 1988), 57–58, graph 4.

127   Bergad *Escravidão e história econômica*, 92–93.

128   Ibid., 201–205, 221–222; Libby, *Transformação e trabalho*, 86–90, 139–140.

129   In 1735 and 1749, 70 percent of slaves lived in the mining villages or in their neighbouring areas. Bergad, *Escravidão e história econômica*, 148–171.

130   Libby, *Transformação e trabalho*, 86–90, graph 6; Bergad, *Escravidão e história econômica*, 74, 85, 92–94, 97.

Slave labour was as pervasive in towns as in rural parishes, at least from the eighteenth century, when Brazilian cities became large and densely populated.[131] Evidence on Brazil's population is presented in Table 2.5 and on Rio de Janeiro's urban population in Table 2.6. Foreigners travelling through Brazil described the different types of slaves who worked and plied their crafts in city streets. There were many activities in which slaves were engaged. Female slaves predominated in domestic work, as well as in selling groceries and candy. Male slaves were porters, carrying people, goods such as sugar crates, coffee sacks, and cotton bales, and heavier items, and commonly worked in groups, known as *cantos* ('corners'). There were skilled slaves working as blacksmiths, shoemakers, coopers, and in other crafts, labouring in their masters' workshops as much as roaming the streets in search of anybody who wished to hire their labour. In addition, slaves were engaged in seafaring jobs, and were to be found working on slave ships as well as in coastal

TABLE 2.5   *Brazil's population in the early nineteenth century*

1810				1819		
Captaincy	Free[b]	Slave	Slave/Total (in percent)	Free	Slave	Slave/Total (in percent)
Pernambuco	286,934	105,052	27	270,832	97,633	26
Bahia	190,502	168,935	47	330,469	147,263	31
Minas Gerais	292,403	202,356	41	463,342	168,543	27
Rio de Janeiro	124,204	105,378	46	363,940	146,060	29
São Paulo	175,398	33,409	16	160,656	77,667	33
Maranhão	42,584	36,276	46	–	–	–
Total[a]	1,303,826	720,409	35	2,488,743	1,107,389	31

Sources: For 1810: Maria Luiza Marcilio, "A população do Brasil colonial," in Leslie Bethell, ed., *História da América Latina* (São Paulo; Brasília, df: Edusp; funag, 2004), 2: 338, table 5. For 1819: Dauril Alden, "Late colonial Brazil, 1750–1808," in Leslie Bethell, ed., *Colonial Brazil* (Cambridge: Cambridge University Press, 1987), 290, table 4.
Note:
a. Other captaincies included;
b. Including whites, Indians, mulattos and blacks.

131   The three major towns in Brazil were among the biggest urban populations in America, even when compared with British towns; Dauril Alden, "O período final do Brasil colônia: 1750–1808," in Leslie Bethell, ed., *História da América Latina: America Latina Colonial* (São Paulo: Editora da Universidade de São Paulo, 1999), 2: 533.

TABLE 2.6   *Population of the city of Rio de Janeiro, 1821*

Areas	Total Population	Free Population	Slave Population	Slave/Total (in percent)
Urban	86,323	45,947	40,376	47
Rural	30,121	12,948	17,173	57
Total	116,444	58,895	57,549	49

Source: José Carlos Soares, *O "povo de Cam" na Capital do Brasil: escravidão urbana no Rio de Janeiro do século XIX* (Rio de Janeiro: FAPERJ, & 7 Letras, 2005), 363, table 1

or river navigation.[132] One consequence of such activities is that they improved the chances of slaves liberating themselves. Manumission was relatively common in colonial Brazil compared to other slave-owning societies in the Americas, but in the urban world of Brazil, slaves found more opportunities to buy themselves out of bondage, paying their masters prices settled by the authorities. Through urban work, slaves could amass sufficient money to make self-emancipation more probable than in other forms of work.[133]

In sum, Brazil's status as one of the major slave-owning colonies in the early nineteenth century in the Americas was reflected in the continuing high share of slaves in its total population at that time. Figures relating to the proportions of slaves in Brazil's population are presented in Tables 2.5 and 2.6.

---

132   A.J. Russell-Wood, *The black man in slavery and freedom in Colonial Brazil* (New York, NY: Macmillan Press, 1982), 33–35; Freyre, *Casa Grande e Senzala*, 464, 469, 477. Freyre pioneered analyses on urban slave labour, resorting to several reports from contemporary travellers and colonial dwellers; see, among others, Daniel P. Kidder and J.C. Fletcher, *Brazil and the Brazilians, Portrayed in Historical and Descriptive Sketches* (California, CA: Elibron, 2005); Louis F. Tollenare, *Notas Dominicais tomadas durante uma viagem em Portugal e no Brasil em 1816, 1817 e 1818* (Recife: Secretaria de Educação e Cultura, 1978); Henry Koster, *Travels in Brazil* (London: Longman, 1817).

133   On manumission practices in colonial Brazil, see: Stuart B. Schwartz, "The Manumission of Slaves in Colonial Brazil: Bahia, 1684–1745," *Hispanic American Historical Review* 54:4 (1974): 603–635. In this case, female and mulatto slaves were the majority among freed slaves; see also: José Carlos Soares, *O "povo de Cam" na Capital do Brasil: escravidão urbana no Rio de Janeiro do século XIX* (Rio de Janeiro: FAPERJ & Letras, 2005), 276–287. Based on a set of 977 manumission letters, Soares made clear that manumission with no financial compensation was more usual than paid manumission in 1808–1888.

Commodities and Manufactured Goods in the Luso-Brazilian Slave Trade: the Total Supply

The Portuguese slave trade that supplied Brazil with African labour was unusual in that the great majority of the slaves disembarking in Brazil in the eighteenth and nineteenth centuries were carried away from Africa in ships that had left from Brazil rather than from Europe.[134] The route of the Atlantic slave trade to Brazil was thus primarily a bilateral rather than a multilateral one of the sort attributed to the European-based slave trade. Given this pattern, some historians have assumed that this branch of Atlantic slave commerce was under the control of Brazilian merchants, who, relying upon local tobacco, sugarcane rum, and, for some decades, gold to exchange for slaves in Africa, superseded Portugal's traders. However, two comments on this issue are necessary.

First, as Joseph Miller has argued, from the 1720s the import and export trade in Luanda was controlled by the leaseholders of custom duties relating to slave exports. These were all Lisbon businessmen, whose gained advantages in trade from their financial power and their close relations with metropolitan and colonial authorities. Nevertheless, though those businessmen financed most slave dealers in Luanda, they avoided converting their investments into slaves, because they were aware of the risks that such investments in overseas human trafficking entailed.[135] A report to the Portuguese Crown about the feasibility of a proposal relating to the Crown's possible direct participation in Angola's slave trade sums up the inbuilt risks of this kind of deal:

> What is true is that the trade of Angola is not a deal in which one can be sure to garner profits, because it is restricted to Negroes [that is, slaves], who run away, eat, and die. And the losses have been so great, that there are few dwellers [in Lisbon] who wish to risk their goods. And when they send them [i.e. goods to Angola], it is only goods which cannot be traded in this kingdom, and nobody requires the returns in Negroes, except when Letters [of Exchange] are unavailable.[136]

In order to avoid dealing with 'merchandize' that *fled, ate and died,* backers of Luanda's slave trade put off the risks of slave ownership to Angolan and Brazilian

---

134 In the eighteenth century, the mainland British colonies also sent slave ships straight to Africa, but their number was never greater than British shipping.

135 Miller, *Way of Death*, 257, 264, 274, 285–286, 295–296, 299–300, 311–312, 315–317. See also: Miller, "Capitalism and Slaving," 1–56.

136 From earlier years, these risks became a structural feature of Portuguese slave trade. AHU, *Angola*, cx. 9. doc. 13: 1666-02-19: 'Consulta do Conselho Ultramarino sobre o papel que se deu a Sua Magestade acerca do comércio que se deve conceder em Angola aos Genovezes'.

merchants, whose vessels transported African slaves to Brazil. The Luso-Brazilian slave dealers, in turn, made remittances from Brazil in order to cover the bills of exchange that their African business partners had charged against Brazilian merchants' accounts.

Second, it is useful to note how the Portuguese procured slaves in Africa. Like others they exchanged goods for slaves, but their trade showed some peculiarities. Textiles (including Asian cotton fabrics) accompanied by guns, brass and pewter wares, other metalwares, and liquor, overwhelmingly made up European slave ship cargoes, and the same was true regarding Portuguese traders.[137] What distinguished Portuguese from other European slave traders is the fact that slave ships clearing from Brazil usually carried tropical goods to barter in Africa for slaves.[138] Moreover, during the first half of the eighteenth century, Luso-Brazilian slavers were successful in Bight of Benin markets in part because they brought tobacco sweetened with molasses but even more importantly because they traded with gold taken illicitly from Brazil. With this Brazilian gold, Bahian and Pernambuco traders purchased from northwestern European traders manufactured goods required to engage with Africans in purchasing slaves.[139]

As regards Brazil-Angola trade, it has been demonstrated that the part played by Brazilian *cachaça* (sugar-cane rum) in Portuguese barters for slaves in Angolan markets has been overestimated.[140] Furthermore, comparing custom data for Portuguese, Angolan, and Brazilian ports, one scholar has estimated that from 1796 to 1807 Portugal supplied 56–62 percent of Luanda's imports.[141] Furthermore, as the data presented in Tables 2.7 and 2.8 show,

---

137   Eltis, *The Rise of African Slavery in the Americas*, 168–169, 184–190; Curtin, *The Rise and Fall of Plantation Complex*, 133–135.

138   The slave trade from Rhode Island, one of the mainland British colonies, also resorted to home produced goods, namely rum, distilled out of molasses.

139   Lopes, "Negócio da Costa da Mina," 148–164. Based on contemporary reports and ship cargoes, I argue that at least 50 percent of slave cargoes were purchased with manufactured goods. It should be noted that Bahia and Pernambuco imported close to 40 percent of the slaves exported from the Bight of Benin in the years 1700–1760, while the Brazilian tobacco exports toward West Africa accounted for only five to 10 percent of the Bight of Benin imports; see: Lopes, Ibid., 200 and also: Eltis, *The Rise of African Slavery in America*, 173–174; Silva and Eltis, "The Slave Trade to Pernambuco," 108–109. Although these authors claim that gold enabled the Luso-Brazilian slave traders "to outbid their English and French competitors for slaves in West Africa," that overestimates the role of Luso-Brazilian merchants among European slave dealers in that African region.

140   Curto, *Álcool e Escravos*, 305; Lopes and Menz, "Resgate e Mercadorias," 68–70.

141   Maximiliano M. Menz, "As "Geometrias" do Tráfico: o comércio metropolitano e o tráfico de escravos em Angola (1796–1807)," *Revista de História* 166 (2012): 185–222. Besides

68 LOPES

TABLE 2.7   *Origin of goods imported into Luanda, 1785–1809*

Years	Europe (in percent)	Brazil (in percent)	Asia (in percent)
1785–1797	44	22	34
1795–1797	41	32	38
1798–1799	40	18	42
1802–1803	49	16	35
1808–1809	33	28	39

Source: Lopes and Menz, "Resgate e Mercadorias," 54

TABLE 2.8   *Portugal's contribution to supplying the Angolan slave trade (in Réis)*

	(A)	(B)	(C)	(A)/(B)	(A)/(C)
Years	Portuguese exports	Gross Angolan imports	Slaves exports	(in percent)	(in percent)
1796	147.576.210		621.834.000		24
1797	126.063.218		549.427.000		23
1798	202.270.993	355.565.753	643.184.000	57	31
1799	427.829.486	581.280.590	512.034.000	74	84
1800	444.749.540		494.710.000		90
1801	665.781.400		618.540.000		108
1802	531.446.477	998.801.831	730.658.000	53	73
1803	480.789.012	995.372.678	874.862.000	48	55
1804	586.978.155	988.522.000	823.378.000	59	71
1805	548.620.485	1.063.412.000	949.953.000	52	58
1806	597.642.320		931.165.000		64
1807	486.255.200		741.272.000		66

Source: Menz, "As "Geometrias" do Tráfico," 195, table 1

demonstrating the role of Portugal's merchant capital in Angola, the article indicates that several slave voyages included in TSTD2 that appeared to be bilateral (i.e. Brazil-Africa-Brazil) are in fact classical triangular voyages. The author has kindly granted me permission to use and quote these important materials and research findings. I would like therefore to thank him.

most of the goods imported into Angola's slave market, principally through Luanda, came from Europe and Asia, not from Brazil.[142] The data in the tables strongly suggest that the majority of Angolan slaves sold to Brazilian merchants (especially those from Rio de Janeiro) were procured using Portuguese merchant capital, even though the slaves were usually loaded on to the decks of Brazilian slave ships. In short, to claim that slaves for Brazil's economy were obtained by bartering tropical goods for them is misleading.

Conclusion

From the early decades of Portuguese settlement in America, African forced labour underpinned development of the colonial economy. Even though from the sixteenth to the nineteenth centuries the colonial territory expanded, its population grew, and its internal economic spaces and relations became denser and complex, the development of Brazil's economy remained largely export-led; that is, its centre of gravity was the export producing sectors. If other branches of Brazil's colonial economy were – directly or otherwise – influenced by the performance of its export sectors, so, too, were trends in slave imports, for these were a function of exports as long as forced labour was an input into colonial production.

The plentiful supply of African slaves in Brazil made the cost of obtaining slaves bearable even to households not directly involved in commodity production, ensuring that slave labour became widespread in fields and towns. However, the more branches of colonial production became increasingly mercantile – and particularly if attached to export generation – the greater became the average size of slave property ownership and more concentrated slave ownership, that is, it came to resemble a plantation system.[143]

The number of slaves entering Brazil from Africa throughout the era of the Atlantic slave trade has been estimated at 4,810,353.[144] This figure is probably

---

142 For the general share of Asian or European textiles in Central West Africa imports, see: Eltis, *The Rise of African Slavery in America*, 168, 191; for Angola's imports, see: Lopes and Menz, "Resgate e Mercadorias," 68–70.

143 Although slave ownership in Brazil seldom was as great as in the Caribbean, nor the ratio of slaves to free people in the population as high as in the West Indies. On the Caribbean plantation and slave ownership, see: Dunn, *Sugar and Slaves*, 164–165, 170–171; Richard Sheridan, *Sugar and slavery: an economic history of the British West Indies, 1623–1775* (Barbados: Canoe Press, 1994), 230–231; Blackburn, *A Construção do Escravismo*, 280–314.

144 Out of 5,361,096 enslaved Africans transported from Africa; there is, however, one slight difference between my own calculation – based on Eltis and Richardson's data – and

subject to some future reappraisal. Nonetheless, the slaves who survived the middle passage sowed and harvested sugar cane, ground and refined it in sugar mills, and carried the sugar crates to waiting ships. They planted and harvested tobacco, cotton, coffee and food crops. They dug and sifted for gold and diamonds. They made and sold candies and victuals. They carried goods, merchandize, and white people up and down the streets of town and cities. It is not surprising, therefore that the authorities and royal councillors in Portugal consistently asserted that as a colonial supplier of exports as well as a consumer of Portuguese exports, Brazil could not have existed without Angola and *Costa da Mina*.

---

those they break down in each column. This figure represents 45 percent of the transatlantic slave trade arrivals; Eltis and Richardson, "A new assessment," 16–17, table 1.3, 21, 48–51, table 1.8. Our knowledge on the overall African forced migration in this period has been strongly improved since Curtin's milestone in 1969 and received a valuable contribution from the TSTD project. Nevertheless, the debate on this issue still rages on, since the TSTD editors derive their estimates mainly from shipping data, a methodological approach that has raised criticism. See: Joseph E. Inikori, "Measuring the Atlantic Slave Trade: An Assessment of Curtin and Anstey," *Journal of African History* 17:2 (1976): 197–223; idem, "Measuring the Atlantic Slave Trade: a Rejoinder," *Journal of African History* 17:4 (1976): 607–627. One higher estimate of the total volume of the Atlantic slave trade is presented in J.E. Inikori and Stanley L. Engerman, "Introduction: Gainers and Losers in the Atlantic Slave Trade," in Inikori and Engerman, eds., *The Atlantic Slave Trade*, 5–6.

CHAPTER 3

Private Businessmen in the Angolan Trade, 1590s–1780s

Insurance, Commerce and Agency[1]

Filipa Ribeiro da Silva

On 7 August 1782, Christiaan Ketner, master of the Danish ship *Anna Bolette*, granted power of attorney to Clement Denijs, merchant in Ostende to sign a freight contract with Liebert Baes Derdeyn & Co. also based in Ostende. Ketner was to command the vessel and its crew of 45 to 50 men. The ship was to sail from Amsterdam to Angola, thence to America and finally return to Europe. The ship was to carry slaves and ivory (or elephant tusks) from Africa. The ship's officers were to be paid according to the number of slaves sold, with the master receiving four guilders per slave, the first pilot and the chief-surgeon each 24 *stuivers* per slave, the second pilot 10 *stuivers*, and the third pilot 6 *stuivers*. To oversee the slaves' health, two 'good' surgeons were to be appointed as part of the crew, and provisions, salt, barrels of water, and medicines were to be carried on board.[2] Like Ketner, in the eighteenth century, ship's officers together with small- and mid-size firms were often organizers of and participants and agents in the preparation of commercial ventures to Western Africa, and more specifically Angola. This was not, however, always the case. Throughout the early modern period the organization of the Angolan trade (as well as western African trade more generally) underwent changes in the number and profile of the business people involved as well as in the mechanisms used to insure, finance and manage this commerce and its complex links between Europe, Western Africa, and the Americas.[3] The purpose of this essay is to unveil some of the complexities, continuities and changes of the

---

1   This article is an extended version of a paper presented at the Annual Meeting of African Studies Association (ASA) held in Washington DC on 17–19 November 2011, in the Panel "Cross-Cultural Exchange on the West Central African Coast, 1600–1850" organized by Mariana P. Candido and Stacey Sommerdyk. I would like to thank all participants in the panel and the discussion for their suggestions. I would also like to thank David Richardson for editing and commenting on earlier versions of this essay.

2   Amsterdam City Archive (former Gemeente Archief van Amsterdam, hereafter cited as SAA), *Notarialen Archiven* (hereafter cited as *Not. Arch.*) 16371/463: 1782-08-07.

3   SAA, *Not. Arch.* 16371/463: 1782-08-07.

© KONINKLIJKE BRILL NV, LEIDEN, 2015 | DOI 10.1163/9789004280588_004

insurance, finance and commercial organization underlying Angolan trade during the early modern period.

Although the transatlantic slave trade database has provided us with an impressive collection of data on slave voyages, including details of ship owners and captains, relatively little is still known about private merchants' involvement in the transatlantic slave trade. This contrasts with other areas of Atlantic commerce in which private businessmen's activities have been examined. In the last two decades, private entrepreneurship has become an important research area in the field of Atlantic history.[4] Various studies have shown the role played by private business in the making of the early modern Atlantic economy.[5] Initially, private entrepreneurship was typically studied separately from imperial entities but recently scholars have started to look at private enterprise in various branches of Atlantic colonial trade, in the process broadening our understanding of when and how private business operated sometimes simultaneously in different colonial settings. The works of Schnurmann, Studnicki-Gizbert, Ebert, Trivellato, and Antunes are some of the most important contributions.[6]

---

4   Some of the materials presented here are also partially integrated into my PhD dissertation, titled "The Dutch and the Portuguese in West Africa: Empire Building and Atlantic System: 1580–1674," defended at Leiden University in June 2009 (published with the title *Dutch and Portuguese in Western Africa: States, Merchants and the Atlantic System, 1580–1674* (Leiden: Brill, 2011; Atlantic World Series, no. 22)).

5   See, for example: Peter A. Coclanis, ed., *The Atlantic Economy During the Seventeenth and Eighteenth Centuries: Organization, Operation, Practice, and Personnel* (Columbia, SC: University of South Carolina Press, 2005); John J. McCusker and Kenneth Morgan, eds., *The Early Modern Atlantic Economy: Essays on Transatlantic Enterprise* (Cambridge: Cambridge University Press, 2000); Diogo Ramada Curto and Anthony Molho, eds., *Commercial Networks in the Early Modern World* (Firenze: European University Institute, 2002).

6   Claudia Schnurmann, "Atlantic Trade and Regional Identities: The Creation of Supranational Atlantic Systems in the 17th Century," in Horst Pietschmann, ed., *Atlantic History: History of the Atlantic System: 1580–1830* (Göttingen: Vandenhoeck & Ruprecht, 2002), 179–198; idem, "Representative Atlantic Entrepreneur: Jacob Leisler, 1640–1691," in Johannes Postma and Victor Enthoven, eds., *Riches from the Atlantic Trade: Dutch Transatlantic Trade and Shipping, 1585–1817* (Leiden: Brill, 2003), 259–286; Daviken Studnicki-Gizbert, "Interdependence and the Collective Pursuit of Profits: Portuguese Commercial Networks in the Early Modern Atlantic," in Curto and Molho, eds., *Commercial Networks*, 90–120; Daviken Studnicki-Gizbert, "La 'nation' portugaise. Réseaux marchands dans l'espace atlantique à l'époque moderne," *Annales* 58:3 (2003): 627–648; idem, *A Nation upon the Ocean Sea. Portugal's Atlantic Diaspora and the Crises of the Spanish Empire, 1492–1640* (Oxford: Oxford University Press, 2007); Christopher Ebert, "Dutch Trade with Brazil before the Dutch West India Company, 1587–1621," in Postma and Enthoven, eds., *Riches from the Atlantic Trade*

Most of the historiography on European engagement in the transatlantic slave trade and the inter-continental commerce of African goods has focus primarily on the volume of voyages, slaves and African commodities.[7] Until now scholars examining merchants' participation in these trades have largely focussed attention on the activities of state-sponsored commercial companies such as the Dutch West India Company (hereafter WIC), and the Middleburg Commercial Company (hereafter MCC).[8] Beyond the studies of

---

49–76; idem, *Between Empires: Brazilian Sugar in the Early Atlantic Economy, 1550–1630* (Leiden: Brill, 2008); Francesca Trivellato, *The Familiarity of Strangers. The Sephardic Diaspora, Livorno, and Cross-Cultural Trade in the Early Modern Period* (New Haven, CT: Yale University Press, 2009); Cátia Antunes, "Investimento no Atlantico: redes multiculturais de negocio, 1580–1776," in *XV Congresso Internacional de ahila, 1808–2008: Crisis y problemas en el mundo Atlántico* (Leiden: AHILA, Depto. de Estudios Latinoamericanos, 2010).

7 Philip D. Curtin, *The Atlantic slave trade; a census* (Madison, WI: University of Wisconsin Press, 1969); David Eltis, "The volume and structure of the transatlantic slave trade: a reassessment," *William and Mary Quarterly* 58:1 (2001): 17–56; David Eltis *et al*, *The trans-Atlantic slave trade a database on CD-ROM* (Cambridge: Cambridge University Press, 1999); David Eltis and David Richardson, *Routes to slavery: direction, ethnicity, and mortality in the transatlantic slave trade* (London: Frank Cass, 1997); idem, "A New Assessment of the Transatlantic Slave Trade," in David Eltis and David Richardson, eds., *Extending the frontiers: essays on the new transatlantic slave trade database* (New Haven, CT: Yale University Press, 2008), 1–60; Herbert S. Klein, *The middle passage: comparative studies in the Atlantic slave trade* (Princeton, NJ: Princeton University Press, 1978).

8 P.C. Emmer, "The Dutch West India Company, 1621–1791: Dutch or Atlantic?," in Leonard Blussé and Femme Gaastra, eds., *Companies and Trade: Essays on Overseas Trading Companies During the Ancien Regime* (Leiden: Leiden University Press, 1981), 71–95; Henk den Heijer, *De geschiedenis van der WIC* (Zutphen: Walburg Press, 1994); W.S. Unger, *Het Archief der Middelburgsche Commercie Compagnie* ('s-Gravenhage: Ministerie van onderwijs, kunsten en wetenschappen, 1951); H.A. Gijsbertsen and P.F. Poortvliet, *Middelburgsche Commercie Compagnie: genealogische aantekeningen uit de ventilatieboeken van aandelen 1720–1840* ([S.l.]: [Nederlandse Genealogische Vereniging-Afd: Zeeland], 1995); Corrie van Prooijen, "Van goederenhandel naar slavenhandel: de Middelburgse Commercie Compagnie 1720–1755" (unpublished PhD Diss. Leiden University, 2000); H.A. Gijsbertsen and P.F. Poortvliet, eds., *Middelburgsche commercie compagnie: testamenten en stukken betreffende het transport van actiën 1748–1770 en 1804–1856* ([Kapelle]: Nederlandse Genealogische Vereniging – Afd., Zeeland, 1994); D. Schoute, *Scheepschirurgijns-journaal van een slavenschip der Middelburgsche Commercie Compagnie* ([Haarlem]: [s.n.], 1948); P.F. Poortvliet, *De bemanningen der schepen van de Middelburgsche commercie compagnie 1721–1803* ([Kapelle]: Nederlandse Genealogische Vereniging – Afd. Zeeland, 1995); Adriaan Wisse, *De Commercie-compagnie te Middelburg van haar oprichting tot het jaar 1754* (Utrecht: Druckkeri, F. Schotanus & Jens, 1933); H.A. Gijsbertsen and P.F. Poortvliet, eds., *Middelburgsche Commercie Compagnie: procuratiën, testamenten,*

Miller and of Newson and Michin on Portuguese private engagement in this commerce, little is known about private merchants' involvement in the long-distant trade between Europe, Western Africa and the Americas.[9] This contrasts with other Atlantic trades where private businessmen activities have been examined and well documented [10] This study partially fills this void in

---

    volmachten, assignatiën van schepelingen tot het ontvangen van maandgelden, 1721–1803 ([S.l.]: Nederlandse Genealogische Vereniging – Afd., Zeeland, 1994); Johan Francke, *Armazoen voor cargazoen: slavenhandel door de Middelburgsche commercie compagnie (1732–1804)* (Middelburg: J. Francke, 1996); R.A. Hezemans, *De Atlantische slavenhandel der Middelburgsche Commercie Compagnie* (Leiden: Leiden University Press, 1985); J.P. van de Voort, *Handel en handelsbetrekkingen met West-Indië: wording en bedrijf van de Middelburgsche Commercie Compagnie 1720–1780* (Nijmegen: [s.n.], 1967); P.C. Emmer, *De laatste slavenreis van de Middelburgsche Commercie Compagnie* ('s-Gravenhage: Nijhoff, 1971); W.S. Unger, *Een belangrijke bron voor de geschiedenis van onze scheepvaart: de journalen der Middelburgsche Commercie Compagnie, 1720–1809* ([S.l.: s.n., [1962]); idem, *Bijdragen tot de geschiedenis van de Nederlandse slavenhandel II: de slavenhandel der Middelburgsche commercie compagnie 1732–1808* ('s-Gravenhage: Nijhoff, 1961); M.J. Eijgenraam, *Menschlievenheid en eigen belang: de behandeling van de slaven aan boord van de schepen van de Middelburgsche Commercie Compagnie* ([Middelburg: Koninklijk Zeeuwsch Genootschap der Wetenschappen], 1990); Paul Koulen, *De eerste reis van het snauwschip "de vigilantie" naar Guinee en Suriname voor de Middelburgsche Commercie Compagnie 9 augustus 1778–8 september 1779* (Terneuzen: [s.n.], 1975); Simon J. Hogerzeil and David Richardson, "Slave Purchasing Strategies and Shipboard Mortality: Day-to-Day Evidence from the Dutch African Trade, 1751–1797," *Journal of Economic History* 67:1 (2007): 160–190; Victor Enthoven, "Dutch Crossings," *Atlantic Studies* 2:2 (2005): 153–176.

9   Joseph C. Miller, "Capitalism and slaving: The financial and commercial organization of the Angolan slave trade, according to the accounts of Antonio Coelho Guerreiro (1684–1692)," *International Journal of African Historical Studies* 17:1 (1984): 1–56; Linda A. Newson and Susie Minchin, *From Capture to Sale: The Portuguese Slave Trade to Spanish America in the Early Seventeenth Century* (Leiden: Brill, 2007). See also: Enriqueta Vila Vilar, "La sublevacíon de Portugal y la trata de negros," *Ibero-Americanks Archiv* 2 (1976): 171–192; idem, Vila Vilar, *Hispanoamerica y el comercio de esclavos* (Sevilla: Escuela de Estudios Hispano-Americanos, 1977); Marisa Vega Franco, *El trafico de esclavos con Americas. asientos de Grillo y Lomelini, 1663–1674* (Sevilla: Escuela de Estudios Hispano-Americanos, 1984).

10   Coclanis, ed., *The Atlantic Economy*; McCusker and Morgan, eds., *The early modern Atlantic economy*; Curto and Molho, eds., *Commercial Networks*; Schnurmann, "Atlantic Trade and Regional Identities," 179–198; idem, "Representative Atlantic Entrepreneur," 259–286; Studnicki-Gizbert, "Interdependence and the Collective Pursuit of Profits," 90–120; idem, "La 'nation' portugaise," 627–648; idem, *A Nation upon the Ocean Sea*; Ebert, "Dutch Trade with Brazil," 49–76; idem, *Between empires*; Trivellato, *The Familiarity of Strangers*; Antunes, "Investimento no Atlantico."

the literature by examining the involvement of private businessmen based in the Dutch Republic (hereafter the Republic) in the trade with Angola between the 1590s and 1780s.

In looking at privately organized trade with Angola in this period, we shall focus on insurance, finance, commercial partnerships and agency. We shall also explore the cross-cultural character of private trade with Angola, both in the Angolan context and at European levels. We start with a brief note on sources, on geography, on chronology and with a brief insight into the composition of Amsterdam private entrepreneurs and businessmen. We then look at changes in the legal framework regulating private participation in the Angolan trade, before finally offering an analysis of the activities of insurers, financers, merchants and their agents in the Angolan trade.

The silence in the historiography of private merchant involvement in Angolan commerce is not surprising since most of the merchants engaged in such activity failed to leave organized and extensive personal collections of business papers. It was states and state-sponsored companies which generated, in fact, most of the source materials relating to colonial trades available in European and Asian archives, and as a result it was their involvement in such trades that has pre-occupied scholars. Records produced by States and chartered commercial companies still offer insights into the activities of private merchants in the Atlantic and other trades, in part because private businessmen often operated as partners with the state and state-sponsored companies in such activities, and in part because they sometimes sought to compete with them. This chapter illustrates the possibilities of discerning the activities of private merchants in colonial trades through the study of company records as well as other records.

At the heart of this paper are the records of Amsterdam's Notarial Archives (hereafter SAA). This extensive collection includes various types of notary acts covering the entire early modern period and comprises thousands of notary books. It is a paramount collection for the study of private entrepreneurship not only in the Dutch Republic, but for other areas of the early modern economy, as various studies have recently shown. The SAA materials used in this paper have been extracted from a larger sample of 16,000 notary acts generated by myself and Catia Antunes for the study of economic activities and cross-cultural trade with Western Africa and within the Atlantic World between the 1590s and 1780s. Given the centrality of these notorial records to this paper, it is important to explain briefly what materials have been collected and how were they selected.

The sampling of the SAA records was essential given the scale of the collection of notary books and acts available. To create the sample, we consulted the inventory files of the SAA available for the period 1590s–1640s and we sampled a specific number of notary books for every other decade. We particularly focussed on acts referring explicitly to economic activities, such as insurances, loans, bottomry arrangements, commercial partnerships, commercial credit, freight contracts, powers of attorney, and labour contracts. Given our research interests geographically, our sample is centred on the Atlantic, north and south, including Western Africa. Within this geographical space, we also focussed our search on names of businessmen known to have engaged in Atlantic and African trades. This second focus of research led us to collect data on activities in the Baltic and sometimes in Asia as many of those participating in Atlantic trades were engaged in worldwide commercial and financial activities. For Western Africa, in particular, we uncovered from the SAA collection data relating to the activities of more than 200 businessmen in regions ranging from Senegambia and Cape Verde in the north to Loango and Angola in the south as well as to the Gulf of Guinea and São Tomé and Príncipe in between.

The use of African place names in European sources poses at least three main problems. First, there are difficulties in matching European geographical names with the real location of those places in Africa. Second, there are variations in usage of names through time. And, third, the meaning of even identical African place names among European merchants, companies and States in relation sometimes differed. Here, I address the last two points, especially in what concerns the geographical names of 'Angola' and 'Loango'.

The terms Angola and Loango became known in Europe, both south and north, through Portugal-based merchants as they first began trading in these areas, as well as by the Portuguese state. As other private merchants and state-sponsored companies engaged in trade with these regions, they, too, also used the terms 'Angola' and 'Loango'. However, the same name often referred to slightly different regions in West-Central Africa. For example, for the Portuguese state, Portugal-based merchants, and businessmen of Portuguese origin living elsewhere (including the Republic), 'Angola' was the stretch of coast between the mouth of the Congo River and Benguela in the south. So, in notary acts involving Portuguese Sephardic Jews based in Amsterdam, the term 'Angola' tends to have this geographical definition. But, for the WIC and Christian merchants of various European origins based in the Republic, the geographical borders of Angola were different, and they changed through time. In the WIC collection, for instance, prior to 1641, the term 'Angola' or 'the coast of Angola' referred mainly to the area between Cape Lopez and Loango, excluding the stretch of coast further south under Portuguese control. During WIC rule over the entire coastal region (1641–1648), 'Angola' encompassed the whole area from Cape Lopez to Benguela, which was also known as the WIC 'Southern district of Africa'. After the 1650s, 'Angola' again referred mainly to the Loango region, but from the 1660s and especially after the Dutch peace treaty with Portugal in 1662, there seemed to be an increasing distinction between 'Angola' as the area controlled by the Portuguese state, and Loango, north of the Congo river, as the area of Dutch commercial influence in West-Central Africa.

Various changes in the meaning of 'Angola' and its geographical limits can also be found in the notary acts involving Christian merchants of Dutch, German, Flemish and other origins based in the Republic. In the period from the 1590s to the 1620s prior to the establishment of the WIC, 'Angola' seems to have referred to a vast and vague stretch of coast between Cape Lopez and Luanda, whereas during Dutch-Portuguese warfare in the South Atlantic from the 1620s onward, the term 'Angola' was used to refer to the area under WIC control. And, after the 1650s, like in the WIC records, the term 'Angola' seems to refer increasingly to the area controlled by the Portuguese state and Portuguese-Brazilian merchants, while 'Loango' appears associated with the coastal region between the mouth of the Congo River in the south and Cape Lopez in the north, where the Dutch centred their commercial activities.

Given the different understandings of the term 'Angola' in the Dutch sources, and their changes over time, it is important to define the geographical scope of this essay. To safeguard the reliability of our record sample, we have adopted the broader definition of the term 'Angola' that we have found in Dutch sources. This decision also took in consideration the purpose of this paper, which aims to identify and explain some long-term trends in insurance, finance, commercial participation and agency in this trade.

Our analysis of these issues takes into consideration changes in the political and military context of trade in the Atlantic as well as changes in the legal framework regulating private participation in Atlantic commerce. Accordingly, we look at four main chronological periods. The first period from the 1590s to the 1620s was a period of free trade, where all merchants based in the Republic were authorized to participate in the overall Atlantic trade, including the Angolan region. The second period, centring on the 1630s and 1640s, coincided with the WIC monopoly chartered by the States General in 1621, the charter of which came into force after 1624, and was forcibly pursued in the 1630s and 1640s. The third period, from the 1650s to the early eighteenth century, was mainly an era in which a company monopoly co-existed with private trade in a sort of love-hate relationship, since collaboration between the WIC and private businessmen based in the Republic went hand-in-hand with harassment, seizure and confiscation of assets owned by merchants engaged in commercial activities within the Company monopoly area without permission, being therefore deemed 'illegal traders' by the Company. The final period, from the

1720s onwards, witnessed the emergence of multiple independent private
commercial firms of small, medium and large size, free of state sponsorship,
which engaged in intense commercial activities with the Angolan region.
The MCC was one such firm, but smaller firms like Liebert Bacs Derdeyn &
Co., cited earlier, also played an important role in this trade during the eighteenth century.

Private Business and Political and Military Contexts

The participation of private businessmen from the Republic in the Angolan
trade was directly affected by the political, military and diplomatic situation in
Europe and the Atlantic between the 1580s and the 1780s. Several main events
influenced the activities of these merchants. They included the Dutch Revolt
and the opening of formal hostilities between the Republic and the Habsburg
Empire in 1621, when the Twelve Years' Truce, signed in 1609 ended and in 1640
the independence of Portugal from Spain and the subsequent negotiations
leading to the Peace Treaty of 1662, with its effects in Europe, the Atlantic and
Asia. The Anglo-Dutch Wars between 1652 and 1682 and the War of Spanish
Succession in 1702–1713 also hampered substantially the involvement of private businessmen in the Republic in the Atlantic trade, though their effects
were probably greater in the North Atlantic than in the South.

The Dutch Revolt of 1568 against taxation and centralization policies implemented by Philip II of Spain dragged the Republic into a war against Spain and
its Empire. For private merchants in the Republic the first effects of this conflict emerged soon after. They intensified when in 1598, Philip II imposed a
total embargo on all Dutch ships sailing to Iberia. Portuguese and Spanish
ships were also barred from anchoring at Dutch ports by a reciprocal embargo
decreed by the Republic's States-General. Such measures forced private
businessmen to find strategies to safeguard their business interests. Among
other things, merchants in the Republic trading in colonial goods started to
re-organize their own inter-continental routes from the Republic to the South
Atlantic, sailing to Venezuela, the Caribbean, Brazil, and western Africa, including the Angolan coast.

The arrival of the Dutch ships in the South Atlantic triggered conflicts
between merchant ships from the Republic and Portugal, as well as naval
attacks by the officials and military placed in various posts along the coast to
safeguard the Portugal's monopoly of trade with western Africa. At the Angolan
coast, merchant ships were attacked by armed vessels sent out from Luanda.
Pieter van den Broecke's diary of his voyages to Africa refers to such conflicts,

which had a disruptive effect on trade in the South Atlantic. After two decades of violence and economic loss for the economies of Spain, Portugal, and the Republic as well as for the businesses of private merchants, the main parties involved in the conflict negotiated a ceasefire – the Twelve Years' Truce – which ended the embargoes. Seemingly a positive measure for private merchants, another reality would, however, unfold during the Truce as both the Republic and the Habsburg Empire used the ceasefire to strengthen their military positions in Europe and overseas and at the end of the Truce to resume open conflict and mutual embargoes. The first move of the States-General was to charter a state-sponsored commercial company (WIC) in 1621 and provide it with a monopoly over Dutch Atlantic trade. The intention was to use the WIC as a weapon against the overseas possessions of the Habsburg emperors in the Atlantic, including the Spanish and Portuguese colonies in the Americas and their western posts and settlements in Africa. The Company began operations on the ground in 1624, with private businessmen being formally banned from trading with the regions under its control.

During the following two decades, the WIC seized territory from Portugal, notably in Brazil and Angola. Following the restoration of Portugal's independence from Spain on 1 December 1640, the newly crowned king, John IV, tried to re-establish peaceful relations with the Republic. On 12 June 1641, a 10 year treaty was signed in The Hague, under which the Republic and Portugal would observe a truce, starting in Europe immediately after the document had been ratified (as it was on 12 November 1641), one year afterward in India, and six months after the arrival of the news in Brazil. In Asia and Europe, Dutch ships freighted by private merchants or serving under the WIC were allowed freedom of navigation and commerce.

In spite of the truce signed in 1641, troops of the WIC and of the Portuguese state had more bloody military encounters in Angola and Brazil between 1645 and 1654. These events had a tremendous impact on trade, since Angola was the major source of slave labour for Brazil and the latter was at the time the major producer of sugar for northern European consumption. Private merchants felt the effects severely.[11] Only in 1662 did the Republic sign a peace treaty with Portugal. Sporadic disputes between WIC officials and private merchants from the Republic, on the one hand, and representatives of the Portuguese state, however, continued well into the eighteenth century, especially in the Gulf of Guinea. In Loango and Angola, by contrast, conflict was less evident, mainly due to the decline of Portuguese influence north of the Bengo

---

11   SAA, *Not. Arch.* 1498/190: 1639-08-17.

region and the resulting divide between the areas economically controlled by
the Portuguese and by the Dutch.

Private Trade and Legal Frameworks for the Atlantic Commerce

The political, military, and diplomatic events just described brought changes
to the juridical framework that regulated private businessmen in the Atlantic.
Those changes affected, directly and indirectly, the business prospects for private merchants in the Republic and the level of risk involved in financial and
commercial transactions associated with the organization of Angolan and
other trades.

In the Republic, trade with western Africa, including the Angolan trade, was
dominated by private partnerships until 1621. In the main Dutch port cities,
there were a handful of private 'companies' and several independent businessmen involved in these commercial branches.[12] These partnerships had no formal commercial organization comparable to the later Dutch WIC, as they had
only hired merchants and accountants aboard ships, onshore or aboard *leggers*
(floating trading posts) to conduct trade in western Africa.[13] The establishment
of the WIC by the States-General in 1621 brought to an end this initial period of
free trade, as the Company was granted a monopoly over all Atlantic trade, as
already mentioned.[14]

From its outset, the chartering of the Company was met with great opposition from the merchants of Amsterdam and the northern port cities of the
Republic, who had important investments in the North Atlantic fisheries,

---

12 W.S. Unger, "Nieuwe gegevens betreffend het begin der vaart op Guinea, 1561–1601,"
    Economisch-historisch Jaarboek 21 (1940): 194–217; Enthoven, "Early Dutch Expansion,"
    17–48.

13 "Andreas Josua Ulsheimer's voyage of 1603–4," in Adam Jones, ed., *German Sources for
    West African History, 1599–1699* (Stuttgart: Franz Steiner Verlag, 1983), 21–29; "Samuel
    Brun's voyages of 1611–1620," in ibid., 45–96; J.D. La Fleur, ed., *Pieter van den Broecke's jour-
    nal of voyages to Cape Verde, Guinea and Angola (1605–1612)* (London: Hakluyt Society,
    2000), 28, 47, 83–103. See also: Filipa Ribeiro da Silva, "Dutch vessels in African waters:
    Routes, commercial strategies, trading practices and intra-continental trade (c.1590–
    1674)," *Tijdschrift voor Zeegeschiedenis* 1 (2010): 19–38.

14 Emmer, "The West India Company," 1–95; Heijer, *De geschiedenis van de WIC*, Chapters 1, 2,
    and 3. See also: Ernest van den Boogaart and P.C. Emmer, "The Dutch Participation in the
    Atlantic Slave Trade, 1596–1650," in Henry A. Gemery and Jan S. Hogenborn, eds., *The
    uncommon market: Essays in the economic history of the Atlantic slave trade* (New York,
    N.Y.: Academic Press, 1979), 353–375.

Brazilian sugar and dyewood, the salt trade with South America, and the African gold, ivory and slave trades. Some branches of Atlantic trade were therefore detached from the Company monopoly soon after its establishment, but the Brazilian and African trades remained under Company control. In combination with the policies pursued by the WIC, this had implications for profits of both the Company and the private merchants. In particular, the military activities of the WIC brought disruption to African and Brazilian trade. For several years after the Dutch takeover of the captaincies in north-eastern Brazil (1630), sugar production decreased, causing major losses for the sugar refiners in the Republic.[15] In the years immediately after the occupation of Luanda (1641), Company officials also failed to secure a regular supply of slave labour to the city and consequently to Dutch Brazil.[16]

During this same period, the burden of paying for the Dutch military campaigns against the Portuguese possessions began to be felt.[17] The Company lacked cash flow to operate the businesses in Brazil, western Africa, the Caribbean, and North America, and struggled to ensure the transport of commodities, personnel, and weaponry between its posts and settlements. To mitigate its losses, the Company granted individual shareholders permission to participate in the trade with Brazil and the Caribbean in 1638. In 1647, the Company also agreed to open the slave trade from Angola to Brazil, the Caribbean, and the Spanish Americas to private businessmen in the Republic. Finally, in 1648, the trade with North America, including the slave trade, was opened to private businessmen from the Republic. The only branch of Atlantic trade that remained as a Company monopoly was the trade in gold.[18]

The bankruptcy of the first Dutch Company in 1674 and the process leading to the chartering of a second company under the same name, did not introduce major changes to the legal framework already in place. Although the second WIC held a nominal monopoly over Dutch trade in western Africa, including commercial activities in Loango and Angola, and

---

15   Ebert, "Dutch Trade with Brazil," 49–76; idem, *Between empires*, Chapters 3, 5 and 6.
16   Klaas Ratelband, *Nederlanders in West Afrika (1600–1650): Angola, Kongo en São Tomé* (Zutphen: Walburg Pers, 2000) [Portuguese Trans. *Os Holandeses no Brasil e na Costa Africana. Angola, Kongo e São Tomé (1600–1650)* (Lisboa: Vega, 2003)].
17   Michiel A.G. de Jong, *'Staat van oorlog': wapenbedrijf en militaire hervorming in de Republiek der Verenigde Nederlanden, 1585–1621* (Hilversum: Verloren, 2005).
18   Emmer, "The West India Company," 79–81; Cornelius C. Goslinga, *The Dutch in the Caribbean and on the Wild Coast, 1580–1680* (Assen: Van Gorcum, 1990), 110; J.G. van Dillen, *Van rijkdom en regenten, handboek tot de economische en sociale geschiedenis van Nederland tijdens de Republiek* ('s-Gravenhage: Martinus Nijhoff, 1970), 169.

had administrative, fiscal and military authority to enforce this monopoly,[19] more often than not intercontinental trade and shipping remained in the hands of private entrepreneurs and businessmen in the Republic. In time, the Company became primarily an administrative and military organisation, with responsibility for the maintenance and administration of outposts in western Africa, while private firms appeared to dominate trade itself. This was reflected in the increasing activities of interlopers in the Company monopoly.[20] It continued with the formation of multiple small, medium and large-sized companies in Dutch ports and their increasing role in the commerce between the Republic, western Africa, and particularly the Loango and Angolan regions. The MCC, founded in 1720, was the best known example of such private independent concerns.[21]

The failure of state-sponsored companies to be able to enforce their monopolies opened up broad opportunities for business in the Republic. It meant that for substantial periods of the sixteenth, seventeenth and eighteenth centuries, private merchants in the Republic controlled most Dutch Atlantic commerce, including the Angolan trade.

Private Mercantile Community in Amsterdam

In the period under study, the Republic was home to two main groups of merchants with economic interest in the Angolan trade. The first was a group of Christian merchants of Dutch, Flemish, and German origin.[22] The second was the Portuguese Sephardim established in Amsterdam and other Dutch cities.[23]

---

19   Heijer, *De geschiedenis van der WIC*; idem, *Goud, ivoor en slaven: scheepvaart en handel van de Tweede Westindische Compagnie op Afrika, 1674–1740* (Zupten: Walburg Pers, 1997).

20   Ruud Paesie, *Lorrendrayen op Africa: de illegale goederen- en slavenhandel op West-Afrika tijdens het achttiende-eeuwse handelsmonopolie van de West-Indische Compagnie, 1700–1734* (Amsterdam: De Bataafsche Leeuw, 2008).

21   For references on the MCC, see note 8.

22   On the mercantile groups in the Republic, see, for example: Cátia Antunes, *Globalisation in the Early Modern Period: the economic relationship between Amsterdam and Lisbon, 1640–1705* (Amsterdam: Aksant, 2004); Oscar Gelderbloom, *Zuid-Nederlandse kooplieden en de opkomst van de Amsterdamse stapelmarkt (1578–1630)* (Hilversum: Verloren, 2000); C. Lesger and L. Noordegraaf, ed., *Entrepreneurs and Entrepreneurship in Early Modern Times: merchants and industrialists within the orbit of the Dutch staple market* (Den Haag: Stichting Hollandse Historische Reeks, 1995).

23   On the Portuguese Sephardim in the Republic, Western Europe and the Atlantic in general, see: Jonathan I. Israel, *European Jewry in the Age of Mercantilism, 1550–1750* (London:

The first began to develop economic activities in the South Atlantic in the late 1580s, investing mainly in the Brazilian sugar and dyewood trades and in African commerce in gold, ivory and leather. In the late sixteenth century, Dutch participation in the slave trade was minimal, as several studies have shown.[24] Nevertheless, the notarial contracts of the Amsterdam City Archives provide examples of ships trading from the Republic to Western Africa, in particular Angola, and travelling back to Europe via Brazil, Spanish America, as well as via Martinique and the Guianas, transporting slaves. These voyages were commonly organized by members of the Portuguese Sephardic community based in Amsterdam and other Dutch ports, as we have shown elsewhere.[25] Many Sephardim had already been engaged with the Angolan trade prior to their arrival in the Republic as they fled persecution from the Iberian Inquisition.

The establishment of the first WIC by the States-General on 3 June 1621 changed this situation, at least for the following two decades. By 1623, all private merchants in the Republic with interests in the Atlantic had been forced to put their activities on hold. Many protested, and others devised strategies to continue operations in these areas, as we shall see later. However, the enforcement of the monopoly proved difficult and from the 1640s increasing numbers of merchants of Dutch, Flemish and German origin began to work with the WIC in order to guarantee supplies of enslaved Africans to the Americas, as well as other commodities, foodstuffs, ammunition and medicines needed to service Dutch Atlantic trade. By contrast, the Portuguese Sephardim no longer appeared to be directly engaged in such activities. They tended instead to become buyers and holders of Company shares, usually through the Chamber of Amsterdam. The closest direct relationship of the Portuguese Sephardim to the Angolan trade, including the slave trade,

Clarendon, 1998); idem, *Diasporas within the Diaspora: Jews, Crypto-Jews, and the world maritime empires (1540–1740)* (Leiden: Brill, 2002); Y. Kaplan, *An Alternative to Modernity. The Sephardi Diaspora in Western Europe* (Leiden: Brill, 2000); Daniel M. Swetschinski, *Reluctant Cosmopolitans: The Portuguese Jews of Seventeenth-century Amsterdam* (London: The Littman Library of Jewish Civilisation, 2000).

24   Johannes Postma, *The Dutch in the Atlantic slave trade, 1600–1815* (Cambridge: Cambridge University Press, 1990), Chapter 1; idem, "A Reassessment of the Dutch Atlantic Slave Trade," in Postma and Enthoven, eds., *Riches from the Atlantic Trade*, 158–138; Jelmer Vos, David Eltis and David Richardson, "The Dutch in the Atlantic World: New Perspectives from the Slave Trade with Particular Reference to the African Origins of the Traffic," in Eltis and Richardson, eds., *Extending the Frontiers*, 228–249.

25   Filipa Ribeiro da Silva, "Crossing Empires: Portuguese, Sephardic, and Dutch Business Networks in the Atlantic Slave Trade, 1580–1674," *The Americas* 68:1 (2011): 7–32.

probably continued through their connections with the Sephardic Jews and
Dutch planters of the Caribbean and Dutch Guiana and through their financial investments in these plantation economies. In practice, therefore, the
participation of the Amsterdam Sephardim in the Angolan slave and other
trades became increasingly indirect, and took the form of financial support
and it was Dutch private merchants who assumed active participation in
trade itself.

The organization of Angolan trade was a complex operation, which involved
not only businessmen, but also insurers, financers, ship owners, outfitters, captains, pilots, attorneys, supercargoes and factors. In the rest of this essay we
shall look at some of these activities, explaining their organization and highlighting changes and continuities over time. We begin with insurance of voyages, then move to an analysis of their funding, before finally examining their
commercial organization in Europe and the creation of agencies throughout
the Atlantic as key elements for their success.

Insurance

During the early modern period the insurance of the Angolan trade
underwent various changes. These involved a gradual shift from multi-party
insurances to insurance partnerships and finally to specialist insurance
firms. These transitions were not unique to Angolan trade, but seem to have
been directly related to the 'risks of the sea' and the more general 'risks of the
market' or the business.

In the late sixteenth and early seventeenth centuries when private businessmen based in the Dutch Republic started to participate in the trade with Africa,
vessels and cargoes were often insured by various businessmen. Voyages
between Europe, Angola and the Spanish West Indies were a case in point. In
1614, Diogo Nunes Belmonte, Portuguese Sephardic Jew and merchant in
Amsterdam, had a 'cargo' of slaves and a return cargo of gold, silver, and other
goods insured by a total of 35 partners. The cargoes were to be transported on
board *De Engel Michiel*, commanded by Sebastião Ribeiro, on route between
Amsterdam, Lisbon, Luanda, Spanish America and Seville. Jan Janss Smit,
Albert Schuijt, Gerrit van Schoonhoven, Baerent Sweerts, Jan Jansen van
Helmont, all prominent businessmen in early seventeenth-century Amsterdam
were among the insurers.[26]

---

26   SAA, *Not. Arch.* 254/188-188v: 1614-05-22.

Voyages simply between Europe and Angola (or Western Africa) involved smaller risks and often were insured by small consortia of merchants or insurance companies (*compagnies van assurantien*). In November 1615, Hendrick Wounterss, Van Veen, and Samuel Trezel, all merchants in Amsterdam, owned an insurance company, which offered insurance for vessels sailing between Amsterdam (or other Dutch ports) and Angola. Samuel Bloemert and Frans Jacobsen Hinlopen, two active merchants in the Angolan trade at the time, were their clients. The insurance premium for their ships sailing from the Republic to Angola and back was eight percent.[27]

This type of multi-party insurance partnership seems to be directly related to the risks associated to the trade with Angola, Western Africa more generally, and the Americas. In the early years, the Angolan commercial market was relatively unknown to entrepreneurs and merchants in the Republic with investment in the insurance business; it was deemed, therefore, as relatively risky. This was for several reasons. On the one hand, there was no control over demand of goods and their prices on the African coast; these were matters largely determined by the African merchants and leaders of the chieftaincies. On the other hand, there was no control over the supply and price of African commodities and enslaved Africans, due to the control of Africans over these issues. To these risks of market exchange were added other risks arising from naval and military attacks carried out by representatives of the chieftaincies or of the Portuguese State, which aimed to protect its monopoly of the Angolan trade from foreign merchants. Moreover, there were naval attacks carried out at sea by corsairs from various bases around the Atlantic, sometimes acting on their own interests, other times sponsored by European states or by the Ottoman authorities. In this context, insurance by multiple parties as well as high premiums appeared to be the strategies followed by Amsterdam-based insurers to provide cover for commercial ventures to Angola (or Africa, and more generally), while safeguarding their own investments. Similar practices were followed in other branches of trade as the Dutch initiated their Atlantic-wide trading activities.

In the course of the seventeenth century, the organization of insurance for the Angolan trade underwent change. Earlier multi-party insurance arrangements began to be replaced by insurance through small or medium sized partnerships of insurers. This trend became evident from the late 1640s with the opening up of the WIC monopoly to participation by private businessmen in the Republic. In the following decades, most merchants operating in the Angolan trade or in other branches of trade within the Company monopoly

---

27   SAA, *Not. Arch.* 199/134-137v: 1617-04-08.

had their vessels and cargoes insured by such insurance partnerships. This applied regardless of whether the merchants traded in tandem with the WIC or separate from it. In the mid-1650s, Jan van de Velde of Amsterdam owned an insurance company and provided cover to merchants operating in various branches of Atlantic trade. Henrico Mathias, a powerful merchant of German origin based in Amsterdam and active in the trade with Angola, was, as we have shown elsewhere, one of Van de Velde's clients. For goods shipped on the route Faro (Portugal) – Angola – Bahia (Brazil) – Lisbon, Mathias paid an insurance premium of 24 percent; this compared to premiums for cargoes transported on the route from Cadiz to Havana and Vera Cruz, of just 10 percent.[28] Such differences in premiums reflected perceptions and understandings of different risks in Atlantic trade at this time, one factor in which was warfare between Portugal and the Republic.

Amsterdam-based insurers offered their services not only to merchants residing in the Republic but also to those living elsewhere. For example, throughout the seventeenth century, merchants based in Iberia had their vessels and cargoes insured in Amsterdam. In 1615, for instance, Jan Snell de Jonge (Jan Snell Junior), merchant in Lisbon, had cargoes of money, gold, silver and other commodities transported on board several ships insured in Amsterdam. His insurers were Claes Andriesz and Hendrick Voet. The maximum cover per cargo was 1,000 guilders.[29] Amsterdam-based insurers also provided cover at sea for merchants of Portuguese, Spanish and other origin, often through such merchants' representatives in the Republic. Iberian merchants often attracted representatives within the *Portugees Natie van Amsterdam*, i.e. the Portuguese Sephardic Jewish Community in the city. For example, in 1615, Jan Janss Smit, Albert Schuijt and Jan Jansen van Helmont of Amsterdam insured the hull of the ship *St. Pieter* for a voyage from Lisbon to Angola. The insurance contract was signed by Gaspar de Rodrigues Nunes, Portuguese merchant in Amsterdam, on behalf of Francisco da Costa Brandão and Simão Rodrigues Lobo, both of Lisbon.[30]

In the eighteenth century, however, Amsterdam-based insurers would lose their key role to London not only in the Angola trade but also in most branches of western African, Atlantic and world trade. The rise of London as the major eighteenth-century world trade, finance and insurance centre is reflected in the activities of the merchants in the Republic with interests in the Angolan trade. Despite their shipping firms being based in Amsterdam and other Dutch

---

28   SAA, *Not. Arch.* 1115/17v: 1655-10-05.

29   SAA, *Not. Arch.* 138/210-211v: 1615-03-25.

30   SAA, *Not. Arch.* 378A/339: 1615-05-29; *Not. Arch.* 317/339: 1615-05-29.

cities, and having their vessels sail under Dutch flag, insurance for Angola-bound vessels for the Low Countries was no longer bought in Amsterdam but in London instead. The firm Pieter and Stephanus Locquet is a case in point. The main office of the firm was in Amsterdam, but cargoes transported on their behalf from Europe to Angola and the Americas were insured in London through Charles Loubier & Tessier. The cargoes owned by the firm and shipped on board the *De Mars* and the corvette *De Cupion* which both sailed between Angola and the French West Indies in 1756 and 1758 were both insured in London.[31]

The evidence shows a gradual transition from multi-party insurance arrangements to insurance by small and medium sized firms in the case of the Angolan trade (as well as other trades). It also highlights the key role played by Amsterdam-based insurers in covering risks at sea for merchants based in the Republic and elsewhere who participated in the Angolan trade in the seventeenth century but their decline as insurance providers to Dutch African voyages in the eighteenth century in the face of competition from London. Evidence from the SAA accounts also underscores the complexity of insurance arrangements in long-distance trade in the early modern period. Partners to insurance agreements or in insurance companies could take different shares in insurance underwriting activities, as in the insurance contract signed between Jan Snell de Jonge, Claes Andriesz and Hendrick Voet, in which Andriesz was responsible for 2/3 of the insurance and Voet only for 1/3.[32] Insurance cover could be made only for the ship's hull, like in the case of the *St. Pieter*, noted earlier, for the ship and its cargo, or just for a part of the cargo, as the examples of the ships *De Engel Michiel*, *De Cupion*, and *De Mars* cited earlier show. Moreover, insurance could be arranged for both outbound and return voyages or just for one-way journeys.

Finance

Like insurance, the financial organization of the Angolan trade underwent change throughout the early modern period. There were not many changes in the type of financial instruments used by private businessmen to fund the trade. Bottomry bonds, loans, and commercial credit remained as the most commonly used instruments. But their values did increase through time, which largely reflected expansion of this trade as a branch of commerce. Moreover,

---

31   SAA, *Not. Arch.* 10475/1638: 1756-10-14; *Not. Arch.* 10493/983: 1758-07-04.
32   SAA, *Not. Arch.* 138/210-211v: 1615-03-25.

during the period under study, there was a noticeable change in the suppliers and receivers of funds, and in their inter-relationships and their involvement in the commercial activities themselves.

In the early years of Dutch participation in the Angolan trade bottomries, loans and commercial credit were often obtained through merchant-financiers resident in Amsterdam to finance voyages, whereas by the eighteenth century ship captains and other officers who served on board ship commonly used such instruments to finance their involvement in ventures. In 1597, for instance, to organize one of the first known commercial ventures between the Republic and Angola, Barent Sas, merchant in Amsterdam, secured a bottomry to the value of 524,11 Flemish Pounds from Volckert Sioucxz, also of Amsterdam. The funds were used to purchase the trade goods shipped by the *De Vliegende Raven* on its voyage from Amsterdam to Lisbon and thence to Angola, before returning to Lisbon and Zealand or Holland under the command of Marten Hermissen, from Hoorn.[33] One hundred years later, however, we find ship officers among users of bottomry bonds. In 1698, for example, shipmaster Dirck Cock acquired a 2,000 guilders bottomry loan from Philip de Flines at 30 percent interest to help fund the venture of the *De Gideon*, offering as guarantee the commodities to be loaded in the return voyage on his own account. On this occasion, the voyage involved a journey from Rotterdam to Angola and thence to Suriname, before returning to Amsterdam or Rotterdam.[34] In other cases we find officers taking loans against the outward value of ship and cargo. One example was the bottomry obtained by captain Nanning Kagias, chief-pilot Willem Boon and third pilot Harmen Bos, from Reinier van Broeckhuysen and Son, merchants in Amsterdam, in 1698 and 1699 on the intended voyage for the *Eva Maria* from Hoorn to Angola and Curaçao and back to Hoorn.[35]

Such changes in patterns of finance indicate how private participation in the Angolan trade shifted from being a high-investment activity involving potentially several financial partners to a low-investment and high-return business in which ship officers could afford to take bottomries and loans to finance activities, using trade goods, return cargoes, or even the ship itself as collateral. Such trends tell us much about the lowering of perceived risks associated with this business. They also remind us that, as with insurance, those providing credit and finance typically remained detached from the day-to-day

---

33   SAA, *Not. Arch.* 78/155: 1597-11-06; *Not. Arch.* 78/155v-156v: 1597-11-06.

34   SAA, *Not. Arch.* 4183/341: 1698-10-07.

35   SAA, *Not. Arch.* 6008/48: 1699-09-08; *Not. Arch.* 5765/750: 1699-10-08.

activities of commerce associated with the Angolan trade. We turn now to look at how that commerce was organized.[36]

Organization of Commerce

Organizing voyages to Angola involved several parties, including ship-owners, freighters, outfitters, captains, pilots, supercargoes, accountants, and agents operating in Africa, the latter often being of African or Eurafrican descent. Bringing these parties together involved multiple forms of associations and partnerships relating to the purchase or lease of vessels, assembling of cargoes, freighting and equipping ships, and identifying and hiring crew, supercargoes, factors and commercial representatives to safeguard commercial exchanges in Europe and overseas. In time, forms of association and relationships between the parties involved were subject to change.

Those involved in the early years of Dutch participation in the Angolan trade often appear to have formed commercial partnerships to purchase the vessels to be used in their ventures. For instance, in 1622, the ship *St. Mauritius*, which was to sail from the Republic, to Angola and the West Indies and thence to Iberia was co-owned by six men, Michiel Pau, Charles Latseur, Abraham de Velaer, Pieter Jansz Coninck, Jan Sijbrantsz de Bont, and P. Servaes Bruijn.[37] In other cases, partnerships hired the vessels to be used in the Angolan trade, as in 1607, when Elias Trip, merchant in Dordrecht, Jan Kuysten, merchant in Amsterdam, and Manuel Telles Barreto, Portuguese merchant in Madeira, jointly hired the vessel *De Maecht,* commanded by Hendrick Reijerss, for a voyage from the River Maas to the Congo and the coast of Angola.[38] In this early period, too, ships were outfitted by partnerships of merchants, as for example, in 1609 when, through Dionijs Bave, Lowys Delbeque contributed 300 Flemish pounds in outfitting two ships and a yacht owned by Cornelis and Lucas van de

---

36   There were of course exceptions. In 1671, for instance, Jacob Abendana, merchant in Amsterdam and member of the *Portuyees Natie,* offered a bottomry to his brother David Abendana to the value of 350 guilders. David was to travel as supercargo on board *De Salamander,* via Middelburg-Angola-Curaçao and Middelburg, under the command of skipper Bastiaen Pietersz. Given the close family ties between bottomry provider and taker, and the fact that the latter was supercargo on the ship, it is likely that Jacob had direct commercial interests in the outcome of the venture. SAA, *Not. Arch.* 4073B/...: 1671-11-30.

37   SAA, *Not. Arch.* 700/...: 1622-11-01; *Not. Arch.* 658-2/909: 1623-01-26.

38   SAA, *Not. Arch.* 107/66-66v: 1607-06-27.

Venne, Gerrit Reijnst, and Hans Francx.[39] We also find evidence of merchants serving as passive or 'silent' investors in voyages largely organised by others and apparently without formal partnership arrangements. Thus, in 1599, Pieter van der Haegen, merchant in Rotterdam, organized a merchant fleet comprising three ships and two yachts and bound for Angola, Brazil and Sofala under the command of Melchior van den Kerckhoven. Total investment in cargo and outfit for the venture was 22,000 Flemish pounds. Among those investing were Nicollas Seys, who invested 2,250 Flemish pounds as well as Roberto Strossi, Hans Broers and Jan de Vries, the last two investing 2,000 and 750 Flemish pounds, respectively.[40]

Associations between private merchants in the purchase, freightage, and outfitting of vessels for the Angolan trade continued in later periods, even when trade was under the auspices of the WIC. Moreover, the level of participation of private merchants grew from the late 1640s, with the opening up of the WIC monopoly in Angolan trade to others. Involvement of private venture capital took two main forms. In some cases, it involved collaboration with the WIC; in other cases, it was in defiance of the WIC monopoly, a practice that opened up private traders to attack by the WIC and legal disputes over the recovery of ships and cargoes. The second type of participation in Angolan trade was in fact a constant from the establishment of the Company by the States General in 1621 onwards.[41] But, in this period, relationships between the private traders and the WIC were not always marked by conflict. Indeed, in the 1620s, the WIC often relied on privately-owned vessels to ship its personnel and equipment, as for instance, in November 1623, when Joris Andriaenssen, Hendrick Broen and Samuel Bloemert, on behalf of the WIC Chamber of Amsterdam, hired three private ships to transport soldiers and goods from Amsterdam to WIC settlements. The ships concerned were the *De Haen*, 250 *last*, owned by Elias Trip, Hans Franx, and Jacob Jansen; the *Concordia*, 250 *last*, owned by Elias Trip and Aernout van Lybergen; and the *Nassau*, 190 *last*, owned by Abraham van Beeck.[42]

The progressive relaxing of the WIC monopoly in the Brazilian and Caribbean trades in 1638, the Angolan trade in 1647, and later in trade with Dutch North America enhanced the opportunities for legal participation in

---

39   SAA, *Not. Arch.* 115/30-30v: 1609-02-03.

40   SAA, *Not. Arch.* 53/505: 1599-10-02; *Not. Arch.* 264/182: 1608-05-02; *Not. Arch.* 197/479v-480v: 1613-01-21.

41   Silva, *Dutch and Portuguese in Western Africa*, Chapter 7.

42   SAA, *Not. Arch.* 170/28v-30v: 1623-11-10; *Not. Arch.* 170/30v: 1623-11-10; *Not. Arch.* 170/30v: 1623-11-10.

such trades by private merchants, thereby easing the almost constant conflict between them and the WIC of former decades. From the mid-seventeenth century onwards various private traders based in the Republic signed commercial deals with the WIC to supply goods to Company settlements. These included slaves in the case of the Angolan trade. Such agreements comprised personal contracts as well as ones made on behalf of third parties based elsewhere. A case in point were agreements between the WIC and the holders of the Spanish *asiento* in the years 1662–1669, Domingos Grillo and Ambrosio Lomellini, of Madrid, who, through their representative and partner in Amsterdam, Francisco Ferroni, agreed to supply slaves to Cartagena via Curaçao.[43] Such types of agreements continued under the second WIC. In 1695, for instance, several directors of the second WIC signed a contract on behalf of the Company with Samuel Cohen Nassij for him to supply 500 slaves to Suriname at a fixed price of 210 guilders per slave. The slaves were to be acquired in Angola and transported to Suriname in four ships, each one carrying 125 slaves.[44] This anticipated another contract in 1697 for the supply of slaves to Suriname signed between the WIC and Jan Baptist van Maesen and associates. The latter included Tobias Ansicq, Thomas de Pinedo, Marcellus Broen, Hendrick Reijgerbis, and Nicolaas and Willem Fernandes de Miranda, who, together with Van Maesen, agreed to supply 101 slaves to Suriname, at a price of 210 guilders per slave. As in the contract made in 1695 the slaves were to be acquired in Angola.[45]

With the decline of the second WIC in the eighteenth century forms of contract between organizations and private traders continued to evolve. Accompanying these were changes in both the parties to and form of agreements, as organizations representing planters and slave buyers in Dutch America were brought into the equation. Equally, there were changes on the slave-supply side, as multi-party partnerships were succeeded by small or medium sized commercial companies or firms. Thus, in 1768, for example, Josua van Ouderkerk and Christiaan van Tarelinkm, directors of the colony of Berbice, signed on their own behalf and that of other directors of the colony, an agreement with the Dutch firm Christiaan Cruijs & Son for the supply of

---

43 SAA, *Not. Arch.* 1148/205: 1664-03-12; *Not. Arch.* 231/82-89: 1669-09-09; *Not. Arch.* 3678B/919:1669-07-01. For further details on the Grillo and Lomellini *asiento*, see: Vega Franco, *El Trafico*, 194–202; Vila Vilar, "La sublevacion," 171–192; Postma, *The Dutch in the Atlantic Slave Trade*, 33–38, and appendix 3, 349–353. See also: Silva, "Crossing Empires," 31–32.

44 SAA, *Not. Arch.* 4774: 1695-10-26.

45 SAA, *Not. Arch.* 4774/346: 1697-12-03.

slaves to the colony. The enslaved were to be purchased in Angola by agents hired by the Dutch firm who would travel on board the ship *Wulpenburg*, under the command of Hans Barends. The agents involved were Jac. Tobiassen Coulphert & Co. of Flushing (Vlissingen).[46]

Such contracts reflected a broader trend towards increasing specialization in Dutch Atlantic trade in which maritime trade, accounting, and transport become distinct, though inter-related activities. The practice of hiring a third party to take care of the outfitting and accounting for commercial ventures emerged clearly from the mid-seventeenth century. In time, captains of ships became more responsible for the equipping of ships, while merchants with commercial interests took shares in such ships, bought their own trade goods, and hired supercargoes to travel on board the vessels and carry out trade at different ports. In 1659, for example, the ship *St. Jan Baptista* left Amsterdam for Angola and thence for Rio de la Plata and Buenos Aires, under the command of Jan Symonsz de Voocht from Zierikzee. The master, together with supercargo David Lemque, outfitted the vessel, financing this through a bottomry of 2,100 guilders from Pieter Uijlenburgh of Amsterdam and offering goods as collateral. Several merchants freighted cargo space on the *St. Jan Baptista* and hired their own supercargoes to represent their interest on board as well as in ports visited by the ship. The merchants included Albert Lubbertsen Coningh and Lord (Cavallier) Jacob Jansen Pelgrom. They entrusted to their supercargoes, David Lemque and Gerrit Hartman, commodities valued in 2,016 guilders. Jan Broers, Hendrick Dusterloo, Louis Quickelenburgh and Anthoine Maire, all merchants in Amsterdam, also freighted space, entrusting their affairs jointly to the same two supercargoes and a third one, Wouter Abrahamsen de Vries. Yet another investor was Abraham Clocker, whose cargo was valued at 4,370 guilders and was entrusted to David Lemque.[47]

The evidence presented above points, on the one hand, to a widening of the base of investment in the trade on the part of private individuals as a way to spread risks by investing their funds in several voyages simultaneously. On the other hand, the shift described earlier might also indicate an increasing specialisation of the business where those involved played a distinct role. Finally, it also shows an increase in ships' cargo capacity.

It was noted earlier that collaboration between private merchants and State-sponsored monopoly companies was not the only form of interaction

---

46   SAA, *Not. Arch.* 14314/409: 1768-07-30.

47   SAA, *Not. Arch.* 2757/133: 1661-04-08; *Not. Arch.* 2757A/149: 1661-04-09; *Not. Arch.* 2757A/153: 1661-04-09.

between these two parties. Conflict remained an ever-present threat even after the opening of the monopolies to non-company investors. In 1648, for instance Gerhard van Hetlingh, Isaac Graswinckel, Willem Graswinckel and Dirck Pietersz Wittepaart saw their ship *St. Jan* and her cargo confiscated by the WIC. The vessel was expected to sail between the Republic, Angola and the West Indies, and return to the Maas River, but was held before it could do so. To release the *St. Jan* and her cargo Isaac Graswinckel was forced to pay a warranty of 10,000 guilders to the WIC.[48] Litigation between private businessmen and the Company for the recovery of seized or confiscated goods, for release of arrested crew, and for demand for compensation for losses or damages was very common, not only for cases related to the Angolan trade, but also to other commercial branches and regions where the company insisted on defending its monopoly rights.[49]

Commercial Agency

Commercial networking and agency were key aspects of the organization of long-distance trade between the Republic, the Angolan Coast, and the Americas. In the context of the time, with its slow and erratic mechanisms of communications, having reliable and efficient agents or representatives in each area of trade as well as on board ship itself was paramount for success. Within Europe, private merchants in the Republic often granted power of attorney and appointed proxies in other European ports and markets to protect and promote their commercial interests. Such agents took responsibility for arranging for the loading and unloading of vessels and the onward movement of commodities to market or to storage in warehouses. In February 1620, for instance, Frans Jacobsen Hinlopen and Samuel Bloemert, merchants in Amsterdam, gave power of attorney to Jelmer Jelmersz to allow him to unload and forward to Amsterdam commodities just arrived at Hoorn from Angola in the ship *De Jager* commanded by Marten Cornelisz.[50] Other responsibilities of agents included the recovery of commodities seized by interlopers or corsairs at sea or overseas, and payment of returns to partners in joint commercial ventures or of salaries and wages to mariners, officers, and supercargoes. To give just one example, in 1657, to recover goods seized by English privateers, Henrico

48   SAA, *Not. Arch.* 1085/378: 1648-12-18.
49   Silva, *Dutch and Portuguese in Western Africa*, Chapters 2, 6 and 7.
50   SAA, *Not. Arch.* 215/99v: 1620-02-11.

Mathias, merchant in Amsterdam, gave power of attorney and credit to Jacob Luce (de Luz?) in London.[51]

If agents were vital to the operation of commercial exchange within Europe, they were equally so in the Republic's inter-continental routes linking Europe, Angola and the Americas. Investors seeking to protect and promote their interests in such had several choices. They could choose to reside themselves in trading places overseas, an option they rarely exercised. They might elect to have one of their partners travel with the ship, again an option that few merchants chose to exercise, or to have a commercial agent do so. The last might be the master of ship or a supercargo. They might also elect to co-opt into their partnership an agent already living, permanently or temporarily, overseas or to hire someone overseas to act on their behalf. In reality, such were the risks of long-distance trade that combinations of such practices were often adopted.

By the the eighteenth century, the most commonly adopted solution used by private merchants in the Angolan trade to protect their interests was to rely on shipmasters or other officers. In the case of slaving voyages, they were remunerated for their services according to the number of slaves delivered alive in the Americas. Christiaan Ketner, master of the *Anna Bolette* in 1782, noted earlier, was paid in this way, receiving a fixed payment per slave disembarked at the port of destination.[52] This practice, however, had evolved through time; it was not the most commonly used means adopted by investors in slaving voyages before the eighteenth century.

In the earliest years of Dutch participation in Angolan trade, the Republic's private merchants sometimes preferred to travel themselves, or have one or more of their commercial partners travel, on board ship. In 1609, for instance, Cornelis and Lucas van de Venne not only owned and co-financed the outfitting of a fleet to sail to Angola but also decided to take command of the fleet's two principal ships.[53] Similarly, in the case of the voyage of the *De Maecht* in 1607, it was agreed by the partners Elias Trip, Jan Kuysten and Manuel Telles Barreto that the last would travel on board the vessel to conduct trade and safeguard their interests.[54] This practice was also common among the Portuguese Sephardic Jews based in Amsterdam. In 1604, for example, Manuel Lopes Homem, merchant in Amsterdam, organized a trading voyage together

51   SAA, *Not. Arch.* 2120/167-169: 1657-05-25.
52   SAA, *Not. Arch.* 16371/463: 1782-08-07.
53   SAA, *Not. Arch.* 115/30-30v: 1609-02-13.
54   SAA, *Not. Arch.* 107//66-66v: 1607-06-27.

with Afonso and Rodrigo Fidalgo, Portuguese merchants from Madeira (but then residing in Antwerp), and Gabriel Pais, merchant in Lisbon, among other participants. The partners agreed that Afonso Fidalgo would sail on board the *São Pedro* from the Republic to Lisbon, Angola, and Pernambuco in Brazil before returning from Amsterdam via Lisbon. He was given responsibility for all commercial transactions during the trip, including the purchase of slaves in Angola and a return cargo of sugar from Brazil.[55]

As business with the Angolan coast expanded and this market became better known in the Republic, merchants opted more often for staying in Europe and hiring a representative to travel on board the vessels. Sometimes, they even employed an agent based in Angola to act on their behalf. Evidence of this is provided in the early seventeenth century by the practices of the Dutch merchant, Lucas van de Venne, who in 1613, entrusted a cargo of trade goods to Bartolomeu Rodrigues Molina bound to Angola for delivery to Gonçalo da Costa, who resided at Luanda. The last would take responsibility for trading them at the Angolan coast and the Congo River.[56] Lucas van de Venne was not alone in following such practices. In 1620, Frans Jacobsen Hinlopen and Samuel Bloemert, merchants in Amsterdam, hired Claes Baenen and Jeremias Cornelisz to act as commercial assistants (*assistenten*) to shipmaster Marten Cornelisz, commander of the *De Jager* in her voyage from Hoorn to Angola.[57]

Having agents in place on the Angolan coast was a well-considered strategy by Dutch merchants anxious to reduce voyage times, including time on the African coast. By recruiting merchants and factors and retaining them on the coast on a more or less permanent basis, private merchants hoped that men on the spot with local knowledge and connections would be able to expedite transactions more efficiently than others. It was a practice not only implemented in the Angolan trade but also in the Petite Côte of Senegal and Cape Mount, as we have argued elsewhere.[58] It is echoed, too, by Pieter van den Broeck in his accounts of his various voyages to Western Africa, in which he provides precious information on merchants at the coast acting as factors to merchants and commercial firms based in Amsterdam and other ports in the Republic. In his second voyage, on the Loango Coast, for example, Van den Broecke went to 'the house of the factor Jacques van der Voorde, who had come

---

55 SAA, *Not. Arch.* 61/487-489: 1604-09-16.
56 SAA, *Not. Arch.* 376/114-115: 1613-03-06.
57 SAA, *Not. Arch.* 200/513: 1620-04-09.
58 Filipa Ribeiro da Silva, "Dutch trade with Senegambia, Guinea and Cape Verde, c.1590–1674," in Toby Green, ed., *Brokers of Change: Atlantic Commerce and Cultures in Pre-colonial Western Africa* (Oxford: Oxford University Press, 2012), Chapter 4.

here [Loango] with a barque [probably *Mercurius*]. The aforementioned barque', he remarked, 'lay near the river Congo'.[59]

There is evidence presented that in this initial period of contact between the Republic and Angola those employed as agents by private merchants to travel on board vessels sometimes comprised men organised in a more or less hierarchal way. They might include a chief merchant or senior trader (*upperkoopman*), one or more junior traders (*onderkoopman*), accountants (*boekhouders*), and assistant staff (*commiesen or assistenten*). Each of them had distinct functions in the organization and conduction of trade in the Angolan Coast and other regions of Western Africa.[60] Junior merchants or factors, together with support staff, were known to be placed in charge of a small cottage or warehouse with a small sloop at the coast, or left in command of floating trading posts – or *leggers* – anchored off the coast while the principal vessel sailed between Africa and the Republic. On his fourth voyage to Loango and Congo as chief-merchant, Van den Broecke left in February 1612 his junior factor, Marten van Colck, ashore in Mayoumba to live and trade. He remained there while Van den Broecke returned to Holland late that year.[61] Even during the stay of the larger ships on the coast, commercial agents onshore played key roles as they assisted in coordinating business and sailing times of such ships to ensure their fastest possible dispatch. Pieter van den Broecke again gives us a glimpse of this complex process of coordinating the activities of larger and smaller ships in the service of the same trading company.[62]

In the second half of the seventeenth century, as private merchants restarted their participation in the Angolan trade under the aegis of the WIC monopoly, this intricate hierarchical organization of commercial staff on board the vessels operating in the Angolan trade and on the coast seems to have become more simplified. By that time, private merchants in the Republic had come to rely on shipmasters and supercargoes to represent their interests in ships trading to Angola. In 1661, Jan Broers, Hendrick Duysterloo, Louis Quickelenburgh and Anthoine Maire employed Jan Symonsz de Voocht, from Zierikzee, as master of the *St. Jan Baptist*, and Wouter Abrahamsen de Vries, Gerrit Hartman and David Lemque as supercargoes. De Voocht was given a monthly wage of 80 *carolus golden*, plus two percent of the net income of the

---

59   Fleur, ed., *Pieter van den Broecke's journal*, 47 and 74.
60   Silva, "Dutch vessels in African waters"; idem, *Dutch and Portuguese in Western Africa*, Chapter 5; idem, "Dutch trade with Senegambia, Guinea and Cape Verde."
61   Fleur, ed., *Pieter van den Broecke's journal*, 79, 88–89.
62   Ibid., 87–91.

voyage. By contrast, the supercargoes received a percentage of the net income of the venture, ranging from 4.5 percent in the case of De Vries to 7 percent in that of the other two.[63] Lemque and Hartman also acted as supercargoes for merchants Aldert Lubbertsen and Jacob Jansen Pelgrom, receiving from them half of the net profit from commodity returns.[64]

This shift towards shipboard rather than land-based agency was to some extent facilitated by the establishment of the WIC, which set up its own commercial organization in Western Africa. This was modelled on the system earlier adopted by private merchants in the period of free trade before 1621. With the monopoly in place, private merchants were banned from having agents of their own on the coast, and when again authorised to trade in Angola, tended therefore to rely on the WIC network of commercial officers. For private merchants, this brought several benefits. By reducing employment costs associated with multiple parties and by giving supercargoes payments related closely to commercial performance, there were potentially improvements in efficiency and thus in profit margins. On the downside, however, reliance on Company officials increased scope for conflict with the same, giving rise to confiscations of cargoes and arrests of crews. In time, and to some extent reflecting the decline of the second WIC in the eighteenth century, a further transformation in terms of commercial agency occurred, with, as noted earlier, an increasing trend towards employing ship captains and pilots as commercial agents. This was to become commonplace in the Dutch eighteenth-century trade with Angola, as the example of Ketner quoted at the outset of this essay reveals.[65]

Paramount, however, to the ultimate success of any commercial venture organized by private merchants in the Republic to Angola was another layer of economic actors. These were the agents that established connections between the African coastal areas and the markets for slaves and other African goods located deeper in the continent. These agents comprised Africans, Eurafricans and, very occasionally, Europeans. Given the Euro-centric nature of most of our primary sources, it is extremely difficult to identify who these men were. Travel accounts sometimes, however, provide us with some references to these traders and their key role. Van den Broecke, for example, during his second voyage to West-central Africa established contacts with several Portuguese and Eurafricans at different points on the coast. He reported meeting on

---

63   SAA, *Not. Arch.* 275A/149: 1661-04-09; *Not. Arch.* 2757A/157: 1661-04-09; *Not. Arch.* 2757A/165: 1661-04-09.
64   SAA, *Not. Arch.* 2757/133: 1661-04-08.
65   SAA, *Not. Arch.* 16372/463: 1782-08-07.

1 November 1609 Hans de Haesse, who, he suggested, was Portuguese, and his own agent at Portudal (Petite Cote of Senegal). Further south, at Mayoumba, he reportedly bought from an Eurafrican of Portuguese descent named Lowies Mendes (or Luís Mendes) redwood, elephant tusks and *taccola* (takula, a dye-yielding plant) on 26 May 1610. During the same voyage, on 17 May, 1610, Van den Broecke also reported that the master of the ship *Mauritius* trading under his supervision went up the Cacongo River to do business with a Portuguese merchant named Manuel da Costa. Finally, on his third voyage to Angola, Van den Broecke met at Mayoumba another Portuguese, who he described as his 'great friend Francisco Delmende Navero'.[66]

The Angolan Trade: A Trans-National Business

The evidence presented in this essay highlights the range and nature of connections between private businessmen in geographical spaces and locations around the Atlantic world and operating under different political and other jurisdictions and across religious and cultural boundaries. In these respects it speaks to the trans-national character of private involvement in the Angolan trade, and indeed in other branches of the African commerce.[67] Insurers, suppliers of credit, shipowners, freighters, outfitters, captains, pilots, proxies, and factors had different geographical origins and citizenships and self-identified themselves as members of different European States. But, despite these and other differences in geographical background, they came together to participate in the development of Dutch commerce with Angola and in doing so contributed to the growth of the Atlantic slave trade as a business enterprise.

This trans-national perspective on Angolan trade raises questions about its identification with and commonly assumed division among European nations. Such labelling becomes problematical when, as we have shown, those involved in European voyages to Angola – whether as insurers, freighters of goods, shipowners, or in other capacities – came from different European countries or places. Nowhere is this better illustrated than in the insurance contract issued by Diogo Nunes Belmonte and his 35 insurers for the voyage of the *Engel Michiel* in 1614 commanded by Sebastião Ribeiro.[68] Belmonte himself was a Portuguese Jew but based in Amsterdam, as was skipper Ribeiro. The collective of insurers comprised people of Dutch, Flemish, and German origin. The ship

---

66   Fleur, ed., *Pieter van den Broecke's journal*, 71, 73, 76, 87.
67   Silva, "Crossing Empires"; idem, *Dutch and Portuguese in Western Africa*, Chapter 7.
68   SAA, *Not. Arch.*, 254/188-188v: 1614-05-22.

itself was owned by a Dutch-Flemish merchant and was to sail from Amsterdam to Lisbon and thence to Seville, to Spanish America and back to Seville. Another case in point is that of the voyage of the *Anna Boleta* commanded by Christiaan Ketner with which we began this essay.[69] Organized in ways that clearly transcended national boundaries, such voyages took forms of super-national economic co-operation within private enterprise to wholly new levels, anticipating forms of multinational endeavour that we commonly associate with the modern world.

---

69   SAA, *Not. Arch.* 16371/463: 1782-08-07.

CHAPTER 4

Angola and the Seventeenth-Century South Atlantic Slave Trade

Arlindo Manuel Caldeira

The field of Atlantic History has stimulated new scholarly work, but its impact has been mainly visible in the Anglo-Saxon world.[1] Accordingly, most scholarship has focused on the North Atlantic, with relatively little attention being devoted until recently to the South. The last was mainly under Portuguese influence. There are exceptions to this pattern, however. John Thornton, author of *Africa and the Africans in the making of the Atlantic World*, a groundbreaking study within the Atlantic History paradigm, has either single-handedly or in collaboration with Linda Heywood re-shaped our understanding of the history of West-Central Africa and has discussed important elements in the cultural formation of South America.[2] Similarly, Luiz Felipe de Alencastro's book *O trato dos viventes* interlinks the different areas and cultures of the South Atlantic in order to explain the origins of Brazil.[3] Also worth mentioning in this context are the publications of Marina de Mello e Souza and James H. Sweet, though, unlike Thornton and Heywood, their focus has been on more circumscribed cultural themes.[4]

---

1 Alison Games, "Atlantic History: Definitions, Challenges, and Opportunities," *American Historical Review* 111: 3 (2006): 741–757; Bernard Bailyn, *Atlantic History. Concepts and Contours* (Cambridge, MA: Harvard University Press, 2005); Douglas R. Egerton, *et al, The Atlantic World* (Wheeling, IL: Harlan Davidson Inc., 2007); Silvia Marzagalli, "Sur les origines de l' 'Atlantic History': Paradigme interprétatif de l'histoire des espaces atlantiques à l'époque moderne," *Dix-Huitième Siècle* 33 (2001): 17–31.

2 John K. Thornton, *Africa and Africans in the Making of the Atlantic World, 1400–1650* (Cambridge: Cambridge University Press, 1992); idem, "Demography and history in the Kingdom of Kongo, 1550–1750," *Journal of African History* 18:4 (1977): 507–530; idem, *The Kingdom of Kongo: Civil War and Transition, 1641–1718* (Madison, WI: The University of Wisconsin Press, 1983); idem, *Warfare in Atlantic Africa, 1500–1800* (London: University College of London, 1998); idem and Linda M. Heywood, *Central Africans, Atlantic Creoles and the Foundation of the Americas, 1585–1660* (Cambridge: Cambridge University Press, 2007); Linda M. Heywood, ed., *Central Africans and Cultural Transformations in the American Diaspora* (Cambridge: Cambridge University Press, 2002).

3 Luiz Felipe de Alencastro, *O trato dos viventes: Formação do Brasil no Atlântico Sul, séculos XVI e XVII* (São Paulo: Companhia das Letras, 2000).

4 Marina de Mello e Souza, *Reis negros no Brasil escravista: história da festa de coroação de Rei Congo* (Belo Horizonte: Editora UFMG, 2002); James H. Sweet. *Recreating Africa: Culture,*

© KONINKLIJKE BRILL NV, LEIDEN, 2015 | DOI 10.1163/9789004280588_005

Although there is no lack of primary sources for the study of the
seventeenth-century South Atlantic slave trade, there are few regular serial collections of data. This may explain the relatively small number of studies for
this period in comparison with the eighteenth century and the absence of an
overview of the seventeenth-century trade similar to Joseph Miller's *The Way
of Death* for eighteenth-century slavery.[5]

Despite focusing on the eighteenth century, Miller's work has, nevertheless,
aroused scholarly interest in Angolan history more generally in the English-
speaking world as the research carried out by several scholars based in North
America attests. Two excellent examples are José C. Curto, whose work examines, among other things, the role of alcoholic beverages in the Angolan slave
trade, and Roquinaldo Ferreira, whose doctoral dissertation examined the
Angolan slave trade between 1650 and 1800, focussing on the influence of military campaigns and of effective control of territory over the trade itself, resulting in the decentralization of slave exports from Luanda to Benguela.[6] Also
paramount to understand sixteenth- and seventeenth-century Angola is the
work of Beatrix Heintze, whose contributions over twenty years can be found
in a wide range of publications. In 1996, a first compilation of Heintze's works
was edited in Germany and ten years later, a revised and extended version was
translated into Portuguese and published in Luanda.[7] Both compilations are
excellent reference books for everyone interested in Angolan history. Equally,
for studying the links between Angola and Spanish America under Portuguese
control of the Spanish *asiento*, the detailed studies of Germán Peralta Rivera
and Enriqueta Vila Vilar are now seen as vital.[8]

    Kinship, and Religion in the African-Portuguese World, 1441–1770 (Chapel Hill, NC: University of
    North Carolina Press, 2003) [Trad. portuguesa: *Recriar África: cultura, parentesco e religião no
    mundo afro-português 1441–1770* (Lisboa: Edições 70, 2007)].

5 Joseph C. Miller, *Way of Death. Merchant Capitalism and the Angolan Slave Trade, 1730–1830*
    (Madison, WI: University of Wisconsin Press, 1988).

6 José C. Curto, *Álcool e Escravos. O comércio luso-brasileiro do álcool em Mpinda, Luanda e
    Benguela durante o tráfico atlântico de escravos (c.1480–1830) e o seu impacto nas sociedades da
    África Central Ocidental* (Lisboa: Vulgata, 2002). [English edition: *Enslaving spirits. The
    Portuguese-Brazilian Alcohol trade at Luanda and its hinterland, c. 1550–1830* (Leiden: Brill,
    2005)]. Roquinaldo Amaral Ferreira, "Transforming Atlantic slaving: trade, warfare and terri-
    torial control in Angola, 1650–1800" (unpublised PhD Diss., University of California, 2003).

7 Beatrix Heintze, *Studien zur Geschichte Angolas im 16. und 17. Jahrhundert. Ein Lesebuch*
    (Köln: Köppe, 1996); idem, *Angola nos séculos XVI e XVII* (Luanda: Kilombelombe, 2007).

8 Germán Peralta Rivera, *El comercio negrero en América Latina (1595–1640)* (Lima: Editorial
    Universitaria, 2005); Enriqueta Vila Vilar, *Hispano-America y el comercio de esclavos. Los
    asientos portugueses* (Sevilha: Escuela de Estudios Hispanoamericanos, 1977).

In addition, during the past decades, a number of articles and essays published in journals and edited collections have also focussed on the Angolan slave trade during the period under analysis here. Among the more important was Joseph Miller's first overview in the 1970s of the Kongolese and Angolan slave trade from its origins to abolition. Twenty five years later, Miller prepared a similar synthesis but this time focussing more on the economic, social and cultural reality of the slave trade suppliers.[9] Complementing this, Rosa Cruz e Silva and Maria da Conceição Gomes Pereira wrote on the fairs of Ndongo-Angola.[10] Both their articles offer overviews of the subject, but from different perspectives. The works by Maria Luísa Esteves and Filipe Nunes de Carvalho are equally worthy of mention for addressing specific historical questions about Angola using mainly previously untapped archival sources.[11]

More recently, the launching of the *Transatlantic Slave Voyages Website* has given scholars access to a prodigious body of information on the slave trade on a global scale, facilitating the development of comparative and highly contextualised studies. Unfortunately, the slave trade from West-Central Africa (in particular Luanda) is still underrepresented in the database due to lack of sources or difficulties in accessing them.[12] Although the authors of the database have attempted to estimate the number of voyages for the entire region during the seventeenth century, by using projections based on figures reported in the sources, similar procedures have not been adopted to calculate the number of voyages from Luanda or its share of the transatlantic slave trade. Many

---

9   Joseph C. Miller, "The Slave Trade in Congo and Angola," in Martin L. Kilson and Robert I. Rotberg, eds., *The African Diaspora* (Cambridge, MA: Harvard University Press, 1976), 75–113; idem, "Central Africa during the Era of the Slave Trade, c. 1490s–1850s," in Heywood, ed., *Central Africans and Cultural Transformations*, 21–69.

10   Rosa Cruz e Silva, "As Feiras do Ndongo. A Outra Vertente do Comércio no Século XVII," in *Actas do Seminário 'Encontro de povos e culturas em Angola' Luanda, 3 a 6 de Abril de 1995* (Lisboa: Comissão Nacional para as Comemorações dos Descobrimentos Portugueses, 1997), 405–422; Maria da Conceição Gomes Pereira, "As Feiras – Sua importância no contexto comercial de Angola. Sécs XV a XIX," *Africana: Revista da Universidade Portucalense* 6 (1990): 211–233.

11   Maria Luísa Esteves, "Os Holandeses em Angola: decadência do comércio externo e soluções locais encontradas," *Studia* 52 (1994): 49–82; idem, "Para o estudo do tráfico de escravos em Angola (1640–1668)," *Studia* 50 (1991): 79–108; Filipe Nunes de Carvalho, "Aspectos do tráfico de escravos de Angola para o Brasil no século XVII. 1. Prolegómenos do inferno," in José Marques and Mário José Barroca, eds., *In memoriam de Carlos Alberto Ferreira de Almeida* (Porto: Faculdade de Letras, 1996), 1: 236.

12   *Voyages: The Trans-Atlantic Slave Trade Database*: http://www.slavevoyages.org, 12 October 2010.

of these questions as well as others of methodological nature are discussed at length and justified in David Eltis and David Richardson's introduction to the collection of essays *Extending the Frontiers: Essays on the New Transatlantic Slave Trade Database* they have edited.[13] In addition, to this introductory chapter, which also offers us a first analysis of the global results of the project, other chapters in this edited collection contain useful information for the topic under scrutiny here in terms of both quantitative and qualitative analysis of primary source materials. In this sense, the essays on the transatlantic slave trade to Spanish America and the Brazilian ports of Pernambuco and Bahia are of particular interest.[14] More recently, the database formed the basis of the *Atlas of the Transatlantic Slave Trade* that Eltis and Richardson have published. Maps 3, 11, 25 35 and 100 are particularly relevant to our purpose.[15]

As for unpublished primary sources, the main collections for the history of seventeenth-century Angola and the South Atlantic can be found in the Portuguese Overseas Archive located in Lisbon and the Angolan National Historical Archive in Luanda. The source materials found in the latter rarely pre-date 1650 and are overall less known to scholars.[16] The Ajuda Library and the Portuguese National Archive (in particular the collections of *Corpo Cronológico* and the *Conselho da Fazenda*), both in Lisbon, as well as various Brazilian and Spanish Archives, such as the Bahia Public Archive in Salvador, the Rio de Janeiro National Archive, and the Indies National Archive in Seville, also have in their collections rich materials for the study of this subject.

As for published primary sources, their number remains small. Particularly noteworthy, however, are *Monumenta Missionaria Africana*, edited by António Brásio, which covers more than missionary activities, as well as collections

---

13   David Eltis and David Richardson, "A New Assessment of the Transatlantic Slave Trade," in David Elits and David Richardson, eds., *Extending the Frontiers: Essays on the New Transatlantic Slave Trade Database* (New Haven, CT: Yale University Press, 2008), 1–60.

14   António de Almeida Mendes, "The Foundations of the System: A Reassessment of the Slave Trade to the Spanish Americas in the Sixteenth and Seventeenth Centuries," in ibid., 63–94; Daniel Barros Domingues da Silva and David Eltis, "The Slave Trade to Pernambuco, 1561–1851," in ibid., 95–129; Alexandre Vieira Ribeiro, "The Transatlantic Slave Trade to Bahia, 1582–1851," in ibid., 130–154.

15   David Eltis and David Richardson, *Atlas of the Transatlantic Slave Trade* (New Haven, CT: Yale University Press, 2010).

16   Selma Pantoja, "O Brasil colónia no acervo do Arquivo Histórico Nacional de Angola," *Revista de História* 140 (1999): 123–131.

published by Alfredo Felner and by Ruela Pombo.[17] Other relevant materials can be found in the journal *Arquivos de Angola* published in 1933–1970 by the Museum of Angola. The excellent and annotated collection of reports, orders and correspondence from Fernão de Sousa, governor of Angola (1624–1630), published by Beatrix Heintze is also vital for understanding the seventeenth century slave trade of the Portuguese.[18]

Finally, reference should be made to a few literary sources of outstanding value to understanding seventeenth-century Angola. They include the writings of Cavazzi and Cadornega, as well as the account book of António Coelho Guerreiro, merchant and royal official in Angola. Because of its rarity as well as its historical importance, the last source merits an updated critical edition.[19]

On the basis of these source materials and the available secondary literature, I propose in the rest of this essay to offer a general overview of the slave trade in seventeenth-century Angola and its connections to the wider Atlantic Ocean.[20] I start by looking at the aquisition of slaves in the interior and their transport to the coast. This will be followed by an analysis of the accommodation of slaves at the coast and their embarkation on board ship. I then examine some technical, commercial and financial issues relating to the Angolan slave trade, and finally look at the terrible conditions under which slaves were transported across the Atlantic.

---

17   António Brásio, ed., *Monumenta Missionaria Africana: África Ocidental* (hereafter *MMA*), 1st series (Lisboa: Agência Geral do Ultramar/Academia Portuguesa de História, 1952–1988), 15 vols.; Alfredo de Albuquerque Felner, *Angola: apontamentos sobre a ocupação e início do estabelecimento dos portugueses no Congo, Angola e Benguela extraídos de documentos históricos* (Coimbra: Impr. da Universidade, 1933); Ruela Pombo, *Anais de Angola: 1630–1635* (Lisboa: Empresa da Revista «Diogo-Cão», 1945).

18   Beatrix Heintze, ed., *Fontes para a história de Angola do século XVII* (Stuttgart: Franz Steiner Verlag Wiesbaden, 1985–1988), 2 vols.

19   Padre João António Cavazzi de Montecúccolo, *Descrição Histórica dos três reinos de Congo, Angola e Matamba* (Lisboa: Junta de Investigações do Ultramar, 1965), 2 vols.; António de Oliveira de Cadornega, *História geral das guerras angolanas: 1680* (Lisboa: Agência-Geral do Ultramar, 1972), 3 vols.; Virgínia Rau, *O "Livro de Rezão" de António Coelho Guerreiro* (Lisboa: Companhia de Diamantes de Angola, 1956). See also: Joseph C. Miller, "Capitalism and Slaving: The Financial and Commercial Organization of the Angolan Slave Trade, according to the Accounts of António Coelho Guerreiro (1684–1692)," *International Journal of African Historical Studies* 17:1 (1984): 1–56.

20   Arlindo Caldeira, "Escravos de mar em fora. As condições de transporte no tráfico negreiro do Atlântico Sul durante o século XVII," in Centro de Estudos Africanos da Universidade do Porto, ed., *Trabalho Forçado Africano. O Caminho de Ida* (Porto: Húmus, 2009), 13–48.

The Angolan Slave Market

The presence of European slave merchants in the Mbundu kingdom of Ndongo, called Angola by the Portuguese, started much earlier than any attempts at political control by the Portuguese Crown. Certainly before 1530, merchants from São Tomé had already begun trading on the Angolan coast.[21] A growing demand for slave labour in São Tomé linked to a rise in sugarcane cultivation and demand for labour in new markets, especially in Spanish America, prompted the lease holders of the Portuguese Crown monopolies and the ship owners[22] of São Tomé to extend their trading activities south of Mpinda, despite protests by the King of Kongo.[23] Initially, their trading vessels visited only the mouth of the Kwanza River, which remained their main destination for many years. Later, however, these ships started to trade at the Bay of Luanda as well. In 1575, the fleet of Paulo Dias de Novais found there seven ships from São Tomé "which had come to trade." At that time, too, "40 very rich Portuguese men" already lived on the island.[24] Map 4.1 shows the location of these early as well as later Portuguese activities in Angola.

As early as 1534 São Tomé ships had sailed southwards "beyond Angola" (i.e. south of the Kwanza River) "to look for" new trading spots along the coast, reaching as far as the Longa River, if not Benguela.[25] In 1546, the brother of King John III sent an official expedition to this region calling it "my River of Alonga."[26]

In Angola, the pattern of trade of São Tomean merchants followed that they had adopted in the Gulf of Guinea. Seeking to exchange slaves for consumer goods, predominantly of European origin, but without directly interferring in internal trade circuits, the merchants tried to attract local African merchants to coastal areas where ancient or recently founded fairs existed. In Ndongo as in other African polities, slavery and slave trade pre-dated the arrival of European merchants, though it assumed forms and characteristics different from those found in later periods. The dominant political system, based on

---

21   "Regimento do feitor do trato de São Tomé: 1532-08-02," in *MMA*, 2: 14.
22   The *armador* (freighter or ship outfitter) was the one who financed and organised commerical operations for the ship whether or not he owned it. The word *armação* (rigging) was often associated with the transport of labour and can simply refer to the transport of slaves.
23   "Inquirição sobre o comércio de S. Tomé com Angola: 1548-11-12," in *MMA*, 2: 197–205; "Carta do padre Cornélio Gomes, 1553-10-29," in ibid., 2: 302–303.
24   "História da Residência dos Padres da Companhia de Jesus em Angola: 1594," in ibid., 4: 554.
25   Instituto dos Arquivos Nacionais/Torre do Tombo (hereafter IAN/TT), *Corpo Cronológico*, II-187-18: 1534-11-02: 'Caderno do recebedor da ilha de São Tomé'.
26   Felner, *Angola*, 98.

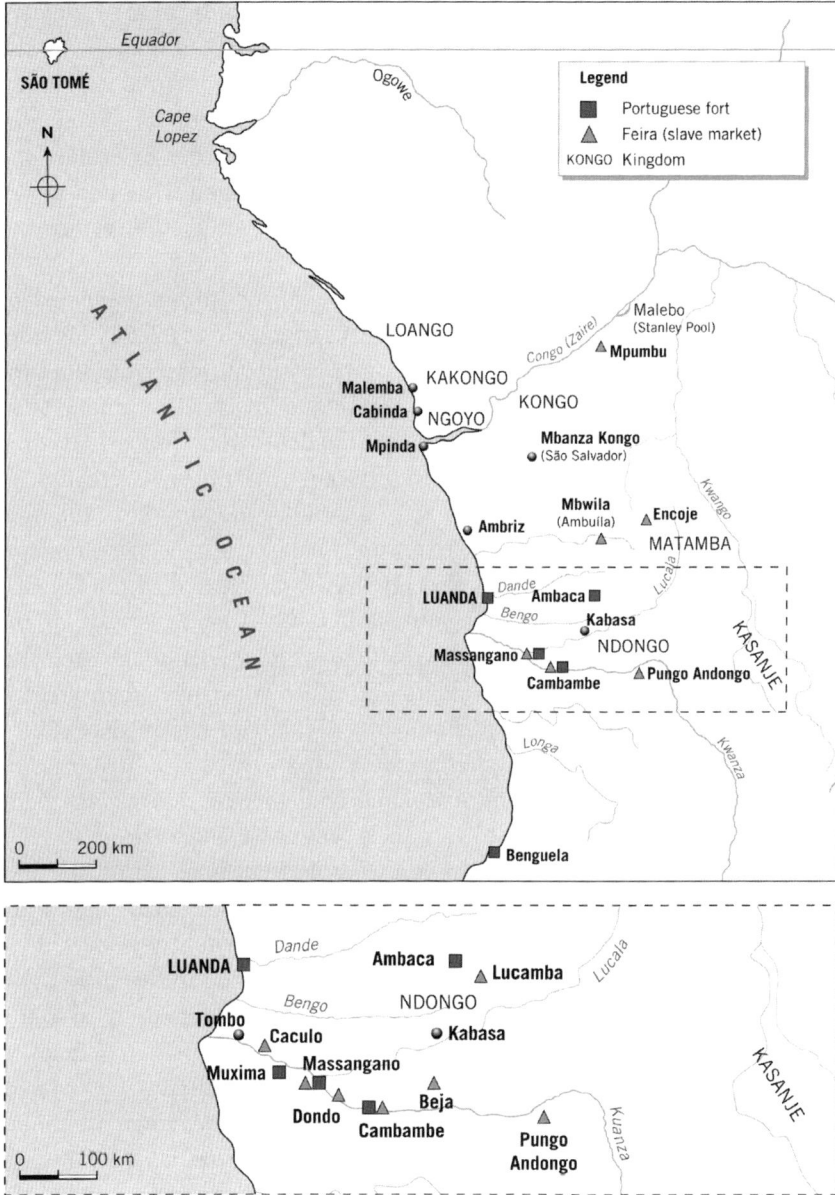

MAP 4.1   *Angola – seventeenth century*
Author: Arlindo Caldeira, 2013

personal and arbitrary power, allowed chiefs freely to dispose of their subjects, facilitating their transformation into 'commodities' and, prompted by the desire for European goods, thereby encouraging an exponential rise in the number of enslaved individuals. The range of crimes carrying the sentence of slavery was broadened and the scale of war grew in order to enslave the defeated. As a result, instability in the Angolan heartland increased as the Portuguese crown became interested in the slave trade of the region, and attempted to bring it under royal control.

In 1575, Paulo Dias de Novais, the first governor of Angola appointed by the crown, arrived in Luanda. Four years later, in 1579, the first military offensive against the Ndongo began and, in 1587 the Crown leased out, for the first time, the royal monopoly over the Angolan trade, granting to leaseholders, among other commercial privileges, permission to collect royal duties from slave exports from Luanda.[27] Map 4.1 highlights Luanda's central location in Portuguese activities.

The appointment of the governor was followed by the transfer of the royal bureaucratic apparatus to Luanda. To ensure a balance of power, a municipal government with inherent rights and privileges was created in the recently established town of Luanda. However, unlike the Atlantic islands or the Brazilian captaincies, Angola was not a settlement colony. Although the noble patron (*donatários*), their descendants and other Portuguese men arriving there had often been granted large amounts of land, for reasons beyond the scope of this study agricultural performance rarely exceeded subsistence levels. Consequently, for Europeans, Angola became a region that specialized in the "production" of slaves. Most likely, there was not a single European man, whatever his social status or profession, who was not engaged in the slave trade. Not even those involved in the church were exempt. Both Franciscans and Jesuits became involved in the business, either as owners or dealers.[28]

In time, the Portuguese crown also became interested in the slave trade, regarding it as a new source of revenue for the royal treasury. Central to this was its monopoly of slave exports from Angola and its imposition of taxes on exports by private merchants who held trading licences. Initially, in 1579–1587, and for a short period of time thereafter in 1606–1608, the crown attempted to manage the monopoly and tax collection directly. The results were unsatisfactory, encouraging the crown to opt for another method, namely, the

27   Felner, *Angola*, 487.

28   Arlindo Manuel Caldeira, "Os jesuítas em Angola nos séculos XVI e XVII: tráfico de escravos e 'escrúpulos de consciência,'" in Centro de Estudos Africanos da Universidade do Porto, ed., *Trabalho Forçado Africano – Articulações com o poder político* (Porto: Campo das Letras, 2007), 47–82.

leasing or farming out of contracts, under which private entrepreneurs could bid at public auction for the monopoly and the right to collect taxes for a fixed term on Angolan trade. As, however, Angolan exports were mainly slaves, leaseholders were given permission not only to collect taxes on slave exports from Luanda but also to engage in slave trade in their own right as well as to sell trading licences (*avenças*) at pre-determined rates to other merchants. In practice, the contractors did not hold a formal monopoly on the slave trade, but rather a monopoly *de facto*, since they came to control the entire dispatch of vessels at Luanda.

A splitting of the royal monopolies on the Angolan and São Tomean trades into two separate contracts first occurred in 1579. However, the first private contract in the Angolan trade was only granted to Pedro de Sevilha and António Mendes de Lamego in 1587. Throughout the seventeenth century, the annual sum paid for leasing rights was about 25,000.000 *réis*; only one contract exceeded 30,000.000 *réis*.[29]

By this means, the Portuguese crown secured an important fixed source of income and the contractors a business that, although requiring large capital investments, could reap huge dividends. In fact, besides being involved in the slave trade under outwardly very favourable conditions, contractors still had permission to charge other merchants 4,000 *réis* for each slave destined for Brazil, Portugal or São Tomé[30] and 7,000 for those bound for Spanish America.[31] Despite these levies, in the course of the seventeenth century, Luanda became the main port for the export of slaves into the Atlantic world, supplying a majority of the enslaved Africans embarking in Angola for Brazil and Spanish America. Some data on slave departures from Angola for the Americas between 1575 and 1693 are set out in Table 4.1.

---

29   Henrique Gomes da Costa leased the contract, in 1624–1628, for 40 million, but he ended up going bankrupt. For further information on the contract and contractors see: *Razões do réu Duarte Dias Henriques contratador, que foi do trato de Angola* (Lisboa: Pedro Craesbeeck, 1619); Celme Coelho da Cruz, "O tráfico negreiro da 'Costa de Angola', 1580–1640" (unpublished BA Diss., Universidade de Lisboa, 1966), 14–86; Frédéric Mauro, *Le Portugal et l'Atlantique uuXVIIe siècle (1570–1670): étude économique* (Paris: S.E.V.P.E.N., 1960), 157–158.

30   This tax, which was originally 3.000 *réis*, was raised unilaterally by the contractor and governor-general João Rodrigues Coutinho (1601–1603) and ended up being fixed at a new value in subsequent contracts, although not always peacefully. After the expulsion of the Dutch, in 1648, a 'new law' was created, with the government enforcing a levy on slave exports: each slave was taxed at 3.000 *réis* regardless of the destination. This "new law" was still in force at the end of the seventeenth century.

31   "Relação de António Dinis, c. 1622," in *MMA*, 11: 67–74.

TABLE 4.1   *Annual total of slaves leaving Angola (1575–1693)*

Periods	Total no. of slaves	Annual average	Source
1575–1587	32,123	2,677	(1)
1576	–	12,000	(2)
1587–1591	20,130	5,033	(1)
1606	–	12,000–13,000	(3)
1611	–	10,000–12,000	(4)
1618	–	10,000–12,000	(5)
c. 1620	–	15,000	(6)
Dec. 1624–Oct. 1626	18,507	10,095	(7)
c.1630	–	12,000–14,000	(8)
c. 1640	–	15,000	(9)
1650	–	15,000–16,000	(10)
Oct. 1654–Feb. 1656	13,945	10,459	(11)
1668–1671	25,271	6,318	(12)
c. 1680	–	8,000–10,000	(13)
c. 1690	–	5,000	(8)
1693	–	5,000–6,000	(14)

Sources:

(1)   Domingos de Abreu e Brito, "Sumário e descripção do Reino de Angola, 1592," in idem, *Um inquérito à vida administrativa e económica de Angola e do Brasil em fins do século XVI, segundo o manuscrito inédito existente na Biblioteca Nacional de Lisboa* (Coimbra: Impr. da Universidade, 1931), 30–34;

(2)   "Carta do padre Garcia Simões ao padre Luís Perpinhão: 1576-11-7" in MMA, 3: 146;

(3)   "Caderno do governador Manuel Cerveira Pereira: 1606-10-27," in ibid., 5: 224;

(4)   "Carta do padre Luís Brandão: 1611-08-21," in Alonso de Sandoval, *Naturaleza, policia sagrada i profana, costumbres i ritos, disciplina i catechismo evangelico de todos etiopes* (Sevilla: Francisco de Lira impressor, 1627), folio 66;

(5)   "Carta do capitão Baltasar Rebelo de Aragão: c. 1618," in MMA, 6: 338;

(6)   Sandoval, *Naturaleza*, fl. 54 v;

(7)   "Rendimento do contrato de Angola, 1624–1626," in Cruz, "Tráfico negreiro," 69;

(8)   AHU, *Angola*, cx. 14, doc.109: 1693-01-29: 'Consulta do Conselho Ultramarino';

(9)   "Carta [sobre o tráfico português] do Alto Conselho do Brasil às autoridades de Angola: Recife, 1641-12-03," in *L'ancien Congo et l'Angola: 1639–1655: d'après les archives romaines, portugaises, néerlandaises et espagnoles*, edited by Louis Jadin (Bruxelles/Rome: Institut Historique Belge de Rome, 1975), 1: 138;

(10)   "Arbítrio dado por Manuel Fernandes da Cruz: 1650-08-20," in Virgínia Rau & Maria Fernanda Gomes da Silva, *Os manuscritos do arquivo da Casa de Cadaval respeitantes ao Brasil* (Coimbra: Universidade, 1956), 1: 90–96;

(11)   AHU, *Angola*, cx. 6, doc. 128: 1656-02-25: 'Carta do governador Luís Manuel Chichorro';

(12)   AHU, *Angola*, cx. 10, doc. 40: 'Receita e despesa referente aos anos de 1668, 1669, 1670 e 1671';

(13)   Cadornega, *História geral*, 3: 31, 254;

(14)   AHU, *Angola*, cx. 14, doc. 121: 1693-03-13: 'Consulta do Conselho Ultramarino'.

Despite their mixed origins and incompleteness, the figures in Table 4.1 allow us to draw two immediate conclusions. Firstly, the average number of slaves leaving Angola throughout the entire period ranged from 10,000 to 15,000 individuals before 1660.[32] Thereafter there seems to have been a fall in the annual level of departures, but this may reflect weaknesses in the sources underlying Table 4.1 rather than reality. Secondly, judging from the low number of slave ship departures registered in the royal books, the tax collection in Luanda must have been difficult to enforce, with smuggling being apparent. This was known at the time. We estimate that during the period under analysis between a third and a half of slave ships escaped official control.

The data gathered in Table 4.1 show an increase in the annual departures of slaves, notably between 1620 and 1650, followed by a visible decrease in the 1660s and 1670s. As noted earlier, the *Transatlantic Slave Trade Database* only includes a limited number of seventeenth-century voyages. However, it is worth noting that in the first half of the century the annual average of slaves recorded as embarking at Luanda was higher than in the second; 2,162 voyages were recorded in the former, against 625 voyages in the latter.[33] The growth of exports over the first decades of the seventeenth century was not only due to an increasing demand for manpower in Brazilian sugar mills, but also to the involvement of Portuguese merchants in the management after 1595 of the Spanish *asiento* to supply Spanish America with slave labour. This was facilitated by the Union of the Iberian Crowns (1580–1640).[34] During the Dutch rule over Bahia (1623–1625), this circumstance also allowed contractors and *asientistas* to direct slave ships, initially destined to northeast Brazil, to the Spanish Indies. This fact may explain the reduced effects of Dutch presence in Bahia on the volume of Angolan slave trade.[35]

---

32   The annual total of slaves leaving Angola includes all enslaved boarding at the port of Luanda, regardless of their place of origin.

33   *Voyages: The Trans-Atlantic Slave Trade Database* [http://www.slavevoyages.org] 15 September 2011. For the period 1601–1650, the total number of slaves registered in the database as embarked in the port of Luanda is 108,103, and for the years 1651–1700 it is 31,249. Estimates provided by the Transatlantic Slave Voyages Database, and summarized in the *Atlas of the Transatlantic Slave Trade*, however, point to much higher levels of activity through Luanda after 1660 than these figures suggest, underlining our point about smuggling noted above.

34   The record of the *asientos* granted by the *Casa de la Contratación*, in Seville, gave us a better idea of the slave trade to Spanish American than the trips to Brazil, which leads to occasional over-analysis of the former.

35   "Carta do governador Fernão de Sousa: 1626-09-20," in Felner, *Angola*, 300.

With the end of the Union in 1640, the Spanish American markets were closed off to the Portuguese the following year and the network of Portuguese merchants, almost all New Christians, which had until then controlled the main ports, was displaced. To make matters worse for the Portuguese, between 1641 and 1648 the Dutch gradually took over the coastal ports of Angola of Luanda, Mpinda, and Benguela, forcing the Portuguese to seek refuge in Massangano between the Lucala and Kwanza Rivers. The sugar mills of Bahia soon experienced a temporary shortage of new labour recruits, reflected in a rise in the price of slaves from 30,000 to 80,000 réis.[36] The Angolan slave trade did not collapse altogether, however. In 1643 the Overseas Council argued that "all ships from this kingdom [Portugal] and the *Estado do Brasil* [Brazil] that sail to Angola should do so now in the same way as before," taking in slaves near the Kwanza River.[37] In 1645, several private ships also tried to break a Dutch blockade of the Kwanza River. Two fleets were sent to help Massangano. The first in 1645 brought reinforcements to the beleagured Portuguese. The second in 1648 succeeded in expelling the Dutch. Both fleets arrived in Brazil crammed with slaves.[38] Futhermore, during Dutch rule in Angola, the Portuguese maintained control over the internal slave trade and a fair number of slaves exported by the Dutch (between 3,000 and 5,000 per year) were supplied by the people of Massangano.[39] After the Dutch left Angola (1648) and Pernambuco (1654), the scale of slave exports from the region returned to levels similar to the 1630s. It was clear that the Spanish American market had been lost, but a greater demand in Brazil through Rio de Janeiro, Bahia, and Pernambuco offset this together with smuggling to Río de la Plata, as shown by the figures in Table 4.2.[40] There were, therefore, structural adjustments in the Portuguese slave trade between 1640 and 1660 linked to the growth of the Brazilian market and the decline of mainland Spanish American markets previously serviced under the *asiento*.

In the last three decades of the seventeenth century, things changed, especially on the African side of the trade. The impact of a century of slave-trade related warfare on the population of Ndongo prompted a decline of the

---

36   Arquivo Histórico Ultramarino (hereafter AHU), *Angola*, cx. 4, doc. 17: 1643-01-08: 'Consulta do Conselho Ultramarino'.

37   ibid.

38   Esteves, "Os Holandeses em Angola," 70–75.

39   Pedro Puntoni, *A mísera sorte: a escravidão holandesa no Brasil holandês e as guerras do tráfico no atlântico sul, 1621–1648* (São Paulo: Hucitec, 1999), 162.

40   J.H. Galloway, *The sugar cane industry: an historical geography from its origins to 1914* (Cambridge: Cambridge University Press, 1989), 77.

TABLE 4.2   *Slave arrivals into Brazil and Spanish America, 1641 and 1650*

Years		1641	1650
Regions		No. of slaves imported	No. of slaves imported
Brazil	Pernambuco	4,400	5,000
	Bahia & Rio de Janeiro	4,000	–
	Bahia	–	4,000
	Rio de Janeiro	–	3,000
Spanish America	Antilles, Spanish America mainland	5,000	–
	Río de la Plata & Buenos Aires	1,500	3,300

Sources:

(1)   C.R. Boxer, *Salvador de Sá and the struggle for Brazil and Angola – 1602–1686* (London: University of London Press, 1952), 225.

(2)   "Arbítrio dado por Manuel Fernandes da Cruz: 1650-08-20," in Virgínia Rau and Maria Fernanda Gomes da Silva, *Os manuscritos do arquivo da Casa de Cadaval respeitantes ao Brasil* (Coimbra: Universidade, 1956), 1: 90–96.

prosperity of markets closest to Luanda, forcing the *pombeiros* (African and Eurafrican slave brokers) to travel further to acquire slaves, thereby increasing costs. Luanda began to lose its hold over the trade, a process that was to culminate in Beneguela's emergence as a slave export centre.[41] Meanwhile, rivalry between the English, French and Dutch grew. Their presence on the Loango Coast, north of Angola, expanded[42] while they also increased activity in the Gulf of Guinea, thereby raising the share of slaves supplied from West Africa relative to West-Central Africa and ending the latter's former dominance of the trade.[43]

Throughout the seventeenth century hundreds of thousands of Africans from the hinterland of Angola made the journey of no return to the Americas. It was a journey that took them from their homeland to the African coast and

41   Ferreira, "Transforming Atlantic slaving," 104–143.

42   Phyllis Martin, "The trade of Loango in the seventeenth and eighteenth centuries," in J.E. Inikori, ed., *Forced migration: the impact of the export slave trade on African societies* (London: Hutchinson, 1982), 202–220.

43   *Voyages: The Trans-Atlantic Slave Trade Database*, http://www.slavevoyages.org, 12 October 2010.

thence in the hull of a slave ship to the plantations and mines of the Americas. The continuous flow of slave exports was sustained by three factors: these were war, taxation and trade. Each merits attention

Within the framework of successive military campaigns, which with gaps lasted over a century and culminated in the destruction of the Ndongo kingdom and the conquest of Kongo and Matamba, Portuguese governors in Angola often declared war against local rulers with the sole purpose of obtaining slaves. Captains of the various *presídios*[44] also acted in a similar fashion, directly leading raids of pillage or creating conflicts between neighbouring chieftaincies.

In order to create this climate of warfare favourable to capturing slaves, the Portuguese often used the services of African auxiliaries (the so-called *guerra preta*) with the collaboration of Jaga or Mbangala groups, fearless and cruel warriors who would sell their prisoners to slave traders. For those triggering these conflicts, there were immediate and positive results, but their consequences were catastrophic in the long term, causing the destruction of cultures, the disappearance or displacement of populations, and disruption to established trade circuits. Protests against these predatory practices were filed by the residents of Luanda, who advocated a commercial solution, and often obtained the support of the central government in Lisbon.

Although in certain circumstances, warfare proved a profitable means of increasing the number of slave captives for captors, we agree with Beatrix Heintze that slaves obtained through warfare and plunder represented "a relatively small part" of the total number of slaves exported in the seventeenth century.[45] Other means of recruiting slaves were thus important, one of which was taxation. This could take various forms, including tribute. This was especially so in relation to *sobas*[46] that comprised territories that had become "subjugated" to Portuguese authority, whether voluntarily or through force, and from which various obligations, among them tribute in slaves, were regularly demanded. Such tribute was known as *baculamento,* and from the days of the earliest governors it came to be regarded as a source of fixed income that might be given away or sold.[47] The first governor Paulo Dias de Novais (1575–1589) and his successors had freely donated *sobas* to private individuals and to

---

44   Fortified military posts.
45   Beatrix Heintze, "O comércio das 'peças' em Angola," in idem, *Angola,* 491–492.
46   Africans chieftans.
47   A Jesuit even compared it to the royal estates in Alentejo. "Apontamentos do padre visitador Pêro Rodrigues e dos padres da Companhia em Luanda: 1593-06-15," in *MMA,* 15: 333–340.

Jesuits. It was only after a general rebellion of the *sobas* that King Philip III of Portugal decided in 1607 to revoke previous donations and make *sobas* subject only to royal authority, thereby requiring them to pay tribute to the royal treasury.[48] Even so, the greed of the royal officials and of previous recipients of tribute led them to demand very high levels of tribute from *sobas*. In the long term, this proved counter-productive as the payments became irregular, *sobas* became heavily in debt, and under threat of military retaliation, resorted to abandoning their territories and fleeing to the heartlands. According to Governor Fernão de Sousa, in 1626 there were 81 "obedient *sobas*," paying annually to the royal treasury 320 slaves.[49] In 1630 the number of such *sobas* was said to have increased to 204, with their tribute reaching 698 slaves.[50] In practice, however, such claims need to be viewed with scepticism for payments in most years tended to be lower and more erratic than these claims suggest.

Given the problems associated with warfare and tribute as methods of acquiring slaves, it is not surprising that commerce became the third and most practical and common way of obtaining slaves. In time, however, rising overseas demand for captives placed mounting pressure on traders to find new sources of slaves in Angola. Thus, vessels of Luanda traders sometimes conducted port-to-port commerce along the coast, sailing southward to Benguela and northwards to Soyo, Mayoumba and Loango.[51] These ships also navigated up the Kwanza, Bengo and Dande Rivers, the main waterways supporting Luanda's trade.[52] At the same time, Luanda traders also negotiated for slaves and provisions at fairs, or *pumbos*, which took place across the Kongolese and Angolan hinterland. There was at least one fair in each *sobado* to which European traders were granted free access, according to the *contratos de vassalagem*.[53] In addition, to these local and regional fairs, there were also others of greater economic significance on a supra-regional level.[54] The fairs most frequently visited by European as well as local merchants who has assimilated European culture were the Dondo, Beja and Lucamba (see Map 4.1), located

---

48   In 1611 the measure was reinstated and from then on appears to have been adhered to.

49   "Carta de Fernão de Sousa: 1626-07-08," in Heintze, *Fontes*, 363.

50   Heintze, "O fim do Ndongo como estado independente," in idem, *Angola*, 377.

51   AHU, *Angola*, cx. 14, doc. 15: 1690-03-08 and doc. 44: 1690-04-27: 'Consultas do Conselho Ultramarino'; cx. 15, doc. 100: 1697-08-23: 'Consulta do Conselho Ultramarino'.

52   AHU, *Angola*, cx. 9, doc. 62: 1666-10-20: 'Carta do governador Tristão da Cunha'.

53   *Sobado* was an African territory ruled by a chief. AHU, *Angola*, cx. 8, doc. 69: 1664-11-15: 'Consulta do Conselho Ultramarino'.

54   "...Besides the individual fairs that each Lord held in their lands, there are other general fairs in certain places, to which [people] for all parts come..." "Informação acerca dos escravos de Angola: 1582–1583," in *MMA*, 3: 227.

along the Kwanza River and its tributaries, which benefited from the protection of Portuguese fortresses. Other fairs visited included those at Matamba, Kassanje and Pumbo of Okanga (*Mpungu*) situated further east. The last was in fact near the Congo River in the eastern frontier of the Kingdom of Kongo and at the extreme edge of Luandan *pombeiros'* trade networks.[55]

African merchants (or *guenzes*[56]), who were commissioned by their own political chiefs to sell groups of slaves, visited *pumbos*, travelling sometimes hundreds of kilometres to do so.[57] There they would meet with *pombeiros* who came from the coast with large quantities of European and African merchandise, sometimes also after having travelled several hundred kilometres.[58] The *pombeiros* were usually enslaved or manumitted individuals of African or mixed descent, who had been hired as agents by Luandan traders and residents to purchase slaves in the interior. Usually, they faithfully discharged their contracts, though sometimes they absconded with the merchandise consigned to them.[59] According to Governor Fernão de Sousa, every week 200 to 300 slaves were traded at the fairs, a figure equivalent to almost 12,000 slaves per year and consistent with the number of slave exported in 1624–1626 reported in Table 4.1.[60]

The military, royal officials and European merchants often interfered with activities in the *pumbos* by making demands or prompting negotiations that disturbed the normal way of operating. Abuses by royal officials,[61] together with misbehaviour by private merchants of European, mixed and African descent, especially the so-called "shod blacks,"[62] were common. Consequently, many local African merchants abandoned the fairs, forcing *pombeiros* to travel further inland in search of slaves. According to the by-laws for the governors of Angola, under no circumstances were "white men" allowed at the fairs as a

---

55 Heintze, "O comércio das 'peças' em Angola," 493; Adriano Parreira, *Economia e sociedade no tempo da rainha Njinga* (Lisboa: Editorial Estampa, 1990), 118–123; Cruz, "O tráfico negreiro," 94.

56 *Guenze* (from the kimbundu *ngenzi*): traveller, merchant.

57 Alonso de Sandoval, *Naturaleza, policia sagrada i profana, costumbres i ritos, disciplina i catechismo evangelico de todos etiopes* (Sevilha: Francisco de Lira impressor, 1627), 68.

58 "...At the end of the seventeenth century most slaves came from small areas within a three to four hundred kilometers radius from the coast..."; David Birmingham, *A conquista portuguesa de Angola* (Lisboa: A Regra de Jogo, 1974), 51.

59 "Memórias de Pedro Sardinha ao Conselho de Estado: c.1612," in *MMA*, 6: 105.

60 "Relação: 1625-09-06," in Felner, *Angola*, 304.

61 Royal officials were often accused of "wanting the fair just for them and for their servants." "Carta de Baltazar Rebelo de Aragão: c.1618," in *MMA*, 6: 337.

62 Acculturated Africans who formed part of the European merchant group at the fairs.

means of "protecting justice and maintaining order."[63] Some governors, like Fernão de Sousa (1624–1630), issued orders locally with the same purpose, but abuses, sometimes quite severe, continued to take place regularly. As late as 1664 the residents of Luanda continued to complain to the Overseas Council about commercial losses stemming from "white and dark-skinned men" trading in the *pumbos* and fairs," a complaint that the Council considered as "very old and almost unsolvable."[64]

Merchandise used to barter for slaves did not have the same value in all *pumbos*. Knowledge of this was essential for buyers of slaves. Generally, slaves were bought with Indian cottons, alcoholic beverages (a trade item that was not always authorized), other fabrics, and many other products of European origin. There were also products of African origin and from various regions, like cloths made from palm thread (*libongo*), elephant's tails (*nsinga*) and metal hoops (*malunga*).[65] Trading in arms and munitions was formally prohibited, but many merchants, including the contractors, could not resist selling them, given that it offered the prospects of high profits.[66]

From the *pumbos* to Luanda was often a long trip, adding many kilometres to the many hundreds already covered by the slave caravans before arriving at the fair.[67] The journey was undertaken on both water and land.[68] Travel by land involved an arduous and relentless walk under sun or rain with little rest. Food and water were very poor. The slaves, particularly the men, walked chained to each other with *libambos* or wooden racks. According to the priest Gonçalo de Sousa, the slaves were "brought from far away in racks" and "lacking basic nourishment" many died on this journey.[69]

In Luanda, the main dock used for housing and embarking slaves was located on the island across the bay and separated from the mainland by a narrow channel. Ships were offloaded in this island. Here, also, were docked all slave vessels awaiting a cargo, while their crews were busy acquiring slaves at auctions. Once the ships were loaded with slaves, it was also on the island that

---

63 Beatrix Heintze, "Problemas de interpretação de fontes escritas," in idem, *Angola*, 111.
64 AHU, *Angola*, cx. 8, doc. 69: 1664-11-15: 'Consulta do Conselho Ultramarino'.
65 Parreira, *Economia e sociedade*, 88–89.
66 AHU, *Angola*, cx. 14, doc. 15: 1690-03-18: 'Consulta do Conselho Ultramarino'.
67 "...in order to trade, the slaves from the Portuguese need to go inland for many months and put in a lot of effort to obtain slaves..." "Carta do Padre Gonçalo de Sousa: 1633-07-06," in *MMA*, 8: 243.
68 Even when they got to Kwanza they had to disembark in Tombo and carry on a further 50 kilometres by foot.
69 "Carta do Padre Gonçalo de Sousa: 1633-07-06," in *MMA*, 8: 243.

they awaited permission to depart.[70] Caulkers, coopers and other craftsmen employed in ship repairing and outfitting lived on the island close by the shacks (*quibangos*) rented out or built by ship owners to house slaves. In these the slaves were usually separated by gender and collected together in groups of 300–400 individuals. Slaves already acquired by ships waiting to complete their cargo were housed on the ship itself, but every morning were brought to the beach bound in chains to wash in the sea and spend the day on dry land sitting on big straw mats weaving baskets or performing other similar tasks.[71] By feeding slaves with manioc flour, beans (*encassa*) and occasionally dried fish or meat, owners hoped they would recover somewhat from their long trek to the coast before starting their arduous transatlantic journey.[72] Before that journey, the bodies of slaves were branded, with owners' personal stamps being burnt on their shoulder or chest with a brass rod.[73]

The Slave Ships

In the port of Luanda, near the island "over twenty ships (...) all merchant ships"[74] were permanently docked, causing at times great delays in completing loadings as well as competition among ship-owners for preference in dispatch. Loading ships with slaves could take up to a year or longer, especially when ship masters lacked leverage with the local Portuguese authorities. The Spanish ship *N.S. de la Candelaria y San Francisco* took almost two years to complete its loading of over 1,000 slaves in 1677–1678, arriving in Luanda in February 1677 and only leaving on 5 December 1678.[75] And in 1690 a trader from Pernambuco had to sell his ship after failing several times to obtain permission to leave.[76]

In principle, the dispatch of slave ships in Luanda should have followed their order of arrival at the port. Regulations relating to this were introduced

---

70 Cadornega, *História geral*, 3: 35.
71 Aleixo de Abreu, *Tratado de las Siete Enfermedades* (Lisboa: Pedro Craesbeeck, 1623), 151v.
72 Felner, *Angola*, 302.
73 In some instances this painful experience was not new. African authorities sending slaves to sell at the markets often also used identifying marks of some kind. Dating the origin of this practice seems impossible, however. Heintze, "O comércio das 'peças' em Angola," 495.
74 Cadornega, *História geral*, 3: 31.3.
75 Enriqueta Vila Vilar, "Aspectos maritimos del comercio de escravos con Hispano-America en el siglo XVII," in Klaus Friedland, ed., *Maritime Aspects of Migration* (Köln: Böhlau, 1989), 193.
76 Ferreira, "Transforming Atlantic slaving," 28.

by Governor Fernão de Sousa (1624–1630) at the beginning of his term of office in the face of opposition from contractors.[77] Despite this, ship masters continued to circumvent the order, using any pretext to obtain permission to depart immediately after their cargo was completed. The most common argument used and accepted by the authorities was that the ship had earlier arrived in Luanda carrying cargo purchased elsewhere and as a result should be allowed to leave port when they wished.

Those who had been given rights of preference in dispatch, a privilege only granted by the monarch, also did everything to defend their privileges to the utmost. The privilege was especially advantageous at ports of embarkation, reducing substantially loading time and increasing the likelihood of profit from sale of slaves at market through removing competition from other ships. Departures for the Americas of ships without privilege were commonly delayed while those with privileges were still awaiting departure.[78] Contractors of the Angolan monopoly and tax collection were most favoured by such privileges.

Governors also invoked privileges for their own vessels, whether wholly or partly owned. Governor Luís Lobo da Silva (1684–1688), for example, was accused of abuses of this nature. His own ships were said to have by-passed several vessels with rights of preference in loading as well as others that were "with their crew already in action, receiving cargo." His vessels were known for entering and leaving the port in record times of just eight to 10 days.[79] Protests against the Governor's abuses were justified as his ships were not entitled to preferential treatment.

By 1693 only contractors and the captain of the cavalry held this privilege. Contractors were entitled to use the privilege while exporting up to 1,500 slaves a year, while, as compensation for transporting horses from Brazil to Angola, the captain of the cavalry was entitled to claim privilege in exporting up to 600 slaves.[80] Additionally, each year a preference in departure was to be granted at auction to a brigantine with a capacity to carry 700 slaves and the income arising therefrom was to be donated to missionaires.[81] In 1695, the ship *Misericórdia* was also offered the right of preference for the export of 500 slaves under similar

77 Heintze, *Fontes*, 1: 232, 305.

78 AHU, *Angola*, cx. 14, doc. 44: 1689-09-03: 'Carta do contratador Diogo da Fonseca Henriques'.

79 AHU, *Angola*, cx. 14, doc. 67: 1691-06-16: 'Auto de queixas do cabido contra o governador Luís Lobo da Silva'.

80 In some earlier contracts there was no reference to any set limit.

81 AHU, *Angola*, cx. 14, docs. 121, 122, 18: 1693-03-13: 'Consultas do Conselho Ultramarino'.

circumstances.[82] Occasionally, preferences were also given to ships, which the authorities wished to reward for special services, as happened, for example, in 1693 with a brigatine transporting Italian Capucin monks to Angola.[83]

Compared to eighteenth-century slave vessels, those transporting slaves between Angola and the Americas in the seventeenth century were small, with most being no more than 100 tons and sometimes significantly less. Between 1616 and 1640, almost 57 percent of ships carrying slaves to Spanish America weighed less than 100 tons; many were less than 80 tons. Tonnages were increasing, however, even within this period. In 1610–1630, over 71 percent weighed less than 100 tons, whereas in the 1630s fewer than 27 percent were under 100 tons.[84] Reflected in numbers of slaves carried per ship, this trend towards employing larger ships continued beyond 1650, as the figures in Table 4.3 suggest. The most common types of vessels recorded were brigantines (*patachos*), caravelles, smacks (*sumacas*) and *navios*.[85] The proportion of other vessels, including three-masters (*charruas*), frigates and flagships (*naus*), gradually increased, however, in the second half of the century.

Information on ship tonnages remains fairly limited in Portuguese sources, and interpretation of its meaning can be problematical. Particularly difficult is the relationship between the recorded or registered tonnage of ships and their tons burthen or in the case of slave ships, their capacity to carry slaves. The last might be described as the usable tonnage or the space available to carry goods or slaves.[86] This was not a universal measurement at the time and the way in which it was calculated varied from place to place and depended on other circumstances. Moreover, it was far from clear which tonnage measurement was recorded in sources. So precisely how many slaves could be transported per ton, and what space per slave this represented is unclear. Using diverse sources of information, Enriqueta Vila Vilar has nevertheless concluded that "a ship weighing 60 tons could carry on average 120 to 200

82   "Carta régia: 1695-03-05," in *MMA*, 14: 393–394.

83   AHU, *Angola*, cx. 14, doc. 110: 1693-02-26: 'Consulta do Conselho Ultramarino'.

84   Calculations based on Vila Vilar, *Hispano-America*, 130.

85   As well as being used in a generic sense, the term *navio* (ship) was also used to designate, at that time, a specific type of vessel similar to a brigatine or a caravelle. Leonor Freire Costa, *O transporte no Atlântico e a Companhia Geral do Comércio do Brasil (1580–1663)* (Lisboa: Comissão Nacional para as Comemorações dos Descobrimentos Portugueses, 2002), 1: 182–184.

86   The total capacity of the interior of a ship calculated here was its usable tonnage or the volume of the ship space used to transport cargo or passengers. This is the sense in which 'usable' tonnage is used in what follows.

TABLE 4.3   *Number of slaves leaving Angola (average per ship), 1601–1688*

Periods	No. of voyages	Destination	No. of slaves	No. of slaves (average per ship)	Sources
1601	15	Cartagena/Vera Cruz	2,959	197	(1)
1604–1610	18	Vera Cruz	4,848	269	(2)
1611–1617	18	Vera Cruz	4,053	225	(2)
1618–1624	15	Vera Cruz	3,394	226	(2)
1622	5	Bahia	1,211	242	(3)
1623–1636	5	Brazil/Spanish West Indies	1,410	282	(4)
1624–1626	37	Brazil	7,923	214	(5)
1624–1626	31	Spanish West Indies	9,400	303	(5)
1654–1656	25	Brazil/Spanish West Indies	13,945	558	(6)
1667–1671	73	Brazil/Spanish West Indies	29,332	402	(7)
1684–1688	20	Brazil	8,750	438	(8)

Sources:

(1)   Vila Vilar, *Hispano-América,* 250–251, table 2. These values refer to the number of slaves disembarked at the port of destination;

(2)   ibid., 256–259, table 3;

(3)   "Certidão dos escravos enviados de Angola pelo governador João Correia de Sousa," in Cruz, "O tráfico negreiro," doc. 7;

(4)   Joannes de Laet, *Historia ou annaes dos feitos da Companhia Priviligiada das Indias Occidentaes...1644* (Rio de Janeiro: Officinas Graphicas da Bibliotheca Nacional, 1916–1925), 1: 621–635.

(5)   "Rendimento do contrato de Angola, 1624–1626," in Cruz, "O tráfico negreiro," 69–70;

(6)   AHU, *Angola,* cx. 6, doc. 128: 1656-02-25: 'Carta do governador Luís Manuel Chichorro';

(7)   AHU, *Angola,* cx. 10, doc. 40: 'Receita e despesa referente aos anos de 1667, 1668, 1669, 1670 e 1671';

(8)   AHU, *Angola,* cx. 14, doc. 67: 1691-06-16: 'Relatório de Jerónimo da Cunha Pimentel'.

slaves."[87] This encompassed a significant range, varying from 2 slaves per ton to over 3 per ton.

A 1684 by-law for the dispatch and loading of slave ships in Luanda established a limit of 5 to 7 slaves per 2 tons for slaves in the hold and "five young boys" per ton in the upper part.[88] If the usable area of the upper part was the

---

87   Vila Vilar, "Aspectos maritimos," 196.

88   AHU, *Angola,* cx. 12, printed document: 1684-03-18: "Regimento sobre o despacho dos negros cativos de Angola e mais conquistas e sobre a arqueação dos navios," in MMA, 13: 551–558.

same as the deck (in reality it was smaller), a ship of 60 tons could, by law, carry 220 to 255 slaves, including adults and children. Although this is rather higher than what Vila Vilar estimated, comparisons remain diffcult between what was established by law in 1684 and what had previously happened. For example, in 1619 the *São Francisco*, a vessel of 30 tons, was authorized to carry no less than 150 slaves or five slaves per ton.[89] In any case, during the seventeenth century, many shipmasters and royal officials began recording tonnages by reference to numbers of slaves per ship. Thus, by about 1685, we find records of ships with usable tonnages ranging from 220 to 1,000 slaves.[90] In these cases, the calculation of the carrying capacity of ships was apparently made using a conversion rate of three adults per ton, figures consistent with the law of 1684.

Investing in Shipping and the Slave Trade

Although information on ship owners is limited, we know that owners of slave ships were commonly based in Portuguese, Brazilian and Angolan ports. In the early seventeenth century, they were mainly found in Portugal but by the second half were largely found in Brazil and Angola, though numbers in Angola were smaller than in Brazil.

In Luanda the main owners were the governors. It was reported in 1611 that Governor Manuel Pereira Forjaz owned at least one brigatine and a "new and very well-designed" flagship. There were others too.[91] The contractors of the royal monopoly of Angola and of tax collection were also important ship owners. In 1690, Diogo da Fonseca Henriques, for example, owned a brigantine amongst other vessels, all of them used in the slave trade.[92] Several other high officials of the Portuguese royal government in Angola owned vessels and had shares in ships operating from Lisbon and various Brazilian ports. Fernão Vogado Sotomayor, who served as factor of the royal treasury in Angola in 1622

---

89   Vila Vilar, *Hispano-America*, 132.

90   AHU, *Angola*, cx. 14, doc. 67: 1691-06-16: 'Conclusões do inquérito de Jerónimo da Cunha Pimentel'.

91   Felner, *Angola*, 429. Two other good examples were Governor Luís Lobo da Silva, who c. 1685 owned a brigantine, two smacks, a quarter of a three-master and partially owned another frigate, and his successor, João de Lencastre (1688–1691), who had at least one ship "that he sent to Brazil with a cargo of slaves." AHU, *Angola*, cx. 14, doc. 67: 1691-06-16: 'Auto de queixas do cabido'; doc. 71: 1691-11-28: 'Carta do governador Gonçalo de Menezes'.

92   AHU, *Angola*, cx. 14, doc. 20: 1690-04-20: 'Treslado da devassa levantada no ano de 1689: testemunho de João Pereira da Fonseca'.

and later as general-auditor and general-treasurer, had large sums invested in "profitable ships [sailing] to Brazil and the [Spanish] Indies."[93]

Some merchants investing directly or through middlemen in the transatlantic slave trade freighted ships from other parties. The charge of freighting ships was determined by the number of slaves delivered alive in the Americas and was paid at the port of disembarkation. For a long time, the freight rates were 4.000 *réis* per slave, but after 1684, when new regulations on ship carrying capacities were introduced, freight rates rose a quarter, to up to 5.000 *réis*. In 1692, the Luanda City Council, which represented the interests of its residents and local slave shippers, opposed this increase, highlighting the divergence of interests between Angolan investors in the slave trade and ship owners and businessmen based elsewhere.[94]

Slave trading was highly risky. Ships and their human cargo could be lost through shipwreck, rebellion, or attacks by corsairs.[95] Slave mortality in the middle passage or Atlantic crossing fluctuated widely but was commonly abnormally high by the standards of the day. Given these risks, mark-ups on prices between Africa and Brazil were modest. The average price of a slave bought at the port of Luanda in the seventeenth century was c. 20.000 *réis* and the average selling price in Bahia or Pernambuco c. 30.000 *réis*.[96] Often this was barely sufficient to cover insurance, freight and maintenance costs, not to mention the "risks at sea" and shipboard mortality.[97] It was possible, however, sometimes to buy slaves at a lower price as well as to reduce freight costs.[98] Slave prices could also increase as a result of market forces and slave sales in

---

93   Similarly, in the years that followed, the Governor's secretary, active tradesman António Coelho Guerreiro, was co-owner of various ships. At the same time the Portuguese soldier Rodrigo da Costa de Almeida, who had married in Luanda and started a prosperous career as a tradesman, had at least three slave ships: the brigantine *Nossa Senhora dos Mártires,* the *navio Corpo Santo e Almas,* and the ship *Nossa Senhora do Cabo*. "Relação de António Dinis: c.1622," in *MMA*, 11: 44, 67–74.

94   AHU, *Angola,* cx. 14, doc. 102: 1692-11-14: 'Consulta do Conselho Ultramarino'.

95   At the time, slave merchants calculated a loss rate at 10 percent. "Avença entre Pero Roiz de Abreu e Manuel Fernandes Ferreira: 1638," in Mauro, *Le Portugal et l'Atlantique,* 163.

96   In 1650, one expert calculated the price a 'piece' could demand in Brazil was around 60.000 *réis,* but he felt the price was excessively high. His calculations might have been still influenced by slave prices during Dutch rule in Luanda. "Arbítrio dado por Manuel F. da Cruz: 1650-20-08," in Rau and Silva, *Os manuscritos,* 1: 95.

97   The prices reported here refer to the first decades of the seventeenth century. Felner, *Angola,* 429; Rau, *O "Livro de Rezão,"* 46; Mauro, *Le Portugal et l'Atlantique,* 172–173.

98   *Pombeiros* could obtain slaves for c.10.000 *réis.* "Relação de António Dinis: c.1622," in *MMA*, 11: 67.

Spanish America could be more lucrative than in Brazil. Profits could also be
increased by illegal means, as we will explain later.

With respect to capital investment in the transatlantic slave trade, Virgínia
Rau and Joseph Miller have argued that this commerce was almost exclusively
controlled by merchants in Brazil and Angola, with metropolitan investors
being little involved directly.[99] This view largely derives from the accounts of
António Coelho Guerreiro (1683–1696) and may be valid for the period covered
by Guerreiro's accounts and later. It does not reflect, however, reality during
the first half of the seventeenth century.

In the early seventeenth century, many slave ships left Lisbon and other
Portuguese ports, following a triangular route that linked Portugal, Angola, and
Brazil. Although the scale of this trade soon dropped in intensity, trade circuits
linking Lisbon with Angola and Brazil did not wholly disappear. Ships departing from Lisbon and calling at Madeira, the Canaries or the Azores to top up
their cargos with wine, then sailed to Angola to acquire slaves. These, in turn,
would then be sold in Bahia for sugar, which would constitute a return cargo
on the ship's return to Europe.[100] Even more complicated trade circuits existed,
with ships carrying European goods and leaving Lisbon heading first to Rio de
Janeiro where they would load flour and other goods to be exchanged in Angola
for slaves. These again were dispatched to Brazil, where they would be sold for
sugar, which would be shipped back to Lisbon.[101] Merchants based in Portugal
also invested, of course, indirectly in the South Atlantic slave trade, mainly
by financing the slave trading activities of the governors of the colony and
the contractors of the Angolan monopoly – the biggest players in the business
throughtout the century. In their view, the transatlantic slave trade was far
more interesting than it was to an average middle-sized merchant, who could
hardly compete in this business.

In this commerce, profit margins could be expanded if: (a) slaves were transported in vessels owned by the investors; (b) cargoes did not pay taxes to the
Crown or the tax farmer; (c) ship owners avoided higher duties on cargoes
bound to Spanish America by declaring an intention to go to Brazil but subsequently diverted to Spanish America; and (d) ships heading to Spanish America
circumvented local duties on slave imports by diverting to ports where duty
collection was inefficient. Other practices which helped to boost profits

---

99   Rau, O "Livro de Rezão," 43; Miller, "Capitalism and Slaving," 1–4.
100   For further details on the Madeiran merchant, Diogo Fernandes Branco, who took part in
      this triangular trade between 1649 and 1652, see: Alberto Vieira, O público e o privado na
      história da Madeira (Funchal: Centro de Estudos de História do Atlântico, 1996), 11.
101   Rau, O "Livro de Rezão," 43.

included accessing information and adopting best practice in relation to the
seasonality of trade; improving turnaround times of ships in port; and after
1684 evading restrictions on the slave carrying capacities of ships. Only highly
organised and experienced merchants in the business had the financial means
and knowledge efficiently to circumvent the bureaucratic apparatus created
by the Iberian Crowns for taxing and monopolising the Iberian slave trade. Vila
Vilar has calculated that during the Portuguese management of the Spanish
asientos the illegal slave trade accounted for more a half to two-thirds of the
cargoes officially registered.[102]

The contractors of the Angolan monopoly and the governors of the colony
also took advantage of their posts and power in the local royal government to
attract sizeable amounts of mainly Portuguese investment into the slave business. Alfredo Felner claimed, though without firm evidence, that behind every
contractor, there was a group of capitalists.[103] His argument seems plausible
for several reasons. First, the amount of capital involved required a good number of investors to participate in the business as well as a network of overseers
and attornies based at Atlantic ports. Second, a large majority of contractors
were New Christians linked to the business world who, for professional and
family reasons, had good contacts with merchants and bankers in Northern
Europe.[104] Third, contractors of the Angolan monopoly took part in other businesses, which also demanded big investments. Between 1595 and 1630 the
asientistas for Spanish America were contractors of the Angola monopoly.[105]
Moreover, at least one of them, António Fernandes de Elvas, leased simultaneously the royal contract of Cape Verdean trade between 1616 and 1624.[106]
Finally, most contractors rarely went to Angola, but instead oversaw the business from Lisbon or Madrid, itself a strong indicator of where the roots of
investment lay.

Although governors belonged to another social sphere and had other kinds
of relationships, they were rarely able to resist the economic opportunities
identified with the slave trade. With few exceptions we find evidence of them

---

102   Vila Vilar, *Hispano-America,* 180–181.
103   Felner, *Angola,* 300.
104   This is particularly evident with contractors such as António Fernandes de Elvas (1616–
       1622) and Manuel Rodrigues de Lamego (1623–1624). In the second half of the seven-
       teenth century, contracts with New Christians with good international links continued to
       dominate the market. Jerónimo Teixeira da Fonseca, his brother Lopo da Fonseca
       Henriques (1669–1676) and the nephew and son Diogo da Fonseca Henriques (1676–1693)
       are all cases in point.
105   Vila Vilar, *Hispano-America,* 104–114; Rivera, *El comercio negrero,* 44–124.
106   Mauro, *Le Portugal et l'Atlantique,* 161.

outfitting ships, seeking out deals with slave brokers, and even participating in smuggling. For instance, João Rodrigues Coutinho (1601–1603) was simultaneously governor and contractor of royal duties while his brother, Gonçalo Vaz Coutinho, who succeeded him in business, also leased out the *asiento* for the Spanish Americas.[107] Another good example is Manuel Pereira, nobleman and member of the Royal Council. Before setting off to serve his term as governor in Angola (1607–1611), Pereira made a partnership with the new Christian, João de Argomedo, resident and merchant in Lisbon.[108] Under this agreement, the latter provided the initial capital for their slave trade operation.[109] Like Coutinho and Pereira, many holders of the governorship as well as other high officials in the local royal government adopted similar practices as a way to increase their income while serving the Crown overseas.[110] In fact, between 1688 and 1692 the Crown discussed the possibility of increasing the then Governor's income up to 10.000 *cruzados*, provided he suspended all commercial activities. This measure, supported by businessmen and officials in Luanda, was not carried through because of the difficulty in raising such an amount "without levying the residents."[111]

---

107   Vila Vilar, *Hispano-America*, 106–108.
108   Argomedo had already been a proxy to the contractor of the Angolan monopoly in Luanda between 1594 and 1600. *Razões do réu Duarte Dias Henriques*, 16v.
109   Argomedo sent wine to Luanda from the Canary islands and other places; the Governor would send slaves to Brazil and the Spanish Indies. Profits were returned to Portugal in the form of artwork and goods. To ensure the trade went well there was an extensive network of overseers stretching across Cartagena, New Spain, Bahia, Pernambuco, Seville, Porto and Viana. The Governor died in 1611 leaving a big personal fortune and many debts to the State in duties owed to Brazil and to the Spanish Indies. Felner, *Angola,* 427–432.
110   Manuel Cerveira Pereira, Governor between 1603 and 1606, was also involved in the slave trade with Brazil and Spanish America. Luís Mendes de Vasconcelos, son-in-law of the influential New Christian trader, Manuel Caldeira, was Governor of Angola between 1617 and 1621 and was also engaged with slave trading. Another excellent example is Luís Lobo da Silva, Governor between 1684 and 1688, who was involved in the transport of slaves. Finally, Luís César de Menezes, Governor in the years 1697 and 1701, borrowed capital from known traders in Lisbon to participate directly and openly in the slave trade. The ships owned by Lobo da Silva completed close to 20 slave voyages to Brazil between 1684 and 1688, carrying some 8,458 adult slaves and 292 children. For further details on the cases mentioned above, see: Felner, *Angola,* 424–425; José Gonçalves Salvador, *Cristãos-novos e o comércio no Atlântico meridional* (São Paulo: Pioneira, 1978), 311; Heintze, "O fim do Ndongo," 292–293; AHU, *Angola,* cx. 14, doc. 67: 1691-06-16: 'Conclusões do inquérito'; Ferreira, "Transforming Atlantic slaving," 25–27.
111   AHU, *Angola,* cx. 13, doc. 79: 1688-06-15: 'Consulta do Conselho Ultramarino'; cx. 14, doc. 102: 1692-11-14: 'Consulta'.

The muncipality of Luanda, as the representative of the residents, frequently protested against embezzlement and abuses of "the powerful ones," seeing them as a form of unfair competition. However the Council's room for manoeuvre was very small. From an economic point of view the number of ship owners and traders with means to invest was small among the residents. Most residents of European origin lived fairly well, possessing large numbers of slaves employed in their households as well as in agriculture and crafts. These generated considerable income for their owners, improving their living standards. However, apart from this small elite group, most families had no capital to invest.[112] Most of them had only one or two slaves employed as *pombeiros* who were sent to the inland markets with trade goods. These were supplied on credit by "non-resident" merchants trading at the port.[113] If things went well, such investors should have been able to make enough money from the sale of slaves, either directly or through an agent in Spanish America or Brazil, to cover their debts to suppliers of trade goods and still make a profit. But as such profit was usually spent on luxury goods, they were probably unable to accumulate capital of their own, and therefore continued to have to rely on credit to fund their trade. While those in positions of power locally had their own means of engaging in slave trafficking, most Luandan residents of European and mixed descent acted as intermediaries for small and medium-sized ship owners and merchants, some based in Portugal and Angola, the majority based in Brazil.

The end of Dutch rule in Angola in 1648, achieved with an expedition outfitted and financed by slavers and planters from Rio de Janeiro, helped to consolidate Brazilian interests in the Angolan trade.[114] With easy access to some of the trade goods used to buy slaves in Africa, including, among others, manioc flour, sugar-cane rum, and Indian cotton, "Brazilian" traders with networks on both sides of the Atlantic played an ever-growing role in the second half of the seventeenth century.[115] By comparison, Portugal-based investors, sometimes operating in tandem with groups in other European ports, were only able to sustain any challenge after 1650 to "Brazilian" and "Angolan" interests in the trade through using the political influence in Angola of the governors of the colony and contractors of the monopoly.

---

112   AHU, *Angola*, cx. 14, doc. 76: 1692-01-29: 'Carta do Governador Gonçalo da Costa e Menezes'.

113   "Carta do padre Jesuíta Gonçalo de Sousa: 1633-07-06," in *MMA*, 8: 242.

114   Alencastro, *O trato dos viventes*, 231–236.

115   The "West Indies route" often stopped off in Bahia.

Ships' Overloading: Legislation and Practice

Usually, ship owners did not accompany ships on their slave voyages. The ship captain or master, instead, acted as their agent, taking responsibilty for overseeing the cargo, paying freight, and purchasing the required trading licences (*uvenças*) from the contractors of the Angolan monopoly in order to embark a given number of slaves.[116]

The number of investors for each ship varied substantially.[117] However, lack of capital and a need to spread risks helped to ensure that the number of slaves transported for each investor was limited. In 1689, Bernardo de Berganha, "resident and citizen" of Luanda embarked in two separate vessels two groups of slaves bound for Pernambuco. One comprised 35 slaves, the other 15. Two of Berganha's fellow citizens sent separate groups of 40 and 38 slaves to Rio de Janeiro about the same time.[118]

The ship captain or master had sole commercial responsibilities on board the slave ship. He was in fact committed by surety to the ship owner and was to be held responsible for the outcome of the voyage, whether it was good or bad. In some cases, masters were part-owners of ships. The ship pilot's responsibilities, by contrast, were confined to navigational matters. In discharging his tasks, the captain or master was often assisted by a deputy master (*contramestre*) and a steward (*despenseiro*).[119] As for the rest of the crew, their number depended on the ship tonnage, varying between 15 and 30 sailors. To them might be added several cabin-boys (*grumetes*), mostly of African descent and some enslaved.[120] In 1708, the *Nossa Senhora do Cabo*, carrying 742 slaves, had nearly 50 "black and white men serving on board."[121]

Passengers, in particular freighters and agents of the ship owners, were also sometimes counted as crew. Their main task was to ensure the safe arrival of their principals' slaves at market and their sale at a good price. Evidence exists of Africans on board ships acting as overseers of the cargo and representatives

---

116   The difference between "captain" and "master" is not very clear in the sources. It appears to be more related to the size of the ship than with the roles played by these two officers.

117   Normally investors were designated as "freighters."

118   AHU, *Angola*, cx. 14, doc. 20: 1690-04-20: 'Treslado da devassa…: testemunhos de Bernardo de Berganha, capitão Manuel Lobo Barreto e Manuel da Costa Romano'.

119   Vila Vilar, *Hispano-America*, 135.

120   Vila Vilar, "Aspectos maritimos," 181–204.

121   Jean Cuvelier, *Relations sur le Congo du père Laurent de Lucques, 1700–1717* (Bruxelles/Rome: Institut Royal Colonial Belge, 1953), 282.

of freighters. Prior to 1642, Luís, slave of António Bruto, completed two voyages to Brazil accompanying a few hundred captives on behalf of his master.[122]

The ship master, whether or not he was the ship owner, often carried illegally a few more slaves on board to sell on his own account and authorised other crew members to do the same, thereby exceeding after 1684 the maximum cargo allowed.[123] The interests of the freighters and ship masters often differed. Although both were interested in making sure the slaves on board arrived safely at their destinations, ship masters, perhaps because of low freight rates, were tempted to try to increase profits by overloading the ships beyond what was assumed reasonable. The results were in most cases averse: overloading could incresae risks of slave mortality on board ship and the chances of such disasters were compounded if the packing of slaves on board occurred at the expense of space for water supplies and provisions. The search for good returns, however, encouraged ship captains and their crew to approach the Atlantic crossing with optimism and to minimise risks of unexpected incidents. Sometimes, freighters, contractors and royal officials were instigators of ideas to maximise loadings of ships. In other cases ship masters were pressurised by ship owners to overload the ship or were expected to do so under the protection, and with the complicity, of ship owners. In 1689, the frigate *Santa Teresa*, commanded by Inácio Nogueira, only had a licence to take on 270 slaves and this was the number recorded as officially dispatched. However, despite many deaths during the journey due to the lack of water, the ship arrived in Pernambuco with over 270 slaves. The intervention of local authorities was only prevented by the "powerful" position of the ship owner, Manuel da Fonseca Rego, in the city.[124]

In fact, throughout the seventeenth century, slave vessels sailing to Brazil and Spanish America were usually loaded up to their maximum loading capacity. Ship overloading had always been a problem, but it worsened from the beginning of the century in response to growing demand for captives.[125] Even

122   "Relatório de Pieter Moortamer ao Conselho do Brasil: 1642–10," in Louis Jadin, ed., *L'ancien Congo et l'Angola: 1639–1655: d'après les archives romaines, portugaises, néerlandaises et espagnoles* (Bruxelles/Rome: Institut Historique Belge de Rome, 1975), 1: 353.

123   AHU, *Angola*, cx. 14, doc. 20: 1690-04-20: 'Treslada devassa...: testemunhos de Domingos Gonçalves Rola e Domingos Trigo'.

124   ibid: 'Testemunho de Bernardo de Berganha'.

125   By 1638, the Angolan treasurer was aware of the problem: "Currently many ships gather at this port and those that were previously happy to leave with 400 slaves, now do not want to take less than 700 or 800, contributing in part to a slower crossing and causing hundreds to perish due to the cramped conditions and lack of water." "Carta do feitor da Fazenda: 1638-03-16," in Cruz, "O tráfico negreiro," 131.

though freighters were not always innocent in this matter, they were the ones who most often rebelled against the excessive loading of ships, which they felt threatened their interests. In 1664, in a petition to the Portuguese monarch the "residents of Angola" declared that after the restoration of Portugal's independence in 1640, slave ships started to leave Luanda with double the number of slaves that their tonnage would allow. They also argued that since carrying capacities were assessed by individuals appointed by the ship masters themselves, allowances of space for water and provisions were often neglected, leading to "the death of many and great losses" for the businessmen involved. For these reasons, they requested permission from the King for the City Council of Luanda to appoint a municipal official to co-inspect "the cargoes and provisions on board the ships," together with the royal official appointed by the royal treasurer of Angola.[126] After examining the petition, the Overseas Council deliberated against the interference of the City Council with regard to the dispatch of ships, but it recommended "that the governers and treasurers of Angola should take particular care to oversee the dispatch of ships to make sure that no vessel would leave the port of São Paulo [of Luanda] without carrying at least 25 fully filled barrels of good water for every 100 slaves."[127]

These recommendations were taken into account by the King and incorporated in the regulations issued on 23 September 1664. These also stipulated "that no ship should be allowed to load more slaves than the number that it could comfortably carry."[128] One year later, in a resolution on the dispatch of slaves in Luanda, the King once again "specially demanded" royal officials in charge of dispatching ships "that ships should not be loaded with more slaves then the vessel could carry comfortably" and ordered governors "not to allow these laws and by-laws to be broken."[129] The zeal of the Portuguese monarch on these matters was, however, far from being matched by the praxis of royal officials and slaving entrepreneurs in Angola. Following this truly pioneering but ineffective legislation, in 1684, the King promulgated the "By-law on the dispatch of Black captives from Angola and other conquests, and on the tonnage of ships," the first systematic set of laws aimed at regulating the slave trade.[130] As summarised in the preamble to the by-law, King Peter II was said to

---

126   AHU, *Angola*, cx. 8, doc. 35: 1664-08-12: 'Consulta do Conselho Ultramarino'.

127   ibid.

128   "Provisão: 1664-09-23," in *MMA*, 12: 499–500.

129   AHU, *Angola*, cx. 8, doc. 111: 1665-08-06: 'Resolução régia sobre consulta do Conselho Ultramarino de 1665-05-28'.

130   AHU, *Angola*, cx. 12, doc. 137: 1684-03-18: 'Regimento sobre o despacho dos negros cativos de Angola e mais conquistas e sobre a arqueação dos navios'.

have taken this initiative because "freighters and ship masters use violence in the transport of Black captives from Angola to the *Estado do Brasil* [Brazil] and pack them so tightly that not only do they not have enough air to breathe and stay alive – life being a natural right for all men, either free or enslaved – but also they end up mistreating each other, which leads to many deaths and terrible injuries for those that survive." The 23 articles of this by-law regulated, sometimes in great detail, issues concerning water and food supply, the treatment of disease, and the spiritual support provided to slaves. However, the key problem that the by-law tried to tackle was the overloading of ships, as the preamble quoted earlier illustrates. In seeking to do so, rules on ship tonnages and carrying capacities per ton were established as well as penalties aimed at disciplining transgressors at any stage of the process, whether they be ship masters, guards or high royal officials. However, the enforcement of these regulations required a bureaucratic apparatus and efficiency in its operation on the part of the Portuguese Crown and its officials that did not exist at that time anywhere in the Portuguese empire and least of all in Luanda, which remained at the very edge of that empire.

Seeking to circumvent these restrictions on loading rates of slaves imposed by the 1684 legislation, ship owners and masters resorted to several stratagems. The most obvious, and not necessarily the most expensive, was to bribe individuals directly or indirectly responsible for the inspection of tonnage and cargo, and for the dispatch of ships.[131] There were, however, more subtle ways to circumvent the legislation, whether during the evaluation of tonnage, loading or the final dispatch of the ship. Throughout the entire process, slaves were hidden in the most unlikely places on board, including the storeroom.[132] Some slaves were counted as sailors and cabin boys to the authorities.[133] In other cases, whenever ship owners, captain or masters had leverage with the local authorities, they simply omitted to declare a part of the cargo. Usually, this required an informal agreement with the contractor of the royal monopoly and the tax collector in Angola. During the term of Governor Luís Lobo da Silva, the *Santa Teresa*, heading to Pernambuco, followed this strategy, secretly carrying 80 slaves more than the 280 slaves it was authorised to transport. In short, almost a quarter of its slaves were carried illegally.[134]

---

131   Elias Alexandre da Silva Correia, *História de Angola* (Lisboa: Ática, 1937), 1: 56.
132   AHU, *Angola*, cx. 14, doc. 20: 1690-04-20: 'Treslado da devassa...: testemunho de Bernardo de Berganha'.
133   ibid., 'Testemunho do capitão Manuel de Sousa Benevides'.
134   ibid., 'Testemunhos de Domingos Trigo e do capitão Manuel Lobo Barreto'. The ship *Almiranta* sailing from Luanda to Rio de Janeiro in April 1689 also carried 100 slaves more

Yet another strategy used to evade the law was to declare adult slaves, the so-called *peças da Índia*, as children (*crias*). Doing so provided a double gain, for not only did it allow more slaves to be carried per ton but as slave children valued at less than 12.000 *réis* were exempt from taxation, it also permitted carriers to reduce their tax liabilities. Between 1668 and 1670, of 18,662 slaves embarked in Angola, 3,133 or 17 percent, were declared as children (*cabeças pequenas*) and thus exempt from taxes.[135] In May 1689, over 40 adults were dispatched as if they were 'children' on board the brigatine *Bom Jesus*.[136] In an attempt to stop abuses and their consequent tax losses to the Royal Treasury in Angola, Governor João de Lencastre ordered on 29 October 1689 that "only toddlers still being breast fed by their mothers were to be dispatched as children free of duty."[137] Nothing, however, discouraged offenders: every effort was made to circumvent the 1684 law, which, at the time, represented a clear step forward with respect to recognizing the humanity of the enslaved and in embodying this in the trade.

Ships from Hell

In the seventeenth century slave ships were rarely specialised, being often used for trades other than slaving. In fact, in their return voyages such vessels could be found transporting Brazilian sugar and tobacco to Portugal. Despite being unspecialized, many ships employed in the slave trade had their hold redesigned to facilitate slave carrying. Many had installed in the hold high wooden platforms on which slaves would sleep, thereby avoiding direct contact with water that might enter the ship as well as with the filth that accumulated there. We have, however, no information for the seventeenth century of the use of the "false bridge" system in which a stationary platform was installed at mid-height on the deck, allowing the cargo area to be extended. This was a device widely used on eighteenth-century slave ships to fit in a few extra slaves.[138]

------

than its usable tonnage permitted. ibid., 'Testemunhos de Bernardo de Berganha e João Cardoso'.

135 AHU, *Angola*, cx. 10, doc. 40: 'Receita e despesa referente aos anos de 1667, 1668, 1669, 1670 e 1671'.

136 AHU, *Angola*, cx. 14, doc. 20: 1690-04-20: 'Treslado da devassa…: testemunho de João Roiz Porto'.

137 ibid., 'Portaria': 1689-10-29.

138 Jean Boudriot, "Le navire négrier au XVIIIe. Siècle," in Serge Daget, ed., *De la traite à l'esclavage: actes du Colloque International sur la Traite des Noirs* (Nantes: Société Française d'Histoire d'Outre-mer, 1988), 159.

In loading slaves on board ship, male slaves were typically housed in the hold, partly because they were thought more resistent to harsh conditions, and partly because, in the hold, they were more remote from the control centre of the ship.[139] Fear of insurrections resulted, in many cases, in slaves being chained to one another by the ankles (and sometimes with chains and rings around their necks), especially when the ship remained in sight of land.[140] The upper part of the ship on the deck or even the bridge was usually allocated to women and children and, although they could at least breathe freely there, they still suffered from lack of space and exposure to the weather.

The worst conditions, however, were to be found inside the hold. Even on ships in other trades, sailors sleeping in the hold experienced great discomforts. "Many mornings they would wake up swimming in water that came through the gun holes; if they chose to close them, however, the hold would be on fire and they would die from the heat, with the lack of ventilation; and if they chose to open them there would be so much water that if they did not drown they would be severely weakened by the conditions they experienced and were likely to become ill."[141] Slaves accommodated in the hold, however, could not choose to leave, and in many cases were so tightly packed that they did not have space enough to move or to lie down.[142] Furthermore, in smaller vessels there were no portholes or ventilation, apart from the hatch from the deck to the hold. The question of ventilation was highlighted in the 1684 legislation, which insisted that, in cases where there were no portholes or forms of ventilation, ships were to be allowed no more than 5 slaves per 2 tons, whereas those with "portholes with ventilation" were permitted to carry 7 slaves per 2 tons, or 40 percent more.[143] In some ships, especially the larger ones, captives housed in the hold were brought on deck at least once a day to get air, but in many cases this was not possible. One factor inhibiting this was fear of revolt or of attempts at suicide by jumping overboard among the enslaved. Such attempts often happened.[144]

---

139   Louis Jadin, *Pero Tavares, missionnaire jésuite, ses travaux apostoliques au Congo et en Angola: 1629 1635* (Bruxelles/Rome: Institut Historique Belge de Rome, 1967), 388.

140   Louis Jadin, *Les flamands au Congo et en Angola au XVIIe siècle* (Coimbra: Instituto de Estudos Históricos Doutor António de Vasconcelos, 1965), 69–70; Sandoval, *Naturaleza*, 72v.

141   José Rodrigues Abreu, *Luz de cirurgiões embarcadiços* (Lisboa: Oficina de António Pedroso Galram, 1711), 35.

142   Cavazzi, *Descrição Histórica*, 1: 426.

143   'Regimento sobre o despacho dos negros cativos...' (1684), Chapter 6.

144   Jerónimo Lobo, *Itinerário e outros escritos inéditos* (Lisboa: Livraria Civilização, 1971), 639.

Most slaves travelled naked or nearly so and slept directly on wooden boarding. Olfert Dapper, when referring to the main differences in the ways in which Portuguese and Dutch treated the slaves, praised the attitude of the Portuguese, who provided the slaves with straw mats to lie on and changed them every 10 days.[145] The Portuguese Jesuit, Pero Tavares, also referred to the use of straw mats, but in less positive terms, noting that carriers gave the slaves a "single straw mat for each three slaves, which served as a bed and cover, but after the first few nights the straw mat was in bits." He went on to note that the slaves "slept naked like animals."[146]

The biggest source of discomfort for the enslaved, however, was thirst. It was also the biggest threat to their survival while on board ship. Problems with water began at the port of embarkation of captives. In the vicinity of Luanda, springs of drinking water were scarce and poor in quality. On the island, where boarding took place, it was only possible to get water by digging wells, known as *quicimas* or *cacimbas* (from Kimbundu, *kixima*). These had limited capacity and duration as they quickly filled with sea water, thereby becoming unfit as a source of water for human consumption.[147] Some ships, however, remained reliant on the island *cacimbas*, which meant that the water they took off was usually of poor quality.[148] An alternative source of water was the Bengo (or Zenza) river, but as this was located 6–7 leagues north of Luanda, procuring water there entailed additional costs as well as other risks.[149]

Access to drinking water of sufficient quality was not the only problem faced by masters of slave ships. Another was managing the use of water on board ship. The water needed to sustain both slaves and crew on slave ships occupied a significant proportion of the cargo space of such ships, and balancing the numbers of slaves taken on board with water requirements involved careful calculation. Two barrels (*pipas*) of water, amounting to perhaps 1,000 litres, typically consumed one ton burthen of cargo space, but, allowing for the use of two litres per slave per day, was sufficient only to satisfy the needs of 20 slaves for just 25 days. As most slaves ships carried ten to twenty times that number of slaves and voyage times often lasted 50 days or more, it is clear that

---

145   Olivier Dapper, *Description de l'Afrique, contenant les noms la situation & les confins de toutes ses parties, leurs rivieres, leurs villes & leurs habitations, leurs plantes & leurs animaux; les moeurs, les coutumes, la langue, les richesses, la religion & le gouvernement de ses peuples* (Amsterdam: chez Wolfang, Waesberge, Boom, Van Someren, 1686), 367.

146   Jadin, *Pero Tavares*, 387.

147   "Carta do padre Garcia Simões para o provincial: 1575-10-20," in *MMA*, 3: 131.

148   AHU, *Angola*, cx. 14, doc. 67: 1691-06-16: 'Auto de queixas do cabido'.

149   Cavazzi, *Descrição Histórica*, 1: 160–161; Cadornega, *História geral*, 3: 32–33.

water supply could occupy up to 40 tons of cargo space. Faced with this, masters needed to weigh the desire to maximise loading rates of ships with slaves
against the uncertainties of voyage times between Angola and the Americas
and the risks of leakages and contamination of water on the voyage. These
were not easy calculations to make, and as there were financial incentives to
maximise loadings of slaves, water supply could sometimes run low, intensify-
ing risks of dehydration among the human cargo tightly packed in almost suf-
focating conditions during the Atlantic crossing. Water contamination itself
could cause illness, of course, but it was inadequate water supply and the
resulting dehydration of captives which contributed most to distress and death
of captives in the voyage to the Americas.

Luandan residents involved in the slave trade who were concerned by high
mortality on slave ships complained not only about overloading (which ultimately affected everything) but also specifically about the inadequate supplies
of water to slaves on board. In a petition to the King in 1664, they complained
that there was no "inspection of water supplies" prior to the dispatch of
ships.[150] To accommodate their demands, the King issued legislation ordering
that "no [ship] could leave the port of São Paulo [of Luanda] without taking on
25 barrels (*pipas*) of good quality water for every 100 slaves."[151] This was equivalent, in principle, to about 125 litres per captive. On a trip to Bahia, it would
amount to about three litres of water per slave per day, and on voyages to
Vera Cruz or Cartagena to about two litres. These amounts were considered
reasonable, given that some of the water allowance would be used for purposes other than drinking, such as preparing food. How adequately the law of
1664 was policed, however, is unclear and it is likely that non-compliance was
common.

Further regulations relating to water supply on board ship were included in
the 1684 by-law, which obliged ship masters to "carry enough water to give
slaves a jug (*canada*) to drink each day without fail."[152] Each jug was assumed
to hold four pints, or roughly two litres, of water. At that time, the voyage from
Angola to Pernambuco was estimated to take at 35 days on average, while those
to Bahia and to Rio de Janeiro were estimated to take 40 and 50 days, respectively.[153] Assuming 200 jugs per barrel, this was equivalent to 14–20 barrels per
100 slaves. It falls to 12–17 barrels per 100 slaves if we assume 250 jugs per barrel.
On the evidence available, it is impossible to assess whether these regulations

---

150   AHU, *Angola*, cx. 8, doc. 35: 1664-08-12: 'Consulta do Conselho Ultramarino'.
151   "Provisão de 1664-09-23," in *MMA*, 12: 499–500.
152   'Regimento sobre o despacho dos negros cativos...(1684)', Chapter 7.
153   Ibid., Chapter 8.

were enforced, but complaints about scarcity of water on board and news of resulting deaths continued after 1684.[154]

As for the diet of slaves on board ship, testimonies of priests and others who travelled on slave ships suggest that, exceptional circumstances apart, ship masters tried to provide slaves with food sufficient to ensure their survival. This does not mean that the food quality or quantity was good. Moreover, the restricted size of ship kitchens and the need to economize on firewood for cooking (storage of which represented a 'dead' weight compared to slaves) underline the difficulties involved in preparing food each day for a month or two for several hundred people. Food preparation was, nevertheless, a routine operation on board slave ships. In 1594, the Florentine merchant, Francesco Carletti, travelling from Cape Verde to Cartagena, via Africa, reported that slaves were given two meals each day, one in the morning and the other around midday, the latter consisting of cooked food, including corn maize cooked in water and seasoned with oil and salt. Occasionally, the latter might be mixed with fresh fish, though this was "badly cooked or almost raw."[155] In 1643, Pieter Moortamer, director of the Dutch West India Company in Luanda, in attempting to prompt his own colleagues to adopt more commercially sound practices, claimed, in a somewhat idealized way, that slaves on board Portuguese ships were provided each day with two hot meals seasoned with palm oil and sometimes dry fish. During the day they would be even given a small amount of manioc.[156] The 1684 by-law, noted earlier, also tried to regulate slave diet on board, by requiring that slaves should be served three meals daily.[157] Reality, however, did not reflect the law.

Although beans and corn flour played an important role in slave diets on board ship, manioc flour was the main staple. Some of the manioc was cultivated in Angola. The Jesuits were said to have had big manioc-growing plantations in the Bengo River area, for example.[158] But most manioc was shipped from Brazil, and in seventeenth-century Brazilian-Angolan bilateral trade, manioc flour came to play a key role, often being the return cargo to Africa of

154   See, for example: AHU, *Angola*, cx. 14, doc. 35: 1690-04-02: 'Carta do Procurador da Fazenda de Angola'.

155   Paolo Carile, ed., *Voyage autour du monde de Francesco Carletti, 1594–1606* (Paris: Chandeigne, 1999), 67–68.

156   "Relatório de Pieter Moortamer à câmara da Zelândia: 1643-29-06," in Jadin, *L'ancien Congo et l'Angola*, I: 359; Boxer, *Salvador de Sá*, 232.

157   AHU, *Angola*, cx. 12, doc. 137: 1684-03-18: 'Regimento sobre o despacho dos negros cativos de Angola e mais conquistas e sobre a arqueação dos navios', Chapter 7.

158   Caldeira, "Os jesuítas," 58–59.

vessels transporting slaves to the sugar mills. In the early seventeenth century Rio de Janeiro exported annually almost 680 tonnes of manioc flour to Angola.[159] Accordingly, manioc flour, cooked and seasoned with palm oil or just cooked plain (or even, in some cases, left raw), was undoubtedly the basis of slave subsistence during the journey between Angola and the Americas. According to Moortamer, the Portuguese had as a rule loaded one bushel of flour per slave taken on board, and on some occasions, some dried fish was added to the daily ration of manioc.[160] In 1635, the Jesuit priest, Pero Tavares, travelling on a slave ship between Luanda and Rio de Janeiro, witnessed "manioc flour and salted sardines" being served to slaves.[161] According to Cadornega, one of the main activities on the island of Luanda during the last quarter of the seventeenth century was the "salting of fish for slave ships setting sail from there."[162]

Despite all the problems caused by ship overloading and by logistics on board slave vessels, there was a clear concern on the part of ship owners, captains and masters to ensure that slaves were sufficiently well fed to survive as a bare minimum. In most cases, however, this was done more for commercial than for humanitarian reasons. The death of a slave represented a significant loss. At the same time, the appearance of thin or emaciated slaves on arrival at their American destination would tend to lower their price at market. The image of hundreds of skeletal Africans, which has become part of the iconography of slavery, was in many cases not far from reality. The condition of slaves, however, stemmed not merely from lack of food on board, but also from the impact of other factors, among them their health after captivity in Africa and their general treatment thereafter. Many slaves boarded ship already weakened by illness and exhaustion caused by their lengthy journey from their African homeland to the coast. Once on board ship, parasites, sharp changes in temperature, poor water quality, and terrible conditions of hygiene fostered infections and illnesses such as dysentery, which had devastating effects. Even those unaffected by serious illness would fall sick with nausea and vomiting throughout the entire journey. Having been raised far from the coast, most of the slaves found it difficult to travel on the open sea on small ships. Matters were made worse by the kind of food available on board, which was

---

159 Calculations by Alencastro, *O trato dos viventes*, 251.

160 "Relatório de Pieter Moortamer ao Conselho do Brasil: 1642-14-10," in Jadin, *L'ancien Congo et l'Angola*, I: 354. The bushel was a unit of measurement which could vary beween 13.8 litres (in Lisbon) and 18 litres.

161 Jadin, *Pero Tavares*, 387.

162 Cadornega, *História geral,* 39.

surely far from appetizing or otherwise suitable under the circumstances they encountered.

Sickness, panic and despair led many slaves to reject food, as a way to accelerate death, which in their minds seemed preferable to the terrible life awaiting them at disembarkation.[163] On board those responsible for slaves tended to interpret the refusal by captives to eat as a form of stubborness and resistence. Therefore, they would do everything they could to counter this attitude, which they regarded as a crime. Although the use of violence to force slaves to eat might seem paradoxical, it was a reality. As the Jesuit Pero Tavares saw it, this type of violence could have tragic consequences. In 1634, he filed a complaint against a man who had slyly killed two of his slaves with punches "only because they did not want to eat, as they were ill."[164]

The stench throughout the entire ship, but especially in the hold, was one of the features of slave ships most noticed by missionaires who travelled on them. A combination of poor ventilation, humidity, faeces, and filth produced a horrendous smell. Even for seventeenth-century individuals, more accustomed perhaps to noxious smells than people today, conditions in the hold of slave ships produced an unbearable stench.[165] Less serious in terms of health but equally disturbing in other ways was the deafening noise that filled the slave ships, which made rest difficult. Some slaves beat their hands or the chains that bound them against the boards of the ships, "others would shout on one side, or the other. Some cried and complained, others laughed. It was total chaos," as one contemporary observed.[166]

Mortality rates are an important indicator of conditions on board. Ideally, one would like evidence on the relative mortality rates of crew and slaves, but the required data are not available for the period under study here. Evidence on slave mortality between Luanda and Vera Cruz and between Luanda and Rio de Janeiro and Bahia is, however, available and allows some conclusions to be made. The data are presented in Table 4.4.

---

163   "Slaves are convinced that once they arrive in those lands [Brazil and New Spain], they would be killed by their buyers and these would make gunpowder from their brains and bones, and the olive oil from Ethiopia from their flesh." Cavazzi, *Descrição Histórica*, 1: 160–161.

164   Jadin, *Pero Tavares*, 387–388.

165   C.A. Walckenaer, ed., *Collection des relations de voyages par mer et par terre en différentes parties de l'Afrique depuis 1400 jusqu'a nos jours* (Paris: Chez l'Editeur, Rue Laffitte, 1842), 13: 385; Jadin, *Les flamands au Congo*, 69–70.

166   Cuvelier, *Relations*, 283.

TABLE 4.4   *Slave mortality on Portuguese and Spanish ships during the middle passage between Angola and the Americas, 1605–1668*

Year	Ship name	Destination	Duration of journey (days)	No. of slaves onboard	No. of slave deaths	Percentage	Sources
1605	*Nª Sª do Rosário*	Vera Cruz	c. 60	341	72	21.1	(1)
1605	*Santo António*	Vera Cruz	c. 60	231	102	44.1	(1)
1606	*Nª Sª da Lapa*	Vera Cruz	c. 60	200	35	17.5	(1)
1608	*Nª Sª da Piedade*	Vera Cruz	c. 60	214	17	7.9	(1)
1608	*S. João Baptista*	Vera Cruz	c. 60	235	8	3.4	(1)
1608	*S. Ildefonso*	Vera Cruz	c. 60	320	67	20.9	(1)
1608	*Santo António*	Vera Cruz	c. 60	247	29	11.7	(1)
1608	*Cinco Chagas*	Vera Cruz	c. 60	290	38	13.1	(1)
1608	*Nª Sª da Nazaré*	Vera Cruz	c. 60	300	176	58.7	(1)
1609	*S. Jerónimo*	Vera Cruz	c. 60	218	26	11.9	(1)
1610	*S. Pedro*	Vera Cruz	c. 60	307	88	28.7	(1)
1610	*S. João Baptista*	Vera Cruz	c. 60	356	70	19.7	(1)
1610	*Santo António*	Vera Cruz	c. 60	157	3	1.9	(1)
1610	*Nª Sª da Nazaré*	Vera Cruz	c. 60	192	24	12.5	(1)
1611	*S. Gonçalo*	Vera Cruz	c. 60	286	78	27.3	(1)
1611	*S. Ildefonso*	Vera Cruz	c. 60	313	144	46.0	(1)
1613	*Santiago*	Vera Cruz	c. 60	292	109	37.3	(1)
1613	*S. Francisco*	Vera Cruz	c. 60	229	64	27.9	(1)
1613	*S. Diogo*	Vera Cruz	c. 60	184	39	21,2	(1)
1613	*Nª Sª do Porto Salve*	Vera Cruz	c. 60	250	160	64.0	(1)
1614	*Nª Sª do Rosário*	Vera Cruz	c. 60	240	107	44.6	(1)
1616	*S. Francisco*	Vera Cruz	c. 60	235	63	26.8	(1)
1617	*Nª Sª da Ajuda*	Vera Cruz	c. 60	150	37	24.7	(1)
1617	*Santiago*	Vera Cruz	c. 60	156	40	25.6	(1)
1617	*Nª Sª do Rosário*	Vera Cruz	c. 60	170	50	29.4	(1)
1618	*Três Reis Magos*	Vera Cruz	c. 60	125	44	35.2	(1)
1618	*Nª Sª da Ajuda*	Vera Cruz	c. 60	186	66	35.5	(1)
1618	*S. João Baptista*	Vera Cruz	c. 60	162	48	29.6	(1)
1618	*S. Boaventura*	Vera Cruz	c. 60	166	47	28.3	(1)
1618	*Santa Catarina*	Vera Cruz	c. 60	189	49	25.4	(1)
1619	*S. Francisco*	Vera Cruz	c. 60	150	39	26.0	(1)
1619	*Nª Sª do Amparo*	Vera Cruz	c. 60	150	10	6.7	(1)

TABLE 4.4   *Slave mortality on Portuguese and Spanish ships during the middle passage between Angola and the Americas, 1605–1668* (cont.)

Year	Ship name	Destination	Duration of journey (days)	No. of slaves onboard	No. of slave deaths	Percentage	Sources
1622	-*	Bahia	c. 40	195	85	43.6	(2)
1622	-*	Bahia	c. 40	220	126	57.3	(2)
1622	-*	Bahia	c. 40	357	157	44.0	(2)
1622	-*	Bahia	c. 40	142	51	36.0	(2)
1635	–	Rio	30	590	130	22.0	(3)
1649		Bahia	c. 40	900	250	27.8	(4)
1668	–	Bahia	50	630	33	5.2	(5)

Souces and Observations

(1)   Vila Vilar, *Hispano-América*, 256–259, table 3;
(2)   "Certidão dos escravos enviados de Angola pelo governador João Correia de Sousa," in Cruz, "O tráfico negreiro," doc. 7;
(3)   Jadin, *Pero Tavares*, 387 (the crew is included in the number of people onboard);
(4)   Cavazzi, *Descrição Histórica*, 1: 379;
(5)   *La Mission au Congo des Peres Michelangelo Guatini et Dionigi Carli (1668)*, edited by John K. Thornton (Paris: Chandeigne, 2006), 153–159.
* This vessel belonged to the governor João Correia de Sousa.

The data in Table 4.4 confirm that seventeenth-century missionaries' accounts of slave transport and their human costs were not far from the truth. Mortality levels on board were often appallingly high. Although our sample is limited, it reveals great variations in percentage losses of captives in transit, with losses ranging from just under 2 percent to 64 percent. The lack of full information on ship tonnages prevents us from exploring linkages between ship loading rates of slave levels and mortality and cautions us against making hasty generalisations on the issue. Equally, the variations in shipboard mortality question the value of making estimates of mean mortality on seventeenth-century slave ships operating between Angola and the Americas. Even if we choose to use median rather than mean mortality, however, the outcome is, at 26.4 percent, still high. Such a calculation, moreover, suggests that the highest values found in Table 4.4 may have been atypical outcomes, resulting from exceptionally adverse situations.[167]

---

167   For example, in 1622 the four ships sent to Brazil by the governor João Correia de Sousa (1621–1623) recorded a very high mortality rate. They took prisoners of war with them

Such exceptional outcomes were probably linked to outbreaks of contagious disease or navigational problems that resulted in unusually long voyages and resulting catastrophic consequences for the enslaved in terms of mortality. To some extent, as would be seen in the eighteenth century, greater prudence on the part of shipmasters in ensuring less crowding, improved hygiene, and adequate food and water supplies may have been a factor in moderating shipboard mortality in the Portugueses slave trade. But such actions by masters were far from predictable, and mortality levels on ships taking slaves from Angola to the Americas after 1700, though lower than in the seventeenth century, still remained high by most historical standards.[168]

Conclusion

During the seventeenth century Luanda was the main African gateway for slave exports, accommodating much of Brazil's demand for slaves as well as that in Spanish America, especially during the period of the Portuguese *asiento* (1595–1640). After 1640, the Portuguese slave trade to Spanish America became secondary, only remaining significant in terms of smuggling via the Río de la Plata.

At the beginning of the seventeenth century, an important part of the slave trade connecting Angola to the Americas followed triangular patterns emanating from the European ports of Lisbon and Seville. During the course of the century, however, Brazilian merchants, based in Pernambuco, Bahia and Rio de Janeiro, played an ever-growing role in this commerce and the bilateral routes between the two sides of the South Atlantic triumphed over the European-based triangular ones. Despite this, in Angola governors and contractors were able to use their political status and support from European captains of slave ships to continue to play a significant role in the South Atlantic slaving business.

---

from Cassanje, together with the slaves, including a large percentage of elderly people and children. Cruz, "O tráfico negreiro," doc. 7.

168 The *Transatlantic Slave Trade Database* registers the following average percentage mortality levels on board ships disembarking slaves in Brazilian ports: 1601–1650: 12.4 percent; 1651–1700: 22.5 percent; 1701–1750: 13.6 percent; and 1751–1800: 7.6 percent. This trend is even more evident if you look only at the region of Pernambuco: 1601–1650: 12.4 percent; 1651–1700: 32.2 percent; 1701–1750: 14.6 percent; 1751–1800: 6.8 percent. *Voyages: Trans-Atlantic Slave Trade Database* [http://www.slavevoyages.org] 15 September 2011.

Throughout the century the trade was carried out in small vessels of about 100 tons, though over time there was a discernible increase in the size of ships employed in the Angolan slave trade. The greed of ship owners and masters, however, gave rise to high slave packing rates and horrendous conditions on board ship and contributed to slave mortality levels in transit that remained extremely high.

CHAPTER 5

Trade Networks in Benguela, 1700–1850

Mariana P. Candido

Benguela was connected to the Atlantic economy from the early seventeenth century. The bay between the Katumbela and Kaporolo Rivers provided a natural harbour that favoured settlement and anchorage of ships. Before the arrival of the Portuguese, inland populations sent caravans into the littoral to acquire dry fish and salt. After the establishment of the colony in 1617, the coastal demand for cattle, zebra skins, and ostrich plumes increased. Some products remained in the town, while cattle, slaves, salt, and *nzimbu* shells were exported to Luanda.[1] The movement of caravans pushed the colonial state to build fortresses inland during the seventeenth century in the attempt to control the flow of trade. The establishment of Caconda in 1680 and its transfer to a safer location in 1768 demonstrated the Portuguese efforts and failures to enforce land and commercial control.[2] The colonial garrisons in Benguela and Caconda were small and insufficient to enforce domination of local people. Unlike in the Americas, the Portuguese colonial state did not manage to extend its control inland, although traders circulated freely. Strong African states and tropical diseases kept Europeans close to the coast, discouraging their expansionist agendas.

Benguela was originally established as a commercial post, but quickly evolved into an urban centre. Africans who lived nearby relocated into the region around the fortress, drawn there by trade opportunities.[3] New economic activities opened, such as salt mine exploitation, sale of foodstuff, and porterage. The settlement expanded, yet life in town revolved around the Atlantic

---

1 António de Oliveira de Cadornega, *História Geral das Guerras Angolanas, 1680–1681* (Lisboa: Agência Geral das Colónias, 1972), 3: 171; Beatrix Heintze, *Fontes para a História de Angola no Século XVII* (Stuttgart: F. Steiner Verlag Wiesbaden, 1985), 2 vols. For the use of *nzimbu* in the Kingdom of Kongo, see: David Birmingham, *Central Africa to 1870* (Cambridge: Cambridge University Press, 1981), 28–30.

2 Joseph Miller, "Angola Central e Sul por Volta de 1840," *Estudos Afro-Asiáticos* 32 (1997): 23; Ralph Delgado, *Ao Sul do Cuanza, Ocupação e Aproveitamento do Antigo Reino de Benguela* (Lisboa: [s.n.], 1944), 1: 234–235.

3 António Manuel Hespanha and Maria Catarina Santos, "Os Poderes num Império Oceânico," in António Manuel Hespanha, ed., *História de Portugal, O Antigo Regime* (Lisboa: Estampa, 1993), 4: 401; Catarina Madeira Santos, "Luanda: A Colonial City between Africa and the Atlantic, 17th and 18th centuries," in Liam Brockey, ed., *Portuguese Colonial Cities in the Early Modern World* (New York, NY: Ashgate, 2010), 249–270.

slave trade. Portuguese merchants established in the home country or in its colony in the New World, Brazil, stopped in the port of Benguela and bartered imported goods for captives. Traders from other parts of Europe had also been visiting the port since the seventeenth century in search of minerals and slaves.[4]

By the early eighteenth century, traders based in Brazil requested licences to sail directly to Benguela, indicating that it was seen as a profitable slave market. Unlike other regions along the coast of Africa, by the 1700s Portuguese and Brazilian traders started travelling inland and settled in and around Caconda, although the power of the colonial state was limited. The establishment of Caconda did not result in political control of African states but increased the participation of foreign and Luso-African merchants based in Benguela in the internal trade. Due to vassalage treaties signed with African rulers, coastal merchants and their associates could circulate in the interior.[5] They could also live under the protection of African rulers obeying laws and paying tribute in order to trade.

This essay focuses on trade networks in Benguela, including the evolution of the merchant community in Benguela during the eighteenth and the first half of the nineteenth centuries. Local Africans played vital roles in the actions of foreign traders, helping them to expand their trade inland. Women were also key agents in the establishment of the commerce of human beings along the coast and the interior. This study focuses on the Atlantic trade network that connected Benguela and its population to other parts of the world, and also on the internal routes that linked the littoral and the hinterland. This essay explores the introduction of new consumer practices in the central highlands and the establishment of new commercial elites associated with the international slave trade and the colonial state.

The Evolution of Benguela from and during the Eighteenth Century

During the eighteenth century, the settlement of Benguela and its population expanded directly with the growth of its importance in the Atlantic trade.

---

4   Joseph Miller, "The Paradoxes of Impoverishment in the Atlantic Zone," in David Birmingham and Phyllis Martin, eds., *History of Central Africa* (London: Longman, 1983), 118–151; Johannes Postma, *The Dutch in the Atlantic Slave Trade, 1600–1815* (Cambridge: Cambridge University Press, 1990).

5   For vassalage treaties, see: Beatriz Heintze, "Luso-African Feudalism in Angola? The Vassal Treaties of the 16th to the 18th Century," *Revista Portuguesa de História* 18 (1980): 111–131.

Initially, it was a commercial outpost, fortified to defend its garrisons from attacks by inland Africans and by other European traders.[6] Located between the Katumbela and Kaporolo Rivers, the town was surrounded by swamps, which encouraged mosquitoes and spread of diseases. Nearby, the jungle of Cavaco hosted animals that wandered around the settlement.[7] Deadly fevers hit European administrators and traders hard, giving Benguela the nickname of "white man's grave." In 1717, the Governor of Angola, Paulo Caetano de Albuquerque, described the settlement as being in a "miserable condition, with the number of soldiers reduced to 30 people in consequences of diseases, lack of medication and care."[8] Another problem was a lack of food, which resulted in its import from Luanda, neighbouring African states, and even Brazil.[9] In the early eighteenth century, the colonial administration and the merchant community focused on quick profits and short-term stays, neglecting agriculture.

During the eighteenth century, increasing numbers of colonial officers were sent to Benguela. Some of them acted as traders, which explains the increase on the volume of slave trade and the importance of Benguela in the South Atlantic world. Despite being a Portuguese settlement, Africans were the majority of the population, offering vital contacts to foreign traders. Local Ndombe men and women who lived in Benguela acted as intermediaries, translators and cultural brokers between Europeans located in the coast and

---

6   On the Dutch invasion see: C.R. Boxer, *Salvador de Sá and the struggle for Brazil and Angola* (London: Athlone Press, 1952); Postma, *The Dutch in the Atlantic Slave Trade*, 77; Luiz Felipe de Alencastro, *O Trato dos Viventes: A Formação do Brasil no Atlântico Sul, Séculos XVI e XVII* (São Paulo: Companhia das Letras, 2000).

7   Ralph Delgado, *Reino de Benguela. Do Descobrimento à criação do Governo Subalterno* (Lisboa: Imprensa Beleza, 1945), 235–237. For the early Portuguese contact in West-Central Africa, see: Miller, "The Paradoxes of Impoverishment," 118–159; David Birmingham, *Trade and Conflict in Angola* (Oxford: Oxford University Press, 1966).

8   Delgado, *Reino de Benguela*, 374 and 379. Scholars have analyzed the impact of the environment on the European expansion. See: Philip D. Curtin, *Disease and Empire* (Cambridge: Cambridge University Press, 1998); idem, *Death by Migration: Europe's Encounter with the Tropical World in the Nineteenth Century* (Cambridge: Cambridge University Press, 1989). For a study that focuses on West-Central Africa, see: Joseph C. Miller, "The Significance of Drought, Disease and Famine in the Agriculturally Marginal Zones of West-Central Africa," *Journal of African History* 23:1 (1982): 17–61.

9   Arquivo Histórico Ultramarino (AHU), *Angola*, cx. 8, doc. 45: 1664-09-23. New studies are stressing the importance of crops produced in Brazil in feeding Portuguese colonial settlements along the coast of Africa. See: Nielson Bezerra, "Mosaicos da Escravidão: Identidades Africanas e Conexões Atlânticas no Recôncavo da Guanabara (1780–1840)" (unpublished PhD diss., Universidade Federal Fluminense, Niterói, 2010).

inland African states. Portuguese merchants, and later Brazilian slavers, concentrated on the transatlantic slave trade, which included fostering diplomatic and commercial relationships with their homologous inland and African states' rulers. *Pombeiros*, itinerant traders based in Benguela or in the interior, linked the littoral to the markets, which were controlled by African rulers.[10] Sometimes they commanded caravans. Their main task was to transport locally produced goods to the coast and carry imported commodities to the interior. *Pombeiros* reached the markets closed to foreign traders and were in charge of bringing slave coffles to the coast. Some of these individuals were Luso-Africans who spoke some Portuguese, dressed in western fashion, and lived in Portuguese controlled settlements.[11] Luso-Africans also acted as agents or brokers stationed in Benguela on behalf of merchants based overseas.[12] Eventually, Luso-Africans acquired the skills, the contacts, and the capital to join the transatlantic commerce. The society that emerged in Benguela during the eighteenth century was similar to that in other African ports along the littoral, such as Luanda, Ouidah, Saint Louis and Gorée.[13]

---

10   On *pombeiros*, see: Willy Bal, "Portugais Pombeiro 'Commerçant Ambulant du Sertão'," *Annali: Istituto Universitario Orientale, Sezione Romana* 7:2 (1965): 123–161; Miller, "Paradoxes of Impoverishment," 89; Isabel Castro Henriques, *Percursos da Modernidade em Angola. Dinâmicas Comerciais e Transformações Sociais no Século XIX* (Lisboa: Instituto de Investigação Científica Tropical, 1997), 765; Beatrix Heintze, "Long-distance Caravans and Communication beyond the Kwango (c. 1850–1890)," in Beatrix Heintze and Achim von Oppen, eds., *Angola on the Move. Transport Routes, Communication, and History* (Frankfurt am Main: Lembeck, 2008), 144–162.

11   For more on Luso-Africans in Angola, see: Beatrix Heintze, "A Lusofonia no Interior da África Central na era pré-colonial. Um contributo para a sua história e Compreensão na Actualidade," *Cadernos de Estudos Africanos* 6:7 (2005): 179–207; Joseph C. Miller, *Way of Death: Merchant Capitalism and the Angolan Slave Trade, 1730–1830* (Madison, WI: University of Wisconsin Press, 1988), 246.

12   See: Mariana Candido, "Merchants and the Business of the Slave Trade, 1750–1850," *African Economic History* 35 (2007): 3–4; António Luis Alvares Ferronha, "Angola. A Revolta de Luanda de 1667 e a Expulsão do Governador Geral Tristão da Cunha," in Júnia Ferreira Furtado, ed., *Diálogos Oceânicos. Minas Gerais e as Novas Abordagens para uma História do Império Ultramarino Português* (Belo Horizonte: Humanitas, 2001), 269.

13   See: James Searing, *West African Slavery and Atlantic Commerce* (New York, NY: Cambridge University Press, 1993); Robin Law, *Ouidah, The Social History of a West African Slaving 'Port'*, *1727–1892* (Athens, OH: Ohio University Press, 2004); George Brooks, *Eurafricans in Western Africa. Commerce, Social Status, Gender, and Religious Observance from the Sixteenth to the Eighteenth Century* (Athens, OH: Ohio University Press, 2003); Peter Mark, *"Portuguese" Style and Luso-African Identity. Precolonial Senegambia, Sixteenth-Nineteenth Centuries*

By the early eighteenth century, slave traders based in Brazil had started requesting permission to sail to Benguela. The first one was António Francisco de Oliveira, captain of the galley *Nossa Senhora da Monsarrata e Liberdade*, who, in January 1716, requested the Overseas Council to grant him a licence to sail from Bahia to Benguela. Oliveira asked to "do his business without the interference of the governor." It remains unclear if he made the voyage or not.[14] But the increased demand in Brazil for slaves encouraged the emergence of new ports on the African coast that could compete with the Luandan slave embarkations.[15] In 1722, Rio de Janeiro traders sent a ship to acquire slaves in Benguela. On board were one hundred *pipas de cachaça*, or 500 litre barrels, of sugar cane-distilled alcohol, produced in mills in Brazil, to be exchanged for captives. The voyage underlines the existence of a local African market for distilled alcohol.[16] These initial expeditions were followed by voyages by other traders who intended to take advantage of the rising price of slaves in Brazil. António de Almeida e Souza, captain of the ship *São Pedro e São Paulo*, asked royal permission to sail to Benguela in 1725. In his appeal, Almeida e Souza declared he intended to acquire slaves in Benguela and to sail to Bahia without stopping at Luanda to pay taxes. He also requested the collaboration of the governor of Benguela in expediting his trip and negotiations.[17] A few months later, another trader from Bahia, José de Carvalho, looked to follow the same plan in sending a ship directly to Benguela.[18] The Board of Commerce granted both traders permission to stay in Benguela for as many days as they

---

(Bloomington, IN: Indiana University Press, 2002); José Curto, *Enslaving Spirits: The Portuguese-Brazilian Alcohol Trade at Luanda and Its Hinterland, c. 1550–1830* (Leiden: Brill, 2004).

14 Roquinaldo Amaral Ferreira, "Transforming Atlantic Slaving: Trade, Warfare and Territorial Control in Angola, 1650–1800" (unpublished PhD diss., University of California-Los Angeles, 2003), 79.

15 Charles Ralph Boxer, *O Império Marítimo Português* (São Paulo: Companhia das Letras, 2002), 167–173; Laura de Mello e Sousa, *Desclassificados do Ouro. A Pobreza Mineira no Século XVIII* (Rio de Janeiro: Graal, 1985). For the importance of Luanda in the Atlantic slave trade, see: Curto, *Enslaving Spirits*; and David Eltis and David Richardson, "A New Assessment of the Transatlantic Slave Trade," in David Eltis and David Richardson eds., *Extending the Frontiers: Essays on the New Transatlantic Slave Trade Database* (New Haven, CT: Yale University Press, 2008), 1–60.

16 José C. Curto, "Luso-Brazilian alcohol and the legal slave trade at Benguela and its hinterland (1617–1830)," in Hubert Bonin, ed., *Négoce Blanc en Afrique Noire: L'évolution du commerce à longue distance en Afrique Noire du 18ᵉ aux 20ᵉ siècles* (Paris: Société Française d'Histoire d'Outre-mer, 2001), 356.

17 AHU, *Angola*, cx. 22, doc. 58: 1725-01-25.

18 AHU, *Angola*, cx. 22, doc. 64: 1725-03-20.

needed to conduct business, thereby initiating the direct slave trade between Benguela and the Brazilian ports.[19] Although these requests for licences are found in archives in Portugal, the *Transatlantic Slave Trade Database* lists only two slave voyages from Benguela around this time, carrying 331 slaves to Rio de Janeiro in 1728 and 636 to Bahia in 1729.[20] Thus, either the database overlooks some early voyages to Benguela or some of the requests were not necessarily followed by an actual completed voyage to the port for slaves.

From the early eighteenth century, merchants based in Benguela were exporting slaves to Brazil. In the 1730s and 1740s, several traders based in Rio de Janeiro sailed straight to Benguela to acquire slaves.[21] Decades later, the Portuguese state created large trading companies such as the *Companhia Geral do Grão Pará e Maranhão* and *Pernambuco e Paraíba*, to control and tax the trade. Together, these companies were granted a monopoly over the supply of African slaves and the export of minerals and agricultural products to Portugal.[22] The goal of the Portuguese crown was to maintain tight control over overseas trade, taxing and controlling exports, in order to prevent the participation of interlopers. Individual traders, however, were not excluded from the commerce, as long as they obtained royal permissions.[23] The short sailing distance between Benguela and Brazil made it an attractive port at which to trade. In the first half of the eighteenth century, slave ships took an average of 45 days to sail from Benguela to Salvador in Bahia, and this fell slightly to 41 after 1750. Data for voyage times to Rio de Janeiro are not available for the first half of the eighteenth century, but the mean time from the 1750s was 50 days. Official records indicate average mortality was less than 10 percent.[24] Brazilian schooners were also faster and required fewer crew than the galleons employed

---

19   AHU, *Angola*, cx. 22, doc. 158: prior to 1725-12-22.

20   See: http://www.slavevoyages.org/tast/database/search.faces, voyages ID 47231 and 49540.

21   AHU, *Brazil, Rio de Janeiro*, cx. 30, doc. 8: prior to 1735-01-27; cx. 32, doc. 106: prior to 1736-12-17; cx. 33, doc. 2: prior to 1737-02-07; cx. 34, doc. 42: prior to 1738-04-15; cx. 45, doc. 48: prior to 1746-04-01; cx. 46, doc. 34: 1746-09-28.

22   António Carreira, *As Companhias Pombalinas de Grão Pará e Maranhão e Pernambuco e Paraíba* (Lisboa: Presença, 1983).

23   Leonor Freire Costa, *Império e Grupos Mercantis: entre o Oriente e o Atlântico (século XVII)* (Lisboa: Livro Horizonte, 2002); Stuart Schwartz, "Prata, Açucar e Escravos: de como o império restaurou Portugal," *Tempo* 12:24 (2008): 206; A.J.R. Russell-Wood, *The Portuguese Empire, 1415–1808. A World on the Move* (Baltimore, MD: John Hopkins University Press, 1998), 29–30.

24   Transatlantic Slave Trade Database. http://www.slavevoyages.org/tast/database/search .faces based on recorded voyages.

by Portuguese traders.[25] In sum, the slave voyages from Benguela to Rio de Janeiro and from Benguela to Salvador were shorter and more profitable for Brazilian traders than for the owners of ships originating from Lisbon.[26]

The Atlantic economy offered a market for African commodities that had previously not been exchanged in long-distance trade, such as wax, ivory, and orchil, used for dyestuff. Also important were exports of wild animals, as well as feathers, skins, and shells that nowadays decorate museums in Europe.[27] The authorities in Lisbon demanded zebras, elephants, copper and any other product that could be sold into European markets. A whole range of goods gained new economic values and allowed the emergence of new African elites who controlled the collection or production of natural resources and the commercialization of imported goods. Inland, beads, alcohol, textiles and paper acquired new meaning and became goods of consumption.[28] In Benguela, wholesale merchants organized the trade. Imported goods were assembled and assorted according to the proportion of textiles, beads, salt, alcohol, and gunpowder that would be used to purchase captives. In the hinterland, slaves were purchased both singly and in lots in markets controlled by African rulers.[29] Luso-African traders,

---

25   Miller, *Way of Death*, 368.
26   Herbert Klein, "The Portuguese slave trade from Angola in the XVIII century," *Journal of Economic History* 32:4 (1972): 538–540; Manolo Florentino, *Em Costas Negras. Uma História do Tráfico de Escravos entre a África e o Rio de Janeiro* (São Paulo: Companhia das Letras, 1997), 78–82; Joseph Miller, "The Numbers, Origins, and Destinations of Slaves in the 18th Century Angolan Slave Trade," in Joseph E. Inikori and Stanley L. Engerman, eds., *The Atlantic Slave Trade: Effects on Economies, Societies, and People in Africa, the Americas, and Europe* (Durham, NC: Duke University Press, 1992), 100.
27   For long distance trade routes in West-Central Africa before the arrival of Portuguese, see: Jan Vansina, "Long-Distance Trade Routes in Central Africa," *Journal of African History* 3 (1962): 375–390. On the importance of the commerce on "exotic" pieces see the catalog of the exhibition *Encompassing the Globe: Portugal and the World in the 16th & 17th Centuries* (Washington, DC: Arthur M. Sackler Gallery, Smithsonian Institution, 2007). For the expansion of legitimate trade in the nineteenth-century, see: Mariana Candido, "Trade, Slavery and Migration in the Interior of Benguela. The Case of Caconda, 1830–1870," in Heintze and von Oppen, eds., *Angola on the Move*, 70–76.
28   Curto, *Enslaving Spirits*, 365; Ana Paula Tavares and Catarina Madeira Santos, "Uma Leitura Africana das Estratégias Políticas e Jurídicas. Textos dos e para os Dembos," in *Africae Monumenta. A Apropriação da Escrita pelos Africanos* (Lisboa: Instituto de Investigação Científica Tropical, 2002), 243–260.
29   Candido, "Merchants and the Business," 15–19; Miller, *Way of Death*, 298. See also: Linda Heywood, "Slavery and Forced Labor in the Changing Political Economy of Central Angola, 1850–1949," in Suzanne Miers and Richard Roberts, eds., *The End of Slavery in Africa* (Madison, WI: Wisconsin University Press, 1988), 417.

who visited markets controlled by African rulers, transported the assorted goods inland. *Pombeiros* exchanged the imported commodities for slaves and brought them to the coast. Those who did not work on credit could sell their slave coffle to transatlantic slave traders directly or to local brokers. Itinerant traders were not obliged to display slaves bought directly from the *gentio* or "heathen lands" to Portuguese authorities.[30]

The port of Benguela grew in importance as an alternative slave port for slave traders not willing to pay the prices asked in Loango and Luanda.[31] Although legally a Portuguese possession, few Portuguese officers ever lived in Benguela, making it very attractive to merchants in search of the loose fiscal controls over their business that gave them more freedom to manoeuvre.[32] Between 1700 and 1750, 22,596 slaves were dispatched from Benguela.[33] A small number of merchants commercially controlled their shipment. A record of 1762 offers us some insight into how slave trading operated on the coast. In the months of October and November in that year, Captain Manoel Gonçalves Bastos bought 410 slaves from different traders in Benguela (see Table 5.1). He was captain of the ship the *Nossa Senhora da Guadalupe e Bom Jesus dos Navegantes*, destined for Rio de Janeiro. Bastos acted on behalf of Lisbon traders Joaquim Rodrigues Vale, João Lourenço Peres and the brothers Manoel and José António da Costa Pinheiro. During 30 days, from October 27 to November 27, he acquired slaves from different traders, some of them colonial officers, most of the time in small lots until he was able to fill up his ship. Bastos bought 150 slaves, or 36.5 percent of the ship's load, from just two traders, Lieutenant Colonel Inácio Rodriguez da Cruz and Captain José M. Santa Torre. Exchanges occurred on a number of occasions, with dealings sometimes restricted to four or five slaves. Two other traders, Ensign Manoel Dias Leite and José Gomes Carlos sold more than forty slaves each. Another group of three Benguela based merchants sold Captain Bastos 86 (or 20 percent) of his human cargo: Francisco José de Ferreira and João Rodrigues sold 30 and 29 slaves, respectively, while the priest Manoel Gomes traded 27 slaves, including

---

30   AHU, *Angola*, cx. 159, doc. 55: 1828-08-09. For the purchase of slaves directly from *gentio* see: AHU, *Angola,* Correspondência dos Governadores, Pasta 1B: 1837-09-12.

31   Arquivo Histórico Nacional de Angola (hereafter AHNA), cód. 1, fls. 92v-93: 1730-04-12; AHU, *Angola*, cx. 24, doc. 36: 1728-04-17; cx. 27, doc. 159: 1734-12-22. On lower prices for Benguela slaves see: Birmingham, *Trade and Conflict in Angola*, 140–141; and Miller, *Way of Death*, 222–225.

32   See: Candido, "Merchants and the Business," 10; Ferreira, "Transforming Atlantic Slaving," 75–77; Curto, *Enslaving Spirits*, 94; Miller, "Paradoxes of Impoverishment," 260–262.

33   For the calculation on the estimates see: Eltis and Richardson, "A New Assessment," 1–60.

TABLE 5.1   *Manoel Gonçalves Bastos' slave acquisitions in Benguela, 1762*

Benguela Trader	Adults	Children	Total	Percentage
Lieutenant Colonel Inácio Rodriguez da Cruz	77		77	18.78
Captain José M. Santa Torre	69	4	73	17.80
Ensign Manoel Dias Leite	44		44	10.73
José Gomes Carlos	43		43	10.49
Francisco José de Ferreira	30		30	7.32
João Rodrigues	29		29	7.07
Priest Manoel Gomes	26	1	27	6.59
Constantino José de Faria	10		10	2.44
First Sergeant António Carneiro de Magalhães	9		9	2.20
Captain Luis de Magalhães	9		9	2.20
Captain José Caetano de Araújo	8		8	1.95
Unidentified Soldiers	6	1	7	1.71
Dona Isabel	6		6	1.46
José Machado Forte	5		5	1.22
António Paulo	5		5	1.22
Lieutenant António Pereira de Siqueira	4		4	0.98
Unidentified black men	3	1	4	0.98
Unidentified Sergeant		4	4	0.98
Soldier Sebastião	3		3	0.73
Francisco de Azevedo	3		3	0.73
Maria Teresa	2		2	0.49
Captain Manoel dos Reis	2		2	0.49
Ensign Caetano de Carvalho Velho	2		2	0.49
José Machado da Costa	1		1	0.24
Lieutenant Simão Batista		1	1	0.24
Surgeon		1	1	0.24
Captain António Rodrigues Algarve		1	1	0.24
	396	14	410	100

a child. Overall, Captain Bastos bought 78.7 percent of his slave cargo, or 323 individuals, from just seven Benguela merchants, thereby showing how the bulk of the trade was in few hands. The remaining 88 slaves were bought from 22 other coastal traders who each negotiated the sale of between one and ten

slaves.[34] Before leaving Benguela, thirty-two slaves died, reducing the number
of slaves at the time of sailing to 378. This single set of slave transactions
reveals how colonial officials were involved in slave sales and the length of
time needed to fill up a single slave ship in Benguela. Trade was shared
between large and small merchants who provided the captives demanded by
transatlantic slavers. The pressure from such slavers probably encouraged the
kidnapping of local slaves and free black people, who could be sold regardless
of their status in order to make a quick profit, a process which may explain
episodes of one or two slaves being traded.[35] The people on board *Nossa
Senhora de Guadalupe e Bom Jesus dos Navegantes*, however, never made it to
the Americas. After reaching Luanda, the slaves revolted and it never reached
its intended destination, Rio de Janeiro.[36]

Local Merchant Networks at the Height of the Slave Trade

Between 1751 and 1800, local merchants shipped off 305,057 slaves from
Benguela. Most of those who survived the Atlantic crossing landed in Rio de
Janeiro and Bahia.[37] The volume of the slave trade grew exponentially during
the eighteenth century, thanks to the demand in the Americas and the local
African conditions characterized by political instability, which generated warfare and captives. The expansion of the slave trade and its profits attracted
traders from Bahia, Rio de Janeiro and Lisbon.[38] Some of traders based
in Benguela were exiled criminals or were colonial officials. Yet important

---

34   AHU, *Angola*, cx. 48, doc. 19: Prior to 1768-06-24.
35   AHNA, cód. 509, fl. 215v: 1837-03-17; cód. 450, fls. 49v-50: 1837-02-20. Between 1834 and 1839
     a series of "crioulos of Benguela," "crioulos" and "crioulos of Angola" arrived in Rio de
     Janeiro. See: Arquivo Nacional do Rio de Janeiro (hereafter ANRJ), cód. 184, vol. 3. Escravos
     Emancipados. See also: Luciano Raposo, *Marcas de Escravos. Listas de escravos emancipa-
     dos vindos a bordo de navios negreiros* (1839–1841) (Rio de Janeiro: Arquivo Nacional, 1990).
     Robin Law also notes that the slave trade relied on relatively few merchants. Law,
     "Introduction," in Robin Law, ed., *From slave trade to "legitimate" commerce. The commer-
     cial transition in nineteenth-century West Africa* (Cambridge: Cambridge University Press,
     1995), 12.
36   For the slave uprising on board of the ship see: AHU, *Angola*, cx. 46, doc. 6: after 1763-01-20.
     This ship is also identified in the Transatlantic Slave Trade Database as voyage ID 8898.
37   Calculation based on estimates. See: the Transatlantic Slave Trade Database (http://www
     .slavevoyages.org/tast/database/search.faces).
38   For a discussion on the size of the merchant community in Benguela, see: Candido,
     "Merchants and the Business," 9–10.

numbers of merchants moved to Benguela in search of business opportunities.
The colonial settlement and its proximity to Brazil made Benguela more attractive and relatively safer than ports in West Africa, such as Ouidah, which were
not under Portuguese nominal control. As in Luanda, the merchant community at Benguela could rely on the Portuguese administration and its local
forces to protect traders and to raid neighbouring populations when there was
demand for slaves. Some acted as agents on behalf of overseas traders receiving credit to lubricate the commerce with the interior, while others relocated
to Benguela in order to participate in the trade. Custódio José Ribeiro, for
example, was a Portuguese trader established in Benguela by the turn of the
eighteenth century. Originally from Porto, he arrived in Benguela sometime
around the late 1780s. By 1803, he had already acquired a two-story house in
Benguela and maintained business operations in Quilengues, a region with a
colonial fortress in the interior.[39] Some foreign traders even travelled inland
despite the prohibition issued by the Overseas Council against the wandering
of white men, mulattoes or blacks wearing pants and carrying canes in the
interior.[40] Traders such as the Portuguese Francisco Lopes de Andrade ignored
the law. By the 1750s, Andrade was trading in slaves in the Benguela highlands,
expanding his commercial contacts inland.[41] Other traders, such as Manoel da
Fonseca e Sá, remained at the coast while in Benguela. Based in Lisbon, he
sailed to Benguela in 1779, and probably remained in the littoral, without venturing inland. In Benguela, he carried on his slave business and headed to Pará
in the north of Brazil.[42]

Brazil and Benguela maintained strong links, in part because of the ocean
currents and wind system of the South Atlantic and because they were territories under Portuguese control. By the end of the eighteenth century, many of
the traders based in Benguela were born in Brazil. Like their Portuguese counterparts, some of them occupied positions in the military or administration
and enjoyed the facilities their official status gave them in the trade. Among
them was Hipólito Ferreira da Silva, tradesman and soldier in the infantry
company, born in Rio, who was 31 and single in 1798.[43] Other Brazilian traders
in Benguela at the end of the eighteenth century were the Bahian-born Crispim

39 IAN/TT, *Feitos Findos, Juízo das Índias e Mina, Justificaçõs Ultramarinas, Terras Diversas*
    (hereafter *FF, JIM, JU*), mç. 7, doc. 20: 1803-10-24. For more on traders who acted as agents
    of merchants based in Brazil or Portugal see: Candido, "Merchants and the Business,"
    1–30.
40 AHU, cód. 544, fls. 7–9: 1676-02-12.
41 IAN/TT, *FF, JIM, JU, África*, cx. 19, mç 10, doc. 12, 1756.
42 IAN/TT, *FF, JU, África*, cx. 2, mç. 1, doc. 9, 1791.
43 AHU, *Angola*, cx. 89, doc. 67: 1798-12-21.

de Silveira e Souza, Ignácio da Silva, João Coelho da Cunha, Joaquim Jozé de
Andrade e Silva Menezes, Manoel Ramos Fernandes e Cunha, and Nazário
Marques da Silva.[44] Some of these traders also operated inland, among them
Bahian-born José da Assumpção e Mello, who was based in Caconda. By the
late 1790s, he had already made three commercial trips to the Lovale, probably
to buy slaves.[45]

The arrival of other new traders brought increased competition from
European merchants. The authorities in Lisbon were keen to prevent the internationalization of trade that had characterized the ports of Loango and
Cabinda, to the north of the Congo River and to deter this, they built the fortress of Novo Redondo. In between Luanda and Benguela, this fortress was
built to establish Portuguese occupation of the coast and to prevent English
and French merchants from landing.[46] However, these measures were not
wholly successful. In the 1760s and 1770s, English interlopers were present in
the region of Benguela buying slaves. Moreover, some of the slaves employed
in the French colonies in the Caribbean at the end of eighteenth century were
also acquired in Benguela, probably by French merchants.[47] On November,
1785, Navy lieutenant António José Valente reported,

> This town [Benguela] looks more French than Portuguese. From July 8 to
> August 4, four different French vessels anchored in Benguela harbour.
> As soon as they arrived, the crew landed and the officers visited the gov-
> ernor in his house; the town then was under the influence of the officials
> and their sailors who walked freely across the town, day and night, as

44   See: Mariana Candido, "Transatlantic Links: The Benguela-Bahia Connections, 1700–1850,"
      in Ana Lúcia Araújo, ed., *Paths of the Atlantic Slave Trade. Interactions, Identities, and
      Images* (Amherst, NY: Cambria Press, 2011), 234–272.

45   Instituto Histórico Geográfico Brasileiro (hereafter IHGB), DL 32, 02.01: 1798: 'Relação dos
      sobas potentados, souvetas seus vassalos e sobas agregados pelos nomes das suas terras,
      que tem na capitania de Benguela', fls. 5v–6.

46   For Loango and Cabinda, see: Susan Herlin, "Brazil and the Commercialization of Kongo,"
      in José Curto and Paul Lovejoy, eds., *Enslaving Connections: Changing Cultures of Africa
      and Brazil during the Era of Slavery* (Amherst, NY: Humanity Books, 2004); Phyllis Martin,
      The External Trade of the Loango Coast, 1576–1870 (Oxford: Clarendon Press, 1972);
      Roquinaldo Ferreira, "Dos Sertões ao Atlântico: Tráfico Ilegal de Escravos e Comércio
      Lícito em Angola, 1830–1860" (unpublished MA diss., Universidade Federal do Rio de
      Janeiro, 1996). On the visits of French and English traders to the coast see: AHU, *Angola*, cx.
      59, doc. 29: 1769-05-16; cx. 59, doc. 44: 1769-08-01; cx. 59, doc. 57: 1769-09-06; cx. 59, doc. 73:
      1769-11-28; cx. 61, doc. 14: 1776-05-14; cx. 61, doc. 18: 1776-06-17; cx. 123, doc. 67: 1811-12-22.

47   Miller, "Central Africa during the era of the slave trade," 29.

comfortable as our Portuguese men. ...The first of the four ships stayed
anchored for 17 days, and embarked more than 700 slaves, and lots
of ivory.[48]

The scale of the trade in Benguela, as well as its risks and distance from Lisbon
and Luanda invited merchants to stray outside of loyalty to the state. Within a
trading empire characterized by commercial flexibility, traders from Portugal
joined forces with merchants from other places to reinforce their position in
the market and expand profits.[49] While this could be seen as a betrayal of loyalty to the homeland, merchants were able to create a web of trade connections in the Atlantic that surpassed state, language or religious allegiance.[50]
Remoteness favoured the emergence of Benguela as an iconic place where
trade was in great part multinational and decentralized, an outcome not necessarily welcome to the authorities in Lisbon.[51] While it seemed logical to merchants to strengthen commercial links with those of different national origins,
the empire and its agents understood such behaviour as corrupt and parasitical
and urged control over such trade operations. Administrators in Luanda complained on numerous occasions about the behaviour of Benguela administrators. In 1790, the Governor of Angola José de Almeida e Vasconcelos (1790–1797),
also known as the first Barão de Mossâmedes, declared that smuggling was

immense throughout the town [of Benguela] and its surrounding
area, provoking severe losses to the crown's share of tribute,...the French

---

48   AHU, *Angola*, cx. 70, doc. 56: 1785-11-11.
49   Russell-Wood, *Portuguese Empire*, 95–96.
50   For scholarship that emphasizes the multicultural and multinational trade relationships
     in the early Atlantic economy see: Daviken Studnicki-Gizbert, *A Nation Upon the Ocean
     Sea. Portugal's Atlantic Diaspora and the Crisis of the Spanish Empire, 1492–1640* (Oxford:
     Oxford University Press, 2007), 41–66; see also his "La *Nacion* among the Nations.
     Portuguese and Other Maritime Trading Diasporas in the Atlantic, Sixteenth to Eighteenth
     Centuries," in Richard L. Kagan and Philip Morgan, eds., *Atlantic Diasporas. Jews,
     Conversos, and Crypto-Jews in the Age of Mercantilism, 1500–1800* (Baltimore, MD: Johns
     Hopkins University Press, 2009), 75–98; Francesca Trivellato, "Juifs de Livourne, Italiens
     de Lisbonne, Hindous de Goa: Reseaux Marchands et Échanges Interculturels a l'Époque
     Moderne," *Annales* 58 (2003): 581–603; and Christopher Ebert, *Between Empires: Brazilian
     Sugar in the Early Atlantic Economy, 1550–1630* (Leiden: Brill, 2008).
51   For a similar case see: David Hancock, "The Emergence of an Atlantic Network Economy
     in the 17th and 18th Centuries: The Case of Madeira," in Diogo R. Curto and Anthony
     Molho, eds., *Commercial Networks in the Early Modern World* (Florence: European
     University Institute, 2002), 23–24.

vessels harbour in the town under cover of excuses, such as a need for ship repair, and clandestinely slaves are purchased from local sellers during the night. After this, the vessel quickly sails.[52]

In Benguela, the merchants and authorities contested Crown attempts to impose control over trade. European interlopers had participated in the trade between Portugal and ports in Africa since the early seventeenth century, and Benguela was no exception.[53]

The size of the merchant community in Benguela varied, in part because it was decentralized and crossed imperial boundaries, attracting merchants from Brazil, Portugal, France and Holland. Cooperation between merchants from different states and imperial systems favoured trade expansion, overcoming barriers that might have existed to prevent commerce. Restrictions in the transport sector precluded the official involvement of French and Dutch traders, for example, but their alliance with Portuguese-born merchants allowed their involvement in commerce in Benguela.

During the nineteenth century, changes in the transatlantic slave trade and its eventual prohibition forced the reorganization of the merchants established in the port of Benguela. After the 1826 treaty signed between the British and Brazilian government, Governor Aurélio de Oliveira warned that Benguela merchants would probably react negatively. According to him, news that the export of slaves was close to an end would result in protests and uprisings inland. It could also incite violence in the hinterland and lead to the murder of itinerant traders. He also feared for the safety of the settlement in Benguela. Some *sobas*, or African rulers, had suggested that "if your majesty is not interested in slaves anymore, you should leave these lands to other nations interested in buying slaves."[54] In fact, the 1826 treaty did not alter the slave trade in Benguela. Slave merchants continued to operate with relative freedom, among them José Luís da Silva Viana and Manuel António Teixeira Barbosa, who bought and sold slaves until the mid-nineteenth century.[55] Slave exports only came to an end in 1850 with the closure of the Brazilian market.

---

52   AHU, *Angola*, cx. 75, doc. 35: 1790-08-15. For the conflict between merchants and administration over trade see: Studnicki-Gizbert, *A Nation Upon the Ocean Sea*, 12.

53   Leonor Freire Costa, *O Transporte no Atlântico e a Companhia Geral do Comércio do Brasil (1580–1663)* (Lisboa: Comissão Nacional para as Comemorações dos Descobrimentos Portugueses, 2002), 1: 116–122.

54   AHU, *Angola*, cx. 164, doc. 75: 1829-12-01.

55   Maria Emília Madeira Santos, *Viagens e Apontamentos de um Portuense em África: Diário de Silva Porto* (Coimbra: Biblioteca Geral de Coimbra, 1986), 62.

The Role of African Women in the Local Trade Networks

The expansion of the transatlantic slave trade brought more African intermediaries into the network and into Benguela. Auxiliary tasks, such as food vending and porterage, expanded. Although not directly linked to the slave trade, washers, tailors, and street vendors profited from the urban expansion linked to the slave trade, and offered services for the temporary residents.[56] As in other African ports, such as Lagos, Luanda, Cape Town, and Ouidah, foreign traders relied on the work provided by locals to feed themselves and run the town.[57]

Many of the foreign merchants and colonial officials maintained relationships with local women. Some of these women were local Nbombe who lived in Benguela, were already acculturated to the colonial settlement, were able to speak Portuguese and were well connected to trade networks. Others were relatives of African rulers interested in strengthening the contact with the Atlantic economy. Temporary or long-term relationships prompted the formation of groups of descendants of foreign men and local women, who maintained and reinforced good relations between the colonial town and the different neighbouring states. As a result of their involvement with Portuguese and Brazilian men, women could acquire wealth, becoming known as "*donas.*" Like the *signares* of St. Louis or Gorée, the *donas* of Benguela participated in a wide variety of commercial activities, from slave trading to clothes manufacturing.[58]

---

56   Maria Luisa Esteves, "Para o Estudo do Tráfico de Escravos de Angola (1640–1668)," *Studia* 50 (1991): 84.

57   Kristin Mann, *Slavery and the Birth of an African City: Lagos, 1760–1900* (Bloomington, IN: Indiana University Press, 2007); José C. Curto and Raymond Gervais, "The Population History of Luanda during the late Atlantic Slave Trade, 1781–1844," *African Economic History* 29 (2001): 1–59; Law, *Ouidah*; Wayne Dooling, *Slavery, Emancipation and Colonial Rule in South Africa* (Athens, OH: Ohio University Press, 2007); Harvey M. Feinberg, *Africans and Europeans in West Africa: Elminans and Dutchmen on the Gold Coast during the Eighteenth Century* (Philadelphia, PA: American Philosophical Society, 1989), 29.

58   George E. Brooks, "A Nhara of the Guine-Bissau Region: Mãe Aurélia Correia," in Claire C. Robertson and Martin A. Klein, eds., *Women and Slavery in Africa* (Portsmouth, NH: Heinemann, 1997), 295–317; Searing, *West African Slavery*, 113–114; Philip J. Havik, "Comerciantes e Concubinas: Sócios estratégicos no Comércio Atlântico na Costa da Guiné," in *Il Reunião Internacional de História da África* (São Paulo: CEA-USP/SDG-Marinha/CAPES, 1996), 161–179; Larry Yarak, "West African Coastal Slavery in the 19th Century: The Case of the Afro-European Slaveowners of Elmina," *Ethnohistory* 36:1 (1989): 44–60; Lillian Ashcraft-Eason, "'She Voluntarily Hath Come': A Gambian Woman Trader in Colonial Georgia in the 18th Century," in Paul E. Lovejoy, ed., *Identity in the Shadow of Slavery* (New York, NY: Continuum, 2000), 202–221.

As slave owners themselves, they had access to internal markets and could act as independent traders or in partnerships with foreign men. Whether or not they actually married, women attached to foreign men often became "widows" after their deaths. As such, they assumed an ongoing relationship to the deceased partner and claimed part of his inheritance, regardless of whether or not they had born children. In the 1770s, Governor D. Francisco Inocêncio de Sousa Coutinho (1764–1772) commented that many women were widows for the fifth time in Angola.[59] Because of inheritance and strategic partnerships, many women became economically influential, which was recognized in their identity as *donas*. By the early eighteenth century, the offspring of these unions referred to themselves as Portuguese and were identified in Portuguese documents as *filhos da terra* (or sons of the land). This was similar to what happened to Portuguese descendants in other African ports.[60]

Donas and *filhos da terra* became intermediaries *par excellence* between Portuguese and African cultures. Building upon their connections to elites in the interior, they provided commercial contacts to coastal merchants. Eventually they established themselves as traders and mediated the adaptation of African societies to the requirements and domination of the international trade.[61] This was the case of *dona* Ana Aranha. In the 1797 nominal list of Caconda's residents, she was identified as a widow. Ana Aranha lived in the fortress of Caconda. In her compound lived 182 free people and 84 slaves (21 men, 36 women, 14 boys and 13 girls). Most of the free individuals who lived in her property were women, who probably worked in her fields cultivating wheat, corn and beans, which were likely sold to the caravans passing by the fortress.[62] The commerce in provisions addressed a constant need for foodstuff in the port town. *Dona* Aranha also acted as a slave trader or *pombeiro* in her own right. She brought slaves from the interior to the coast and probably moved imported goods inland. In her caravans, she directly controlled the transport operation and managed the porters and guards who protected the

---

59   AHU, *Angola*, cx. 54, doc. 20: 1770-03-15. For more on partnerships between European men and African women see also: Russell-Wood, *The Portuguese Empire*, 96; Searing, *West African Slavery*, 94–98; Brooks, *Eurafricans in Western Africa*.

60   Mark, *"Portuguese" Style*, 14–15. Russell-Wood shows how Portuguese descendents in different parts of the world identified themselves as Portuguese and Catholics; see his: *The Portuguese Empire*, 63–64.

61   Law, *Ouidah*, 6–7 and 126–138.

62   IHGB, DL 31,05: 1797-12-31: 'Relação feita por João da Costa Frade, do Presídio de Caconda em Benguela, sobre moradores, escravos, forros, mantimentos e gados existentes no presídio'.

caravans.[63] Traders like *dona* Aranha were under the protection of African rulers and Portuguese administrators, as these were the people who could protect them and their caravans while crossing the interior.

Donas visited inland markets controlled by African states. By 1811, *dona* Leonor de Carvalho Fonseca was visiting the Mbailundu state, probably to collect debts that local traders had with her deceased husband.[64] Evidence suggests that *dona* Aranha and *dona* Leonor controlled their businesses alone after the death of their husbands, accumulating slaves and textiles. Other women acted in partnerships with their husbands, such as Lourença Santos, a 45-year-old mulatto resident in Caconda in 1797. *Dona* Lourença was married to Joaquim da Silva, a trader based in Luanda. Living inland, *dona* Lourença probably acquired slaves and sent them to Luanda. She was also one of the most powerful residents in the fortress, with large numbers of dependents who produced corn and raised cattle.[65] An association with a powerful woman, who lived inland, offered Joaquim da Silva a chance to rely on a trusted partner who could buy and sell on his behalf, without necessarily relying on credit to trade. Local women acted as translators and caravan leaders and represented the interests of foreign traders in the hinterland.

In Benguela, many of the *donas* were the head of the household, partly because of high mortality rates, but also because of the mobility of the coastal traders, who lived in different places of the Atlantic world.[66] *Dona* Aguida Gonçalves, for example, lived in a two-storey house in Benguela. She owned a tavern where traders and authorities gathered to buy and sell slaves and to organize caravans.[67] *Dona* Aguida hosted numerous dependents, including her daughter, a nephew and his wife, and António Lobo Viana, a carpenter. In addition there were eight young black female dependents who were seamstress' apprentices. Besides these, there were two male slaves, a tailor, a bricklayer, and 10 female slaves.[68] *Dona* Aguida Gonçalves counted on several skilled

63   AHNA, cód. 443, fls. 108-108v: 1802-03-23; fl. 109: 1802-04-23; fl. 109v: 1802-06-15.

64   AHNA, cód. 323, fls. 28v-29: 1811-08-19; fls. 30v-31: 1811-08-20.

65   IHGB, DL 31, 05, fls. 4v-5: 1797-12-31.

66   For the mobility of merchants in the Portuguese empire see: Daviken Studnicki-Gizbert, "La 'Nation' Portuguaise. Réseaux Marchands dans l'Espace Atlantique à l'Époque Moderne," *Annales* 58:3 (2003): 627–648.

67   AHU, *Angola*, cx. 42, doc. 88: 1759-10-30.

68   IHGB, DL 32, 02.02: 1797-11-20: 'Relação de Manuel José de Silveira Teixeira sobre os moradores da cidade de São Felipe de Benguela separados por raça, idade, emprego, título de habitação, ofícios mecânicos e quantos mestres e aprendizes existem', fls. 8v-9.

labourers, especially tailors and seamstresses, who could sew clothes and sell them to a population of less than 3,000 people. *Dona* Gonçalves' ability to train and gather skilled labourers allowed her to dominate certain economic activities. In her case, it was needlework. African women who maintained stable relationships with foreign traders could carry their business even further after they became commercial partners. The goods manufactured or produced in Benguela under their supervision could be sent to the interior to be exchanged for slaves. Households became small industries, where free people and slaves worked side by side in order to increase production.[69]

The *donas* in Benguela exhibited their material wealth and commercial influence in a similar fashion to the *signares* in the Senegambia region. They lived in urban centres and had large numbers of captives and dependents. From their liaisons with foreign traders, *donas* had easier access to imported goods, including textiles and alcohol, which in turn gave them a commercial advantage in their trading enterprises. Like other merchants, their family and social relationships were focused towards benefitting their economic interests, maximizing profits, social connections and personal wealth.[70] Their access to transatlantic networks was maintained even after the death of their partners. In exchange they offered connections, company and attention to foreign traders. They took care of sick partners, cooked, carried on business operations into the interior and raise descendants who could continue to expand the family activities. Since they were commercial partners and not employees of the foreign traders, they enjoyed flexibility and autonomy in administering businesses. They had space to negotiate profits, prices, and costs of transport, and shared the responsibility of operations with their partners. They also maintained businesses while the men were away. Like other merchant women in colonial frontiers, the *donas* of Benguela played a crucial role as culture-brokers between indigenous populations and European traders.[71]

Caconda and the Commercial Network in the Central Highlands

From the first half of the seventeenth century, Portuguese authorities tried to control the slave trade coming from the Benguela highlands. The resistance of

---

69   Philip Havik, "Women and Trade in the Guinea Bissau Region," *Studia* 52 (1994): 103.

70   For similarities with Portuguese merchants see: Studnicki-Gizbert, "La 'Nation' Portugaise," 630.

71   Brooks, "A Nhara of Guine-Bissau," 296. For other cases in the Atlantic world, see: Jennifer L. Morgan, "'Some Could Suckle over Their Shoulder': Male Travelers, Female Bodies, and the Gendering of Racial Ideology, 1500–1770," *William and Mary Quarterly* 54:1 (1997): 167–192.

the rulers of Matamba and Kasanje in providing slaves to Portuguese merchants created difficulties and caused the latter to search for new markets. The solution was to establish a political and commercial alliance with the small polity of Kakonda, on the outskirts of the Benguela central plateau, whose ruler controlled the trade in slaves.[72]

In 1684, Portuguese forces established a settlement in the lands of the ruler of Bongo. Located in fertile land, the place was ideal for the Portuguese Crown to expand its territorial conquest. However, the ruler of Bongo resisted the colonial settlement, and gathering his forces attacked and destroyed it.[73] Initially located in the lands of the Hanya, its location was "in the worst place in the world," according to Governor Sousa Coutinho. Hence, decades after the destruction of the first Caconda, he decided to transfer it to a location further east to the region of Katala,[74]

> ...a few days away from its previous place. ...[T]he artillery, ammunition, and troops were transferred to the new location between the months of January and July, by the end of which the *presídio* already had a fence of pole and mud, a church, and a treasury.

He hoped that "the quality of the air and lands, and the abundance of cattle would transform it into a populous village."[75]

By the end of the eighteenth century, Caconda had become an important commercial *entrepôt* on the fringes of the densely populated central highlands. By the mid-nineteenth century, the fortress comprised an estimated area of 44.4 kilometers by 28 kilometers.[76] Caconda linked the coast to internal trade routes, along which *pombeiros* ventured through the highlands to obtain slaves, ivory, and cattle. The fortress also connected Benguela to the inland states of Ngalenge, Mbailundu, and Viye, among others.[77] By the end of the eighteenth

---

72   Delgado, *Reino de Benguela*, 120–122. Kakonda refers to the African ruler and his settlement, while its Portuguese version, Caconda, refers to the Portuguese *presídio*. See: Rosa Cruz e Silva, "Saga of Kakonda and Kilengues: Relations between Benguela and Its Interior, 1791–1796," in Curto and Lovejoy, eds., *Enslaving Connections*, 245–259.

73   Delgado, *Ao Sul do Cuanza*, I: 230–231. Luiz Alfredo Keiling, *Quarenta Anos de África* (Braga: Edição das Missões de Angola e Congo, 1934), 9; Miller, "Angola Central e Sul," 23.

74   Biblioteca Nacional de Portugal (BNP), *Reservados*, cód. 8553, fls. 92–92v: 1768-08-14.

75   AHU, *Angola*, cx. 53, doc. 71: 1769-10-18.

76   Eduardo Balsemão, "Concelho de Caconda," *Annaes do Conselho Ultramarino*, third series, (1862): 47; Delgado, *Ao Sul do Cuanza*, 1: 241.

77   Balsemão, "Concelho de Caconda," 48; João Francisco, "Explorações do sertão de Benguela. Derrota que fez o tenente de artilharia João Francisco Garcia," *Annaes Marítimos e Coloniaes*,

century, there were 17 white, 54 mulatto and 44 black residents in Caconda
Most of them engaged in trade and held official positions They included
António José Rodrigues, a white trader who lived in a compound with his son
and 300 dependents, including 19 slave men, 29 slave women and 32 slave children. Rodrigues was clearly an important trader who was also responsible for
the production of foodstuffs and raising cattle.[78] Other traders lived around
the fortresses, though not necessarily under Portuguese control. Among them
was the Luso-African trader Pedro Joaquim Ignácio, who lived in the territory
of Kamburo. Francisco António da Glória lived under the control of the *soba* of
Kitata, and Jorge do Porto Ribeiro in Kalukembe. These traders opted to live
apart from the colonial settlement, residing among the "heathens without
respecting the law and regulations," although they clearly maintained commercial links to the port of Benguela.[79]

In the territory of Mbailundu, a Portuguese colonial official was appointed
to regulate trade and provide direct communication between the governor in
Benguela and the ruler of Mbailundu. By 1797, he made an inventory of the
traders who lived under the *soba* control. Manoel José da Costa Arouca,
Francisco José Cordeiro and Manoel A. Sá were the only white traders established in Mbailundu by then, and they probably already had established families, since Arouca was listed with two children and Cordeiro with one. There is
no mention of the names of the mothers, but their children were identified as
mulatto, indicating an African mother.[80] João da Costa Arouca was 10 years old
while Estevão José Cordeiro was 12 years old. Most of the other traders were
listed as black or mulatto.

Markets operated in the highlands independently of the Portuguese fortress
in territories controlled by African rulers. The origin of the trade among highland states was probably linked to the exchange of grains, salt, cattle and other
foodstuffs. Later, Viye, Mbailundu, and Wambu prospered by exchanging textiles, alcohol and other commodities obtained from coastal networks through
the sale of slaves. By 1797, the ruler of Viye wrapped his lower body with

---

fourth series, 6 (1844): 252; Deolinda Barrocas and Maria de Jesus Sousa, "As populações
do hinterland the Benguela e a passagem das caravanas comerciais (1846–1860)," in *II
Reunião Internacional de História da África* (São Paulo/Rio de Janeiro: CEA/USP/SDG
Marinha, 1997), 96–98. See also: Candido, "Trade, Slavery and Migration," 70–75.

78   IHGB, DL 31, 05: 1798: 'Notícias do Presídio de Caconda em Benguela', fls. 3v–4.

79   IHGB, DL 31, 05: 1797-12-31: fl. 10.

80   IHGB, DL 32, 02.05: 1798: 'Relação de António José Fernandes, capitão-mor, a Alexandre
José Botelho de Vasconcelos, governador de Benguela, dos moradores e de seus filhos
desta província (Bailundo)', fl. 35.

imported textiles. He also wore imported trousers, jackets and shirts. His wife dressed in a loose dress made of cotton textiles. Both wore leather belts and remained barefoot.[81] Imported commodities changed highland fashion style and drinking habits. In the 1860s, Silva Porto reported that the *soba* of Kipata kept requesting "*aguardente* to heal his throat. The old *soba* has [his throat] already burnt [by the firewater], and the alcohol does not affect him anyone. One day he will not wake up."[82] The adoption of trousers, shoes, and alcohol distilled from cane sugar demonstrated how regions far from the coast were integrated in the Atlantic economy.

Inland states had their own markets that could attract thousands of people from surrounding areas. In 1771, the Captain of Caconda, José António Nogueira, reported that the *soba* of Humbe did not allow itinerant traders into his market. Afraid of coastal traders, he forbade the entrance of white merchants or their agents into Humbe.[83] In the 1820s, the *soba* of Viye controlled a market in his territory. He allowed the presence of *pombeiros*, but set prices, imposed taxes, and sold his own slaves. The market was in a square surrounded by houses and shops built by Luso-African traders, who exchanged imported goods for slaves held in storehouses.[84] Slaves acquired in the inland markets were lined up in coffles and forced to walk long journeys to the coast. They carried commodities acquired by the *pombeiros* inland. These included beeswax, gum-copal, and ivory tusks.[85] While slaves could walk to the coast, goods had to be transported by free or enslaved porters in caravans that linked the hinterland of Benguela to the Atlantic coast. Thus, imported goods reached people who lived miles away from the coast, and were not necessarily directly involved in the transatlantic slave trade. The commercial networks that crossed Benguela linked merchants in Lisbon, Porto, Rio de Janeiro and Luanda, as well as those located in the inland markets of Viye or Mbailundu.

---

81   IHGB, DL 29, 17: 1797: 'Notícia Geral dos Costumes da Província de Bihé, em Benguela, por João Napomuceno Correia, 1797', fl. 9.

82   Biblioteca da Sociedade de Geografia de Lisboa (hereafter BSGL), Res 2-C 6, vol. 2: 1861-05-12.

83   IHGB, DL 81, 02.18: 1771-06-22: 'Carta do capitão-mor José António Nogueira dirigida a um general, pedindo ajuda para guerrear contra o Soba do Humbe, que impede os negros de buscarem marfim e cera para comercializar', fls. 9–9v.

84   J.B. Douville, *Voyage au Congo et dans l'interieus de l'Afrique Equinoxiale, fait dans les années 1828, 1829, 1830* (Paris: Jules Renouard, 1832), 2: 121–122.

85   IHGB, DL 81, 02.20: 1772-01-15: 'Carta do capitão-mor José António Nogueira dirigida a um general, pedindo ajuda para guerrear contra o Soba do Humbe, que impede os negros de buscarem marfim e cera para comercializar', fls. 62–63.

Conclusion

The slave trade at Benguela was an Atlantic enterprise. Foreign traders provided the credit for the slave trade of Benguela, but also organized the commerce along the coast. Credit moved the commerce and linked elites on both sides of the Atlantic. Most of the commodities imported to Benguela were items to supply the demands of the slave trade. They included textiles, alcohol and gunpowder.

The local population relocated to Benguela and to the Portuguese fortress inland to profit from the Atlantic commerce. Commerce was transformed in the region. New merchant groups arose, among them the *pombeiros*. New trade elites also emerged. *Donas* (or powerful local women) acquired wealth and prestige from their association with transatlantic merchants. They assumed control of economic activities such as food production, textile manufacturing and the sale of foodstuffs. *Filhos da terra* and *donas* operated both near the coast and inland. They were a new and unprecedented element in West-Central Africa. It is not clear how their acquisition of wealth was perceived by African commercial elites inland. Intermediaries between coastal traders and inland markets, Luso-African traders adopted western dress styles and helped to spread new consumption patterns.

The transatlantic slave trade connected people who lived miles away from the coast to the Atlantic. The daily lifestyle of the population changed as part of the widespread consumption of imported goods. New forms of alcoholic beverage, food tastes, and fashion styles were developed. Away from the coast, African rulers and their subjects increased raids and warfare to generate more captives. Addictions to imported commodities eventually led to political instability and social change.

CHAPTER 6

Slave Trade Networks in Eighteenth-Century Mozambique

José Capela

In the eighteenth century, the commercial relationships dominating the slave trade in Mozambique's ports were as much the continuation of ancestral relationships as of those created throughout the century itself. The former were already in force when the Portuguese arrived in the region at the end of the fifteenth century. The Oman Arabs had dominated the coast since the tenth century, after the first Muslims from the Gulf had done the same. Interracial relationships between Arabs and local people, in turn, gave rise to the Swahili civilization on this coast.[1] Although much remains unknown about the history of the coast, it is clear that regular slave trading took place between it and the Indian Ocean. This commerce, in which the key players were *mujojos* (or Swahili traders), would continue until the early years of the twentieth century, mainly involving the Gulf, but also Zanzibar, the Comoros and Madagascar. Whilst prior to the sixteenth century this traffic had not reached as far as Indian ports, thereafter the Portuguese started to promote it quite regularly. Ships bound to India and departing annually from Lisbon embarked slaves for Goa in Mozambique. The same vessels also made the return journey with a large number of slaves, including slaves from Goa and Mozambique's ports. These were taken where?

The French initiated and sustained another branch of the slave trade in this region. Heading initially to the Mascarene Islands, French trafficking in slaves became systematic in the second half of the eighteenth century and continued until the following century, when large numbers of slaves were sent to the French colonies in the Antilles. By that stage another new slave circuit had arisen that started in Brazil and linked Mozambique with Brazil and Spanish America. This traffic would continue until the mid-nineteenth century. Simultaneously, and to guarantee slave supply for this commerce, port-to-port navigation was carried out between smaller ports and Mozambique's port, which was intended to be the centre of all slave exportation. Map 6.1 shows Mozambique's ports and the hinterlands they served in the eighteenth century.

---

1 Auguste Toussaint, *L'Océan Indien au XVIII* siècle* (Paris: Flamarion, 1974), 41.

MAP 6.1   *Mozambique – eighteenth century*
          Author: José Capela, 2014

Slave Trade to the Indian Ocean

At the end of 1498, as Vasco da Gama sailed to India, he encountered traders both in the River of the Bons Sinais and on the island of Mozambique. Their appearance surprised him. Until then he had only found "black barbarians." Between there and Malindi, on the Kenyan coast, he would learn about how long-distance trade was carried out on that coast.[2] The Portuguese who succeeded him in Indian Ocean exploration found forms of slave trading of which they could take advantage. They involved slave supply for the navy.[3] They also provided slaves for domestic service within the region.[4] Between May 1510 and November 1512, more than 600 slaves were sold at the port of Sofala, which by then was under Portuguese rule.[5] This provided a continuing source of slaves for export, which had existed there from a long time before. In the 1540s ships were sent from Cochim to the islands of Mozambique and São Lourenço to buy slaves.[6] The Portuguese settled into and continued the commerce which was already established there.

A lack of documentation prevents us from demonstrating the probable long-term continuity of slave trafficking from ports in southeast Africa and within the Indian Ocean basin, but its omnipresence throughout the eighteenth century is indisputable. In 1754 dhows of Swahili traders travelled from Mombasa and Pate to the Quirimbas Islands to load up with slaves.[7] Quirimbas is the name given to a small number of islands, 55 *léguas*[8] north of Mozambique and immediately south of Cape Delgado. The islands had a good port on the island of Ibo, which was much used by slave traders.[9] Towards the end of the eighteenth century, *mujojos* were assiduous visitors, playing a significant role in the Cape Delgado Islands where they would go inland to kidnap and enslave people to be sold to the French at Kilwa.[10] Kilwa's links to long-distance slave trading in both the Indian and Atlantic Oceans is illustrated in a number of

---

2   João de Barros, *Décadas* (Lisboa: Livraria Sá da Costa Editora, 1982), 1: 22.

3   *Documentos sobre os portugueses em Moçambique e na África Central 1497–1840* (Lisboa: National Archives of Rhodesia and Nyassaland and Centro de Estudos Históricos Ultramarinos, 1963), 2: 100.

4   *Documentos sobre os portugueses*, 5: 412.

5   Eduardo Correia Lopes, *A Escravatura: subsídios para a sua história* (Lisboa: Agência Geral das Colónias, 1944), 32.

6   IAN/TT, *Corpo Cronológico*, part 1, mç. 66, doc. 78: 1540-01-07: 'Carta de Bartholomeo Pires a El-Rei'.

7   Edward A. Alpers, *Ivory & Slaves in East Central Africa* (London: Heinemann, 1975), 132.

8   Old measurement for distance and length in used throughout the entire early modern period in Iberia and the Spanish and Portuguese overseas empires. 1 *légua* equalled circa 4.2 kilometres and circa 2.5 miles.

9   Toussaint, *L'Océan Indien*, 36.

10   AHU, *Moçambique*, cx. 61, doc. 36: 1790-11-08: 'Carta do comandante das Ilhas de Cabo Delgado para o governador-geral'.

ways.[11] The sheik of Quitangonha, close to the Bay of Fernão Veloso, admitted to having personally captured slaves from local residents to be exported.[12] The local commander authorized the sale of slaves from farms to six 'Moorish' (or Arab) dhows from the Anjoane Islands, on condition that Christian slaves would not be sold and that they would pay the rates required by Mozambique customs.[10]

Who were the *mujojos*? It is a term that appears most frequently in records from the nineteenth century, and which is used even today to identify a small group of Swahilis who live in the Mafalala area of Maputo. Judging by eighteenth-century documentation, *mujojos* were Swahili traders raised in the Comores and Madagascar, and who operated in that part of the Indian Ocean. Azevedo Coutinho refers to Catamoio as the "*mujojo* capital of the island of Angoche" and to the "noble families from whom *mujojos* of Angoche are pure Arab descendants."[14] A governor-general of the colony described the *mujojos* who arrived at the Island of Mozambique from different foreign ports as "dark Moors, vagabonds, jobless, surviving by stealing slaves which they sold to other *mujujos* for further general trafficking."[15] Everything leads us to believe that the *mujojos*' activities in southeast Africa intensified with the growth of slave trade in the region during the second half of the eighteenth century. This extended to the supply of slaves to new long-distance routes, notably across the Atlantic.

The increasing frequency of slave trading in the Island of Mozambique port created local problems, especially a shortage of rice, a commodity which *mujojos* began to supply. Payment was made in gold and silver coins. It soon came about that the customs authorities stopped charging import duties for slaves brought to Mozambique by the *mujojo* dhows because the *mujojos* had become their main suppliers.[16] Before this, rice and other goods were supplied from Quelimane port and payment was made with cloth. It was a trade from which *mujojos* had been excluded. At the same time, the *mulales*, inhabitants of the Comoros Islands who were mistaken for *mujojos*, provided other types

---

11   AHU, *Moçambique,* cx. 87, doc. 10: 1801-01-21: 'Carta de António da Silva Pinto para o governador-geral, Ibo'.

12   Nancy Jane Hafkin, 'Trade, Society and Politics in Northern Mozambique, c. 1753–1913' (unpublished PhD diss., Boston University Graduate School, 1973), 97–98.

13   AHU, *Moçambique,* cx. 134, doc. 194: 1810-12-28: 'Carta do comandante das Ilhas de Cabo Delgado para o governador-geral'.

14   João de Azevedo Coutinho, *Memórias de Um Velho Marinheiro e Soldado de África* (Lisboa: Livraria Bertrand, 1941), 470.

15   AHU, *Moçambique,* sala 12, pasta 5, doc. 2: 1840-09-24: 'Relatório em resumo do estado em que se achava Moçambique em Março de 1840, por Joaquim Pereira Marinho'.

16   AHU, *Moçambique,* cx. 166, doc. 54: 1810-11-19: 'Apontamento do governador-geral'.

of food exclusively for slaves. These food supplies were very cheap and paid for with goods from Europe and Asia rather than with money.[17] Rice, however, continued to be the main food source. When this was scarce, two dhows from Mombasa were employed to import it, the rice being exchanged for slaves of low value and who could not be sold to Europeans.[18] This pattern of activity was evident by the second decade of the nineteenth century when the *mujojos* had already settled on the Island of Ibo and were "introducing their doctrine to the people."[19] By then there was a myriad of dhows sailing constantly from the Arabian coast and the Red Sea, going to Madagascar and doing business in all the ports in that part of the Indian Ocean. This trade was controlled and slaves made up a large part of it. It would reach huge proportions, if not in the eighteenth century, then definitely in the first part of the following century. As one contemporary remarked:

> Throughout the year, Mozambique's port is more or less full of dhows as well as caiques from the Algarve, Moors and Arabs from the north who bring corn, rice, dates, coconut oil, contraband gunpowder, mats, some cattle, preserved meat, slaves and other goods, from Arabia, Mombasa, Melinde, Kilwa, the Comoros Islands, the Anjoanes, Madagascar and many other ports along the coast [...] a true cabotage in full action. These Moors leave their ports, which are normally on the Arabian Red Sea coast.[20]

For the Governor of Mozambique in 1825–1829, Sebastião José Botelho, the great smuggling trade was carried out by residents of Madagascar, Arabs from Zanzibar, and dominated by the Imam of Muscat. He observed that

> along the whole of the East African coast to Zanzibar...there are thousands of coastal ships (dhows), which trade from one port to another during every monsoon, and even at the ports under our control...where they do not pay duties, they have an advantage over those who pay them.[21]

---

17   Francisco Santana, *Documentação Avulsa Moçambicana do Arquivo Histórico Ultramarino* (Lisboa: Centro de Estudos Históricos Ultramarinos, 1967), II: 338.
18   AHU, *Moçambique*, cx. 168, doc. 10: 1820-03-08.
19   Santana, *Documentação Avulsa*, I: 843.
20   "Frei Bartolomeo dos Mártires," in Virginia Rau, *Aspectos Étnico-Culturais da Ilha de Moçambique em 1822* (Lisboa: Centro de Estudos Históricos Ultramarinos, 1963), 152 (offprint: *Studia* 11 (1963): 123–162).
21   Arquivo Histórico de Moçambique (hereafter AHM), *Secção especial*, no. 225: 'Copiador de correspondência, Sebastião Xavier Botelho'.

The presence of *mujojos* both at the ports and inland gave them a key role in the growing slave trade, whether as captors, as suppliers, or as dealers at the ports. They would also become great promoters of the slave trade in the second half of the nineteenth century.[22] In 1830 the auditor-general (*ouvidor-geral*) and factor (*feitor*) of Mozambique's Customs House explained that it was becoming impossible to control the Arab ships called "dhows," whose names were unknown, both in that port and many others along the coast, which long distance ships could not reach and where there was no Portuguese authority at all. It would be this dominance of trade in the ports that would allow the strengthening and expansion of slave trading further inland into East African societies over time, including the nineteenth and the beginning of twentieth centuries.[23]

Portuguese Slave Trade to India and to the Atlantic Ocean

Once the Portuguese were established in India, ships from Portugal bound for India loaded slaves on the southeast African coast. This commerce was not limited to ships that made annual journeys from Portugal but was also carried out by ships trading regularly on circuits between India, namely Daman and Diu, and Mozambique.

At the end of the 1500s, Portuguese ships took on, at the Island of Mozambique, supplies of "kaffirs [i.e. slaves] which are sold cheaply there."[24] The same ships, on their return to Portugal, carried great numbers of these slaves home. On the galleon *São João*, shipwrecked at Natal in 1522, it was said that, once the important people had been landed ashore, "the best part of 500 people: 200 Portuguese and the rest slaves" remained on the ship. In another shipwreck, this time in 1554, 224 slaves were said to have managed to reach

---

22   Lieut. H.E. O'Neill, *The Mozambique and Nyassa Slave Trade* (London: British and Foreign Anti-Slavery Society, 1885).

23   AHU, *Moçambique,* sala 12, pasta 5, doc. 2: 1840-09-24: 'Relatório em resumo do estado em que se achava Moçambique em Março de 1840, por Joaquim Pereira Marinho'; cx. 61, doc. 36: 1790-11-08: 'Carta do comandante das Ilhas de Cabo Delgado para o governador-geral'. AHM, *Fundo da Administração Civil de Lourenço Marques,* secção A, diversos, cx. 3: 1902-05-15, Processo apresamento de pangaios em Naburi.

24   Frei João dos Santos, *Etiópia Oriental e Vária História de Cousas Notáveis do Oriente* (Lisboa: Comissão Nacional para as Comemorações dos Descobrimentos Portugueses, 1999), 258.

land.[25] The slaves on board were property of the passengers and crew.[26] Similar situations were reported in the seventeenth century.[27] In 1635, during the shipwreck of the *Nossa Senhora de Belém* off the coast of Natal, there is evidence that the slaves on board tried to save the ship.[28] Jan Huygen van Linschoten, who in 1583 travelled from Lisbon to Goa, where he stayed until 1588, described how, from Mozambique, as well as gold, brown amber, ebony and ivory, the caravels transported to India "many slave men and slave women [prized] for being the strongest in all the Orient, to do the dirtiest and toughest work." Establishing how slavery contributed to the domestic sector is difficult as, in Goa, there were Portuguese people who lived exclusively from the work of their slaves, and it was said, usually owned as many as 36 slaves. The slave men dedicated themselves to a wide range of tasks including selling water in the streets, and the slave women to sewing lace and knitting, as well as to prostitution.[29]

In the late sixteenth century, an attentive eyewitness reports how the Portuguese royal fleets bound for India loaded African blackwood, food and kaffirs [i.e. slaves] sold on the Island of Mozambique. A "large number of slaves" were also to be found on the Island of Inhaca, at Cape Correntes and at Inhambane, Sofala, and the Cuama (present-day Zambezi) and Ibo rivers.[30] The instructions of the King to the Viceroy of India in 1628 show that slaves were a habitual part of supplies from India, as in referring to the cargo, they noted "pepper and bands of men to load the ships."[31]

If the ships sailing in the *Carreira da Índia* were regularly used for the transport for slaves, this was just a fortunate byproduct of a shipping route which

---

25 Bernardo Gomes de Brito, ed., *História Trágico-Marítima, Relação da muy notável perda do Galeão Grande «São João»* [...] *a 24 de Junho de 1552 e Relação sumaria da viagem que fez Fernão d'Alvares Cabral, desde que partiu deste reino por capitão-mor da armada que foi no ano de 1553 às partes da Índia* (Lisboa: Off. da Congregação do Oratório, 1735–1736), 2 vols.; Eric Axelson, *Portuguese in South East Africa 1488–1600* (Johannesburg: Witewatersrand University Press, 1973), 205.

26 Artur Teodoro de Matos, *Na Rota da Índia: Estudos de História da Expansão Portuguesa* (Macau: Instituto Cultural, 1994), 247.

27 Paulo Guinote, Jorge Alves *et al*, *Naufrágios e Outras Perdas da Carreira da Índia, séculos XVI e XVII* (Lisboa: Ministério da Educação, 1998), 347, 363–365.

28 Ibid.

29 Arie Pos and Rui Loureiro, eds., *Itinerário, Viagem ou Navegação de Jan Huygen van Linscoten para as Índias Orientais ou Portuguesas* (Lisboa: Comissão Nacional para as Comemorações dos Descobrimentos Portugueses, 1997), 82, 149.

30 Santos, *Etiópia Oriental*, 299.

31 Guinote, Alves *et al*, *Naufrágios e Outras Perdas*, 340.

was primarily intended to maintain commercial relationships between the metropole and its possessions in India. Paralleling this circuit, another form of slave trade developed which consisted as much of regular slave trading expeditions as it did of expeditions to strengthen normal commercial relationships between the ports of Portuguese India and the ports of Mozambique. In 1555, the Portuguese government in Goa asked permission from the King of Portugal to send a ship to the island of São Lourenço to fetch 80 men.[32] In 1567, the Portuguese fleet took 300 slaves from Mozambique to India. At the end of the century the trips to Mozambique provided Goa with "much gold powder and bars, ivory, enslaved Africans and kaffirs [i.e. slaves]."[33] The supply of slaves to India continued to be sustained by both slaves carried in the ships of the *Carreira* and sporadic slave trading expeditions. In the middle of the eighteenth century, the slave trade to India remained regular but not substantial. In August 1750, the Marquis of Távora, while calling at Mozambique, on his way to India, did not allow the crew to carry more than 35 slaves aboard the ship which carried him, but allowed them to dispatch as many as they wished on the *Carreira's* ships, provided they paid rates and freight costs.[34]

In 1773, two ships left Mozambique for Goa with 800 slaves on board.[35] However, it seems likely that by this time, year by year, "fewer slaves" were carried on this route.[36] Between 1770 and 1791 the French took slaves from Mozambique to Goa and from there to Mauritius. In 1777 a French ship arrived at Goa with 700 slaves from Mozambique. Slaves were being shipped, too, from Mozambique to Macau and Indonesia, specifically Timor, directly and via Goa.[37] Of the 5,500 slaves reportedly exported in 1788 from Mozambique's ports, only 400 to 500 were apparently destined for so-called Portuguese Asia.[38]

---

32   Vitorino de Magalhães Godinho, *Mito e Mercadoria, Utopia e Prática de Navegar, séculos XIII–XVIII* (Lisboa: Difel, 1990), 387.

33   João de Andade Corvo, *Estudos sobre as Províncias Ultramarinas* (Lisboa: Academia Real das Ciências, 1883–1887), 2: 42–43.

34   Biblioteca Nacional de Portugal (former Biblioteca Nacional de Lisboa (hereafter BNP), *Colecção Pombalina*, cód. 742:1750-08-06: 'Bando do Marquês de Távora, Ilha de Moçambique'.

35   'Journal tenu par le sr. De Jean, marchand sur le vaisseau La Vierge de Grace, pour le commerce à la costa de Soffala, 1733," *Recueil Trimestrel de Documents et Travaux Inédits pour Servir à L'Histoire des Mascareignes Françaises* 4 (Apr.–Jun. 1939): 364.

36   BNP, *Reservados*, cód. 8554: 1779: 'D. Francisco Inocêncio Sousa Coutinho'.

37   Rudy Bauss, "The Portuguese Slave Trade from Mozambique to Portuguese India and Macau and comments on Timor 1750–1850," *Camões Center Quarterly* 6–7:1–2 (Summer-Fall 1997): 21–27.

38   AHU, *Moçambique*, cx. 57, doc. 3: 1789-01-14: 'Carta do capitão-general Melo e Castro para o secretário de estado'.

If the first two decades of the nineteenth century followed the pattern established at the end of the eighteenth century, then between four and six ships loaded with goods would likely have departed from Goa, Diu and Daman, and would have arrived in Mozambique in March. There they would have received gold dust from the rivers of Sena, half-*doblas* from Brazil, Spanish *patacas*, ivory, amber, *ponta de abada*, and seahorse teeth, as well as "some slaves." They would most likely set sail at the end of August. Among those pursuing such trade were ships from Goa and Daman, which in 1819, loaded 350 slaves in Mozambique.[39]

The Slave Trade to the French Colonies

In the eighteenth century, slave ships departing from the ports of Mozambique headed systematically towards two main directions other than India. The first was to French colonies in the Indian Ocean and in the West Indies. The second was to Brazil. We shall look at these in sequence.

From the beginning of the colonization of Bourbon in 1665, the French settled there and the *Compagnie des Indes* set its sights on commercial relations with the east coast of Africa. The development of such relations was proposed over several decades but the company finally authorized them on 22 February 1713. In doing so, it confronted the problem of Portuguese rules banning trade with other Europeans on the coast. These included most recently laws of 8 February 1711 and 5 October 1715 stopping foreign ships from entering Portuguese ports, except in emergencies.[40] In April 1721 French privateers boarded a ship sailing near the Mascarene Islands and captured the Viceroy of Portuguese India, the Count of Ericeira, who was subsequently ransomed and released. As part of the ransom agreement the Portuguese were forced to allow the French access to their ports. Ericeira guaranteed that in Mozambique the French would have access to abundant and cheap slave labour supplies. In the same year, the ship *Indien* travelled from Bourbon to Mozambique, returning with slaves.[41] Although the earliest expeditions were not rewarded with high slave prices at market, slaves from Mozambique soon came to be regarded as better than those from Madagascar. In securing slaves in Southeast Africa the

---

39   "Frei Bartolomeo dos Mártires," 151.

40   Fritz Hoppe, *A África Oriental Portuguesa no Tempo do Marquês de Pombal 1750–1777* (Lisboa: Agência Geral do Ultramar, 1970), 265.

41   *Recueil Trimestrel de Documents Françaises*: 318 and ss.

French also opened up new markets for their own goods there. The Company insisted on being able to use the Mozambican coast, and it sent two ships on 5 September 1729 to gather information on ports, rivers, conditions of access, goods in demand, supply of slaves and gold and terms of their procurement.[42] The first major shipload of slaves was secured four years later, when the ship, *Viorgo de Grâce*, arrived in Mozambique on 14 July 1733 and within a month acquired 368 slaves. Upon arrival the ship's captain behaved amicably and the Portuguese authorities reciprocated in turn.[43] This marked the beginning of a more systematic trade in slaves and goods between Mozambican ports and the French Indian Ocean and other colonies, a trade which would continue into the nineteenth century.

From 1720 onwards the pattern of French slave trading in southeast Africa may be divided in five main periods[44] The first, in 1721–1734, was characterised by occasional encounters and failed plans before a viable plantation economy was established in the Mascarenes. The second, in 1735–1770, saw rapid economic growth but erratic Portuguese policies in relation to French commerce in East Africa. The third, in 1771–1784, was defined by greater unity of purpose by all interested parties and by extensions of French activity north of Cape Delgado. The fourth, in 1785–1794, saw French slaving activity in southeast Africa reach its peak, as shipments of slaves round the Cape of Good Hope into the Atlantic grew to meet demand for slaves in the French Caribbean, thereby aligning slave supply systems from southeast Africa with those from the south Atlantic. Finally, in 1795–1810, the repercussions of the Napoleonic wars in the Indian Ocean and the takeover of Mauritius by the English saw a reduction in French activity in southeast Africa, even though the provision of slaves and *libertos* (like the *libres engagés*) to the remaining French colonies in the Indian Ocean would be maintained beyond 1810, and not end formally until 1888.[45]

Relations between Mozambique and the Mascarene Islands, underpinned by demands for slaves, remained extremely cordial throughout the

---

42   Ibid.

43   Archives départementales de la Réunion, ed., *Voyages, Commerce, Comptoirs et Colonies: Bourbon sur la route des Indes au XVIII siècle* (Saint-Denis, Réunion: Archives départementales de la Réunion, 1987).

44   Edward A. Alpers, "The French Slave Trade in East Africa 1721–1810," *Cahiers d'Études Africaines* 10:37 (1970): 80–129.

45   "Portaria de 23 de Junho de 1881," *Boletim Oficial da Província de Moçambique* 28 (1881): 17; AHM, *Governo Geral*, cx. 10, mç. 3, doc. 21: 1881-07-03: 'Carta do director-geral da secretaria de estado do Ultramar para o governador-geral'; Sudel Fuma, *Histoire d'un Peuple: La Réunion 1848–1900* (Saint-Denis, La Réunion: édition du C.N.H., 1994), 252.

Governor-generalship of Bertrand-Francois Mahe de la Bourdonnais between 1734 and 1745 in the Mascarenes. He had been in French service in Portugal in 1729–1732 and cultivated a strong friendship with his counterpart in Mozambique, Nicolau Tolentino e Almeida. The friendship was apparent in the correspondence exchanged by the two. Thanks to La Bourdonnais' policies and to coffee cultivation, the demography of the Mascarene Islands changed radically. In 1714, before coffee production was introduced, Bourbon had 1,200 inhabitants, divided equally between slaves and freemen. Following the start of the coffee cultivation in 1720, the slave population grew rapidly and by 1735 for every one of the 1,716 freemen on the Mascarenes, there were some 8.5 (or 14,600) slaves. The pattern was sustained during La Bourdonnais' government. Under his rule, 8,500 slaves entered the Mascarene Islands, three-quarters of whom went to Mauritius. Bourbon's slave population also grew, and in 1758, of a total population on the island of 19,000, fewer than 4,000 were free.[46] In both cases, the majority of slaves came from Mozambique. The success of the slave supply to French colonies in the Indian Ocean was such that it led the factor of the French factory in Chandernagor to dispatch two merchant ships to the southeast African coast to acquire slaves. Although the *Compagnie des Indes* had sought to reserve Mozambique as a source of slaves for the Mascarene Islands, this did not prevent the factor at Chandernagor from sending the ship *Princesse Émilie* to the coast in 1738 and the Pondicherry Council from doing the same with the *Contorbéry* in 1739.[47]

Despite explicit instructions from Lisbon to stop French commerce in Mozambique,[48] the Portuguese local authorities, with occasional exceptions, failed to do so, since they had a personal interest in the business. In order to enter the ports, ships invariably declared a state of emergency for real or "imagined" accidents. With a brief interregnum between 1746 and 1749, French slave trading continued in southeast Africa, with the support of the Captain General Francisco de Mello e Castro (1750–1758), who exempted trade between the two parties from customs duties.[49] In the middle of the century the traffic was proceeding just as it had done in the times of former governors Nicolau Tolentino (1736–1739), Lourenço de Noronha (1740–1743) and Pedro de Rego Barreto de Gama e Castro (1743–1746). This was confirmed by a royal magistrate

---

46   *Mahé de La Bourdonnais, Conseil Général de La Réunion* (Saint-Denis, Réunion: Archives Départementales de la Réunion, 1987).

47   *Voyages, Commerce, Comptoirs et Colonies.*

48   Hoppe, *A África Oriental Portuguesa*, 262.

49   Ibid., 195.

and auditor (*sindicante*) who carried out an enquiry in 1750–1753 into the history of arrivals of French ships in the port of Mozambique.[50]

In 1752, the Governor-general of the *Compagnie des Indes*, Joseph-Francois Dupleix, proposed an agreement with the Portuguese administration in India, which included a provision for Mozambique to supply 2,000 slaves per year to the French.[51] The proposal was not followed up but at the time the French presence was evident not only in Mauritius but also to the north on the islands of Cape Delgado. The Governor Pedro do Rego had been accused of allowing French access.[52] Dominican priests resided on the islands and according to the local captain-judge, in the 1750s, one of them had monopolized the slaving business there, provoking an uprising among the local people.[53] Around this time, in the middle of the century, the slave trade had been sustained over the years by long-established trade from ports along the coast at the rivers of Sena, Sofala, Inhambane, and the islands of Cape Delgado, supplying it seems, annually, some 1,100 slaves to Mozambique.[54] At the same time, ship owners at Rio de Janeiro in Brazil had established trading posts in Mozambique from which they provided slaves to the French islands and ivory, gold and pearls to India's ports. But the French remained the most active traders in the Quirimba Islands and the port of Mozambique. There they bought slaves, ivory and gold in exchange for cloth from Bengal as well as arms, gunpowder and other goods. *Patacas* (*pesos*) from Spain were the most highly sought means of payment in both the Indian and Atlantic Oceans, and Spanish *patacas* began to dominate long distance trade in the Indian Ocean.[55] The well established French trade in southeast Africa did not require justification. Instead, the Lisbon government and its representatives tolerated it.[56]

---

50   AHU, *Moçambique*, cx. 13, doc. 30: 1754-04-20: 'Cópia da Carta…Dada de Mossambique pelo Desembargador Sindicante ao Marquês de Távora Vice Rey da Índia'.

51   Alpers, "The French Slave Trade," 90.

52   Simões, *O Oriente Africano Português*, 65.

53   AHU, *Moçambique*, cx. 31, doc. 66: 1753-01-05: 'Parte que dao a V. Sra. Snõr Dezembargador Sindicante os moradores da Ilha de Mathemo do que aqui tem acontecido nestas Ilhas, do mez de Novembro de 1751, a esta parte'.

54   IAN/TT, *Ministério do Reino*, no. 604: 1758: 'Memórias Anónimas da Costa da África Oriental'.

55   IAN/TT, *Ministério do Reino*, no. 604: 1773-12-01: Luiz Pinto Figueiredo, 'Noticia do Continente de Moçambique e abreviada relação do seu comércio' (the author had lived more than 20 years in Mozambique); BNP, *Reservados*, cód. 8554: 1779: 'D. Francisco Inocêncio Sousa Coutinho'.

56   Hoppe, *A África Oriental Portuguesa*, 268, 269, 494.

Further intensification of the French presence in southeast Africa occurred when in 1771 commercial slave expeditions began to depart from the French port cities of Bordeaux, Lorient, Nantes, Marseilles and elsewhere to trade in the region and from there to supply slaves to the Mascarene Islands as well as to French colonies in the Atlantic. As the latter demanded large investments, it is not surprising that French ports only decided to outfit slave voyages to the Indian Ocean after colonial trade in the Americas had achieved good results from the 1730s and 1740s onwards. Efforts to promote French slave supplies from the Indian Ocean into the Atlantic were hindered first by continuing success in slaving in the Atlantic Ocean and by the disruptions to French colonial trade in the Americas caused by war with Britain in 1755–1763. With the return of peace in 1763 and with it the restoration of Martinique and Guadeloupe to France, French traders sought to expand their slave trade to the Mascarene Islands to help to meet the demands for slaves in their Caribbean colonies. This was as much a political as an economic decision. As early as 1744, the French Minister of Naval Affairs, Raymond de Sartine, had confirmed an intention to finance French ship owners to participate in the slave trade in the area between the Portuguese territories in southeast Africa and the Cape of Good Hope.[57] Around 1740, the French favoured slaves purchased in the Quirimba Islands as they were seen as more docile than those from Madagascar, but they still sent ships to ports north of Cape Delgado where they dealt with the 'Moors' of that region. After 1773, however, French activity generally in southeast Africa grew. Between 1773 and 1810, there were no less than 142 French slave voyages to ports under Portuguese authority and by 1800 traders from the Seychelles were also making slaving voyages to Mozambique.[58] In 1779, the Portuguese provisional government in Mozambique proposed to the King the creation of an East African Company exclusively for the exportation of slaves to the Mascarene Islands but this course of action was not pursued.[59] The armistice with the British at the end of the War of American Independence in 1783 combined with difficulties in obtaining slaves in Atlantic Africa to encourage French ship owners further to outfit ships to visit the Indian Ocean as a way of supplying slaves to Saint-Domingue in the French Caribbean from 1783 onwards.[60]

57   Éric Saugera, *Bordeaux, port négrier XVII–XIX Siècles* (Paris: Éditions Karthala, 1995), 81.

58   Toussaint, *L'Océan Indien*, 40.

59   IAN/TT, *Ministério do Reino*, no. 604: 1779-08-24: 'Plano da Companhia da África Oriental, do desembargador e Governador Interino de Moçambique, Diogo Guerreiro de Aboim, para o Rei'.

60   Saugera, *Bordeaux, port négrier*, 81.

In 1772, seven or eight French slave ships had visited the ports of Mozambique and the Quirimba Islands.[61] The first registered slave expedition dated from that year, and was by the ship *Digue*, which left Lorient on 17 April 1772, and entered the Indian Ocean, where it loaded slaves at the Quirimba Islands, and then sailed for Saint-Domingue.[62] Until that time there had been an estimated 1,500 to 2,000 slaves taken each year by the French.[63] As French trade grew, so more details of it arose. A description by the captain of a ship anchored in the port of Ibo, dating from 1783, details the conditions and means of exchange used in this commerce as well as the age and gender of the slaves it had taken on. He witnessed the loading of 350 to 400 slaves by a French ship, which was there for four months, and noted the arrival of another for the same purpose. As it was a prohibited business, the governor felt able to levy four Spanish *patacas* per slave. Five or six ships, he observed, moored there each year. The same ship captain went on to Mozambique's port, where he encountered three great ships sailing under the same flag. By 1787 he had been in Mauritius for five months and he had frequently seen slave ships arriving. On the island, he reported, there must have been 60,000 Blacks from the African coast, "Madagascars and Timors."[64]

From 1786 to 1793 there were 55 recorded slave expeditions registered in Bordeaux with Mozambique as their destination. Between 1786 and 1787, 92 expeditions bound for Mauritius probably also stopped at Mozambican ports.[65] Between 1784 and 1791, 15 expeditions left Marseilles for Mozambique. From 1785 to 1792, 10 left Nantes for the same destination. To these were added seven from Lorient from 1769 to 1790, four from Saint Malo from 1777 to 1790, and in different years one each from Saint Brieuc, Dunkirk and Bayonne.[66]

Until 1787, Portuguese dealings with the French remained unregulated, but thereafter were subject to intervention, notably the imposition of a system for collecting all currencies that the ships carried, to be exchanged for stamped *patacas* (the marking increasing the value of the coin). Commerce had, in large

---

61   Alpers, "The French Slave Trade," 99.

62   Jean Mettas, *Répertoire des Expéditions Négrières Françaises au XVIIIe Siècle*, 2 volumes, eds. Serge and Michelle Daget (Paris: L'Harmattan for Société Française d'Histoire d'Outre Mer, 1978–1984), II.

63   IAN/TT, *Ministério do Reino*, no. 602: 1779-08-05: 'Memorando contendo várias memórias e relações sobre Moçambique, Goa'.

64   Biblioteca Nacional do Rio de Janeiro (hereafter BNRJ), I-13, 1, 47: 1783: 'Descripção da Negociação q. os Francezes fazião em Moçambique, Ilha do Ibo, e Querimba com a Compra de Escravatura, e Marfim para conduzirem á Ilha Mauricia por João Baptista Roffe em 1783'.

65   Saugera, *Bordeaux, port négrier*, 351, ss.

66   Mettas, *Répertoire des Expéditions Négrières*, I and II.

part, become monetized. The main reason given for the change was "the great amount of currency which has been coming here" [as a result of] "the great exportation of slaves, the most flourishing commercial activity at this port." In 1788, more than 5,500 slaves had left the port of Mozambique and more than 1,500,000 Spanish *patacas* had entered it.[67]

In France, the *Compagnie des Indes* had its monopoly restored on 15 April 1785, and it was maintained until 1790. Between 1786 and 1789, it issued 119 licences for commercial expeditions to East Africa.[68] In 1790, the French trade with Mozambique was at its peak and alone accounted for one-third of all the revenue collected by local Customs House.[69] In 1793 war in Europe put an end to French slaving activity; it would only be renewed briefly before 1815 in 1802. Because of the European conflict, no French ships entered Mozambican ports from May 1794 until 7 April 1796. This did not stop, however, Portuguese ship owners in Mozambique from continuing their slave trade to the Mascarene Islands. Captain-general Diogo de Sousa Coutinho, Governor at Mozambique in 1793–1797, complained to Lisbon about the distress inflicted on residents by the absence of the French, particularly at Cape Delgado Island which "flourished with the slave trade."[70] His successor, Francisco Guedes de Carvalho Menezes e Costa (1797–1801), decided to attempt to restore trade by sending a slave ship owner, Joaquim de Morais Rego Lisboa, to Mauritius to negotiate with the French an end to privateering off the ports of Mozambique, in return for which French ships would be allowed to enter Mozambican ports under a flag of neutrality. The aim was to counter the reluctance of Portuguese-owned ships to visit Mauritius for fear of being boarded by British privateers.[71] Efforts to restore trade also focused on the activities in the region of privateers from the French islands, whose activities did not reflect local political goals and were not condoned by commercial interests, which kept excellent relations with their Mozambican counterparts. Some six ships had been intercepted by the French, the crew of which had been returned in one of the

---

67   AHU, CX. 57, doc. 3: 1789-01-14: 'Carta do capitão-general Mello e Castro para o secretário de estado'; BNP, *Reservados, Colecção Tarouca*: 1801-02-28: 'Carta do governador Isidro de Sá para D. Rodrigo de Sousa Coutinho'.
68   Alpers, "The French Slave Trade," 111.
69   AHU, *Moçambique*, CX. 62, doc. 58: 1791-08-20: 'Carta do governador-geral para o secretário de estado'.
70   AHU, *Moçambique*, CX. 76, doc. 5: 1796-10-07: 'Carta de D. Diogo de Sousa Coutinho para Luis Pinto de Sousa Coutinho'.
71   IAN/TT, *Ministério do Reino*, no. 499: 1797-12-10: 'Carta de Francisco Guedes da Costa para D. Rodrigo de Sousa Coutinho'.

ships seized.[72] All these concerns were articulated to Lisbon, which fully supported the efforts to restore trade with the French contained in the Mozambican Captain-general's plan.[73] In time, the French duly returned to the ports of Mozambique, with the Captain-general being implicated in discounting local custom rates as a means of encouraging this.[74] On leaving office, Carvalho e Menezes claimed credit for increasing business with the French from Mauritius.[75] At the time, the island was considered to have the greatest share of slave exports from Mozambique, an argument given support by the data in Table 6.1, and in 1806, 40 percent of its population was thought to have originally come from Mozambique.[76]

The slave trade from the ports of Mozambique and Ibo to the Mascarene Islands was made easier by the fact that voyage times of slave ships were short, allowing potentially multiple voyages a year. An outgoing journey from the islands to Mozambique typically took around 15 days and, because of the prevailing easterly winds, a return journey took about 40 days. By the early nineteenth century the slave trade from Mozambique to the Mascarene Islands had been restored. It would continue in various guises well into the nineteenth century.

TABLE 6.1   *Slave trade from Mozambique to the islands of the Indian Ocean*

Periods	Destinations	No. of Slaves embarked/disembarked (imputed values)	
1670–1810	Mauritius	160,000	Disembarked (1)
1733–1799	Mauritius	125,306	Embarked (2)
1773–1810	Île-de-France	64,000	Disembarked(3)

Sources:

(1)   J.M. Filliot, *La traite des esclaves vers les Mascareignes au XVIII siècle* (Paris: OSTROM, 1970), 163 and ss.

(2)   José Capela, *O Escravismo Colonial em Moçambique* (Porto: Edições Afrontamento, 1993), 131.

(3)   Toussaint, *L'Océan Indien*, 49.

---

72   AHU, *Moçambique,* cx. 80, doc. 32: 1798-02-10: 'Carta do governador-geral para D. Rodrigo de Sousa Coutinho'; cx. 81, doc. 90: 1798-11-02: 'Carta de idem para idem'; doc. 98: 1798-11-10: 'Carta de idem para idem'; cx. 83, doc. 41: 1799-08-12: 'Carta de idem para idem'.

73   IAN/TT, *Ministério do Reino,* no. 499: 1799-11-07: 'Carta do secretário de estado da Marinha para o governador-geral'.

74   IAN/TT, *Ministério do Reino,* no. 44: 1800-07-25: 'Carta do desembargador juiz da Alfândega, Manuel José Gomes Loureiro'.

75   IAN/TT, *Ministério do Reino,* cx. 89, doc. 7: 1801-09-21: 'Carta do governador cessante, Carvalho e Menezes para D. Rodrigo de Sousa Coutinho'.

76   Toussaint, *L'Océan Indien*, 36.

Slave Trade to Latin America

Interest among slave traders from the Atlantic world in taking slaves from East Africa only really emerged after the conquest of Angola by the Dutch in 1641. The Captaincy of Mozambique came to be seen as a source of slaves able to mitigate the difficulties caused by the Dutch takeover of Angola in supplying slaves to Brazil. This is attested by the first known Royal permission, dated 12 December 1642, opening ports on the East African coast under Portuguese jurisdiction to Portuguese and Brazilian ship owners. On 30 April 1643, a licence was granted under special conditions to Gaspar Pacheco, Francisco Furna, António Roiz Figueiredo and Rui da Silva Pereira to recruit a Portuguese crew and sail a large and well-armed Flemish ship to Mozambique, to collect slaves there, and then to proceed to Brazil. This was "a new journey and unknown trading area" to these merchants.[77] For traders in Lisbon this was indeed a new venture, for there is no evidence of any previous expedition to southeast Africa to load slaves for Brazil. There is evidence of one earlier voyage in 1624 to southeast Africa from Lisbon to procure slaves for sale in the Americas.[78] This was captained by Jerónimo Monteiro, and probably traded at Ibo and other places along the coast, but the destination of the slaves was not Brazil but Cartagena.

In 1644, two ships from Rio de Janeiro were used in expeditions to the coasts of Mozambique and Madagascar. The expeditions did not produce the desired results because the length of the journey cancelled out the difference in prices between the east and west coasts, and because the slaves from the east did not have a good reputation in Brazil. This did not stop continuing loads going onto the so-called *náus da Índia* (Portuguese royal fleets bounded for India).[79] The following year Gaspar Pacheco, who had sent one of his ships to Mozambique for slaves in 1644, requested a licence for a new expedition, although he considered it "risky and expensive." He justified the expedition by citing a lack of available labour for sugar plantations. He was granted a licence to be used before March 1646, with further licences dependent on the results.[80] The Portuguese recovery of Angola in 1648 would contribute to Brazil's waning interest in slaves from the East African coast. Although the ship owners who used these ports were reluctant to establish a systematic transatlantic slave trade, they were also attracted by the opportunities available within the Indian Ocean itself. They ended up establishing

77   Lopes, *A Escravatura*, 77, 165, 166.
78   http://www.slavevoyages.org.
79   Lopes, *A Escravatura*, 165, 166.
80   AHU, *Moçambique,* cx. 2, doc. 68: 1645-08-09: 'Consulta do Conselho Ultramarino'.

themselves to supply the islands of the Indian Ocean with slaves and Indian ports with gold, ivory and pearls.[81]

There were few other recorded seventeenth-century slave expeditions from Brazil to the Indian Ocean; two left Bahia, one in 1664, with no known return date, another in 1690. Rather more voyages left Britain and British America, however. Indeed, from 1664 to the end of the century, 47 British expeditions sailed from London or from ports in British America such as New York and Boston.[82] The slaves were chiefly taken aboard in Madagascar, but most probably originated from ports throughout southeast Africa.

As in the seventeenth century, the presence of Portuguese or Brazilian slave traders in the ports of Mozambique remained sporadic before the closing years of the eighteenth century. In 1718 and 1722 there were expeditions from Bahia to Mozambique, but these apparently did not return with slaves.[83] It appears that in 1759–1761 four voyages from southeast Africa went to Bahia and were followed by one each in 1767 and 1776. In 1767 one voyage went to Rio de Janeiro. This pattern persisted until the last 15 years of the century, when the level of sailings between southeast Africa and Brazil rose sharply, reaching 12 a year in 1786, 1790 and 1797.[84] In the meantime, with one or two exceptions, British interest in slave exports from southeast Africa to the Americas essentially ended.

Whilst en route to India on 22 August 1744, Pedro Miguel de Almeida Portugal, who had been Governor of São Paulo, wrote to Lisbon asking why slaves were not imported into Brazil from Mozambique, since they were far cheaper there than at the Coast of Mina in West Africa.[85] In 1753, Lisbon ship owner, Félix von Oldenburg, gained a monopoly on transport to Mozambique, with the aim of trading with Goa and other ports in Asia and stopping in Bahia on the home journey.[86] In the same year the ships *Nossa Senhora da Piedade* and *Nossa Senhora da Atalaya* loaded 119 slaves; those loaded including slaves for the Royal Treasury destinated for the royal services.[87] Portuguese trafficking in slaves in southeast Africa was still not systematic, however, though there

---

81   Lopes, *A Escravatura*, 167.

82   http://www.slavevoyages.org.

83   Ibid.

84   Ibid.

85   Manuel Artur Norton, *D. Pedro de Almeida Portugal* (Lisboa: Agência Geral do Ultramar, 1967), 39.

86   Hoppe, *A África Oriental Portuguesa*, 208, 212, 213.

87   AHU, *Moçambique,* cx. 8, doc. 51: 1753-11-29: 'Carta do governador de Moçambique para o secretário de estado'; cx. 9, doc. 20: 1753-12-27.

were signs the market for such captives in Brazil was growing. Nowhere was this more evident than in the plan to transform Brazil into the epicentre of the colonial system implemented by the Marquis of Pombal (1750–1777), which had repercussions in Mozambique as a source of slaves for the South American colony. On 4 June 1753, the Portuguese Crown created a local royal government in the captaincy of Mozambique, identical to the ones in Brazil and Angola. The newly appointed Captain-general, Francisco de Mello e Castro, was authorized to impose the first customs duties on imported and exported slaves. These provide us with the first statistics on slave imports and exports from the island of Mozambique between 1753 and 1758 and the income therefrom.[88] Each slave, irrespective of gender, entering the port of Mozambique was to pay five *cruzados*. Only slaves paying entry dues could legally be re-exported. Upon each slave leaving for India, Brazil or Portugal, dues were levied at rates of three *cruzados* for adult slaves (or *grandes*) and two *cruzados* for children (*bichos*). These customs rates were reaffirmed by royal decree seven years later. Although these are the first official customs rates applied to slaves, they were anticipated in 1751–1752 by similar charges by the local governor on the slaves shipped in the vessel *Glorioza*, the rate being three *cruzados* per slave.[89]

The Portuguese in India were granted free trade with Mozambique in 1757 and this was extended to all Portuguese subjects in 1761.[90] In that year a licence was granted to José Rodrigues Vareiro to send a frigate to Mozambique, and from there to sail to Rio de Janeiro and Bahia.[91] To ensure improved provision of slaves to Brazil, on 7 May 1769, free trade was decreed between Brazil and Portuguese East Africa. The slaves procured were expected to be paid for in goods imported from Portugal.[92] The interim governor of Mozambique, who in 1779 advocated a company for slave trade with the French, was of the opinion that the only "goods" from Mozambique of interest to the Brazilians would be slaves, but that these had stopped being competitively priced.[93] Those anticipating to buy slaves in Mozambique to ship to Brazil could not compete at that stage with French buyers in the ports of Mozambique.

---

88   AHU, *Moçambique,* cx. 14, doc. 49.

89   AHU, *Moçambique,* cx. 13, doc. 30: 1754-04-20: 'Cópia da Carta...Dada de Mossambique pelo Dezembargador Sindicante ao Marquês de Távora Vice Rey da Índia'.

90   Hoppe, *A África Oriental Portuguesa,* 213.

91   Ibid.

92   Alexandre Lobato, *Evolução Administrativa e Económica de Moçambique, 1752–1763* (Lisboa: Agência Geral do Ultramar, 1957), 265.

93   IAN/TT, *Ministério do Reino,* 604: 1779-08-24: 'Plano da Companhia da África Oriental'.

When a more systematic slave trade to Brazil was established in the last decade of the eighteenth century, the initiators of it were ship owners from Mozambique. The first, Faustino José Pinto de Lima and José Henriques da Cruz Freitas, residents in the captaincy, had previous experience in the slave trade there. On 23 October 1795, they were authorized by Lisbon to sail a 300-400 ton ship to Portuguese America with slaves, trade with foreign ports was explicitly excluded.[94] Another licence followed, this time of greater importance since it was granted to two of the wealthiest and most famous men in the Mozambique slave business, João da Silva Guedes and Joaquim do Rosário Monteiro. Guedes was a well-established trader. He had been the Customs Major Registrar in 1779 and in 1804 would become Sergeant Major of the local militias (*Ordenanças*).[95] In 1784 his brigantine *Santo António Dois Amigos* set sail for Inhambane where it picked up slaves to be sold in Maranhão or another port in Portuguese America. The ship was commanded by Captain António Caetano Lopes; its pilot was José Ignácio Dias Moreira and its supercargo Domingos Pinto Guerreiro.[96] Monteiro had been raised in Goa before establishing himself in Mozambique in the last quarter of the eighteenth century. From there he ran a long-distance business with connections in India, China, Goa, Macau, the Mascarene Islands, and Madagascar. On 7 September 1796 he continued what earlier pioneers started, and requested a passport to trade in slaves to Portuguese America for his galley *Joaquim*. We do not know if this planned voyage was activated, but in 1798 Monteiro went to Rio de Janeiro and in the early 1800s began a prolonged stay in Montevideo, where he became actively involved in trade, including slaves.[97]

The supply of slaves to Brazil continued to expand after 1800. The Mozambique-based slave fleet and slave trade that Lisbon had long aimed for would come to fruition by the end of the eighteenth century. The Captain-general triumphantly informed the court in 1801: "...currently [there are] 14 ships belong to the traders in this fort (*praça*), including ships with three masts, brigantines, schooners and sloops..." Their tonnage totalled 3,020 tons, the largest vessel weighing 800 and the smallest 80. Three of them sailed to America (seemingly Portuguese America) carrying slaves. The others were used for local

---

94 Santana, *Documentação Avulsa*, 1: 83. AHU, *Moçambique,* cx. 66, doc. 61.

95 IAN/TT, *Chancelaria de D. Maria I*, lv. 61: 1799-12-17; lv. 70: 1804-01-07. *Ordenanças* were para-military regiments formed by civilian males recruited locally.

96 AHU, *Moçambique,* cód. 1365, fl. 34v: 1794-09-11.

97 AHU, *Moçambique,* cód. 1362, fl. 67v; cx. 75, doc. 53; cx. 81, docs. 99, 102; cx. 89, doc. 44.

trade (or cabotage) or were employed in the Indian Ocean.[98] There was also a local shipbuilding industry, with two having been built in Quelimane, two in the Quirimba Islands, and one in Mozambique.

The great ship owner of Lisbon, José Nunes da Silveira, who had been dispatching ships to the Far East since 1795, only risked his first slaving expedition from southeast Africa to Rio de Janeiro in 1816. Among the 20 ships he owned, he committed only three to the slave trade.[99] However, at the turn of the century, a systematic and increasing flow of slaves from Mozambican ports to Brazil became evident and would continue throughout the first half of the nineteenth century. On 10 June 1797 while still in Rio de Janeiro, the Brazilian scientist, Francisco de Lacerda e Almeida, recently appointed Governor of the Rivers of Sena captaincy, advocated the opening of the port of Quelimane to ships exporting slaves to Brazil. According to him, the Governor-general intended not only to allow the French from Mauritius to continue to use the port of Mozambique for slave trading, but also to open trading with Englishmen from the Cape of Good Hope. He advocated that slaves should be sent to Santa Catarina, Rio Grande do Sul, São Paulo and other Brazilian ports, as well as Spanish colonies. He insisted that the permission given to Lisbon merchants to take slaves from Mozambique to Brazil should be extended to Brazilian merchants.[100] It took another 13 years before entry to the port of Quelimane would be expressly opened to Brazilian ship owners in 1810. Table 6.2 underlines the primacy of French and Spanish markets in the Atlantic for slaves leaving Mozambique until 1799.

TABLE 6.2   *Slave trade from Mozambique to the Atlantic*

Periods	Destinations	No. of Expeditions	No. of Slaves embarked/ disembarked
1717–1799	Spanish America	52	16,393/13,373
1759–1793	French Colonies	90	35,697/25,843

Sources: www.slavevoyages.org, 1717–1799; Capela, *O Tráfico*, 304 and ss

---

98   IAN/TT, *Ministério do Reino*, 499: 1801-08-22: 'Carta do capitão-general de Moçambique, Francisco Guedes de Carvalho e Menezes da Costa para o Rei'; AHU, *Moçambique*, cx. 82, doc. 33: 1801-08-18: 'Carta do mesmo para o Secretário de Estado'.

99   Sociedade de Geografia de Lisboa (hereafter SGL), *Reservados*, 5-A, cx. 4 and 5. Carreira, *O Tráfico Português de Escravos*, 3 and ss.

100   AHU, *Moçambique*, cx. 78, doc. 9.

Internal Networks

At the end of the sixteenth century, coastal traffic had been established between the myriad ports along the coast of southeast Africa. The web of sea connections was sustained by Swahili traders using dhows, vessels common employed throughout the Indian Ocean. Once the *Estado da Índia* was consti tuted by the Portuguese, and included the captaincy of Mozambique, annual maritime trading relationships were also established between the ports of Goa, Daman and Diu, on one side, and Mozambique, on the other. This type of commercial relationship was, in turn, extended from the port of Mozambique to the remaining ports belonging to the captaincy. In this way, regular trade circuits linking the port of Mozambique to the ports of Quelimane, Inhambane and the Cape of Correntes appeared. The so-called *náu de viagem* was the ship authorized to trade the goods from India in Mozambique. This privilege was granted by the King to an individual in exchange for a donation made by the beneficiary to the granting body.[101] The captain of Mozambique's fort sent ships, at varying intervals ranging from two months to one year, to the Island of Inhaca (near present-day Maputo), the Cape of Correntes and Inhambane, Sofala, the Rivers of Cuama (Quelimane), Angoche, the Island of São Lourenço (present-day Madagascar), and the Quirimba Islands. These were ships, large flatships or dhows with goods received from India in exchange for other trade items, mainly slaves. From Sofala, Rivers of Cuama, and Angoche came "many slaves" and from the Quirimba Islands "a great number of slaves."[102] The pattern persisted at least until the second decade of the nineteenth century, as one contemporary noted:

> From Mozambique's capital eight to 10 sloops, schooners, *sumacas* and flatships leave every year, and some of these ships do two journeys a year depending on the distance from the port to their destination: such is the number which go to Quelimane, which is the port of Rivers of Sena, and to Cape Delgado; but those which go to Sofala, Inhambane, and Cape of Correntes only make one journey per year. These ships leave packed with goods from India.[103]

Slaves were among the items with which they returned to Mozambique. There was no local slave trade network per se; however, slaves were always among the

101   AHU, *Moçambique*, cx. 166, doc. 10: 1819-11-07: 'Carta do Governador-Geral para a Corte'.

102   Santos, *Etiópia Oriental*, 299.

103   "Frei Bartolomeo dos Mártires," 146.

goods exchanged, in turn supplying the long-distance slave trade from Mozambique. Between 1753 and 1758, Mozambique's customs charged entry taxes for 4,656 slaves and export taxes for 4,628, or some 800–1,000 a year in each direction.[104] According to the customs evidence, coastal trafficking evidently helped to sustain the port of Mozambique's slave export trade.

The first explicit references of slaves being supplied to the ports are also from the sixteenth century. On a few occasions the Portuguese were offered slaves by traditional societies. The presence of the Swahili merchants both on the coast and far inland attests the existence of slave trade networks linking traditional chiefdoms to the coast. In the first half of the seventeenth century, thanks to the military domination of chief Maravi over an area which extended from inland Zambezi to the coast, a trade route ran from Zambezi to Mossuril, fronting the port of Mozambique.[105] In the mid-seventeenth century there were merchants in Mozambique trading with the Makuas, those of Quelimane with the Borores, and those of Rivers of Sena with the traders of Rundo, Tete and Marave.[106] Map 6.1 shows some of these early as well as later connections.

Only during the eighteenth century can we begin to indentify specific individuals who were involved in the slave trade at Mozambique. Between 1742 and 1750, the main suppliers of slaves to the French in the Quirimba Islands were the previously mentioned Dominican friar João de Menezes and the Dominican father Manuel Nunes da Silveira; the latter was an associate of the local judge.[107] In 1751, a Monsieur Bosse, who had lived also at Quirimba Islands, was taking slaves to Mauritius. At the same time, another Frenchman, Captain Lucas Duguly, employed the ship *Gloriosa* to transport slaves from Mozambique to Mauritius. These French had established themselves on the islands and, with the support of the authorities, had proceeded to supply compatriots across the Indian Ocean. The following year, in 1752, Monsieur de Ville Neuve captained a ship which transported and paid rates for 33 slaves.[108] The Captain-general Saldanha de Albuquerque (1758–1763), who was also

---

104 AHU, *Moçambique*, cx. 14, doc. 49; António Alberto de Andrade, ed., *Relações de Moçambique Setecentista* (Lisboa: Agência Geral das Colónias, 1955), 216.

105 Alpers, *Ivory & Slaves*, 52.

106 Frei António da Conceição, "Tratados dos Rios de Cuama," in J.H. da Cunha Rivara, ed., *O Chronista de Tissuary*, 2:14–17 (1867): 15:63. [English edition: Malyn Newitt, ed. and trans., *Treatise on the Rivers of Cuama* (Oxford: Oxford University Press, 2009)].

107 AHU, *Moçambique*, cx. 31: 1751–11: 'Parte que dao a V. Sra. Snôr Dezembargador Sindicante os moradores da Ilha de Mathemo do que aqui tem acontecido nestas Ilhas, no mez de Novembro de 1751, a esta parte'.

108 AHU, *Moçambique*, cx. 13, doc. 30: 1754-04-20: 'Cópia da Carta...Dada de Moçambique pelo Dezembargador Sindicante (Francisco Raymundo de Moraes Pereyra)'.

involved in the slave trade, granted the request made by José Basílio Leitão to carry slaves to Mauritius. Basílio Leitão had apparently come from Brazil as a commercial agent (*despachante*) to conduct trade in the Indian Ocean.[109] He had arrived in Mozambique from Goa. He went inland on a trade expedition to find slaves to transport to Mauritius, where he died.[110] Directly implicated in this slave trade with the French were the Governor-general Baltazar Pereira do Lago (1765–1779) and Joaquim José da Costa Portugal who was Governor of the Islands of Cape Delgado for eleven years until 1786.[111] According to Alexandre Lobato, "[a]s well as governor, [the latter] was a slave trader and ship owner."[112]

In 1772 the first two ships from France arrived with their respective ship owners' agents and began transporting slaves to the French colonies of the Indian and Atlantic Oceans.[113] These were followed by other traders, including Cochon, Troplong and Company, a firm of ship owners from Bordeaux. In 1787 they received permission "to go to the coast of Mozambique, calling at Mauritius, to get 500 Blacks to be taken to the French colonies in America," a voyage which their ship completed in 1788.[114] A similar expedition was carried out by the frigate *Breton*, captained by Monsieur Gendron, which sailed from Nantes to Mauritius and thence to Mozambique, from where it left on 27 March 1787 for French America with a consignment of slaves.[115] Alongside the French were other traders, including Manoel de Souza Guimarães, one of the biggest traders in Luanda with interests in Benguela. In 1798 he was in Mozambique with the ships *União, Rezolução* and *Nazareth,* which took slaves to Mauritius and Montevideo.[116]

Those involved in such commerce, however, were not just merchants. In 1793–1794, Manuel Galvão da Silva, went to Mozambique to study fauna, flora and minerals.[117] Appointed secretary general of the Colony's government, he

---

109   In the sources, Leitão is referred to as "American."
110   AHU, *Moçambique,* cx. 31, doc. 66: 1768: 'Narração do estado em que se acha a Fazenda Real no Governo de Moçambique posta à presença de Sua Magestade por Luiz António Figueiredo'.
111   IAN/TT, *Ministério do Reino*, mç. 604.
112   Alexandre Lobato, *História do Presídio de Lourenço Marques* (Lisboa: Junta de Investigação do Ultramar, 1960), 11.
113   www.slavevoyages.org.
114   W.S. Unger, "Voyage d'un Navire Négrier," *Revue Maritime et Coloniale* 114 (1892): 250.
115   AHU, *Moçambique,* cx. 54, doc. 48.
116   AHU, *Moçambique,* cx. 81, doc. 4; cód. 1365, fls.87, 88, 89.
117   H.H.K. Bhila, "A Journal of Manoel Galvão da Silva's Travels Trough The Territory of Manica in 1790," *Monumenta: Boletim dos Monumentos Nacionais de Moçambique* 8:8 (1972): 79–84.

went on to be engaged in slave trading voyages to Mauritius and Spanish America in partnership with the ship owner Gabriel José Pereira Basto and the pilot João da Luz.[118]

Although the first systematic slave trade with Mauritius was established by the French, they were soon followed by Portuguese ship owners and other residents in Mozambique, as well as parties from Brazil and Angola, and ultimately by French firms operating out of Bordeaux, Lorient, Nantes, Saint Malo, Marseille, Le Havre and La Rochelle. In the case of the Portuguese, their agents and suppliers established trading houses on the Island of Mozambique. The earliest were the trading houses of Joaquim do Rosário Monteiro and João da Silva Guedes.[119] The latter was Major Registrar of Customs in the colony.[120] Both carried out a huge amount of trade inland, where their agents acquired slaves; they also frequented Quelimane and other smaller ports, using their own ships.[121] Another Portuguese trader was José Agostinho da Costa. Born in Portugal, he went to Mozambique as a soldier where he rose to be a lieutenant. In 1790 he was promoted to Mayor of the town of Sena, and later became a colonel in the Quelimane regiment. By then he was owner of a great number of slaves and would later become a ship owner and by 1798 was sending slaves destined for export from Quelimane to Mozambique.[122] Yet another trader was Joaquim José da Costa Portugal, Governor of Cape Delgado for 11 years, who ran a firm which employed three ships in clandestine slave trading to the French islands. He became Governor of Lourenço Marques (present-day Maputo) in 1786, and reputedly built a fortune valued at 60,000 *cruzados*.[123] Others such as José Francisco Ribeiro rose to prominence as slave traders from less exalted positions. Starting out as a ship captain and pilot in 1784, and continuing in those roles through the early nineteenth century, Ribeiro nevertheless became a slave trader of some note, like most other ship owners.[124]

Clergymen were also involved in the business. In April 1785 the convent of São João de Deus was granted a passport for the sloop *Almas Santas* to sail to Quelimane, and in August of the following year, Friar António de São José Nepumoceno collected a cargo of 33 slaves from Quelimane in the galley *Santo*

118   AHU, *Moçambique,* cx. 69, doc. 11; cód. 1365, fls. 22, 34v, 36.

119   AHU, *Moçambique,* cx. 101, doc. 33; cód. 1362, fls. 124, 132, 143, 147.

120   AHU, *Moçambique,* cód. 1362, fl. 166.

121   AHU, *Moçambique,* cx. 80, doc. 101; cód. 1365, fl. 8.

122   Santana, *Documentação Avulsa* , 2: 457, 948; 3: 492. AHU, *Moçambique,* cx. 80, doc. 109; cx. 81, doc. 61, 83; cx. 108, doc. 81.

123   Lobato, *História do Presídio,* 11 and ss.

124   AHU, *Moçambique,* cód. 1365, fls. 3, 29; cx. 71, doc. 36; cx. 73, doc. 63, 67.

António e Dous Amigos. Sebastião José Rodrigues, in 1790, became a prominent figure in coastal traffic, as well as that carried out to India and Mauritius. He was one of the four largest traders in Mozambique, and the governor-general requested a decoration for him. He would become one of the first ship owners in Mozambique to engage in systematic slave trading to Brazil.[125] Yet another clergyman, José Henriques da Cruz Freitas entered the slave trade as a ship pilot and captain of slave ships in 1793, and then became a slave trader, employing ships on freight. In 1795, and in partnership with Faustino José Pinto de Lima, he received permission to export slaves to Portuguese America and later to Mauritius.[126]

Another group clearly involved in the slave trade were the *baneanes* who comprised Muslim traders. Originally from Daman and Diu, they migrated to Mozambique following the creation of the Banyan Company of Diu in the late seventeenth century.[127] With great influence over inland trade, they were well placed to participate in slave trafficking. By the end of the eighteenth century their network was far reaching. It included Velgi Ambaidas and Taibo Valy, who were noted as ship owners in 1784. They were joined in the following year by Govangi Gangadas.[128] All three were involved in coastal trade. By 1789, Caliangy Naviangy and Assane Valley had joined the group.[129] Then, by 1791, Amod Cadry Sanchande Matchande had become involved, in the process extending operations from coastal trade in southeast Africa to trade to Daman in India. He had Portuguese "nationality" and remained involved in trade until his death in 1825.[130] Yet another was Giva Sancargy, who in 1799 went to Mauritius to reclaim the brigantine *Africano Ligeiro*, which had been seized by privateers. In subsequent years he undertook expeditions with Velgy Darcy and with Joaquim do Rosário Monteiro, thereby underlining the scale of *banean* traders' influence on the Mozambican market.[131] Many other *baneanes* sent slaves from smaller ports to Mozambique. They acquired slaves inland and then supplied the large traders in the capital and at the ports.

---

125   AHU, *Moçambique,* cx. 90, doc. 23; cx. 94, doc. 42; cx. 140, doc. 44.

126   AHU, *Moçambique,* cód. 1365, fl. 2v. Santana, *Documentação Avulsa,* 1: 83.

127   Joana Pereira Leite, "Indo-britaniques et indo-portugais: la présence marchand dans le Sud du Mozambique au moment de l'implantation du système colonial portugais," *Revue Française d'Histoire d'Outre-mer* 88:330–331 (2001): 17.

128   AHU, *Moçambique,* cód. 1355, fl. 20.

129   AHU, *Moçambique,* cód. 1362, fls. 152v, 162.

130   AHU, *Moçambique,* cód. 1362, fl. 132; cód. 1365, fls. 2v, 23v; cód. 1365, fl. 218; cx. 93, doc. 21; cx. 114, doc. 62; cx. 166, doc.10; cx. 181, doc. 119; cx. 199ª, doc. 14.

131   AHU, *Moçambique,* cód. 1365, fls. 107v, 139; cx. 89, doc. 16; cx. 93, docs. 44, 45, 78; cx. 96, doc. 8.

Following accusations that they were monopolizing the local trade, efforts began to be made to restrict the influence of *baneanes* over Mozambique commerce. In 1782 and 1785 Royal decrees were issued that prohibited *baneanes* from taking up residence on the Mozambique mainland fronting Mozambique Island. In addition, they were banned from participating in commerce on the continent, and also from owning land, buildings, houses, slaves and cattle. In short, their trading activities were restricted to the city, but this did not prevent them from continuing to grow their influence over coasting and export trade.[132]

During the last decade of the eighteenth century, the capture of slaves was causing significant social disorder in the Zambezi valley. The governor of Mozambique thought that in the Rivers of Sena there was a "slave traffic which is abusive and against the rules of true and healthy policy in the sale of kaffirs [i.e. slaves] by residents." Both slaves and freemen were being sold for export and he wished to put an end to it. He therefore put in place drastic measures to "stop once and for all and abolish the abuse which many landowners carry out in catching and selling kaffirs and free settlers." His goal was to curtail the movement of slaves for "exportation to the capital, or another place outside the Rivers."[133] In doing so, he recognized that it was clearly long-distance slave trading across the Atlantic that pushing the demand for slaves further inland. Recalling the fact that the residents of Rivers of Sena had made the slave trade the main objective of all their activities, he ordered that from August 1792 "no more kaffirs [i.e. slaves] will be exported from the Rivers of Sena," thereby expressly abolishing this trade.[134] If this measure hindered slave trading in inland areas, it was not sufficient to impede its growth in subsequent years. Slave trade continued substantially to alter the social structure of the so-called *Prazos da Zambézia.*[135]

Until 1788, the settlers who managed these lands on long leases did not sell the slaves working on their properties, nor did they feel pressured by the

---

132   AHU, *Moçambique,* cx. 179, doc. 22.

133   AHU, *Moçambique,* cód. 1358, fl. 113: 1791-01-29: 'Carta de António Manuel de Mello e Castro para Christovão de Azevedo e Vasconcellos'.

134   AHU, *Moçambique,* cód. 1358, fls. 120v–121: 'Carta de António Manuel de Mello e Castro para Christovão de Azevedo e Vasconcelos'.

135   This was a system of land leasing implemented by the Portuguese Crown in Mozambique during the seventeenth century. According to this system, land which had been occupied and claimed by Portuguese settlers (who came either from Portugal or Portuguese India) was to be leased out for terms of three generations, and inherited through the female line of descent.

demand for slaves in the port of Quelimane.[136] As the number of ships visiting the port grew, however, they were accommodated by sending trustworthy slaves (*muçambazes*) owned by landlords to carry out expeditions to acquire *caporros*, by which name slaves intended for export were known.[137] Continuing demand encouraged landlords, moreover, to begin selling slaves and settlers (*colonos*) working on their own land, transforming themselves into major slave suppliers, and even prompting them to outfit slave voyages to the Mascarene Islands and to Spanish America in the nineteenth century. Many landowners, regardless of gender, boldly entered into the business of slave trade. In 1794, Pedro Xavier Velasco, owner of the *Prazo* of Tirre, pursued coastal trade and subsequently became an exporter of slaves to Brazil.[138] In the following century, female landowners began to appear as organizers of slave voyages: they included *Dona* Páscoa Maria de Almeida, owner of the *Prazo* of Chupanga;[139] *Dona* Maria Antónia de Mello Virgolino, wife of the Governor of Quelimane, Vasconcelos e Cirne, and owner of the *Prazo* of Boror, as well as owner of the brig *Nossa Senhora da Guia Morgado do Almeo*;[140] *Dona* Maria Luísa Saldanha, owner of the brig *São José Africano,* which sailed between Mozambique and Quelimane;[141] and *Dona* Josepha Natália Pinho, resident of Quelimane and owner of the ship *Leopoldina*, which was eventually decommissioned in Rio de Janeiro in 1848 after it ceased to be seaworthy.[142]

In 1840–1841, the Governor-general Joaquim Pereira Marinho described how all social groups in Mozambique were involved in the slave trade: he included in his description Portuguese, *canarins* (originally from Goa), *baneanes, parces*, Moors, women of all ages, civilians, soldiers, clergymen, and governors of all military districts except one, Inhambane. The port of Mozambique was full of dhows from many ports crewed by *mujojos*, "dark Moors," who had no profession and who invaded the city to steal slaves, carrying them to different ports in the same dhows to be sold to other *mujojos,* who in turn, sold them into the export slave trade. He noted that the trade

> employs all residents without exception and it is the slave trade because it does not require any kind of work with the main employers, nor

136   AHU, *Moçambique,* cx. 36, doc. 31.

137   AHM, cód. 11–5831, fls. 37, 74, 83, 93, 95, 96, 98, 100.

138   AHU, *Moçambique,* cód. 1365, fls. 22, 35; cód. 1376, fl. 265; cx. 70, doc. 70; cx. 74, doc. 81; cx. 208, doc. 63.

139   Santana, *Documentação Avulsa,* 1: 77.

140   AHU, *Moçambique,* cx. 174, doc. 30. Santana, *Documentação Avulsa,* 1: 617.

141   AHU, *Moçambique,* cx. 174, doc. 30.

142   IAN/TT, *Documentos dos Negócios Estrangeiros, Rio de Janeiro,* cx. 3: 1848-08-25: 'Carta de João Baptista Moreira para o Duque de Saldanha'.

bookkeeping for commercial transactions, without sacrificing personal funds. ...The main employers asked *baneanes* for the necessary amount of cloth and clothes to go to the bush and exchange them for slaves. ... Generally, the ladies of the houses received these goods, gave them to different Blacks who were used to the bush[,] so they could go inland and exchange them for slaves. ...Once the consignment of slaves comes in from the bush, each of the contractors puts theirs in their backyard where they are fed corn and water, and kept in order and without any other kind of comfort, until the ships from Brazil and Havana arrived."[143]

This is what the day-to-day world of the slave trade was like, on the Island of Mozambique, in the eighteenth and the early nineteenth centuries.

---

[143]   AHU, *Moçambique*, sala 12, pasta 5, doc. 2.

CHAPTER 7

Trans-Cultural Exchange at Malemba Bay

The Voyages of Fregatschip Prins Willem V, 1755 to 1771[1]

Stacey Sommerdyk

On 23 May 1755, the Fregatschip *Prins Willem V* set sail from the port of
Vlissingen in the province of Zealand in the Netherlands. Engaged by the
Middelburgsche Commercie Compagnie (hereafter MCC), Captain Adriaan
Jacobse and 44 other crew sailed for three months before reaching the Loango
Coast. Between 21 August and 25 December 1755, Captain Jacobse purchased
348 enslaved Africans to fill the cargo decks of his 288 ton vessel. Of these
slaves, 59 percent were male and 37 percent were children. On Christmas day
the ship departed the African coast for the Americas. Four slaves died on its
two-month Atlantic crossing, before on 19 February 1756 the ship reached
Curaçao in the Dutch Caribbean, where the surviving 344 slaves were sold. On
30 July 1756, the ship returned home to Zealand to be re-outfitted for its next
voyage. On the journey one crewman had lost his life. This was the first of six
voyages the *Prins Willem V* would make to the Loango Coast.[2]

Collected from the Slave Voyages website, this fragmented evidence tells a
story of European shipbuilders, crews, purchasers, and investors. The African
actors, both the merchants and the enslaved, exist at the margins of the story.
The former, for the most part, are silent and unexplored actors. The latter are
presented merely as a commodity for trade, quantified and measured for the
purposes of profit. Within the scholarship of the transatlantic slave trade as a
whole, the role of African merchants recently has been elevated to a more
prominent position in conversations about African ports, merchant communities and trade networks. The scholarship includes major contributions by
Robin Law on Ouidah; by Kristin Mann on Lagos; by Paul Lovejoy and David
Richardson on Calabar and Bonny; by Linda Heywood and John Thornton as
well as Joseph Miller on Luanda; and by Mariana Candido on Benguela.[3] In

---

1 I have chosen to use the spelling "Malemba" used by the English and Dutch rather than
   Portuguese spelling "Malembo" as this paper is written in English and makes extensive use of
   Dutch primary sources.
2 *Voyages: The Transatlanic Slave Trade Database* available at: http://www.slavevoyages.org/
   tast/assessment/estimates.faces Query: Voyage Identification Number – 10958.
3 Robin Law, *Ouidah: The Social History of a West African Slaving 'Port' 1727–1892* (Oxford: James
   Currey, 2004); Kristin Mann, *Slavery and the Birth of an African City: Lagos, 1760–1900*

keeping with this trend of emphasising Africa's role in the Atlantic world, this essay will build on Phyllis Martin's analysis of the Loango Coast by expanding our knowledge of economic engagement and political power in Malemba Bay.[4]

To meet this end, this chapter will examine the voyages of the Fregatschip *Prins Willem de Vijfde* (Prince Willem the Fifth) to the Loango Coast. Over a twenty four year period between 30 August 1749 and 7 May 1773, the *Prins Willem V* undertook 12 voyages from the Netherlands to western Africa and thence to the Americas (see Table 7.1 below). Of these 12 voyages, six went to the Loango Coast, and I have created a database of trade transactions relating to them.[5] By combining a contextual account of the MCC trade on the Loango Coast with an analysis of this database, this essay endeavours to reconstruct the trade negotiations between Loango and Dutch merchants. Thus it will broaden our understanding of the agency of Africans in the Atlantic slave trade and in trans-continental trade relations more broadly.

TABLE 7.1   *The voyages of Fregatschip* Prins Willem de Vijfde, *1749 to 1773*

Voyage #	Destination in Africa	Destination in Americas	Departure	Return
1	Guinee[a]	---	1749-08-30	1751-08-14
2	African Coast	Suriname	1751-12-11	1753-04-27
3	African Coast	Suriname	1753-08-11	1754-10-26
4	Loango Coast (Malemba)	Curacao	1755-05-23	1756-07-30
5	Loango Coast (Malemba)	Suriname	1757-04-19	1758-06-17
6	Loango Coast (Malemba)	Suriname	1759-06-20	1760-06-28
7	Guinee	St. Eustatius	1761-03-09	1762-05-16

(Bloomington, IN: Indiana University Press, 2007); Paul E. Lovejoy and David Richardson, "Trust, Pawnship, and Atlantic History: The Institutional Foundations of the Old Calabar Slave Trade," *American Historical Review* 104:2 (1999): 333–355; idem, "The Business of Slaving: Pawnship in Western Africa, c. 1600–1810," *Journal of African History* 42:1 (2001): 67–89; idem, "'This Horrid Hole': Royal Authority, Commerce and Credit at Bonny, 1690–1840," *Journal of African History* 45:3 (2004): 363–392; Linda M. Heywood and John K. Thornton, *Central Africans, Atlantic Creoles, and the Foundations of the Americas, 1585–1660* (New York, NY: Cambridge University Press, 2007); Mariana Candido, *Fronteras de la Esclavización: Esclavitud, Comercio e Identidad en Benguela, 1780–1850* (Mexico: El Colegio de Mexico Press, 2010).

4   Phyllis M. Martin, *The External Trade of the Lonago Coast 1576–1870: The Effects of Changing Commercial Relations on the Vili Kingdom of Loango* (Oxford: Clarendon Press, 1972).

5   The other six voyages, not having traded in West-Central Africa, are not relevant to this study. See: Table 7.1.

Voyage #	Destination in Africa	Destination in Americas	Departure	Return
8	Guinee	Suriname	1762-11-10	1764-04-14
9	Guinee	Suriname	1764-11-24	1766-06-30
10	Loango Coast (Undefined)	Suriname	1767-06-09	1768-10-08
11	Loango Coast (Loango Bay)	Suriname	1769-03-22	1770-09-15
12	Loango Coast (Malemba)	St. Eustatius	1771-06-05	1773-05-07

Sources: Zeeland Rijksarchief (hereafter ZRA), *Middelburgsche Commercie Compagnie* (hereafter MCC), nos. 958, 964, 969, 974, 979, 980, 985, 990, 995, 1000, 1005, 1009, 1014, 1019
Note:
a. In an attempt to maintain consistency and prevent confusion, I have used the spelling "Guinee" found in the Dutch MCC documents.

This essay is divided into three sections. The first section provides a rationale for the division of the West Central African coastal region, which is often seen as a single region of trade, into two distinctive regions: the Loango Coast and the Angolan Coast. In doing so, it highlights the unique pattern of trade that evolved on the Loango Coast. The second section explores the specific and unusual properties of the MCC records and the importance of Malemba as a trading venue on the Loango Coast to Middelburg slave traders. The final section analyses the Malemba and Loango Bay merchants who engaged in slave trading negotiations with Captain Adriaan Jacobse. Overall the essay argues that European traders encountered a unique economic and political context for commerce on the Loango Coast, a context of locally enforced free trade among European traders balanced with an internal system of economic regulation.

Geography and European Competition

This section will begin by focusing on situating Malemba Bay in the broader arena of the Atlantic world. How did the Dutch compare to their European counterparts? Throughout the transatlantic slave trade, c. 1500–1860, the Dutch were responsible for 4.4 percent of slaves shipped, or approximately 545,000 slaves.[6] The importance of the Dutch on the Loango Coast is slightly more pronounced

---

6   See: David Eltis, Stephen D. Behrendt, David Richardson and Herbert S. Klein, *The Transatlantic Slave Trade: A Database on CD-ROM* (Cambridge: Cambridge University Press, 1999) and

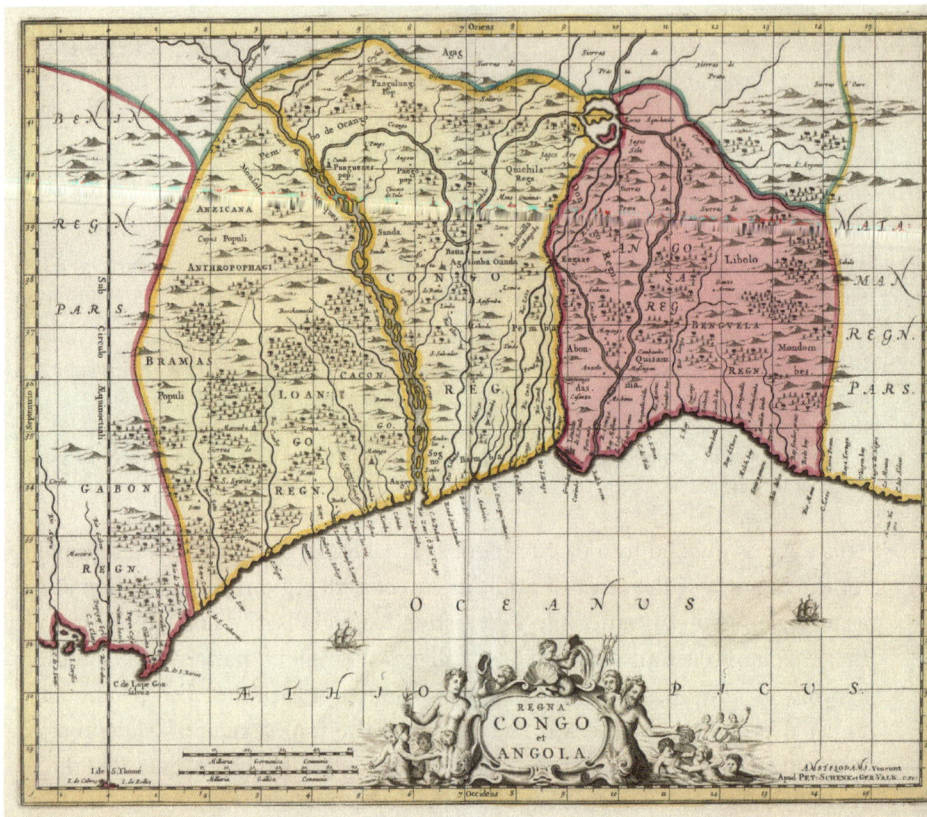

http://www.slavevoyages.org. The 1999 version of the database gives the Dutch has having embarked 527,700 slaves or 4.8 percent of the total. The newer online version of the database, on the other hand, shows the Dutch as embarking 545,808 slaves or 4.4 percent of the total. With the total number of slaves embarked having increased, the Dutch percentage has declined. See: David Eltis and David Richardson, "A New Assessment of the Transatlantic Slave Trade," in David Eltis and David Richardson, eds., *Extending the Frontiers: Essays on the New Transatlantic Slave Trade Database* (New Haven, CT: Yale University Press, 2008), 22–23. For a more in-depth analysis of the significance of these numbers, see: Simon J. Hogerzeil and David Richardson, "Slave Purchasing Strategies and Shipboard Mortalitiy: Day-to-Day Evidence from the Dutch African Trade, 1751–1797," *Journal of Economic History* 67:1 (2007): 160–190; Jelmer Vos, David Eltis and David Richardson, "The Dutch in the Atlantic World: New Perspectives from the Slave Trade with Particular Reference to the African Origins of the Traffic," in Eltis and Richardson, eds., *Extending the Frontiers*, 228–249.

with the Dutch shipping 9 percent of the slaves taken away, the largest exporter being the Portuguese-Brazilians with 21.4 percent of the slaves shipped from the Loango Coast.[7] Graph 7.1 below illustrates the transitions of European trade on the Loango Coast throughout the transatlantic slave trade. Unlike the trading region of Angola to the south, which was dominated by the Portuguese-Brazilians, and Biafra to the north, which was dominated by the British, the Loango Coast was never dominated solely by one European trading power. To the contrary, the Loango Coast went through a series of transitions: between 1660 and 1720 the Dutch were the most prominent traders on the coast, while the British and French traded a smaller number of slaves. In the 1720s the Dutch share of the slave trade fell below that of the French as control of the Dutch slave trade nationally passed from the second West India Company (WIC) to the MCC and other private traders. Though the levels of Dutch trade thereafter recovered, the French maintained the position of the largest traders on the Loango Coast until 1790, after which the British experienced a brief period of supremacy through 1810. Following Britain's abolition of its slave trade effectively from 1808 onwards, Portuguese-Brazilian traders experienced unprecedented success on the coast, virtually monopolizing the trade in the immediate period after the British moratorium on slave trading and continuing to take the largest share of slaves from the region until 1830. From 1831 to 1864, the Portuguese-Brazilians, Americans, Spanish, and French engaged in intermittent trade on the coast. These shifts in patterns of European trade connections with the Loango Coast through time help us to highlight some unique features of trade in the region.

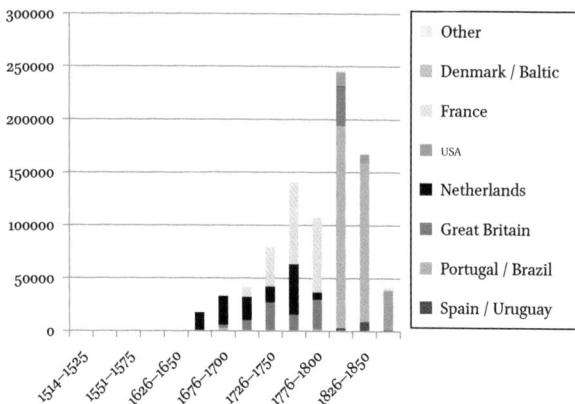

GRAPH 7.1   *Slaves embarked at the Loango Coast by flag*
            Source: www.slavevoyages.org/tast/database/search.faces Query: Principle place of slave
            purchase – Boary, Cabinda, Congo North, Congo River, Rio Zaire, Kilongo, Loango,
            Malembo, and Mayumba. Accessed on 2 May 2014.

---

7 www.slavevoyages.org/tast/assessment/estimates.faces Query: All and Query: Principle
   place of slave purchase – West-Central Africa. Accessed on 2 December 2008.

West-Central Africa, as defined by Curtin in his seminal work *The Atlantic slave trade: a census* and subsequently in the Slave Voyages Database, stretches from Cape Lopez in the north to Cabo Negro in the south. The West-Central African coast exported approximately 5.7 million slaves between 1505 and 1866. As the single largest slaving region in the Atlantic world, West-Central Africa exported 46 percent of the total 12.5 million slaves estimated to have been taken from Africa to the Americas during this period.[8] Along this 1200 kilometre stretch of coast there were 18 known locations for the purchase of slaves. From north to south, these are the locations recorded by European traders from which slaves were embarked: Mayumba, Kiloango, Loango, Malemba, Cabinda, Congo North, Congo River [Rio Zaire], Mpinda, Ambriz, Rio Dande [Dande River], St. Paul de Loanda [Luanda], Salinas, Coanza River [Kwanza River], Ambona, Benguela Velha [Old Benguela], Novo Redondo, Quicombo [Kikombo], and Benguela. Given the Portuguese-Brazilian dominance of the primary port, Luanda, the history of this stretch of the African coast has often been left to Portuguese-speaking scholars to explore. Although scholars have hitherto dealt with this coast as one unit to be compared with the Gold Coast or the Bight of Biafra, the diverging shipping patterns of this region, the differing political systems, and the volume of trade itself all indicate a clear divide between the Loango Coast to the north of the Congo River and the Angolan Coast to the south.

This definition of the Loango Coast rests on the political configuration of the coast at the time of European contact. In the sixteenth century the Loango Coast was divided into three polities: running north to south these were Loango, Kakongo, and Ngoyo. Loango stretched from Cape St. Catherine in the north to the Chiloango River in the south and, under the governance of the Vili, exercised control over territories reaching as far as 200–300 miles inland towards the north-east. Loango Bay was the primary harbour in this region. To the south of Loango was Kakongo, which occupied a coastal stretch of a mere 25 miles between the Chiloango and Mbele rivers. Malemba Bay was the primary port of Kakongo. The southernmost polity was Ngoyo, which was the smallest of the three, and was situated between the Mbele River and the mouth of the Congo River. Within it lay the largest and safest of the Loango Coast harbours at Cabinda. In her history of the Loango Coast, the historian Phyllis Martin concluded that "[t]he people of Ngoyo, Kakongo, and Loango were closely related. The three kingdoms had similar systems of government, laws, and social customs. They spoke very similar dialects of Kikongo."[9] Within this structure,

---

8   www.slavevoyages.org/tast/assessment/estimates.faces Query: All. Accessed on 2 December 2008. Note: these are the estimates, not the hard numbers which are available on another section of the webpage.

9   Martin, *The External Trade of the Loango Coast,* 30.

however, Loango was politically, economically, and socially dominant. This was evident in the payments of tribute to Loango, in the homage given to Loango rulers at their appointment and death, and in the lower status of Ngoyo wives in the Loango ruler's family. Additionally, Martin argued, "[t]he superiority of the Maloango was further emphasized by the titles of the three rulers. The king of Loango [the Maloango] was called *Nunu*, meaning husband, the Manikakongo [ruler of Kakongo] was called *Mokassi*, meaning consort or wife, and the Maningoyo [ruler of Ngoyo] was called *Itemma*, or priest."[10] To the south of the Congo River, the people of the Loango Coast were known as *Mubiri*, indicating a larger common identity among the people loyal to the Loango, Kakongo, and Ngoyo leaders.

The relative political stability of the Loango Coast stood in sharp contrast to the reality Europeans first encountered to the south of the Congo River. In the sixteenth century, the coastline south of the Congo River was marked by a struggle for dominance between the Kongo, Ndongo, and Benguela polities. Although the Mubiri traded on the Angolan Coast, they did not seem to interfere with their politics. In turn, the Kongo occasionally declared but never implemented supremacy over the Ngoyo people. Likewise the Portuguese made some futile attempts to forcefully incorporate Ngoyo into its Angolan trade monopoly, but the lack of resources and the Ngoyo refusal to cooperate quickly crushed these efforts.[11]

The slave trade on the Loango Coast was a barter-based, largely shipboard-based trade which was open to all traders. Local centralized polities, relying on internal financing and local agents, supported commercial engagements with such traders. The slave trading regions of the Angolan Coast to the south and the Bight of Biafra to the north provide contrasting examples of governance and credit. The slave trade on the Angolan Coast focused around permanent Portuguese settlements, relied upon Portuguese capital, and often involved Portuguese agents. Trade at the Bight of Biafra presents yet another pattern: a pattern of ship based trade and European credit, guaranteed in Bonny by a "centralized authority and its law-enforcing powers" and in Old Calabar by a system "linked to the pawning or pledging of human beings as collateral for debt."[12]

10   Ibid., 31.

11   John K. Thornton, *Warfare in Atlantic Africa 1500–1800* (New York, NY: Routledge, 1999), 99–104, 112. Also see: Martin, *The External Trade of the Loango Coast*, 83–91.

12   Paul E. Lovejoy and David Richardson, "African Agency and the Liverpool Trade," in David Richardson, Suzanne Schwarz, and Anthony J. Tibbles, eds., *Liverpool and Transatlantic Slavery* (Liverpool: Liverpool University Press, 2007), 60. For a more detailed analysis of comparative systems of trade see: Stacey Sommerdyk, 'Malemba Merchants:

In the *Atlas of the Transatlantic Slave Trade*, David Eltis and David Richardson have released new estimates for the twenty largest ports of embarkation of African slaves in the transatlantic system. In this list, Cabinda emerges as the fourth most important port of the transatlantic slave trade having supplied an approximate 753,000 slaves to be embarked on transatlantic voyages. Malemba follows closely as sixth largest supplier embarking 549,000 slaves. Loango, despite its decline at the end of the eighteenth century, still sold an approximate 418,000 slaves into the transatlantic slave trade. This places Loango in the position of the eighth largest transatlantic supplier of slaves. Furthermore, Congo River supplied an additional 276,000 slaves and ranks twelfth in the list. These data are displayed in Table 7.2 below. Given the dominance of these ports as transatlantic slave suppliers and their relative absence in the literature, as outlined above, this is a gap that calls to be addressed.

Although the Loango Coast often has been viewed as part of the broader West-Central African coast, which exported approximately 5.7 million slaves, the Loango Coast stands out as having a distinct trading pattern. If the Loango Coast is separated out from the Angolan Coast, an estimated two million (35 percent) of these slaves were embarked at the Loango Coast. One significant factor in distinguishing these coasts is the presence of specific national carriers. Of the slaves embarked on the Loango Coast, there is a substantially

TABLE 7.2   *Estimated number of slaves embarked on the Loango Coast*

Loango Coast Port	Estimated slaves embarked	Percentage of 5.7 Million West-Central African Slaves
Cabinda	753,000	13.21
Malemba	549,000	9.63
Loango	418,000	7.33
Congo River	276,000	4.84
Total	1,996,000	35.02

Sources: David Eltis and David Richardson, *Atlas of the Transatlantic Slave Trade* (New Haven: Yale University Press, 2010), 90

A Repositioning of West-Central Africa in the Transatlantic Slave Trade' (Unpublished paper, Stirling, 2009); John K. Thornton, *Africa and Africans in the Making of the Atlantic World, 1400–1800* (Cambridge: Cambridge University Press, 2nd edition, 1998); James A. Rawley and Stephen D. Behrendt, *The transatlantic slave trade: a history* (Lincoln, NE: University of Nebraska Press, 2nd Revised edition, 2005).

higher percentage embarked by non-Portuguese ships than from the Angolan Coast, particularly in the era before 1807. As shown in Graphs 7.2 and 7.3 below, on the Loango Coast Portuguese-Brazilian traders embarked 39 percent of all slaves leaving the coast, whereas on the Angolan Coast they embarked 97 percent of all slaves. Of the non-Portuguese-speaking traders on the Loango Coast, the Dutch were second only to the French with the former accounting for 16 percent and the latter 22 percent of the trade, respectively. The British followed closely with 14 percent. The disproportionate role of Dutch traders on the Loango Coast makes the Dutch slave trading documents addressed in this article particularly relevant for this region. More generally, the diversity of trade in the Loango area was in stark contrast to the Portuguese-Brazilian dominated trade in Angola, the region south of the Congo River. When figures are separated between the early trade (pre-1800) and the late trade (1800–1867), the Dutch, French and British ships dominated the coast in succession throughout the early period shipping 33 percent, 46 percent, and 20 percent of slaves, respectively. The Portuguese-Brazilians only emerged as the dominate traders circa 1810, following Britain's abolition of its trade, shipping 75 percent of all slaves from the Loango Coast after that date.[13] Based on this difference, the western African coast can be better understood when divided into seven regions: Senegambia, Upper Guinea, Gold Coast, Bight of Benin, Bight of Biafra, Loango Coast, and Angola rather than conflating Loango Coast and Angola together under the category of West-Central Africa. This would be consistent with a number of historical maps as illustrated in Map 7.1 above.[14]

The Sources

Moving on from the geography of the documents, this section will explore the source material that tells the story of the voyages of the Dutch ship *Prins Willem V*. The *Prins Willem V* was owned and operated by the MCC in Zealand. The MCC was a private company set up in the Netherlands in the eighteenth century for the primary purpose of engaging in the slave trade. Between 1733 and 1803, the MCC embarked in Africa over 30,000 slaves on 112 transatlantic

---

13   Stacey Sommerdyk, "Trade and the Merchant Community of the Loango Coast in the Eighteenth Century" (unpublished PhD thesis, University of Hull, UK, 2012), 56–59.

14   For a more detailed discussion on the separation of West-Central Africa into two trading regions see: Stacey Sommerdyk and Filipa Ribeiro da Silva, "Re-examining the Slave Trade on the West-Central African Coast: Looking behind the Numbers," *African Economic History* 38 (2010): 77–106.

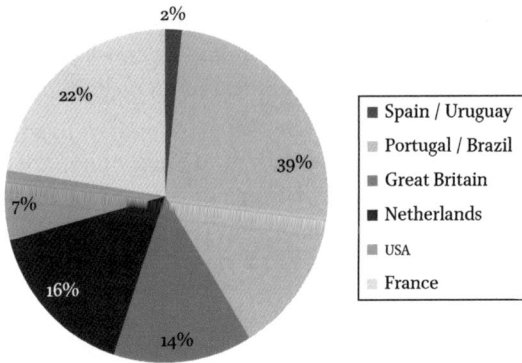

GRAPH 7.2   *The number of enslaved Africans exported from the Loango Coast sorted by ship's flag*
Source: http://www.slavevoyages.org/tast/database/search.faces Query – Principal place of
slave purchase: Cabinda, Congo North, Congo River, Rio Zaire, Kilongo, Loango, Malembo,
Mayumba, and Mpinda. Accessed: 2 May 2014.

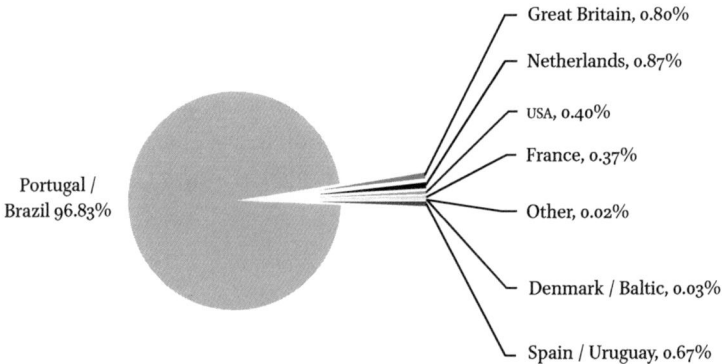

GRAPH 7.3   *The number of enslaved Africans exported from the Angolan Coast sorted by ship's flag*
Source: http://www.slavevoyages.org/tast/database/search.faces Query – Principal place of
slave purchase: Ambona, Ambriz, Benguela, Benguela Velho, Nova Redonda, Quicombo,
Salinas, and Luanda Accessed: 2 May 2014.

voyages. Of these voyages, approximate one-third embarked slaves on the
Loango Coast making it the largest single regional supplier of slaves in western
Africa for the MCC (see Graph 7.4 below). Twenty-one of the MCC's 31 voyages
to the Loango Coast listed their specific place of slave purchase as the Bay of
Malemba. Interestingly, it is not Malemba but Cape Lahou on the Windward
Coast, which was the port most frequented by MCC vessels. Nevertheless,

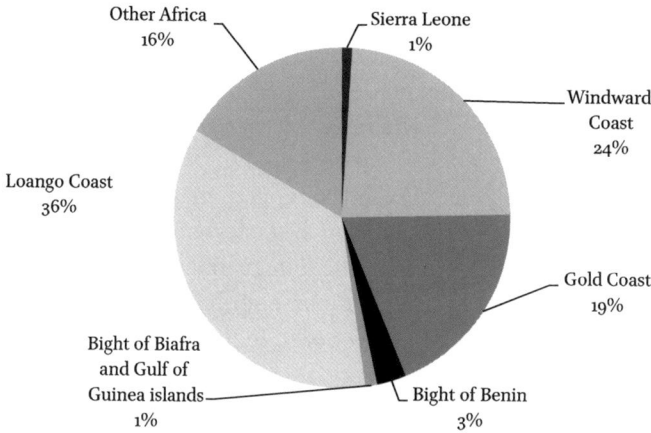

GRAPH 7.4   *Percentage of enslaved Africans embarked by the MCC by port, 1733 to 1803*
Source: http://www.slavevoyages.org/tast/database/search.faces Query: Vessel Owners –
Middelburgsche Commercie Compagnie. Accessed on 2 May 2014.

Malemba was the MCC's largest purveyor of slaves, supplying 7,651 compared to 6,325 slaves embarked at Cape Lahou.[15]

The MCC records show that the 31 slaving voyages that went to 'Angola' (i.e. the Loango Coast) between 1732 and 1797 were made by 19 ships. For each of the 31 voyages there survives a minimum of three different sets of documents. They are a record of trade negotiations, a crew account book, and a miscellaneous collection of papers usually roughly translated as "several pieces concerning this equipage." For some voyages there are additional records, such as captain's journals, cargo books, drafts of trade negotiations, lists of crew, and packets of letters. In this essay, I focus primarily on lists of slave purchases and sales, which are generally found in the records of trade negotiations and sometimes in the miscellaneous papers. Journals are used to verify locations, dates, and personalities involved as well as other details that are unclear or absent in the main records used. I have sorted and organized this information in a database which records each slave purchase including the ship, date, captain, and Loango Coast merchant involved in the transactions as well as the sex, age (i.e. adult or child), and cost (whether in local and Dutch currency) of the slaves involved.

To understand the specific qualities of the MCC data it is useful to compare it to the English Royal African Company records (hereafter referred to as the RAC). In both cases, ship captains kept records, but the MCC records are far

---

15   Sources: http://www.slavevoyages.org/tast/database/search.faces Query: Vessel Owners –
       Middelburgsche Commercie Compagnie. Accessed on 19 September 2010.

more detailed with respect to the purchasing of supplies, the trading of goods for slaves, and the resale of slaves in the Americas. This reflected different trade strategies of the two parties. Due to the predominance of the concentration of the RAC trade at the Gold Coast, where a fort-based system of trade predominated and where factors, not captains, engaged in the bulk of the buying and selling, the RAC trading records tend to be very fragmented.[16] Many English captains left the financial transactions to the factors and other RAC officials. By contrast, the captains of ships *were* the bureaucrats of the MCC. This ensures that the MCC data are an excellent resource for historians seeking to study commercial transactions at the Loango Coast. In this essay I shall focus on trade at Malemba Bay, which was not only the most important source of slaves for the MCC on the Loango Coast but also its principal single source of captives in western Africa as a whole. Within this context, the next section provides a detailed analysis of the voyages of one ship to the Loango Coast, during which it carried some 2,300 enslaved people from Malemba Bay to the Americas.

Malemba Merchants and Fregatschip *Prins Willem V*

Fregatschip *Prins Willem V* traded at Loango in two distinct periods: 1755–1759 and 1767–1771. In each period the ship undertook three voyages to the Loango Coast under the same commander, Captain Jacobse, who purchased a total of 2311 slaves at Malemba, Loango, and another port on the Loango Coast which is unspecified in the MCC documents. In the first period, trade was concentrated at Malemba; in the second period, trade was split between the unspecified port and Loango Bay. The first period of trade produced the most slaves, with 346, 462, and 472 slaves embarked, respectively, on the three voyages concerned. Following this, the *Prins Willem V* did not return to the Loango Coast until 1767, at which point the ship went to Loango Bay rather than Malemba, purchasing 334 slaves. The next voyage in 1769 went to the undefined port on the coast, where 379 slaves embarked. A final voyage to Malemba in 1771 saw the vessel obtain 318 slaves, but, unfortunately, records of the transactions relating to this voyage have not survived (see Graph 7.5 below).[17] Nevertheless, examining the series of transactions relating to the five voyages with complete data provides insights into how the merchant community of the Loango Coast operated in the third quarter of the eighteenth century period and offers the opportunity

---

16   David W. Galenson, *Traders, Planters, and Slaves: Market Behavior in Early English America* (Cambridge: Cambridge University Press, 1986), 23–24, 27.

17   See Table 7.1.

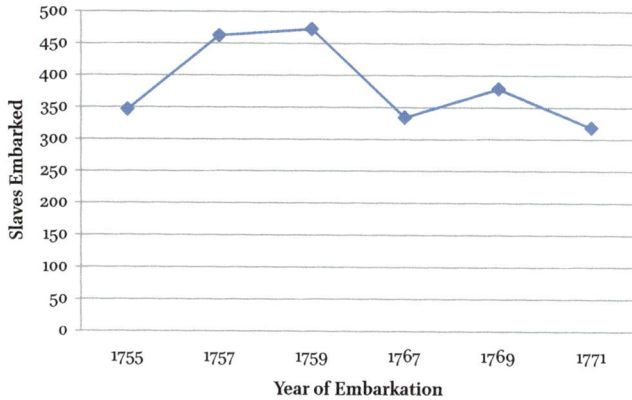

GRAPH 7.5   *Fregatschip Prins Willem V's slave trading voyages to the Loango Coast*
             Sources: ZRA, MCC, nos. 979, 980, 985, 990, 1009, 1014, 1019

to contrast patterns of slave procurement in Malemba with patterns at other parts of the western African coast.

Between 1755 and 1771, the captain of the *Prins Willem V* made 1,456 transactions with 192 named merchants for the purchase of the 2311 slaves on the Loango Coast shown in Table 7.3.[18] The transactions are listed in the appendix to this chapter. Unfortunately there is no merchant information for the last of these six voyages. Transactions with unknown merchants are excluded from the calculations which follow. Among the known merchants, the ratio of merchants to slaves is 1:11; and the mode, or most reoccurring configuration, is one slave per merchant and transaction. So despite the large number of merchants engaging in the trade, the majority of these merchants seem to be engaging on a very small scale while a few merchants engage in a relatively large number of transactions. Thus, the majority of slave suppliers seem to have engaged in slave trafficking with the *Prins Willem V* as one element within a portfolio of activities. These activities could, of course, include selling slaves to other ships visiting the coast at the same time. However, if the picture shown here is representative of the slave trade with other ships and other nations, this could have interesting implications on how we understand the organization of the slave trade. Specifically, the average Malemba merchant may have made a relatively small investment in the trade, or at least a relatively small investment in trade with the *Prins Willem V*. Furthermore, this could indicate

---

18   While the data in the Appendix indicate a total of 1499 transactions, in the case of multiple merchants some transactions show up more than once, thus the discrepancy with the 1,456 total transactions mentioned above.

TABLE 7.3   *Total number of slaves purchased on the*
             Loango Coast per voyage

Voyage #	Slaves Purchased
4	346
5	462
6	472
10	334
11	379
12	318
Mean	385
Total	2311

Sources: ZRA, MCC, nos. 979, 980, 985, 990, 1009, 1014, 1019
Note: # The voyage numbers are in reference to Table 7.1.

a spreading of risk throughout the merchant community with numerous of its members having made a small percentage of the overall investment in slaving activities.

Four merchants stand out, nevertheless, from the rest of those listed in Table 7.4 as major traders: Prins Tom, Mafoeke, Matientie, and Jan Klaase. Cumulatively, these four men accounted for 25.6 percent of all transactions (excluding those with un-named merchants). The most prominent trader in the *Prins Willem V* records is Prins Tom. He was the second Malemba merchant to negotiate a sale of slaves with the *Prins Willem V* upon its first visit to the Loango Coast on 21 August 1755. Between that date and 25 November 1757, Prins Tom engaged in 154 sales, or 11 percent of the total 1,456 slave transactions included in the appendix, providing the *Prins Willem V* with a total of 267 slaves in only two voyages.

Mafoeke was the first merchant at Malemba to negotiate a sale with the *Prins Willem V*. He was involved in 101 transactions, or 7 percent of the *Prins Willem's* transactions, providing a total of 133 slaves between 21 August 1755 and 30 November 1767. During all of these transactions, Mafoeke is listed as being in Malemba or Angola undefined. Interestingly, an additional 49 transactions, involving 68 slaves, included the name 'Mafoeke' as part of the merchant name or a similar spelling (i.e. Mafoeke Bliem, Maboeke, and Mafoeke Robijn). For these it is difficult to tell whether it is a trading partnership between two merchants or whether they are different merchants with a common name. The presence of the names Jonge Mafoeke (or Young Mafoeke) and Mafoeke Cousin seem to indicate something different altogether: a developing trade network based on familial ties. If, in fact, there is a connection between all of these entries containing 'Mafoeke' or a variant spelling, that would seem to indicate that 'Mafoeke' engaged in trade, whether by proxy or directly, at all the locations, specified and unspecified, over the two periods covered by the *Prins Willem V*'s trade at the Loango Coast.

Mafoeke appears to be a political title in use throughout the Loango Coast. In her studies, Martin referred to a position within the Cabinda court that developed about this period: the 'mafouk'. Though not a destination of the *Prins Willem V*, Cabinda was also a slave trading port situated between Malemba to the north and the Congo River to the south. During the eighteenth century, the political and economic systems of Loango Bay, Malemba Bay, and Cabinda Bay were closely linked. Given the corresponding time period and geographical location, the mafouk to which Martin referred may well be the same 'mafoeke' to which the Dutch are referring. Martin described the role of the mafouk as follows: "This appointment, a particularly lucrative one due to the responsibility of overseeing trade, was acquired through payment to the Ngoyo ruler in goods and services."[19] According to Martin, Mbatchi Ncongo appointed Franque Kokelo to this position in the late eighteenth century. She goes on to suggest that "[Kokelo] was the servant of a French slave-trader who died at Cabinda and left his possessions to his African employee...[S]tarting with this small capital, Kokelo moved from being a minor figure in the community to being a successful broker and slave dealer."[20]

The merchant commonly referred to as Matientie presents us with not dissimilar problems of identification. The inconsistencies of the spelling of his name, taken in tandem with antiquated and faded handwriting, the time lag between voyages, and the difficulties of finding a Dutch spelling for African or Africanized names, all present challenges here. In the database I have identified with the name Matientie other variants, such as Matiijnie, Matijnje, Matinie, Matinje, Matintie, Matjnie, Mattijnje, and Mattjnie, on the assumption that spelling of the name varied through time, with single consonants often becoming doubles, 'ie's becoming 'ij's and 'je's or vice versa. Even with these variations, a certain commonality is present throughout. Assuming this identification is correct, Matientie accounted for 54 transactions or 4 percent of the slaves sold to the *Prins Willem V*. This translated into a total of 101 slaves for transatlantic shipment. As with Prins Tom, noted earlier, the transactions

19   Phyllis M Martin, "Family Strategies in Nineteenth-Century Cabinda," *Journal of African History* 28:1 (1987): 71.

20   Ibid.

identified with Matientie were largely grouped between 1757 and 1759 in
Malemba, although a Matientje Andries appears once in Loango in 1769. This
raises possible questions, as with the Mafoeke, noted above, about possible
familial ties through time or even migration of families between ports.

The last of the four major traders was Jan Klaase. As with the two previously
mentioned merchants, there is some ambiguity in the spelling of Jan Klaase's
name as noted in the Appendix. Like Prins Tom and Matientie, however, Jan
Klaase traded primarily with the *Prins Willem V* in 1757–1759, showing up in 52
transactions in that period in the trade at Malemba, and supplying a total of 84
slaves. In addition, a Prins Jan Claasen participated in four transactions, involving four slaves in the 1767 voyage of the ship to Loango, though whether this is
the same merchant or not is difficult to say. Jan is not the only merchant connected to the achternaam (surname) Klaase: Pieter, Jonge, Cabinda, and Nite
are all listed among the Klaases. We cannot be sure but, again, this may indicate larger familial networks within the Loango region.

In this examination of trading patterns which emerge out of the *Prins
Willem V* trading records on the Loango Coast, a distinction between the 1755–
1759 and 1767–1771 market participants becomes readily apparent. All four of
the leading slave suppliers to the *Prins Willem V* in 1755–1771 are to be found in
the first sub-period but not in the second. Their disappearance may have been
partially due to generational change, but the absence of their replacement is
quite obvious. In the first period, 1280 or 55 percent of total number of slaves
purchased by the *Prins Willem V* at the Loango Coast embarked at Malemba. Of
these slaves, 44 percent were bought from just four Malemba traders. This
seems to indicate a larger concentration of market influence in the hands of a
few traders in the earlier period or perhaps a preferential trading arrangement
which did not continue in the second period when MCC traders sought slaves
suppliers in other Loango Coast ports. More likely, the concentration of trade
in the hands of a few traders in the data from the first period may indicate a
more centralized and organized trade between MCC and local merchants in
Malemba in comparison to the other parts of the Loango Coast on which *Prins
Willem V* traded in 1767–1771. This may suggest variations of trading practices
within the Loango Coast region, although the effects of competition from
other European carriers of slaves cannot be ruled out.[21]

---

21   In his voyage journal for 1605–1612 Pieter van den Broeke makes an argument for the pref-
     erential treatment of the Dutch merchants by the people of Loango. See: J.D. La Fleur, ed.
     and trans., *Pieter van den Broecke's Journal of Voyages to Cape Verde, Guinea and Angola
     (1605–1612)* (London: Hakluyt Society, 2000), 54–55. This assertion is supported by
     José Curto's statement in his 2004 book *Enslaving Spirits*: "Most African slave suppliers

Alternatively, the absence of a few dominant suppliers of slaves to the *Prins Willem V* in 1767–1771 could be indicative of a larger societal change. Martin points to the eighteenth-century slave trade in the context of destabilization in the Ngoyo "kingdom." She writes:

> From the last quarter of the seventeenth century, the great men of Cabinda augmented their wealth and power in relation to the government at the capital through their role in the slave trade as dealers and brokers. They also acted as agents of the Ngoyo ruler who was prohibited from approaching the sea and lived sequestered in Mbanza Ngoyo.
>
> A hundred years later Cabinda had emerged as the leading slave-port between the equator and Luanda, through its proximity to the Zaire River and to the slave-markets, in the savanna regions to the south and at Malebo Pool. This was the background for the collapse for the centralized Ngoyo state.[22]

Martin continued on the crisis of Ngoyo leadership: "Unable to participate fully in the trade, too weak to control the powerful families at Cabinda and overburdened with the expenses of the office, the Ngoyo rulers found themselves in an economic and political crisis."[23] Beyond the power of their ruler, she argued, his administrators began to expand their influence in Cabinda through "a judicious mixing of economic activities of a capitalist kind, namely commerce with foreign slave-traders and investments in a more traditional mode."[24] Although the slave trade was one element in the disintegration of central power, changing traditions also played a role, perhaps as a less direct result of contact with Europeans. Although it is difficult to establish to what extent the slave trade stimulated change in the political situation or the political situation shaped the slave trade, it is evident that these two patterns were inextricably linked.

The Franque family of Cabinda was a symbol of how Europeans contributed to the shifting power base in Cabinda. Inheriting his fortune from his European master, Franque Kokelo "moved from being a minor figure in the community to being a successful broker and slave dealer." He thereby obtained the office of

---

preferred to trade with the Dutch, who offered better quality goods at lower prices than Lusitanian competitors" (José Curto, *Enslaving Spirits: The Portuguese-Brazilian Alcohol Trade at Luanda and its Hinterland, c. 1550–1830* (Leiden: Brill, 2004), 62.

22   Martin, "Family Strategies in Nineteenth-Century Cabinda," 69.

23   Ibid., 69–70.

24   Ibid., 70.

mafouk from the Ngoyo ruler. His son and heir Francisco Franque was edu-
cated in the Portuguese tradition in Brazil. Martin suggested: "Of all nineteenth-century Cabinda traders, Francisco (Chico) Franque (c.1777–1875) was
most deserving of the title of 'merchant prince.'"[25]

Amidst the turmoil surrounding the slave trade on the Loango Coast, the
MCC's records of Mafoeke/Mafouk trading in Malemba further substantiate
Martin's earlier arguments that Loango had an active trade policy that included
exporting to the north, east, and south:

> As early as the seventeenth century and probably before, the inhabitants of
> the Loango Coast enjoyed a wide reputation as peripatetic traders and cara-
> vaneers throughout West-Central Africa, from Gabon to Luanda and from
> Pool Malebo to the Atlantic Ocean. Some of these [traders] established settle-
> ment abroad from where they could direct their trading interests.[26]

This also strengthens the argument of connections among the Claases. In addition, the 104 MCC records of joint sales among Loango Coast merchants indicate that trading networks existed among the region's merchants, which made
it desirable to join forces when negotiating with Dutch merchants.

Through examining these six trading voyages of the fregatschip *Prins Willem V*,
it is evident that some Loango Coast merchants played an extraordinary role in
the supplying of slaves to MCC ships. These merchants were mobile within the
Loango Coast region and well networked. This was evident in the 1755 to 1759
period, when a small number of merchants supplied a large share of the slaves
sold to the *Prins Willem V*. As a result, the vessel's voyages help to link the history
of the Loango Coast to a broader story of Dutch and indeed Atlantic history.

Conclusion

By disaggregation of West-Central Africa into two regions of trade, the Loango
Coast emerges as a major contributor of slaves in its own right to the transatlantic trade rather than a periphery of the more dominant Angolan Coast.
The organization of the Loango Coast trade stands out when compared to its
neighbouring regions of Biafra and Angola: first, as a region free from commercial domination by any one European power, relying upon ship trade rather

25   Ibid., 73.
26   Phyllis M. Martin, "The Cabinda Connection: A Historical Perspective," *African Affairs*
      76:302 (1977): 48, 50.

than castle trade; and, second, as a region with a highly organized trade regulated by political agencies and allowing both a few major players and numerous small investors to coexist, particularly, it seems, at Malemba. Additionally, our data suggest the slave trade was linked to shifts in internal political structures, while questioning the role of European credit in such shifts which has been argued for other ports of the Loango Coast. An analysis over a broader time period would be useful to verify these findings.

By emphasizing the agency of African traders in negotiating the terms of trade within the context of the transatlantic slave trade, this essay attempts to move beyond what the sources tell us about European engagement in the Atlantic World and to re-frame the conversation around African contributions. The examination of the history of the trading transactions of the Fregatschip *Prins Willem V* is only the first piece of the puzzle. Within the historiography of the African slave trade, an expansion of this project will add to our understanding of trade negotiations on the Western African coast, and consequently, to our understanding of Africans in the Atlantic World.

APPENDIX *Number of transactions completed with each Loango Coast merchant*

Merchant	Individual Sale	Joint Sale	Total Sales	Percentage of Total Sales*	Total Slaves**
Prins Tom/Prinstom	154		154	10.74	267
Mafoeke/Makoeke	99	2	101	7.04	133
Matientje/Matientie/Matiijnie/ Matijnje/Matinie/Matinje/ Matintie/Matjnie/Mattijnje/ Mattjnie	54	7	61	4.25	101
Jan Claase*/ Clase/Klaafe/Klaas/ Klaase/ Klaasen/ Klaasfe/Klase/ Klassen	52		52	3.63	84
Koffij/Coffij(e)	42	1	43	3.00	46
Tom Aary/Tom Arij/Tomaij/ Tomarij/Tomary	36	4	40	2.79	42
Mabanse	36		36	2.51	36
Joarij/Joo Arij/Joo Ary/Jooarij/ Jooary/Joobry	32		32	2.23	34
Dicke Barend	29		29	2.02	37
Prins Manuel	27		27	1.88	34

APPENDIX   *Number of transactions completed with each Loango Coast merchant* (cont.)

Merchant	Individual Sale	Joint Sale	Total Sales	Percentage of Total Sales*	Total Slaves**
Prins Jeck	26		26	1.81	44
Jan Coni/Conij/Connij/Cooni/ Coonij	23	3	26	1.81	48
Mafoeke bliem/Mafoe bliem/ Mafoeke Cliem	19	6	25	1.74	50
Prins Coffij	22		22	1.53	44
Batje Claad/Batje Claas/ Batij Claas	18	3	21	1.46	33
Jan Zwart	15	3	18	1.26	32
Jan Broer/Groer	12	6	18	1.26	20
Monnebanse Laton/Monnebase Laton	15	2	17	1.19	17
Prins Wabbe	15	2	17	1.19	21
Bon Claaijs Monebee	16		16	1.12	32
Lange Jan	15	1	16	1.12	21
Apollo	15		15	1.05	24
Coubrou	13	2	15	1.05	22
Prins Wiel/Wile/Will	13	2	15	1.05	23
Coubrou Macos	14		14	0.98	14
Jan Prins	14		14	0.98	16
Pieter Mavonge/Pieter Mavongo	14		14	0.98	23
Koning	13		13	0.91	29
Prins Matijello/Matjello/Matiello	11		11	0.77	18
Quini Mattentje/Matienije	10	1	11	0.77	11
Foete Tatie	10		10	0.70	11
Prins Parrij	10		10	0.70	12
Voerdeijn/Vordeijn	10		10	0.70	17
Prins Fernand/Ferdinand	10		10	0.70	21
Coffij Anboe	9		9	0.63	15
Jonge Monnebanse	9		9	0.63	12
Maboek/Maboeka/Maboeke	9		9	0.63	11
Melonde Malos/Melonge Macos	9		9	0.63	10
Pieter Claas/Pieter Claasen/ Pieter Claaven	9		9	0.63	14

Merchant	Individual Sale	Joint Sale	Total Sales	Percentage of Total Sales*	Total Slaves**
Andries	7	2	9	0.63	23
Bikoe		9	9	0.63	11
Mafoek Robijn/Mafoeke Robijn/ Mafoeke Robin	8	1	9	0.63	22
Gouverneur Map(p)ello	8		8	0.56	16
Tom Grieffij/Griffij/Griffin	8		8	0.56	17
Fam Koning	7		7	0.49	11
Jonge Claaijs/Claas	7		7	0.49	7
Lowij	7		7	0.49	7
Pierro Magoffe	7		7	0.49	7
Prins Famel /Famele/Famell/ Famile	7		7	0.49	8
Prins Mabjere/Majere	7		7	0.49	11
Prins Mabotte	7		7	0.49	13
Prins Monwango/Mowango	7		7	0.49	11
Goblet	2	5	7	0.49	20
Monnebanse/Monneb	5	2	7	0.49	11
Tom Vrijman	3	4	7	0.49	12
Gouverneur Matimo/ Matimongoo/Mattimomongo/ Mattimongo/Mattimongoo	6		6	0.42	11
Goveneur Cabende	6		6	0.42	6
Monebee Maboek	6		6	0.42	10
Jan Cabende	5	1	6	0.42	7
Pieter Markadoor	5	1	6	0.42	7
Pieter Macaaij/Maraaij	5	1	6	0.42	9
Siclander	6		6	0.42	6
Wis Gouverneur	5		5	0.35	6
Anthonij (Antonij) van Malemba	5		5	0.35	5
Jonge Fernandes	5		5	0.35	6
Peero Malemba	5		5	0.35	5
Prins C(h)ambo	5		5	0.35	5
Prins Lingo/Prins Linga	5		5	0.35	8
Monnebelle Joba	5		5	0.35	5
Prins Dock/Prins L Dock	5		5	0.35	5
Mabialla/Mabijalla	2	3	5	0.35	8

APPENDIX *Number of transactions completed with each Loango Coast merchant* (cont.)

Merchant	Individual Sale	Joint Sale	Total Sales	Percentage of Total Sales*	Total Slaves**
Mafoeke Cousin	1	4	5	0.35	11
Tate	1	4	5	0.05	5
Boo Coffij	4		4	0.28	7
Commandeur	4		4	0.28	5
Jong Jan Arij (Ary)	4		4	0.28	7
Prins Jan	4		4	0.28	4
Prins Jan Claasen	4		4	0.28	4
Prins Joubert/Joubent	3	1	4	0.28	5
Batje		4	4	0.28	4
Jimi Claaijs	3		3	0.21	3
Koffij Tatij	3		3	0.21	3
Lobbe Claaijs	3		3	0.21	3
Bomba	3		3	0.21	3
Cabende	3		3	0.21	3
Capteijn Moor	3		3	0.21	3
Coubrin Macost/Coubroin Matosi	3		3	0.21	3
Fernande Poo	3		3	0.21	3
Im Arij/Imarij	3		3	0.21	3
Jan Alfret/Jan Alttet	3		3	0.21	3
Jeck Bord	3		3	0.21	8
Maloende Masenje/ Masentie	3		3	0.21	4
Melonde Maros Latoes/Milonde Makos Latoes	3		3	0.21	3
Tom Makasfo/Makosse	3		3	0.21	4
Wie Gouverneur	3		3	0.21	3
Sarsant/Sersant	3		3	0.21	4
Prins Wis Fombe/Prins Wit Tombe	2		2	0.14	2
Maboba/Maboeba	2		2	0.14	3
Comme		2	2	0.14	2
Batte Cansie	2		2	0.14	3
Cabende Claaijs	2		2	0.14	2
Combange Combates	2		2	0.14	2

Merchant	Individual Sale	Joint Sale	Total Sales	Percentage of Total Sales*	Total Slaves**
Coraie/Corail	2		2	0.14	2
Denfeloen	2		2	0.14	2
Fooary (ij)	2		2	0.14	2
Frange Bange/Franke Banges	2		2	0.14	3
Gouverneur Mat(t)endo	2		2	0.14	2
Jaas Koningzoon	2		2	0.14	4
Jan Arij/Janarij	2		2	0.14	3
Jan Bien Opsteeker/Jan Bier Opsteeker	2		2	0.14	2
Jim arij	2		2	0.14	2
Jimie Jars	2		2	0.14	2
Jimmidood	2		2	0.14	2
Jonge Bondes	2		2	0.14	2
Jonge Mafoeke	2		2	0.14	3
Macos Melonge	2		2	0.14	2
Mafoek Calli	2		2	0.14	2
Mafoeke Boosman/Mafoeke Zijn Boosman	2		2	0.14	2
Mamoeba	2		2	0.14	4
Pieter Cinci	2		2	0.14	2
Prins Jansen	2		2	0.14	2
Prins Makaik	2		2	0.14	2
Prins Sangron	2		2	0.14	2
Rotterdam	2		2	0.14	2
Sambo Klaase/Samboo Klase	2		2	0.14	2
Tom Governeur Cabende	2		2	0.14	2
Tom Imica/Jimica	2		2	0.14	3
Robben	1	1	2	0.14	3
Docke		2	2	0.14	4
Jimbi		2	2	0.14	2
Jan Koffij/Coffij	2		2	0.14	2
Jim Baatie/Battie	2		2	0.14	2
Jon(g) Janse Mavongo(o)	2		2	0.14	2
Jong Marck David	2		2	0.14	2
Labeer	1	1	2	0.14	3

APPENDIX   *Number of transactions completed with each Loango Coast merchant* (cont.)

Merchant	Individual Sale	Joint Sale	Total Sales	Percentage of Total Sales*	Total Slaves**
Manuel	1	1	2	0.14	8
Pierro	1	1	2	0.14	3
Prins Pacsent	2		2	0.14	2
Marbeule	1		1	0.07	1
Mafoeke Wis	1		1	0.07	1
Prins Lonne Mojombe	1		1	0.07	1
Amsterdam	1		1	0.07	2
Bonse Mantesse	1		1	0.07	1
Gouverneur Matinde	1		1	0.07	2
Immi Webbens	1		1	0.07	1
Jan Blanco	1		1	0.07	1
Jan Hout	1		1	0.07	1
Jeck Jimike	1		1	0.07	1
Jeck Mafoeke	1		1	0.07	1
Jo Monebee	1		1	0.07	1
Jonge Gouari Maronge	1		1	0.07	1
Joubert	1		1	0.07	1
Kleijn Klaasje	1		1	0.07	1
Kocks Maat	1		1	0.07	1
Maffongo	1		1	0.07	1
Mafoeke Canties	1		1	0.07	1
Magoffe Dick	1		1	0.07	1
Malemba	1		1	0.07	1
Malkadoor Malondu	1		1	0.07	1
Manepoeketa Majobo	1		1	0.07	1
Monbelle	1		1	0.07	3
Montette	1		1	0.07	1
Nite Claaijs	1		1	0.07	1
Pains Lingo	1		1	0.07	1
Peter Griffij	1		1	0.07	1
Pieter Andoensie	1		1	0.07	1
Pieter Jamboeka	1		1	0.07	1
Pieter Koning	1		1	0.07	1
Pieter Lowange	1		1	0.07	1

Merchant	Individual Sale	Joint Sale	Total Sales	Percentage of Total Sales*	Total Slaves**
Princes Meningo	1		1	0.07	2
Prins Feck	1		1	0.07	2
Prins Langro	1		1	0.07	1
Prins Macolle	1		1	0.07	1
Prins Majobo	1		1	0.07	1
Prins Mane Loeketas	1		1	0.07	3
Prins Mapello	1		1	0.07	1
Prins Mapoteko	1		1	0.07	1
Prins Pieter	1		1	0.07	1
Prins Pollo	1		1	0.07	1
Prins Present	1		1	0.07	1
Prins Sambo	1		1	0.07	1
Prins Sonne Majomb	1		1	0.07	1
Prins Taffij	1		1	0.07	1
Prins Was	1		1	0.07	1
Robbert Jan	1		1	0.07	1
Sorme Mayomba	1		1	0.07	1
Tom Fernandes	1		1	0.07	1
Tom Koffij	1		1	0.07	1
Water Boer	1		1	0.07	1
Will		1	1	0.07	1
Wall		1	1	0.07	1
Unknown	64	1	65	(excluded)	366

Totals Excluding Unknown

Sum <5			303	21.13	
Sum 5+			1066	74.34	
Sum			1434		

Sources: ZRA, *MCC*, nos. 979, 980, 985, 990, 1009, 1014, 1019.

Note:

* Excluding transactions with "Unknown" merchant;

** This notes the total number of slaves involved in all purchases, individual and joint. In the case of joint purchases, individual slaves may appear more than once in the Appendix.

CHAPTER 8

Measuring Short- and Long-Term Impacts of Abolitionism in the South Atlantic, 1807–1860s

Roquinaldo Ferreira

In the nineteenth century, Angola, Brazil, and Kongo formed the most travelled route of the transatlantic slave trade. From 1801 to 1850, approximately 1.4 million slaves of the total number of approximately 1.7 million captives taken to the Americas were embarked at ports in Angola and near the River Congo. This number represents an increase of almost 30 percent more than the number of slaves embarked from 1751 to 1800, signalling a southward shift in the centre of gravity of the trade that had been unfolding since the late eighteenth century. The vast majority of these slaves were taken to Brazil, by far the largest destination of the slave trade in the nineteenth century and where the demand for enslaved labour force remained high due to the rise of coffee cultivation in the nineteenth century.[1]

By and large, the early prospects of abolitionism in the south Atlantic were utterly unpromising. As pointed out by David Eltis, while the overall volume of the slave trade declined by about 60 percent in the years immediately following the abolition of the British slave trade in 1807, shipments of slaves soon revived.[2] Much of this resilience related to events in Angola and coastal Congo. In Ambriz, for example, where shipments of slaves had been under the control of the British until 1807, the trade was redirected to Brazil after the end of the British trade. In Luanda and Benguela, two slave ports in Portuguese Angola long under deep Brazilian influence, the end of the British slave trade produced no visible impact whatsoever.

The earliest impact of abolitionism in the south Atlantic occurred in Brazil, largely due to the role that the British played in the crisis that affected Portugal after the invasion of French troops in 1807. To avoid becoming hostage of French troops, the Portuguese court fled to Brazil, turning the South American colony into the centre of the Portuguese empire. The British played a critical role in helping the Portuguese court escape to Rio de Janeiro, even escorting

---

1 David Eltis, "Was the Abolition of the U.S. and British Slave Trade Significant in the Broader Atlantic Context?," *William and Mary Quarterly* 66:4 (2009): 722.

2 Ibid.

the Portuguese fleet that brought the royal family to Brazil.[3] Furthermore, they were also instrumental in helping the Portuguese to expel the French from Portugal.[4] Portuguese dependence on the British was by no means exclusively military. Britain's ability to exert pressure on the Portuguese authorities also derived from the fact that Britain was a key market for Brazilian products.[5]

Brazil offered a formidable challenge to early British abolitionism, since it was from there, not Portugal, that most of the southern Atlantic slave trade was controlled. Brazilian participation included not only funding but also organization of the logistical aspects of the trade in Angola and the Bight of Benin. In 1814, for example, Brazilian merchants were the owners of most of the vessels transporting slaves from Benguela to Brazil. In 1827, a recently-appointed Brazilian council in Luanda estimated that the majority of the slave vessels in Luanda were owned by Brazilian merchants. Eltis has linked the strength of the Brazilian trade with Angola to patterns of ocean currents and winds in the Atlantic, yet much more was at stake. The two former Portuguese colonies developed strong socio-cultural links that provided strength and resilience to the trade in the context of abolitionism. Brazilian geopolitical interest in Angola was so strong that in 1827 the government of newly independent Brazil sent a fleet of three warships to protect Brazilian slave ships in Angola.[6]

Against this backdrop, the British used their diplomatic leverage with the Portuguese government to bring the issue of the slave trade into the spotlight. As early as 1810, they began pressuring for a Portuguese commitment to end imports of slaves into Brazil. In 1815, British pressure led to an early concession from the Portuguese authorities, with the prohibition of the slave trade in

---

3   For the broader context to the Portuguese court's move to Brazil, see: Alan Manchester, "The Transfer of the Portuguese Court to Rio de Janeiro," in Dauril Alden, ed., *Conflict and Continuity in Brazilian Society* (Berkeley, LA: University of California Press, 1973), 148–183; Kirsten Schultz, "The Crisis of Empire and the Problem of Slavery: Portugal and Brazil, c. 1700-c. 1820," *Common Knowledge* 11 (2005): 262–282; idem, "The Transfer of the Portuguese Court and Ideas of Empire," *Portuguese Studies Review* 15:1–2 (2007): 367–391; Jeremy Adelman, *Sovereignty and Revolution in the Iberian Atlantic* (Princeton, NJ: Princeton University Press, 2006), 220–257; Patrick Wilcken, "A Colony of a Colony: The Portuguese Royal Family in Brazil," *Common Knowledge* 11 (2005): 249–261.

4   Martin Robson, "The Royal Navy and Lisbon, 1807–1808," in Malyn Newitt and Martin Robson, eds., *Lord Beresford e a Intervenção Britânica em Portugal, 1807–1820* (Lisboa: Instituto de Ciências Sociais, 2004), 23–47. For the diplomatic dimensions to the relationship, see: Frederick H. Black, "Diplomatic Struggles: British Support in Spain and Portugal, 1800–1810" (unpublished PhD thesis Florida State University, 2005).

5   Alan Manchester, *British Pre-eminence in Brazil, its Rise and Decline: A Study in European Expansion* (New York, NY: Octagon Books, 1973).

6   AHNA, cód. 96, fls. 74v–75: 1826-10-21: 'Carta do Governador de Angola'.

regions north of the Equator. Although this decision deeply affected imports of slaves to sugar-producing Bahia, which drew heavily on captives from the Bight of Benin, it failed to eliminate entirely shipments of slaves from the regions north of Equator and gave further momentum to the slave trade from Angola. In 1825, however, as mediators in the process of recognition of Brazilian independence, the British forced Brazilian elites to agree to ending imports of slaves in 1830 in exchange for the recognition of Brazil as an independent nation.[7] Tellingly, the British began obstructing the entry in Brazil of slave vessels from Angola as early as 1828.[8]

The Effects of Diplomatic Abolitionism

The Brazilian commitment to ending imports of slaves in 1830 soon reverberated across the Atlantic in Angola and Congo. In Luanda, where exports of slaves generated most of the revenues used to pay salaries of the local bureaucracy, news that Brazil had agreed to end imports of slaves resonated almost immediately.[9] Some authorities predicted that "most of the current merchants will seek to leave [Angola]."[10] In the following year, that assessment was no less gloomy: "the idea of a blockage or simple prohibition of funds from Brazil to Luanda makes residents shake since this measure could ruin their fortune with one stroke."[11] To alleviate the predicted fall in tax revenues, the number of workers in the Luanda administration was reduced.[12] Portuguese authorities even contacted the ruler of Congo to inform him about the pending development.[13]

Following the introduction of the anti-slave trade treaty in 1830, the Brazilian government passed legislation prohibiting imports of slaves in 1831. This law

---

7   Jaime Rodrigues, "O Tráfico de Escravos e a Experiência Diplomática Afro-luso-brasileira: Transformações ante a Presença da Corte Portuguesa no Rio de Janeiro," *Anos 90* 15:27 (2008): 112–118. For the British participation in the process of recognition of Brazilian independence, see: Valentim Alexandre, *Velho Brasil, Novas Áfricas: Portugal e o Império (1808–1975)* (Lisboa: Edições Afrontamento, 2000), 35–64.

8   AHU, *Angola*, cx. 158, doc. 58: 1828-03-21: 'Ofício do Governador de Angola'.

9   AHNA, cód. 96, fl. 41: 1826-05-20: 'Carta do Governador de Angola'.

10   AHU, *Angola*, cx. 151: 1826-04-27: 'Ofício do Governador de Angola'.

11   AHU, *Angola*, cx. 160, doc. 43: 1828-10-31: 'Ofício do Governador de Angola'.

12   AHU, *Angola*, cx. 167, doc. 46: 1828-09-20: 'Ofício do Governador de Angola'. AHNA, cód. 97, fl. 45v: 1830-03-01: 'Carta do Governador de Angola'.

13   AHNA, cód. 97, fls. 42–42v: 1830-01-28: 'Carta do Governador de Angola'. See also: Alexandre, *Velho Brasil, Novas Áfricas*, 85–86.

has been dismissed by scholars as an ineffective law that was passed only to appease the British. However, a closer examination demonstrates that it was actually the cornerstone of an impressive, if brief, set of measures to end the trade. In 1831, for example, several ships sailing along the Brazilian coastline or recently arrived from Africa were taken by Brazilian warships.[14] Apprehension of ships continued in the following years. In early 1835, five ships carrying 1,000 slaves were apprehended along the coast of Rio de Janeiro.[15] In the first half of 1837, another nine ships were arrested.[16] As a result of heightened abolitionism, imports of slaves declined significantly. While approximately 250,000 slaves entered Brazil between 1826 and 1830, these numbers dropped to 93,000 slaves between 1831 and 1835.

This brief period of early Brazilian abolitionism culminated with plans to purchase a piece of land in Portuguese Africa to resettle enslaved Africans apprehended from slave ships captured by Brazilian naval vessels.[17] Although Portuguese diplomats in Rio de Janeiro reacted favourably to this plan, the Portuguese government never gave serious consideration to it, also refusing to follow up on a Brazilian proposal to sign an anti-slave trade treaty.[18] Despite its ultimate failure, since imports of slaves resumed by 1835, this brief wave of abolitionism gave birth to a series of measures that later would prove critical to dismantling the commercial networks of the slave trade in Brazil. It was during this time, for example, that the Brazilian government first expelled Portuguese nationals implicated in the slave trade – a precedent widely relied upon two decades later.[19]

Not surprisingly, the impact of the 1831 Brazilian law was also substantial in Angola. In the wake of the formal end of imports of slaves into Brazil, Luanda's economy was dealt a major financial blow and many slave dealers retired to Brazil.[20] Given the drop in the demand for captives, prices of slaves collapsed.

---

14   IAN/TT, *Ministério dos Negócios Estrangeiros* (hereafter *MNE*), cx. 534: 1831-10-18: 'Nota do Cônsul Geral e Encarregado de Negócios Interino Português'.

15   IAN/TT, *MNE*, cx. 536.

16   AHU, sala 12, lv. 1, fl. 4: 1838-03-17: 'Nota do Ministério da Marinha e Ultramar de Portugal'.

17   IAN/TT, *MNE*, cx. 536: 1835-05-10: 'Ofício do Encarregado de Negócio Português no Rio de Janeiro'.

18   João Pedro Marques, *The Sounds of Silence: Nineteenth-Century Portugal and the Abolition of the Slave Trade* (New York, NY: Berghahn Books, 2006), 123.

19   Arquivo Geral da Marinha (hereafter AGM), cx. 311: 1834-12-15: 'Ofício do Secretário de Estado Agostinho José Freire'. IAN/TT, *MNE*, cx. 535: 1834-04-15: 'Ofício do Encarregado de Negócios Português'.

20   AHU, *Angola*, cx. 164, doc. 24: 1830-02-00: 'Ofício'. AHNA, cód. 160, fl. 150v: 1830-06-22: 'Carta do Governador de Angola'; cód. 2310, fl. 16: 1831-10-06: 'Ofício do Governador de Angola'. See also: Alexandre, *Velho Brasil, Novas Áfricas*, 85.

Since most of the products imported into Luanda came from Brazil, a sharp decline in monetary instruments followed the outlawing of the slave trade. This monetary crisis was caused by the fact that Luanda merchants were forced to use currency then circulating in the city to honour financial commitments to Brazilian trading houses. The lack of money in Luanda became so acute that the Luanda administration had to prohibit the transfer of cash to Brazil.[21]

Transformations of the Illegal Slave Trade

By the mid-1830s, the Angolan trade was rekindled anew, due to reasons that can once again be traced to Brazil, where the political landscape was transformed by the rise of political groups that supported the slave trade, thus weakening the government's commitment to suppressing imports of slaves. To ease imports of slaves, there were even attempts to revoke the 1831 anti-slave trade law.[22] More importantly, the revival of imports of slaves reflected Brazil's continuing dependence on slaves as production of coffee intensified in Rio de Janeiro. In the last three months of 1836, for example, thirty-six ships left Rio de Janeiro for Africa. Needless to say, the revival of imports of slaves in Brazil had an almost immediate ripple effect in Angola. While British reports indicated that over 20,000 slaves were shipped in 1835, an Italian traveller reported shipments of at least 13,000 individuals in the first half of 1836.[23] In 1836 alone, the number of slave ships in Luanda stood at 35.[24]

It was against this inauspicious backdrop that Portugal launched its first attempt formally to abolish the slave trade in 1836. Unsurprisingly, it did not work. First, although officially outlawing shipments of slaves to the Americas, the Portuguese anti-slave trade law still permitted the transport of slaves between Portuguese colonies in Africa, effectively creating a loophole that allowed dealers to circumvent the law. Another powerful factor was the high profits generated by the trade, which were estimated at around 50 percent and

---

21   AHNA, cód. 12, fls. 39–41: 1830-10-11: 'Ofício do Governador de Angola'.
22   Jaime Rodrigues, "O Fim do Tráfico Transatlântico de Escravos para o Brasil: Paradigmas em Questão," in Keila Grinberg and Ricardo Salles, eds., *O Brasil Império* (Rio de Janeiro: Civilização Brasileira, 2009), 2: 328. For Brazilian politics at the time, see: Tamis Parron, *A Política da Escravidão no Império do Brasil, 1826–1865* (Rio de Janeiro: Civilização Brasileira, 2011).
23   AGM, CX. 311: 1835-09-00: 'Relatório do Comandante do Brigue Charybolis'; Tito Omboni, *Viaggi nell'Africa Occidentale* (Milano: Stabeliemnto Civelli e Com, 1845), 107.
24   AHNA, cód. 13, fls. 28v–29v: 1836-06-11: 'Ofício do Governador de Angola'. AHU, *Papéis de Sá da Bandeira*, mç. 827: 1839: 'Apontamentos do Tenente Lima'.

continually lured Angolan investors into the business.[25] To make matters worse, the slave trade was widely supported by Angolan local elites, which systematically sabotaged the anti-slave trade law.

Given these circumstances, shipments of slaves remained high in Luanda and Benguela in the later 1830s and early 1840s. In 1838, for example, some 15,000 slaves were carried away from Luanda and another 20,000 were shipped from Benguela.[26] To a large extent, the renewed expansion of the slave trade was made possible by the use of new strategies that in part resulted from the new environment created by abolitionism. For example, to avoid penalties from the anti-slave trade treaty between Brazil and Britain in 1830, owners of ships would frequently use the Portuguese flag on their vessels, often simulating the sale of vessels in Angola or Brazil, so that they could sail with the Portuguese flag. This strategy had been first put into practice in the early 1830s. Between 1827 and 1833, for example, there were at least 16 fraudulent sales of vessels in Luanda that allowed slave ships to sail under the Portuguese flags.[27]

The reason why slave dealers used the Portuguese flag was because Portugal did not sign an anti-slave trade treaty with Britain until 1842. By relying on the use of the Portuguese flag, therefore, slave dealers were able to evade British cruisers, which could not legally seize them.[28] But other evading strategies were also used by slave ships, such as declaring trips from Rio de Janeiro to Montevideo, with stopovers in several African ports, thus seeking to create the impression they were engaging in legal trade.[29] In fact, these ships would then

25 AHNA, cód. 13, fls. 5–10v: 1836-04-08: 'Ofício do Governador de Angola'.

26 AHU, *Segunda secção de Angola*, pasta 2 A: 1838-02-24: 'Ofício do Governador de Angola'. In 1838 and 1839, at least forty ships came to Luanda to embark slaves. See: AHU, *Papéis de Sá da Bandeira*, mç. 827: 1838: 'Apontamento do Tenente Lima'. See also: George Tams, *Visita às Possessões Portuguesas da Costa Ocidental da África* (Porto: Typographia da Revista, 1850), 110; David Eltis, *Economic Growth and the Ending of the Transatlantic Slave Trade* (Oxford: Oxford University Press, 1987), 253.

27 Biblioteca Municipal de Luanda (BML), cód. 37, fls. 92v, 93, 99v, 102, 103, 105v, 108, 112, 118, 119v, 120, 124v, 127v, 129v, 131, 131v: 'Receita da Siza dos Prédios desta Cidade [Luanda] entre 1808–1833'. For further information on the use of the Portuguese flag on slave vessels, see: IAN/TT, MNE, cx. 535: 1834-01-18: 'Ofício do Encarregado de Negócios Português no Rio de Janeiro, Joaquim Barrozo Pereira'; cx. 536: 1835-05-11: 'Ofício do Encarregado de Negócios Português no Rio de Janeiro'.

28 The use of the Portuguese flag by slave vessels was at times opposed by Portuguese diplomats in Rio de Janeiro, to no avail. See: IAN/TT, MNE, cx. 536: 1835-04-30: 'Ofício do Encarregado de Negócios Português no Rio de Janeiro'.

29 Arquivo Histórico do Itamaraty (hereafter AHI), lata 25, mç. 4, pasta 1: 1833–1834: 'Processo do Paquete do Sul'.

return to Uruguay via Brazil, where they would then disembark slaves. According to Alex Borucki, this strategy accounted for 12 percent of slave imports into Rio de Janeiro between 1831 and 1839.[30] In addition, slave dealers would seek to circumvent anti-slave trade laws by declaring that ships carrying slaves from Benguela would sail to Luanda or Mozambique.[31]

After the 1842 Anglo-Portuguese anti-slave trade treaty, slave ships began increasingly relying on the American flag, which also gave them immunity against British cruisers. In the 1810s, British warships had seized vessels sailing under the American flag.[32] However, these seizures were not grounded on a solid legal basis, due to the lack of an anti-slave trade treaty between the British and the North Americans. Accordingly, the American flag was widely used by slave vessels during the last three decades of the slave trade.[33] Between January and April 1847, seven ships, most of them sailing under the American flag and probably built in the United States, left Rio de Janeiro for Ambriz and Cabinda.[34] Between 1821 and 1867, ships sailing under the American flag were responsible for the transport of more than 85,000 slaves across the Atlantic. As noted by David Eltis, if these numbers included ships that used the American flag for just part of their trip, these numbers would likely "rise to well in excess of half a million."[35]

In addition to the use of the America flag, the rise of the slave trade in the 1840s was facilitated by the internationalization of the trade in Angola and Kongo. For example, one of the largest American trading houses in the trade with Angola and Kongo – Robert Brookhouse, of Salem, Massachusetts – played an important role in furnishing slave trading entrepots with commodities to trade in slaves. As well as the slave trade, the Brookhouse trading house also actively engaged in licit commerce in Angola. Ships belonging to this

---

30   Alex Borucki, "The 'African Colonists' of Montevideo: New Light on the Illegal Slave Trade
      to Rio de Janeiro and the Río de la Plata (1830–42)," *Slavery & Abolition* 30:3 (2009): 430.

31   AHI, lata 14, mç. 3, pasta 1: 1839: 'Processo do Navio Especulador'.

32   Holger Kern, "Strategies of Legal Change: Great Britain, International Law, and the
      Abolition of the Transatlantic Slave Trade," *Journal of the History of International Law* 6
      (2004): 233–258.

33   Historian Andrew Lambert has stated that the "the appearance of the American flag para-
      lyzed the naval campaign [against the slave trade]," an assertion that might be an exag-
      geration. Andrew Lambert, "Slavery, Free Trade, and Naval Strategy, 1840–1860," in Keith
      Hamilton and Patrick Salmon, eds., *Slavery, Diplomacy and Empire: Britain and the
      Suppression of the Slave Trade, 1807–1975* (Eastbourne: Sussex Academic Press, 2009), 69.

34   IAN/TT, *MNE*, CX. 314: 1848-04-28: 'Ofício do Cônsul Português no Rio de Janeiro'.

35   David Eltis, "The U.S. Transatlantic Slave Trade, 1644–1867: An Assessment," *Civil War
      History* 54:4 (2008): 371.

trading house accounted for at least one quarter of the approximately 180 American ships visiting Luanda between 1845 and 1860. Complementing the Brookhouse trading houses were several other American nationals, who became involved in the illegal slave trade as operatives and crew of slave ships.[36]

This internationalization of the trade brought not only American nationals but also several other new groups of foreigners to Angola and coastal Congo. By 1830, British ships had resumed trading in coastal Congo, dealing mostly in licit products such as ivory but also selling goods used by local slave dealers to purchase slaves in the interior of the country.[37] In 1835, a report indicated that all ships embarking slaves in coastal Congo were sailing under the Spanish flag.[38] This trade led to the formation of communities of expatriate traders along the African coast. In 1841, American traders were said to be established in Ambriz.[39] In 1845, French and British merchants were also reportedly solidly established in Ambriz.[40] These communities were able to undersell Portuguese merchants that had until then controlled the trade in the region, providing further momentum to the slave trade through the supply of competitively priced products to African and other dealers operating there.

A further stimulus to growth of the illegal slave trade was the process of decentralization of embarkation of slaves along the Angolan coast and coastal Congo. This development had begun with the British withdrawal from the slave trade in 1807 and further gained momentum with the 1831 Brazilian law that formally abolished imports of slaves into Brazil. In places like Ambriz and Cabinda, outside Portuguese control, slave dealers were immune to anti-slave trade legislation and, more importantly, the structure of the slave trade was significantly leaner and more agile than in Luanda and Benguela.[41] In Ambriz,

---

36   Dale T. Graden, "O Envolvimento dos Estados Unidos no Comércio Atlântico de Escravos para o Brasil, 1840–1858," *Afro-Ásia* 35 (2007): 9–35; Don Fehrenbacher, *The Slaveholding Republic: an Account of the United States Government's Relations to Slavery* (Oxford: Oxford University Press, 2002), 176–177.

37   AHNA, cód. 12, fls. 59–61: 1830-12-14: 'Ofício do Governador de Angola'; fl. 83: 1831-08-02: 'Ofício do Governador de Angola'.

38   AGM, cx. 311: 1835-09-06: 'Relatório do Comandante do Brigue Charybolis'.

39   AHNA, cód. 15, fls. 34v–35: 1841-01-18: 'Ofício do Governador de Angola'.

40   AHNA, cód. 16, fls. 125v–126: 1845-08-31: 'Ofício de Joaquim Xavier Bressane Leite'.

41   Jean Baptiste Douville, *Voyage au Congo et dans l'Intérieur de l'Afrique Equinoxiale (fait dans les années 1828, 1829 et 1830)* (Paris: Société de Géographie de Paris, 1832), 3: 278; Tams, *Visita às Possessões Portuguesas da Costa Ocidental da África*, 167–170.

several barracoons existed only five miles away from the ocean, significantly increasing chances to circumvent British and Portuguese cruisers patrolling the area.[42]

The advantages that the region provided to slave dealers were such that part of the trade was based on Ambriz, coastal Congo and Cabinda in the late 1840s and the 1850s. In 1845, British authorities reported that "the Congo River appears at present to be one of the most active and extensive slave depots on the south coast of Africa."[43] Two years later, British authorities reported "that there were at that time several hundred slaves in barracoons near Ambriz ready for shipment."[44] In one of the focal points of the trade, *Cabeça de Cobra*, one of the barracoons could hold up to 1,000 slaves, with a logistical infrastructure that comprised a kitchen and yards where slaves were kept during the day.[45]

Abolitionism and Sovereignty

Even while shipments of slaves were expanding in Ambriz, Cabinda and coastal Congo in the 1840s, an increase in anti-slave operations paved the way for the end of the slave trade by increasing risks and costs of shipments of slaves and prompting investors to turn away from the slave trade. Portugal's participation in the struggle against the slave trade was a critical development. Particularly important were Portuguese fears that the British would seize upon the struggle to end the slave trade to claim Portuguese territories in Angola and thereby thwart Portuguese plans to develop the Angolan economy in the 1840s. These two factors led the Portuguese government to turn against the slave trade in the 1840s.

Portuguese participation in the struggle to end the slave trade is relevant to recent debates about the relationship between abolitionism and colonialism. Recently, Seymour Drescher has suggested that British abolitionism was not driven by imperialistic motivation. According to Drescher, "British intrusions on foreign sovereignty in favor of abolition were more diplomatic and fiscal

---

42   AHNA, cód. 261, fls. 145–145v: 1844-04-27: 'Portaria da Secretaria de Governo da Marinha e Ultramar'.

43   Public Record Office (hereafter PRO), *Foreign Office* (hereafter FO) 84, 572, 1845, fls. 358–375: 1845-12-31: 'Report on the State of the Slave Trade'.

44   PRO, *fo* 84, 630, 1846, fls. 99–101: 1846-11-11: 'Draft of Letter by Palmerston'.

45   *Boletim Oficial do Governo Geral da Província de Angola* (BOGGPA), 602: 1857-03-06: 'Termo de registo da feitoria da Cabeça de Cobra'.

than military."[46] From the point of view of Portuguese administrators, however, the situation was significantly different, with generalized suspicion about
British motivations being compounded by the cordial relations between foreign traders and African rulers. In 1840, for example, Portuguese authorities
remarked that the king of Ambriz was fluent in English and that one of the
members of the Franque Cabinda family had already been in France.[47]
American traders began openly challenging Portuguese claims of sovereignty
in Ambriz, in 1841 claiming that "Portugal did not have more rights over Ambriz
than other nations and that since they have paid duties to African rulers, they
did not need to deal with the Luanda government."[48]

Portuguese suspicions were rooted in acute understanding of debates
among British abolitionists, since leading British abolitionist Thomas Fowell
Buxton advocated direct intervention in regions supplying slaves to the
Atlantic in 1841.[49] Buxton suggested the signing of anti-slave trade treaties with
African rulers and the use of warships to attack African states supportive of the
slave trade. These policies were adopted in 1841 in Sierra Leone, when warships
were used to destroy slave trade barracoons, setting a precedent that would be
repeated in Cabinda and Ambriz in 1842, and later in the Congo River.[50] In
addition to establishing African participation in the struggle against the slave
trade, the treaties that the British signed with African rulers gave the British
the right freely to trade in African territory.[51]

---

46   Seymour Drescher, "Emperors of the World: British Abolitionism and Imperialism," in
      Derek Peterson, ed., *Abolitionism and Imperialism in Britain, Africa, and the Atlantic*
      (Athens, OH: Ohio University Press, 2010), 129–150.
47   AHNA, cód. 259, fls. 174v–174: 1840-07-02: 'Portaria do Ministro da Marinha e Ultramar'.
48   AHNA, cód. 15, fls. 25–25v: 1841-01-17: 'Ofício do Governador de Angola'.
49   Keith Hamilton, "Zealots and Helots: the Slave Trade Department of the Nineteenth-
      Century Foreign Office," in Hamilton and Salmon, eds., *Slavery, Diplomacy and Empire*, 22.
50   For the landing of British troops in Ambriz and Cabinda, see: Roger Anstey, *Britain and
      the Congo in the Nineteenth Century* (Oxford: Clarendon Press, 1962), 13. For an analysis of
      British use of the law and treaties at the time, see: Robin Law, "Abolition and Imperialism:
      International Law and the British Suppression of the Atlantic Slave Trade," in Peterson,
      ed., *Abolitionism and Imperialism*, 150–175.
51   Anstey, *Britain and the Congo in the Nineteenth Century*, 15. For an analysis of the use of the
      British navy as a tool of British imperial expansion, see: Stephen Conway, "Empire, Europe
      and British Naval Power," in David Cannadine, ed., *Empire, The Sea and Global History:
      Britain's Maritime World, c. 1760-c. 1840* (New York, NY: Palgrave Macmillan, 2007), 22–40.
      For an examination of the ideology of free trade, as well as its implications for British
      foreign policy in the first half of the nineteenth century, see: Anthony Howe, "Free Trade
      and Global Order: the Rise and Fall of a Victorian Vision," in Duncan Bell, ed., *Victorian*

Preemptively to avoid possible threats to its territorial aspirations, the Portuguese government considered the establishment of a city in the Congo River region – a project that ultimately was never implemented.[52] In 1838, a Portuguese administrator acknowledged that "the continuation of the [slave] trade is not suitable insofar as Portugal wishes to avoid insults by British cruisers and their direct contacts with African authorities, which means a threat to Portuguese sovereignty."[53] Later, a warship was deployed to Ambriz after rumours that the British had established a base in the region.[54] Also to prevent the increase of foreign presence in Congo, the Luanda administration sent a delegation to the king of Congo, in what turned out to be a failed attempt to convince him to prohibit his subjects from participating in the slave trade.[55] Significantly, Portugal also negotiated treaties with African rulers in Cabinda that would have allowed Cabinda's rulers to issue licences for small boats sailing along the Cabindan coast. This was an attempt to strengthen political alliances with a powerful local family in Cabinda. However, the British refused to recognize Portuguese diplomacy on the ground that Cabinda lay outside Portuguese sovereignty.[56]

Against this backdrop, Portugal shifted from an inconsequential condemnation of the slave trade to active pursuit of the ending of shipments of slaves from Angola. It appointed as Governor of Angola a Lisbon officer who had long opposed the slave trade, António de Noronha. Once he arrived in Luanda, Noronha gave 90 days for Luanda merchants to retrieve investments made in slaving in the interior of Angola.[57] In a letter to Brazil, a dealer stated that "everything related to the slave trade was like hell, since the governor wants the business finished and everything is very tight."[58] Between April and September in 1839, 44 ships were inspected for evidence of slave trading in the port of Luanda.[59]

Visions of Global Order: Empire and International Relations in Nineteenth-Century Political Thought (New York, NY: Cambridge University Press, 2007), 26–47.

52   AHNA, cód. 259, fls. 214–222v: 1838-11-04: 'Instruções (reservadas) para o Governador de Angola'. See also: Alexandre, *Velho Brasil, Novas Áfricas*, 137.

53   AHU, *Segunda Seção de Angola*, pasta 3: 1838-08-06: 'Relatório de Manoel de Noronha'.

54   AHNA, cód. 15, fls. 26–26v: 1841-01-17: 'Ofício do Governador de Angola'.

55   AHU, *Segunda Seção de Angola*, pastas 5 A and 5 B: 1842-03-1y: 'Carta dos Príncipes do Congo'.

56   AHNA, cód. 21, fls. 175v–177v: 1854-12-31: 'Ofício do Governador de Angola'.

57   AHNA, cx. 1359: 1839-05-02: 'Edital'.

58   AHI, *Coleções Especiais*, lata 27, mç. 3, pasta 1: 1839-01-28: 'Mano para Mano Diogo'.

59   AHNA, cx. 148; cx. 142; cx. 1359: 1839-05-02: 'Edital do Governador de Angola'; cx. 1602: 1839-05-29: 'Despacho do Governo de Benguela'; cx. 148: 1840-11-04: 'Ofício do Administrador da Alfândega'.

Several individuals suspected of slaving were held in custody.[60] More importantly, Noronha signed an agreement with British naval forces that significantly expanded their power to seize slave ships off the coast of Angola.[61] However, the drive against the slave trade so antagonized Noronha with Luanda merchants that he left Angola in 1840.

Military Abolitionism and Its Consequences

Repression would only gain momentum again with the appointment of Pedro Alexandrino da Cunha, an official who had built a record of opposition to the slave trade as the commander of the Portuguese naval squadron in Luanda. Almost immediately after the appointment of Governor Cunha, in 1845, a crackdown of slave traders began. Several Luandan slave dealers were put in jail – including the infamous Arcenio Pompílio Pompeu de Carpo.[62] Brazilian nationals, often times slave dealers sent to Angola to work for slave trade firms, were prevented from disembarking in Luanda if they did not have a licence issued by the colonial administration.[63]

According to historian João Pedro Marques, the drive against the slave trade during Cunha's administration was part of the general response of Portugal to an Anglo-French anti-slave trade treaty that led to the deployment of 26 British and French warships along the African coast. Building upon the strategy of military direct intervention that the British had been using since the early 1840s, this treaty called for the use of military force and territorial occupation as means to end shipments of slaves.[64] Portugal reacted to the treaty by requesting detailed information from the British about several of its

---

60   AHNA, cx. 1350: 1840: 'Autos Crimes' and 1840-09-22: 'Requerimento'.

61   PRO, FO 84, 322, fls. 135–136v: 1839-10-10: 'Carta do Comandante do Navio Urania'. Alexandre, *Velho Brasil, Novas Áfricas*, 115; Marques, *The Sounds of Silence*, 123. See also: Anne Stamm, "L'Angola a un Tournant de son Histoire, 1838–1848" (unpublished PhD thesis, Université de Paris I, 1971), 159.

62   AHNA, cód. 65, fls. 1–3: 1845-09-11: 'Ofício do Governador de Angola'. See also: Marques, *The Sounds of Silence*, 174. For cases of other individuals jailed due to involvement with the slave trade, see: AHNA, cx. 145: s/d: 'Registros da Cadeira Pública de Benguela'.

63   AHNA, cód. 104, fl. 65: 1845-11-04: 'Ofício do Secretário de Governo'. As demonstrated by the case of three Brazilians who made their way from Ambriz to Luanda without licence in 1847, the order proved difficult to enforce. See: AHNA, cód. 106, fl. 7: 1848-02-08: 'Ofício do Secretário do Governo de Angola'.

64   Lawrence Jennings, "France, Great Britain, and the Repression of the Slave Trade, 1841–1845," *French Historical Studies* 10:1 (1977): 101–125.

provisions.[65] In Marques' view, this treaty was a clear threat to Portuguese sovereignty and led Portugal to increase the number of warships in Angola from six to 11 between 1843 and 1846 – a rise equivalent to approximately 40 percent of the total number of ships in the Portuguese navy at that time.[66]

In point of fact, the appointment of governor Cunha was not the first time that Lisbon had tried to deal a blow to the slave trade in Angola. As discussed earlier, Portuguese opposition to the slave trade had manifested itself several years before the appointment of Cunha, when Lisbon chose Antonio Manoel de Noronha to become governor of Angola in 1839. However, it is undeniable that the beginning of Cunha's tenure came at time when the stakes were much higher for Portugal, which three years earlier had been forced to sign an anti-slave trade treaty with Britain. At the time, the British had 10 percent of its 200 strong naval force deployed on the campaign to end the oceanic trade in Africans, and this treaty significantly increased the power given to British warships to apprehend ships that did not even have slaves onboard but were suspected of being slave traders.[67]

Under the provisions of the new treaty, British cruisers temporarily blocked the port of Benguela and registered all ships docked there in 1843.[68] In 1845 alone, the British apprehended 81 slave vessels at the Angolan and Congo coasts.[69] Between 1845 and 1850, the British took 400 ships involved in the trade with Brazil.[70] In 1845, according to a British diplomat stationed in Luanda, Portuguese cruisers primarily carried out repression of the slave trade in the vicinity of the city.[71] In addition to engaging in naval operations against the slave trade, the Portuguese administration of Luanda established a heavy tax on slaves brought to the city from the interior. As stated by British diplomats, "the tax for every negro entering the

---

65   "Relatório do Ministério dos Negócios Estrangeiros," *Annaes maritimos e coloniaes*, Parte Oficial, fifth series, 9 (1845): 191.

66   João Pedro Marques, "A Armada Portuguesa no Combate ao Tráfico de Escravos em Angola (1839–1865)," *Anais de História de Além-Mar* 1 (2000): 168.

67   For the overall size of the British navy, see: John Darwin, *The Empire Project: The Rise and Fall of the British World-System, 1830–1870* (New York, NY: Cambridge University Press, 2009), 33.

68   AHNA, cód. 522, fls. 172 v–174: 1843-05-25: 'Edital do Governador Interino de Benguela'; cód. 454, fls. 76–76v: 1843-10-18: 'Ofício do Secretário de Governo de Benguela'.

69   John Beeler, "Maritime Policing and the Pax Britannica: The Royal Navy's Anti-Slavery Patrol in the Caribbean, 1828–1848," *The Northern Mariner/Le Marin du Nord* 16:1 (2006): 17.

70   Lambert, "Slavery, Free Trade, and Naval Strategy, 1840–1860," 71.

71   PRO, FO 84, 571, 1845, fls. 195–197: 1845-08-12: 'Dispatch by Edmond Gabriel'.

city from the interior is so heavy (nine dollars) that few if any are brought in."[72]

As a result of warship patrols, the logistical and trading network of the slave trade in Luanda had been seriously undermined by mid-1840s. Luanda had until then been the largest African port involved in the slave trade over several centuries but anti-slave trade measures were successful in ending shipments of slaves from the city. By then, the strategy of slave traders was to unload their ships in Luanda and later to sail to points towards the north of Angola. Slave ships left Luanda without carrying any cargo in order to load slaves at ports such as Ambriz, Cabinda, and Ambrizete. As naval operations increased, however, links between Luanda and places to the north were severed and ships were forced to arrive to Angola already loaded with provisions for slaves.[73] By thus eliminating the slave trade in Luanda, these operations not only prevented further increase in shipments of slaves but also raised costs of the slave trade. Furthermore, as a result of the rise of anti-slave trade measures in Luanda, slave dealers were forced to move to places such Ambriz, Congo, and Cabinda. As described by the British vice-consul in Luanda, the city had definitely lost importance as a slave seaport: "The slave dealers are thus compelled to confine themselves almost wholly to the system of establishing barracoons in several districts, as near as possible to those spots which offer the readiest means of embarkation."[74]

In 1848, a British official stated that "the measures pursued by the present Governor General of this province appear to have succeeded in suppressing all direct attempts at slave trade by Portuguese vessels."[75] To prevent leaks to slave dealers of confidential information relating to anti-slave trade operations, Lisbon allowed the navy squadron in Luanda to carry out activities without previous consent from the governor of Angola.[76] Governor Cunha supported British requests to land troops in Angola and destroy slave barracoons.[77]

---

72   PRO, FO 84, 671, 1847, fls. 99–111: 1847–02: 'Report on the Slave Trade by Edmond Gabriel and George Jackson'.

73   AHNA, CX. 3723: 1846-02-17: 'Autos do Processo da Sumaca Boa União'; CX. 2400: 1846-04-21: 'Autos do processo da Sumaca Lealdade'; cód. 264, fl. 22v: 1851-03-10: 'Portaria do Ministério da Marinha e Negócios do Ultramar'. IAN/TT, MNE, CX. 374:1847-05-10: 'Ofício do Cônsul Português'.

74   PRO, FO 84, 671, 1847, fls. 99–11: 1847-02-18: 'Report on the Slave Trade by Edmond Gabriel and George Jackson'.

75   PRO, FO 84, 719, 1848, fls. 61–74: 1848-02-14: 'Report on the Slave Trade by Gabriel and Jackson'.

76   AHNA, cód. 263, fls. 38–40: 1849-02-20: 'Portaria do Ministério da Marinha e Ultramar'.

77   PRO, FO 84, 630, 1846, fls. 99–101: 1846-11-11: 'Draft of Letter by Palmerston'. AGM, CX. 311:1847-05-22: 'Ofício do Ministério da Marinha e Ultramar'. AHNA, cód. 262, fl. 59v: 1847-05-22: 'Portaria do Ministério da Marinha e Negócios do Ultramar'.

Despite the Portuguese government's rejection of this request, it still gave the British formal permission to destroy barracoons.[78] As a result of the good relations between Governor Cunha and the British, several joint operations by Portuguese and British cruisers were conducted in the late 1840s. In 1846, they burned several barracoons south of Benguela at Bahia Farta.[79] Two years later, they dealt an especially devastating blow to Luanda merchants by burning barracoons in Mussulo only a few miles to the north of Luanda.[80]

The lack of logistical support from Luanda seriously jeopardized slave dealers' networks and provided a strong disincentive for potential investors in the slave trade. In 1847, the British reported "that the speculation [ie. the slave trade] has become a much more hazardous [endeavour]; that many [slave dealers] engaged in it have been almost ruined, and that none but such as have a large capital at command can venture to carry in it, is however certain."[81] In 1851, British officials reported that "depression and distress are most apparent, the payment of debts by them are now almost hopeless and the greatest distrust is felt in all transactions of a commercial character."[82] In addition to leading investors away from the slave trade, anti-slave trade measures provoked a migration of investors to licit activities then being promoted by the Portuguese administration of Angola. As stated by British officials, "many [slave dealers] had altogether transferred their ships and their capital to trade of a legitimate character."[83] In 1858, it was reported, "the legitimate trade of Luanda has augmented within the last few years nearly in the same ratio as the traffic in human being has been suppressed."[84]

The trade in coastal Congo and Cabinda presented distinct features that seriously increased costs of the business. As stated by John Monteiro, a British national who visited Angola in the 1850s, "there were [in Ambriz] also

---

78   PRO, *FO* 84, 676, fls. 30–33: 1847-05-17: 'Dispatch by Seymour'. AHNA, cód. 262, fl. 59v: 1847-05-22: 'Portaria do Ministério da Marinha e Negócios do Ultramar'. AGM, CX. 311: 1847-05-22: 'Ofício do Ministério da Marinha e Ultramar'.

79   AHU, *Segunda Seção de Angola*, pasta 10 A: 1846-02-17: 'Ofício do Governador de Angola'. AHNA, cód. 7183, fls. 109v–110v: 1846-10-26: 'Ofício do Governador de Benguela'; cód. 523, fls. 16–16v: 1846-10-31: 'Edital do Governo de Benguela'.

80   PRO, *FO* 84, 723, 1848, fls. 27–28v: 1848-06-21: 'Letter by Palmerston'; fls. 46–47v: 1848-08-24: 'Draft of Letter by Palmerston'.

81   PRO, *FO* 84, 671, 1847, fls. 99–11: 1847-02-18: 'Report on the Slave Trade by Edmond Gabriel and George Jackson'.

82   PRO, *FO* 84, 841, fls. 169–172: 1851-01-13: 'Dispatch by Brand'.

83   PRO, *FO* 84, 872, 1852, fls. 62–65: 1852-01-23: 'Report on the slave trade by George Jackson'.

84   PRO, *FO* 84, 1043, 1858, fls. 121–150: 1858-02-25: 'Report on the state of the slave trade by Edmond Gabriel.

established there American and Liverpool houses, trading in gum copal, malachite, and ivory, and selling, for hard cash, Manchester and others goods to the slave dealers from Cuba and Brazil, with which goods the slaves from the interior were all bought by barter from natives."[85] In contrast to Luandan commercial houses, however, foreigners operating in the region refused to sell products on credit and slaves dealers were forced to pay for goods to buy slaves in cash. Evidence of these new logistical problems emerged in letters exchanged by slave dealers in the 1850s: "Mr. Vianna, I have no supply of beans. I am expecting to receive cannon with flour and beans tomorrow. I advise you to be as economical as possible [with the remaining supplies] because there is a shortage of supplies to purchase and the times are critical."[86]

To make matters worse, risks associated with the slave trade now derived not only from cruisers but also from local African rulers or *Mambucos*, who dominated the regions where slave dealers had had to relocate. These rulers would frequently charge taxes to allow dealers to embark slaves. As African rulers commonly provided slaves to dealers, the latter were routinely in debt to the former. The upper hand that African rulers held in such arrangements allowed them to present new demands that strained the relationship. As stated by a slave dealer, "the thief of *Mambuco* should present documents to prove that he was owed debts."[87] Furthermore, in Cabinda and coastal Congo, slave dealers were constantly victims of robberies and attacks by Africans, with commercial disputes souring otherwise friendly relationships and turning into fierce hostility. *Mossorongos*, or local Africans that became famous through their piratical activities, could make careers of kidnapping and become merchants in coastal factories. The difficulties of dealing with African rulers are illustrated by "Guilherme do Zaire," a Portuguese dealer who dominated the trade in the Congo River, and once said to one of the members of his network of dealers: "never tell the people from Cobra [a region in the north of Angola] which ship is arriving to me so that they cannot charge duties."[88]

---

85   Joachim John Monteiro, *Angola and the River Congo* (London: Macmillan and Co., 1875), 1: 152–153.

86   Arquivo Nacional do Rio de Janeiro (ANRJ), IJ 6 472: 1854-10-07: 'Carta de Guilherme José da Silva Correia para João José Vianna'.

87   ANRJ, *IJ* 6 472: 1854-10-23: 'Carta de Guilherme José da Silva Correia para João José Vianna'.

88   ANRJ, *IJ* 6 472: 1855-03-08: 'Carta de Guilherme José da Silva Correia para João José Vianna'.

Conclusion

The initial phase of abolitionism in the south Atlantic had little if any impact on the slave trade to Brazil, since the earliest legislation mostly dealt with the trade north of the Equator and excluded the regions of the south Atlantic that supplied most of the slaves taken across the Atlantic to Brazil. This picture was thoroughly transformed with the establishment of restrictions on the entry of slaves in Brazil in 1830. Not surprisingly, scholars have recently pointed out that two critical fluctuations in shipments of slaves occurred when abolitionism was on the rise.[89] Later, a further set of measures on the African coast, particularly following the growth of naval operations along the Angolan coast in the 1840s, contributed to putting shipments of slaves on a path towards extinction by leading to a gradual shift of the centre of gravity of the slave trade away from Luanda and Benguela, previously the two largest slave port cities in West-Central Africa. With the rise of abolitionism in Luanda, dealers had to conduct their business in places like Ambriz and other places near the Congo River. The shift led to logistical challenges, including increasing difficulties in relying on Luanda as base to resupply other slave embarkation ports, serious erosion of the network that underpinned the slave trade, and, as a result, a rise in the costs of running the business. By straining slave dealers beyond their commitment to shipments of slaves, the rise of abolitionism contributed decisively to end the slave trade.

---

89   Eltis, "Was the Abolition of the U.S. and British Slave Trade Significant in the Broader Atlantic Context?," 721.

Bibliography

Printed Primary Sources

Abreu, Aleixo de, *Tratado de las Siete Enfermedades* (Lisboa: Pedro Craesbeeck, Impressor del Rey, 1623).

Abreu, José Rodrigues, *Luz de cirurgiões embarcadiços* (Lisboa: Oficina de António Pedroso Galram, 1711).

Andrade, António Alberto de, ed., *Relações de Moçambique Setecentista* (Lisboa: Agência Geral do Ultramar, 1955).

Archives départementales de la Réunion, ed., *Voyages, Commerce, Comptoirs et Colonies: Bourbon sur la route des Indes au XVIII siècle* (Saint-Denis, Réunion: Archives départementales de la Réunion, 1987).

Balsemão, Eduardo, "Concelho de Caconda," *Annaes do Conselho Ultramarino*, third series (1862).

Barros, João de, *Décadas* (Lisboa: Livraria Sá da Costa Editora, 1982).

Behrendt, Stephen D., Latham, A.J.H. and Northrup, David, eds., *The Diary of Antera Duke: An Eighteenth-Century African Slave Trader* (Oxford: Oxford University Press, 2009).

Bhila, H.H.K., "A Journal of Manoel Galvão da Silva's Travels through the territory of Manica in 1790," *Monumenta: Boletim dos Monumentos Nacionais de Moçambique* 8:8 (1972): 79–84.

Brásio, António, ed., *Monumenta Missionaria Africana: África Ocidental*, 1st series (Lisboa: Agência Geral do Ultramar/Academia Portuguesa de História, 1952–1988), 15 vols.

Brito, Bernardo Gomes de, ed., *História Trágico-Marítima, Relação da muy notavel perda do Galeão Grande "São João" [...] a 24 de Junho de 1552 e Relação sumaria da viagem que fez Fernão d'Alvares Cabral, desde que partiu deste reino por capitão-mor da armada que foi no ano de 1553 às partes da Índia* (Lisboa: Off. da Congregação do Oratório, 1735–1736), 2 vols.

Brito, Domingos de Abreu e, "Sumário e descripção do Reino de Angola, 1592," in idem, *Um inquérito à vida administrativa e económica de Angola e do Brasil em fins do século XVI, segundo o manuscrito inédito existente na Biblioteca Nacional de Lisboa* (Coimbra: Impr. da Universidade, 1931).

Broecke, Pieter van den, *Pieter van den Broecke's Journal of Voyages to Cape Verde, Guinea and Angola (1605–1612)*, trans. and ed. J.D. La Fleur (London: Hakluyt Society, 2000).

Buxtorf, M.C., ed., *Mahé de la Bourdonnais* (Saint-Denis, Réunion: Archives départementales de la Réunion, 1987).

Cadornega, António de Oliveira de, *História geral das guerras angolanas: 1680* (Lisboa: Agência-Geral do Ultramar, 1972), 3 vols.

Carile, Paolo, ed., *Voyage autour du monde de Francesco Carletti, 1594–1606* (Paris: Chandeigne, 1999).

Cavazzi de Montecúccolo, João António, *Descrição Histórica dos três reinos de Congo, Angola e Mutumbu* (Lisbon: Junta de Investigações do Ultramar, 1965), 2 vols.

Conceição, Frei António da, "Tratados dos Rios de Cuama," in J.H. da Cunha Rivara, ed., *O Chronista de Tissuary* 2:14–17 (1867): 15:63. [English edition: Malyn Newitt, ed. and trans., *Treatise on the Rivers of Cuama* (Oxford: Oxford University Press, 2009)].

Cordeiro, Luciano, *Questões Histórico-coloniais* (Lisboa: Agência Geral das Colónias, 1935–36), 3 vols.

Correia, Elias Alexandre da Silva, *História de Angola* (Lisboa: Ática, 1937), 2 vols.

Corvo, João de Andrade, *Estudos Sobre as Províncias Ultramarinas* (Lisboa: Academia Real das Sciencias de Portugal, 1884), 2 vols.

Coutinho, João de Azevedo, *Memórias de Um Velho Marinheiro e Soldado de África* (Lisboa: Livraria Bertrand, 1941).

Cuvelier, Jean, *Relations sur le Congo du père Laurent de Lucques, 1700–1717* (Bruxelles/Rome: Institut Royal Colonial Belge, 1953).

Dapper, Olivier, *Description de l'Afrique, contenant les noms la situation & les confins de toutes ses parties, leurs rivieres, leurs villes & leurs habitations, leurs plantes & leurs animaux; les moeurs, les coutumes, la langue, les richesses, la relogion & le gouvernement de ses peuples* (Amsterdam: chez Wolfang, Waesberge, Boom, Van Someren, 1686).

——, *Documentos sobre os portugueses em Moçambique e na África Central 1497–1840* (Lisboa: National Archives of Rhodesia and Nyassaland e Centro de Estudos Históricos Ultramarinos, 1963–1989), 4 vols.

Douville, J.B., *Voyage au Congo et dans l'interieus de l'Afrique Equinoxiale, fait dans les années 1828, 1829, 1830* (Paris: Jules Renouard, 1832), 2 vols.

Eltis, David, Behrendt, Stephen, D., Richardson, David, and Klein, Herbert S., *The Trans-Atlantic Slave Trade: A Database on CD-ROM* (Cambridge: Cambridge University Press, 1999).

Elton, J. Frederic, *Travels and Researches among the Lakes and Mountains of Eastern and Central Africa* (London: John Murray, 1879).

Felner, Alfredo de Albuquerque, *Angola: apontamentos sobre a ocupação e início do estabelecimento dos portugueses no Congo, Angola e Benguela extraídos de documentos históricos* (Coimbra: Impr. da Universidade, 1933).

Francisco, João, "Explorações do sertão de Benguela. Derrota que fez o tenente de artilharia João Francisco Garcia," *Annaes Marítimos e Coloniais*, fourth series, 6 (1844).

Gijsbertsen, H.A. and Poortvliet, P.F., eds., *Middelburgsche Commercie Compagnie: procuratiën, testamenten, volmachten, assignatiën van schepelingen tot het ontvangen van maandgelden, 1721–1803* ([S.l.]: Nederlandse Genealogische Vereniging – Afd., Zeeland, 1994a).

Gijsbertsen, H.A. and Poortvliet, P.F., eds., *Middelburgsche commercie compagnie: testamenten en stukken betreffende het transport van actiën 1748–1770 en 1804–1856* ([Kapelle]: Nederlandse Genealogische Vereniging – Afd., Zeeland, 1994b).

Gijsbertsen, H.A. and Poortvliet, P.F., eds., *Middelburgsche Commercie Compagnie: genealogische aantekeningen uit de ventilatieboeken van aandelen 1720–1840* ([S.l.]: [Nederlandse Genealogische Vereniging – Afd., Zeeland], 1995).

Governo Geral de Moçambique, ed., *Boletim Oficial da Província de Moçambique* (Moçambique: Imprensa Nacional, 1860–1911).

Heintze, Beatrix, ed., *Fontes para a história de Angola do século XVII* (Stuttgart: Franz Steiner Verlag Wiesbaden, 1985–1988), 2 vols.

Jadin, Louis, "Journal tenu par le sr. De Jean, marchand sur le vaisseau La Vierge de Grace, pour le commerce à la costa de Soffala, 1733," *Recueil Trimestrel de Documents et Travaux Inédits pour Servir à L'Histoire des Mascareignes Françaises* 4 (1939).

——, ed., *L'ancien Congo et l'Angola: 1639–1655: d'après les archives romaines, portugaises, néerlandaises et espagnoles* (Bruxelles/Rome: Institut Historique Belge de Rome, 1975), 3 vols.

Jones, Adam, ed., *German sources for West African History, 1599–1699* (Stuttgart: Franz Steiner Verlag, 1983).

Kidder, Daniel P. and Fletcher, J.C., *Brazil and the Brazilians, Portrayed in Historical and Descriptive Sketches* (California, CA: Elibron, 2005).

Koster, Henry, *Travels in Brazil* (London: Longman, 1817).

Koulen, Paul, *De eerste reis van het snauwschip "de vigilantie" naar Guinee en Suriname voor de Middelburgsche Commercie Compagnie 9 augustus 1778–8 september 1779* (Terneuzen: [s.n.], 1975).

Laet, Joannes de, *Historia ou annaes dos feitos da Companhia Priviligiada das Indias Occidentaes...1644* (Rio de Janeiro: Officinas Graphicas da Bibliotheca Nacional, 1916–1925), 2 vols.

Linschoten, Jan Huygen van, *Itinerário, Viagem ou Navegação para as Índias Orientais ou Portuguesas*, eds., Arie Pos and Rui Manuel Loureiro (Lisboa: Comissão Nacional para as Comemorações dos Descobrimentos Portugueses, 1997).

Lobo, Jerónimo, *Itinerário e outros escritos inéditos* (Lisboa: Livraria Civilização, 1971).

Matos, Artur Teodoro de, ed., *Documentos Remetidos da Índia ou Livro das Monções 1625–1627* (Lisboa: Centro de Estudos Damião de Góis, 2000a).

Matos, Artur Teodoro de, ed., *Junta da Real Fazenda do Estado da Índia* (Lisboa: Centro de Estudos Damião de Gois, 2000b), 3 vols.

Mello, J.A. Gonsalves de and Albuquerque, Cleonir X., eds., *Cartas de Duarte Coelho a El Rei* (Recife: Imprensa Universitária, 1967).

Mettas, Jean, *Répertoire des Expéditions Négrières Françaises au XVIIIe Siècle*, eds., Serge and Michelle Daget (Paris: Société Française d'Histoire d'Outre-Mer, 1978–1984), 2 vols.

Monteiro, Joachim John, *Angola and the River Congo* (London: Macmillan and Co., 1875), 2 vols.

Montez, Caetano, "Arquivo Histórico de Moçambique. Inventário do Fundo do Século XVIII. Sumários e Transcrições," *Moçambique, Documentário Trimestral* 72:89–92 (1952–1957).

——, "Documentos do Arquivo Histórico Ultramarino relativos à navegação do Oceano Índico," *Studia* 11 (1963): 211–235.

Omboni, Tito, *Viaggi nell'Africa Occidentale* (Milano: Stabeliemnto Civelli e Com, 1845).

O'Neill, Lieut. H.E., *The Mozambique and Nyassa Slave Trade* (London: British and Foreign Anti-Slavery Society, 1885).

Parreira, Adriano, ed., *Dicionário glossográfico e toponímico da documentação sobre Angola: séculos XV–XVII* (Lisboa: Editorial Estampa, 1990).

Pombo, Manuel Ruela, *Anais de Angola: 1630–1635* (Lisboa: Empresa da Revista "Diogo-Cão", 1945).

Rau, Virgínia, *O "Livro de Rezão" de António Coelho Guerreiro* (Lisboa: Companhia de Diamantes de Angola, 1956).

Rau, Virgínia and Silva, Maria Fernanda Gomes da, *Os manuscritos do arquivo da Casa de Cadaval respeitantes ao Brasil* (Coimbra: Universidade, 1956–1958), 2 vols.

Razões do réu Duarte Dias Henriques contratador, que foi do trato de Angola (Lisboa: Pedro Craesbeeck, 1619).

Rego, A. da Silva, Baxter, T.W., and Burke, E.E., eds., "Relatório do Ministério dos Negócios Estrangeiros," *Annaes maritimos e coloniaes*, Parte Oficial, fifth series, 9 (1845).

——, *Documentos sobre os portugueses em Moçambique e na África Central* (Lisboa: Centro de Estudos Históricos Ultramarinos e National Archives of Rhodesia and Nyassaland, 1962–1975), 8 vols.

Sandoval, Alonso de, *Naturaleza, policia sagrada i profana, costumbres i ritos, disciplina i catechismo evangelico de todos etiopes* (Sevilha: Francisco de Lira impressor, 1627).

Santana, Francisco, *Documentação Avulsa Moçambicana do Arquivo Histórico Ultramarino* (Lisboa: Centro de Estudos Históricos Ultramarinos, 1964–1967), 3 vols.

Santos, Frei João dos, *Etiópia Oriental e Vária História de Cousas Notáveis do Oriente* (Lisboa: Comissão Nacional para as Comemorações dos Descobrimentos Portugueses, 1999).

Schoute, D., *Scheepschirurgijns-journaal van een slavenschip der Middelburgsche Commercie Compagnie* ([Haarlem]: [s.n.], 1948).

Silva, José Justino de Andrade e, ed., *Collecção Chronologica da Legislação Portugueza* (Lisboa: Imprensa de J.J.A. Silva, 1854) (http://www.iuslusitaniae.fcsh.unl.pt).

——, "Sobre os navios que despacharem de Angolla para o Rio de Janeiro não tomarem este porto. Lisboa, 6 de novembro de 1679," in "Informação Geral da Capitania de Pernambuco. [1749]," *Annaes da Bibliotheca Nacional do Rio de Janeiro* 28 (1906).

Tams, George, *Visita às Possessões Portuguesas da Costa Ocidental da África* (Porto: Typographia da Revista, 1850).

Theal, George McGall, ed., *Records of South-Eastern Africa* (Cape Town: Government of Cape Colony, 1964), 9 vols.

Thornton, John K., ed., *La Mission au Congo des Peres Michelangelo Guatini et Dionigi Carli (1668)* (Paris: Chandeigne, 2006).

Tollenare, Louis F., *Notas Dominicais tomadas durante uma viagem em Portugal e no Brasil em 1816, 1817 e 1818* (Recife: Secretaria de Educação e Cultura, 1978).

Unger, W.S., "Voyage d'un Navire Négrier," *Revue Maritime et Coloniale* 114 (1892).

——, *Het Archief der Middelburgsche Commercie Compagnie* ('s-Gravenhage: Ministerie van onderwijs, kunsten en wetenschappen, 1951).

——, *Een belangrijke bron voor de geschiedenis van onze scheepvaart: de journalen der Middelburgsche Commercie Compagnie, 1720–1809* ([S.l.: s.n., [1962]).

Voyages: The Trans-Atlantic Slave Trade Database (2008) (http://www.slavevoyages.org).

Walckenaer, C.A., ed., *Collection des relations de voyages par mer et par terre en différentes parties de l'Afrique depuis 1400 jusqu'a nos jours* (Paris: Chez l'Éditeur, Rue Laffitte, 1842), 21 vols.

Secondary Literature

Adelman, Jeremy, *Sovereignty and Revolution in the Iberian Atlantic* (Princeton, NJ: Princeton University Press, 2006).

Alden, Dauril, *Royal Government in Colonial Brazil* (Berkeley, LA: University of California, 1968).

——, "Late colonial Brazil, 1750–1808," in Leslie Bethell, ed., *Colonial Brazil* (Cambridge: Cambridge University Press, 1987), 527–594.

——, "O período final do Brasil colônia, 1750–1808," in Leslie Bethell, ed., *História da América Colonial: América Latina Colonial* (São Paulo: Editora da Universidade de São Paulo, 1999).

Alencastro, Luiz Felipe de, "The Economic Network of Portugal's Atlantic World," in Francisco Bethencourt and Diogo Ramada Curto, eds., *Portuguese Oceanic Expansion, 1400–1800* (Cambridge: Cambridge University Press, 2007), 109–137.

——, *O trato dos viventes: Formação do Brasil no Atlântico Sul, séculos XVI e XVII* (São Paulo: Companhia das Letras, 2000).

Alexandre, Valentim, *Velho Brasil, Novas Áfricas: Portugal e o Império (1808–1975)* (Lisboa: Edições Afrontamento, 2000).

Almeida, A.A. Marques de, ed., *Dicionário dos Sefarditas Portugueses: Mercadores e Gente de Trato* (Lisboa: Campo da Comunicação, 2010).

Alpers, Edward A., *Ivory & Slaves in East Central Africa* (London: Heinemann, 1975).

——, "The French Slave Trade in East Africa 1721–1810," *Cahiers d'Etudes Africaines* 10:37 (1970): 80–129.

Anstey, Roger, *Britain and the Congo in the Nineteenth Century* (Oxford: Clarendon Press, 1962).

Antunes, Cátia, *Globalisation in the Early Modern Period: The Economic Relationship between Amsterdam and Lisbon, 1640–1705* (Amsterdam: Aksant, 2004).

——, "Investimento no Atlantico: redes multiculturais de negocio, 1580–1776," in *XV Congresso Internacional de* AHILA, *1808–2008: Crisis y problemas en el mundo Atlántico* (Leiden: AHILA, Depto. de Estudios Latinoamericanos, 2010).

Araújo, Ana Lúcia, ed., *Paths of the Atlantic Slave Trade: Interactions, Identities and Images* (Amherst, NY: Cambria Press, 2011).

Arruda, José Jobson de A., *O Brasil no Comércio Colonial* (São Paulo: Ática 1980).

Aschcraft-Eason, Lillian, "'She Voluntarily Hath Come': A Gambian Woman Trader in Colonial Georgia in the 18th Century," in Paul E. Lovejoy, ed., *Identity in the Shadow of Slavery* (New York, NY: Continuum, 2000), 202–221.

Axelson, Eric, *Portuguese in South East Africa 1488–1600* (Johannesburg: Witwatersrand University Press, 1973).

——, *Portuguese in South East Africa 1600–1700* (Johannesburg: Witwatersrand University Press, 1960).

Bailyn, Bernard, *Atlantic History. Concepts and Contours* (Cambridge, MA: Harvard University Press, 2005).

Bal, Willy, "Portugais Pombeiro 'Commerçant Ambulant du Sertão'," *Annali: Istituto Universitario Orientale, Sezione Romana* 7:2 (1965): 123–161.

Barickman, Bert J., *Um Contraponto Baiano: açúcar, fumo, mandioca e escravidão no Recôncavo, 1780–1860* (Rio de Janeiro: Civilização Brasileira, 2003).

Barrocas, Deolinda and Sousa, Maria de Jesus, "As populações do hinterland the Benguela e a passagem das caravanas comerciais (1846–1860)," in *II Reunião Internacional de História da África* (São Paulo/ Rio de Janeiro: CEA/USP/SDG Marinha, 1997), 96–98.

Bauss, Rudy, "The Portuguese Slave-Trade from Mozambique to Portuguese India and Macau and Comments on Timor 1750–1850," *Camões Center Quarterly* 6–7:1–2 (Summer–Fall 1997): 21–27.

Beeler, John, "Maritime Policing and the Pax Britannica: The Royal Navy's Anti-Slavery Patrol in the Caribbean, 1828–1848," *The Northern Mariner/Le Marin du Nord* 16:1 (2006): 1–20.

Benot, Yves, *La démence coloniale sous Napoléon* (Paris: La Découverte, 2006).

Bergad, Laird W., *Slavery and the Demographic and Economic History of Minas Gerais, Brazil, 1720–1888* (Cambridge: Cambridge University Press, 1999). [Portuguese

Translation *Escravidão e história econômica: demografia de Minas Gerais, 1720–1888* (Bauru: EDUSC, 2004)].

Bethell, Leslie, *The Abolition of the Brazilian Slave Trade: Britain, Brazil, and the Slave Trade Question, 1807–1869* (Cambridge: Cambridge University Press, 1970; 2009 edition).

Bethell, Leslie, and Carvalho, J.M. de, "1822–1870," in Leslie Bethell, ed., *Brazil: Empire and Republic (1822–1930)* (Cambridge: Cambridge University Press, 1989), 45–112.

Bezerra, Nielson, "Mosaicos da Escravidão: Identidades Africanas e Conexões Atlânticas no Recôncavo da Guanabara (1780–1840)" (unpublished PhD thesis, Universidade Federal Fluminense, Niterói, 2010).

Birmingham, David, *Trade and Conflict in Angola: The Mbundu and Their Neighbours under the Influence of the Portuguese 1483–1790* (Oxford: Clarendon Press, 1966).

——, *A conquista portuguesa de Angola* (Lisboa: A Regra de Jogo, 1974).

——, *Central África to 1870: Zambezia, Zaire and the South Atlantic* (Cambridge: Cambridge University Press, 1981).

Birmingham, David, and Martin, Phyllis, eds., *History of Central Africa* (London: Longman, 1983).

Black, Frederick H., "Diplomatic Struggles: British Support in Spain and Portugal, 1800–1810" (unpublished PhD thesis, Florida State University, 2005).

Blackburn, Robin, *A Construção do Escravismo no Novo Mundo. Do Barroco ao Moderno, 1492–1800* (Rio de Janeiro: Civilização Brasileira, 2003).

Bonin, Hubert, ed., *Négoce Blanc en Afrique Noire: L'évolution du commerce à longue distance en Afrique Noire du 18e aux 20e siècles* (Paris: Société Française d'Histoire d'Outre-mer, 2001).

Boogaart, Ernest van den and Emmer, Pieter C., "The Dutch Participation in the Atlantic Slave Trade, 1596–1650," in Henry A. Gemery and Jan S. Hogendorn, eds., *The Uncommon Market: Essays in the Economic History of the Atlantic Slave Trade* (New York, NY: Academic Press, 1979), 353–375.

Borucki, Alex, "The 'African Colonists' of Montevideo: New Light on the Illegal Slave Trade to Rio de Janeiro and the Río de la Plata (1830–42)," *Slavery & Abolition* 30:3 (2009): 427–444.

Boudriot, Jean, "Le navire négrier au XVIIIe. Siècle," in Serge Daget, ed., *De la traite à l'esclavage: actes du Colloque International sur la Traite des Noirs* (Nantes: Société Française d'Histoire d'Outre mer, 1988), 159–168.

Bowser, Frederick, P., *The African Slave in Colonial Peru, 1524–1650* (Stanford, CA: Stanford University Press, 1974).

Boxer, Charles R., *Holandeses no Brasil: 1624–1654* (São Paulo: Nacional, 1961).

——, *The Portuguese Seaborne Empire, 1415–1825* (New York, NY: Alfred A. Knopf, 1969). [Portuguese Translation: *O Império Marítimo Português* (São Paulo: Companhia das Letras, 2002)].

——, *Salvador de Sá and the struggle for Brazil and Angola – 1602–1686* (London: University of London, 1952).

——, "The Querimba Islands in 1744," *Studia* 11 (1963): 343–355.

Braudel, Fernand, *The Wheels of Commerce* (Berkeley, LA: University of California Press, 1989).

Brockey, Liam, ed., *Portuguese Colonial Cities in the Early Modern World* (New York, NY: Ashgate, 2010).

Brooks, George, "A Nhara of the Guine-Bissau Region: Mãe Aurélia Correia," in Claire C. Robertson and Martin A. Klein, eds., *Women and Slavery in Africa* (Portsmouth, NH: Heinemann, 1997), 295–317.

——, *Eurafricans in Western Africa. Commerce, Social Status, Gender, and Religious Observance from the Sixteenth to the Eighteenth Century* (Athens, OH: Ohio University Press, 2003).

Caldeira, Arlindo Manuel, "Escravos de mar em fora. As condições de transporte no tráfico negreiro do Atlântico Sul durante o século XVII," in Centro de Estudos Africanos da Universidade do Porto, ed., *Trabalho Forçado Africano. O Caminho de Ida* (Porto: Húmus, 2009), 13–48.

——, "Os jesuítas em Angola nos séculos XVI e XVII: tráfico de escravos e 'escrúpulos de consciência," in Centro de Estudos Africanos da Universidade do Porto, ed., *Trabalho Forçado Africano. Articulações com o poder politico* (Porto: Campo das Letras, 2007), 47–82.

Calógeras, João Pandiá, *A Política Externa do Império* (Rio de Janeiro: Imprensa Nacional, 1927), vol. 1.

Campbell, Gwyn R., "Madagascar and the Slave Trade, 1810–1895," *Journal of African History* 22: 2 (1981): 203–227.

Candido, Mariana, "Merchants and the Business of the Slave Trade, 1750–1850," *African Economic History* 35 (2007): 1–30.

——, "Trade, Slavery and Migration in the Interior of Benguela: The Case of Caconda, 1830–1870," in Beatrix Heintze and Achim von Oppen, eds., *Angola on the Move. Transport Routes, Communication, and History* (Frankfurt am Main: Lembeck, 2008), 70–76.

——, *Fronteras de la Esclavización: Esclavitud, Comercio e Identidad en Benguela, 1780–1850* (Mexico: El Colegio de Mexico Press, 2010).

——, "Trans-Atlantic Links: The Benguela-Bahia Connections, 1700–1850," in Ana Lúcia Araújo, ed., *Paths of the Atlantic Slave Trade: Interactions, Identities and Images* (Amherst, NY: Cambria Press, 2011).

——, *An African Slaving Port and the Atlantic World: Benguela and Its Hinterland* (Cambridge: Cambridge University Press, 2013).

Capela, José, "La Traîte au Départ du Moçambique vers les Îles Françaises de l'Océan Indien, 1720–1904" Unpublished paper presented at the *International Seminar on Slavery in the South-West Indian Ocean* (Mauritius, 26 February–2 March 1985).

——, *O Tráfico de Escravos nos Portos de Moçambique, 1773–1904* (Porto: Edições Afrontamente, 2002).

——, *O Escravismo Colonial em Moçambique* (Porto: Edições Afrontamento, 1993).

Capela, José, and Medeiros, Eduardo, *O Tráfico de Escravos de Moçambique para as Ilhas do Índico, 1720–1902* (Maputo: Núcleo Editorial da Universidade Eduardo Mondlane, 1987).

——, ed., *The Structure of Slavery in Indian Ocean, Africa and Asia* (London: Frank Cass, 2004).

Carrara, Angelo Alves, *Minas e Currais: produção rural e mercado interno em Minas Gerais, 1674–1807* (Juiz de Fora, MG: UFJF, 2007).

——, *Receitas e despesas da Real Fazenda no Brasil* (Juiz de Fora, MG: Editora da UFJF, 2009), 2 vols.

Carreira, António, *O Tráfico Português de Escravos na Costa Oriental Africana nos Começos do Século XIX* (Lisboa: Junta de Investigações Científicas do Ultramar, 1979).

——, *As Companhias Pombalinas de Grão Pará e Maranhão e Pernambuco e Paraíba* (Lisboa: Presença, 1983).

Carvalho, Filipe Nunes de, "Aspectos do tráfico de escravos de Angola para o Brasil no século XVII. 1. Prolegómenos do inferno," in José Marques e Mário José Barroca, eds., *In memoriam de Carlos Alberto Ferreira de Almeida* (Porto: Faculdade de Letras, 1996), 1: 233–248.

Centro de Estudos Africanos da Universidade do Porto, ed., *Trabalho Forçado Africano: Articulações com o poder político* (Porto: Campo das Letras, 2007).

——, *Trabalho Forçado Africano. O Caminho de Ida* (Porto: Húmus, 2009).

Coclanis, Peter A., ed., *The Atlantic Economy during the Seventeenth and Eighteenth Centuries: Organization, Operation, Practice, and Personnel* (Columbia, SC: University of South Carolina Press, 2005).

Conrad, Robert E., *World of Sorrow: The African Slave Trade to Brazil* (Baton Rouge, LA: Louisiana University Press, 1986).

Conway, Stephen, "Empire, Europe and British Naval Power," in David Cannadine, ed., *Empire, The Sea and Global History: Britain's Maritime World, c. 1760–c. 1840* (New York, NY: Palgrave Macmillan, 2007), 22–40.

Costa, Leonor Freire, *O transporte no Atlântico e a Companhia Geral do Comércio do Brasil (1580–1663)* (Lisboa: Comissão Nacional para as Comemorações dos Descobrimentos Portugueses, 2002), 2 vols.

Cruz, Celme Coelho da, "O tráfico negreiro da 'Costa de Angola', 1580–1640" (unpublished BA dissertation, Universidade de Lisboa, 1966).

Curtin, Philip D., *The Atlantic Slave Trade: A Census* (Madison, WI: University of Wisconsin, 1969).

——, *Economic Change in Pre-colonial Africa. Senegambia in the Era of the Slave Trade* (Madison, WI: University of Wisconsin Press, 1975).

——, *Cross-Cultural Trade in World History* (Cambridge: Cambridge University Press, 1984).

——, *The Rise and Fall of the Plantation Complex: Essays in Atlantic History* (Cambridge: Cambridge University Press, 1990).

——, *Death by Migration: Europe's Encounter with the Tropical World in the Nineteenth Century* (Cambridge: Cambridge University Press, 1989).

——, *Disease and Empire* (Cambridge: Cambridge University Press, 1998).

Curto, Diogo R., and Molho, Anthony, eds., *Commercial Networks in the Early Modern World* (Florence: European University Institute, 2002).

Curto, José C., "Luso-Brazilian alcohol and the legal slave trade at Benguela and its hinterland (1617–1830)," in Hubert Bonin, ed., *Négoce Blanc en Afrique Noire: L'évolution du commerce à longue distance en Afrique Noire du 18ᵉ aux 20ᵉ siècles* (Paris: Société Française d'Histoire d'Outre-mer, 2001), 351–369.

——, "Alcohol and Slaves: The Luso-Brazilian Alcohol Commerce at Mpinda, Luanda, and Benguela during the Atlantic Slave Trade c. 1480–1830 and its Impact on the Societies of West Central Africa" (unpublished PhD thesis, University of California, 1996); [Portuguese edition: *Álcool e escravos: o comércio luso-brasileiro do álcool em Mpinda, Luanda e Benguela durante o tráfico atlântico de escravos (c. 1480–1830)* (Lisboa: Vulgata, 2002)].

——, *Enslaving Spirits: The Portuguese-Brazilian Alcohol Trade at Luanda and Its Hinterland, C. 1550–1830* (Leiden: Brill, 2004).

Curto José C., and Gervais, Raymond, "The Population History of Luanda during the late Atlantic Slave Trade, 1781–1844," *African Economic History* 29 (2001): 1–59.

Curto, José and Lovejoy, Paul, eds., *Enslaving Connections: Changing Cultures of Africa and Brazil during the Era of Slavery* (Amherst, NY: Humanity Books, 2004).

Curto, José and Soulodre-La France, Renée, eds., *Africa and the Americas: Interconnections during the Slave Trade* (Trenton: Africa World Press, Inc., 2005).

Daget, Serge, ed., *De la traite à l'esclavage: actes du Colloque International sur la Traite des Noirs* (Nantes: Société Française d'Histoire d'Outre-mer, 1988).

Darwin, John, *The Empire Project: The Rise and Fall of the British World-System, 1830–1870* (New York, NY: Cambridge University Press, 2009).

Delgado, Ralph, *Ao Sul do Cuanza, Ocupação e Aproveitamento do Antigo Reino de Benguela* (Lisboa: [s.n.], 1944).

——, *Reino de Benguela. Do Descobrimento à criação do Governo Subalterno* (Lisboa: Imprensa Beleza, 1945).

Dillen, J.G. van, *Van rijkdom en regenten, handbook tot de economische en sociale geschiedenis van Nederland tijdens de Republiek* ('s-Gravenhage: Martinus Nijhoff, 1970).

Dooling, Wayne, *Slavery, Emancipation and Colonial Rule in South Africa* (Athens, OH: Ohio University Press, 2007).

Drescher, Seymour, *Abolition: A History of Slavery and Antislavery* (Cambridge: Cambridge University Press, 2009).

——, "Emperors of the World: British Abolitionism and Imperialism," in Derek Peterson, ed., *Abolitionism and Imperialism in Britain, Africa, and the Atlantic* (Athens, OH: Ohio University Press, 2010), 129–150.

Dunn, Richard, *Sugar and Slaves: The Rise of the Planter Class in the English West Indies, 1624–1713* (New York, NY: Norton, 1973).

Ebert, Christopher, "Dutch trade with Brazil before the Dutch West India Company, 1587–1621," in Johannes Postma and Victor Enthoven, eds., *Riches from Atlantic Commerce: Dutch Transatlantic Trade and Shipping, 1585–1817* (Leiden: Brill, 2003), 49–75.

——, *Between Empires: Brazilian Sugar in the Early Atlantic Economy, 1550–1630* (Leiden: Brill, 2008).

Egerton, Douglas R. et al., *The Atlantic World* (Wheeling, IL: Harlan Davidson, 2007).

Eijgenraam, M.J., *Menschlievenheid en eigen belang: de behandeling van de slaven aan boord van de schepen van de Middelburgsche Commercie Compagnie* ([Middelburg: Koninklijk Zeeuwsch Genootschap der Wetenschappen], 1990).

Eisenberg, Peter, *Modernização sem mudança* (Campinas: UNICAMP, 1977).

Ellison, Thomas, *The Cotton Trade of Great Britain* (London: Effingham Wilson, 1886).

Eltis, David, "The British Contribution to the Nineteenth–Century Transatlantic Slave Trade," *Economic History Review*, second series, 32 (1979): 211–227.

——, *Economic Growth and the Ending of the Transatlantic Slave Trade* (Oxford: Oxford University Press, 1987).

——, "Europeans and the Rise and Fall of African Slavery in the Americas: An Interpretation," *American Historical Review* 98:5 (1993): 1399–1423.

——, *The Rise of African Slavery in the Americas* (Cambridge: Cambridge University Press, 2000).

——, "The Volume and Structure of the Transatlantic Slave Trade: A Reassessment," *William and Mary Quarterly* 58:1 (2001): 17–56.

——, "The Transatlantic Slave Trade: A Reassessment Based on the Second Edition of the Transatlantic Slave Trade Database" (unpublished paper, 2005).

——, "The U.S. Transatlantic Slave Trade, 1644–1867: An Assessment," *Civil War History* 54:4 (2008): 347–378.

——, "Was the Abolition of the U.S. and British Slave Trade Significant in the Broader Atlantic Context?" *William and Mary Quarterly* 66:4 (2009): 662–682.

Eltis, David, Behrendt, Stephen and Richardson, David, "A participação dos países da Europa e das Américas no tráfico transatlântico de escravos: novas evidências," *Afro-Ásia* 24 (2000): 9–50.

Eltis, David and Lachance, Paul, "The Demographic Decline of Caribbean Slave Populations: New Evidence from the Transatlantic and Intra-American Slave Trades," in David Eltis and David Richardson, eds., *Extending the Frontiers: Essays on the New Transatlantic Slave Trade Database* (New Haven, CT: Yale University Press, 2007), 335–365.

Eltis, David, Lewis, Frank D. and Richardson, David, "Slave Prices, the African Slave Trade and Productivity in the Caribbean, 1674–1807," *Economic History Review,* second series, 58:4 (2005): 673–700.

Eltis, David, Morgan, Philip and Richardson, David, "Agency and Diaspora in Atlantic History: Reassessing the African Contribution to Rice Cultivation in the Americas," *American Historical Review* 112.5 (2007): 1329–1358.

Eltis, David and Richardson, David, *Atlas of the Transatlantic Slave Trade* (New Haven, CT: Yale University Press, 2010).

——, "A New Assessment of the Transatlantic Slave Trade," in David Richardson and David Eltis, eds., *Extending the Frontiers: Essays on the New Transatlantic Slave Trade Database* (New Haven, CT: Yale University Press, 2008), 1–60.

——, eds., *Extending the Frontiers: Essays on the New Transatlantic Slave Trade Database* (New Haven, CT: Yale University Press, 2008).

——, *Routes to Slavery: Direction, Ethnicity, and Mortality in the Transatlantic Slave Trade* (London: Frank Cass, 1997).

Emmer, P.C., "The Dutch West India Company, 1621–1791: Dutch or Atlantic?," in Leonard Blussé and Femme Gaastra, eds., *Companies and Trade: Essays on Overseas Trading Companies During the Ancien Regime* (Leiden: Leiden University Press, 1981), 71–95.

——, *De laatste slavenreis van de Middelburgsche Commercie Compagnie* ('s-Gravenhage: Nijhoff, 1971).

Enthoven, Victor, "Dutch Crossings," *Atlantic Studies* 2:2 (2005): 153–176.

Esteves, Maria Luísa, "Para o estudo do tráfico de escravos em Angola (1640–1668)," *Studia* 50 (1991): 79–108.

——, "Os Holandeses em Angola: decadência do comércio externo e soluções locais encontradas," *Studia* 52 (1994): 49–82.

Evans, E.W. and Richardson, David, "Empire and Accumulation in Eighteenth-Century Britain," in Terry Brotherstone and Geoffrey Pilling, eds., *History, Economic History, and the Future of Marxism: Essays in Memory of Tom Kemp (1921–1993)* (London: Porcupine Press), 79–103.

Fehrenbacher, Don, *The Slaveholding Republic: An Account of the United States Government's Relations to Slavery* (Oxford: Oxford University Press, 2002).

Feinberg, Harvey M., *Africans and Europeans in West Africa: Elminans and Dutchmen on the Gold Coast during the Eighteenth Century* (Philadelphia, PA: American Philosophical Society, 1989).

Ferreira, Roquinaldo Amaral, "Dos Sertões ao Atlântico: Tráfico Ilegal de Escravos e Comércio Lícito em Angola, 1830–1860" (unpublished MA thesis, Universidade Federal do Rio de Janeiro, 1996).

——, "Transforming Atlantic Slaving: Trade, Warfare and Territorial Control in Angola, 1650–1800" (unpublished PhD thesis, University of California-Los Angeles, 2003).

——, *Cross-Cultural Exchange in the Atlantic World: Angola and Brazil during the Era of the Slave Trade* (New York, NY: Cambridge University Press, 2012).

Ferronha, António Luis Alvares, "Angola. A Revolta de Luanda de 1667 e a Expulsão do Governador Geral Tristão da Cunha," in *Jornadas de História Moderna: actas* (Lisboa: [s.n.], 1986), 1143–1157.

——, "Angola: 10 anos de história: 1666–1676" (unpublished PhD thesis, Faculdade de Letras da Universidade de Lisboa, 1989), 2 vols.

Filliot, Jean Michel, *La traite des esclaves vers les Mascareignes au XVIII siècle* (Paris: ORSTOM, 1974).

——, "La traite vers l'Ile de France. Les contraintes maritimes," Paper presented at the *International Seminar on Slavery in the South-West Indian Ocean* (Mauritius, 26 February–2 March 1985).

Florentino, Manolo, *Em Costas Negras. Uma História do Tráfico de Escravos entre a África e o Rio de Janeiro* (São Paulo: Companhia das Letras, 1997).

——, "The Slave Trade, Colonial Markets, and Slave Families in Rio de Janeiro, ca. 1790–ca. 1830," in David Eltis and David Richardson, eds., *Extending the Frontiers: Essays in the New Transatlantic Slave Trade Database* (New Haven, CT: Yale University Press, 2008), 275–312.

Fragoso, João L., *Homens de Grossa Aventura. Acumulação e hierarquia na praça mercantil do Rio de Janeiro (1790–1830)* (Rio de Janeiro: Civilização Brasileira, 1998).

——, "A formação da economia colonial no Rio de Janeiro e de sua elite senhorial (séculos XVI e XVII)," in João Fragoso, Maria de Fátima Gouvêa and Maria Fernanda Bicalho, eds., *O Antigo Regime nos Trópicos: a dinâmica imperial Portuguesa, séculos XVI–XVII* (Rio de Janeiro: Civilização Brasileira, 2000), 29–73.

Francke, Johan, *Armazoen voor cargazoen: slavenhandel door de Middelburgsche commercie compagnie (1732–1804)* (Middelburg: J. Francke, 1996).

Freyre, Gilberto, *Casa Grande e Senzala* (São Paulo: Círculo do Livro, 1980).

Friedland, Klaus, ed., *Maritime Aspects of Migration* (Koln: Böhlau, 1989).

Fuma, Sudel, *Histoire d'un Peuple La Réunion 1848–1900* (Saint-Denis, La Réunion: édition du C.N.H., 1994).

Furtado, Júnia Ferrreira, ed., *Diálogos Oceânicos. Minas Gerais e as Novas Abordagens para uma História do Império Ultramarino Português* (Belo Horizonte: Humanitas, 2001).

Galenson, David W., *Traders, Planters, and Slaves: Market Behavior in Early English America* (Cambridge: Cambridge University Press, 1986).

Galloway, J.H., "Nordeste do Brasil, 1700–1750: Reexame de uma crise," *Revista Brasileira de Geografia* 36:2 (1974): 85–102.

Games, Alison, "Atlantic History: Definitions, Challenges, and Opportunities," *American Historical Review* 111:3 (2006): 1741–757.

Gayer, Arthur D., Rostow, Walter W. and Schwartz, Anna J., *The Growth and Fluctuation of the British Economy, 1790–1850* (Oxford: Clarendon Press, 1953), 2 vols.

Gelderbloom, Oscar, *Zuid-Nederlandse kooplieden en de opkomst van de Amsterdamse stapelmarkt (1578–1630)* (Hilversum: Verloren, 2000).

Gerbeau, Hubert, "Quelques Aspects de La Traite Illégale des Esclaves à L'Ile Bourbon au XIX Siècle, in *Mouvement de Populations dans l'Océan Indien* (Paris: Champion, 1980).

Godinho, Vitorino de Magalhães, *Mito e Mercadoria, Utopia e Prática de Navegar, séculos XIII–XVIII* (Lisboa: Difel, 1990).

——, "Portugal, as frotas do açúcar e as frotas do ouro (1670–1770)," *Revista de História da Universidade de São Paulo* 15 (1953): 69–88.

Gorender, Jacob, *O Escravismo Colonial* (São Paulo: Ática, 1978).

Goslinga, Cornelis, *The Dutch in the Caribbean and on the Wild Coast, 1580–1680* (Assen: Van Gorcum, 1990).

Goulart, Maurício, *A Escravidão Africana no Brasil: Das origens à extinção do tráfico* (São Paulo: Martins Fontes, 1950).

Graden, Dale T., "O Envolvimento dos Estados Unidos no Comércio Atlântico de Escravos para o Brasil, 1840–1858," *Afro-Ásia* 35 (2007): 9–35.

Guinote, Paulo Jorge Alves et al, *Naufrágios e Outras Perdas da Carreira da Índia, séculos XVI e XVII* (Lisboa: Ministério da Educação, 1998).

Hafkin, Nancy Jane, "Trade, Society, and Politics in Northern Mozambique, c. 1753–1913" (unpublished PhD thesis, Boston University Graduate School, 1973).

Hall, Gwendolyn Midlo, *Slavery and African Ethnicities in the Americas: Restoring the Links* (Chapel Hill, NC: University of North Carolina Press, 2005).

Hamilton, Keith, "Zealots and Helots: The Slave Trade Department of the Nineteenth-Century Foreign Office," in Keith Hamilton and Patrick Salmon, eds., *Slavery, Diplomacy and Empire: Britain and the Suppression of the Slave Trade, 1807–1975* (Eastbourne: Sussex Academic Press, 2009), 20–41.

Hancock, David, "The Emergence of an Atlantic Network Economy in the 17th and 18th Centuries: The Case of Madeira," in Diogo R. Curto and Anthony Molho, eds., *Commercial Networks in the Early Modern World* (Florence: European University Institute, 2002), 18–58.

Harms, Robert W., *River of Wealth, River of Sorrow: The Central Zaire Basin in the Era of the Slave and Ivory Trades, 1500–1891* (New Haven, CT: Yale University Press, 1981).

Havik, Philip J., "Women and Trade in the Guinea Bissau Region," *Studia* 52 (1994): 83–120.

——, "Comerciantes e Concubinas: Sócios estratégicos no Comércio Atlântico na Costa da Guiné," in *I Reunião Internacional de História da África* (São Paulo: CEA-USP/SDG-Marinha/CAPES, 1996), 161–179.

Hedges, David William, "Trade and Politics in Southern Mozambique and Zululand in the Eighteenth and Early Nineteenth Centuries" (unpublished PhD thesis, School of Oriental and African Studies, University of London, 1978).

Heijer, Henk den, *De geschiedenis van der WIC* (Zutphen: Walburg Press, 1994).

——, *Goud, ivoor en slaven: scheepvaart en handel van de Tweede Westindische Compagnie op Afrika, 1674–1740* (Zupten: Walburg Pers, 1997).

Heintze, Beatrix, "Luso-African Feudalism in Angola? The Vassal Treaties of the 16th to the 18th Century," *Revista Portuguesa de História* 18 (1980): 111–131.

——, *Studien zur Geschichte Angolas im 16. und 17. Jahrhundert. Ein Lesebuch* (Köln: Köppe, 1996).

——, "A Lusofonia no Interior da África Central na era pré-colonial. Um contributo para a sua história e Compreensão na Actualidade," *Cadernos de Estudos Africanos* 6:7 (2005): 179–207.

——, *Angola nos séculos XVI e XVII* (Luanda: Kilombelombe, 2007).

——, "Long-distance Caravans and Communication beyond the Kwango (c. 1850–1890)," in Beatrix Heintze and Achim von Oppen, eds., *Angola on the Move. Transport Routes, Communication, and History* (Frankfurt am Main: Lembeck, 2008), 144–162.

Heintze, Beatrix and von Oppen, Achim, eds., *Angola on the Move. Transport Routes, Communication, and History* (Frankfurt am Main: Lembeck, 2008).

Hemming, John, *Red Gold: The Conquest of the Brazilian Indians* (Cambridge, MA: Harvard University Press, 1978).

Henriques, Isabel Castro, *Percursos da Modernidade em Angola. Dinâmicas Comerciais e Transformações Sociais no Século XIX* (Lisboa: Instituto de Investigação Científica Tropical, 1997).

Herlin, Susan, "Brazil and the Commercialization of Kongo," in José Curto and Paul Lovejoy, eds., *Enslaving Connections: Changing Cultures of Africa and Brazil during the Era of Slavery* (Amherst, NY: Humanity Books, 2004).

Hespanha, António Manuel and Santos, Maria Catarina, "Os Poderes num Império Oceânico," in António Manuel Hespanha, ed., *História de Portugal, O Antigo Regime* (Lisboa: Estampa, 1993), 4: 395–413.

Heywood, Linda M., "Slavery and Forced Labor in the Changing Political Economy of Central Angola, 1850–1949," in Suzanne Miers and Richard Roberts, eds., *The End of Slavery in Africa* (Madison, WI: Wisconsin University Press, 1988), 415–435.

——, ed., *Central Africans and Cultural Transformations in the American Diaspora* (Cambridge: Cambridge University Press, 2002).

Hezemans, R.A., *De Atlantische slavenhandel der Middelburysche Commercie Compagnie* (Leiden: Leiden University, 1985).

Hogerzeil, Simon J. and Richardson, David, "Slave Purchasing Strategies and Shipboard Mortality: Day-to-Day Evidence from the Dutch African Trade, 1751–1797," *Journal of Economic History* 67:1 (2007): 160–190.

Hoppe, Fritz, *A África Oriental Portuguesa no Tempo do Marquês de Pombal 1759–1777* (Lisboa: Agência Geral do Ultramar, 1970).

Howe, Anthony, "Free Trade and Global Order: the Rise and Fall of a Victorian Vision," in Duncan Bell, ed., *Victorian Visions of Global Order: Empire and International Relations in Nineteenth-Century Political Thought* (New York, NY: Cambridge University Press, 2007), 26–47.

Inikori, Joseph E., "Measuring the Atlantic Slave Trade: An Assessment of Curtin and Anstey," *Journal of African History* 17:2 (1976a): 197–223.

———, "Measuring the Atlantic Slave Trade: A Rejoinder," *Journal of African History* 17:4 (1976b): 607–627.

———, *Africans and the Industrial Revolution in England: A Study in International Trade and Development* (Cambridge: Cambridge University Press, 2002).

———, "Review: Herbert S. Klein, *The Atlantic Slave Trade. New Approaches to the Americas* (New York, NY: Cambridge University Press, 1999)," *Hispanic American Historical Review* 82:1 (2002): 130–135.

Inikori, Joseph E. and Engerman, Stanley L., "Introduction: Gainers and Losers in the Atlantic Slave Trade," in Joseph E Inikori and Stanley L, Engerman, eds., *The Atlantic Slave Trade: Effects on Economies, Societies and Peoples in Africa, the Americas and Europe* (Durham, NC: Duke University Press, 1992), 1–24.

Iria, Alberto, *Da Navegação Portuguesa no Índico no Século XVII* (Lisboa: Centro de Estudos Históricos Ultramarinos, 1973).

Israel, Jonathan I., *European Jewry in the Age of Mercantilism, 1550–1750* (London: Clarendon, 1998).

———, *Diasporas within the Diaspora: Jews, Crypto-Jews, and the world maritime empires (1540–1740)* (Leiden: Brill, 2002).

Jadin, Louis, *Les flamands au Congo et en Angola au XVIIe siècle* (Coimbra: Inst. de Estudos Históricos Doutor António de Vasconcelos, 1965).

———, *Pêro Tavares, missionnaire jésuite, ses travaux apostoliques au Congo et en Angola: 1629–1635* (Bruxelles/Rome: Institut Historique Belge de Rome, 1967).

Jennings, Lawrence, "France, Great Britain, and the Repression of the Slave Trade, 1841–1845," *French Historical Studies* 10:1 (1977): 101–125.

Jong, Michiel A.G. de, *'Staat van oorlog': wapenbedrijf en militaire hervorming in de Republiek der Verenigde Nederlanden, 1585–1621* (Hilversum: Verloren, 2005).

Kagan, Richard L., and Morgan, Philip, eds., *Atlantic Diasporas. Jews, Conversos, and Crypto-Jews in the Age of Mercantilism, 1500–1800* (Baltimore, MD: John Hopkins University Press, 2009).

Kaplan, Y., *An Alternative to Modernity. The Sephardi Diaspora in Western Europe* (Leiden: Brill, 2000).

Karasch, Mary C., *Slave Life in Rio de Janeiro, 1808–1850* (Princeton, NJ: Princeton University Press, 1987).

Keiling, Luiz Alfredo, *Quarenta Anos de África* (Braga: Edição das Missões de Angola e Congo, 1934).

Kern, Holger, "Strategies of Legal Change: Great Britain, International Law, and the Abolition of the Transatlantic Slave Trade," *Journal of the History of International Law* 6 (2004): 233–258.

Kilson, Martin L. and Rotberg, Robert I., eds., *The African Diaspora* (Cambridge, MA: Harvard University Press, 1976).

Klein, Herbert, "The Portuguese Slave Trade from Angola in the XVIII Century," *Journal of Economic History* 32:4 (1972): 894–918.

——, *The Middle Passage. Comparative Studies in the Atlantic Slave Trade* (Princeton, NJ: Princeton University Press, 1978).

——, *The Atlantic Slave Trade* (Cambridge: Cambridge University Press, 1999) [Portuguese translation: *O tráfico de escravos no Atlântico* (São Paulo: FUNPEC, 2004)].

Klein, Herbert, and Luna, Francisco Vidal, *Slavery in Brazil* (New York, NY: Cambridge University Press, 2009).

Kulikoff, Alan, *Tobacco and Slaves* (Chapel Hill, NC: University of North Carolina Press, 1986).

Lambert, Andrew, "Slavery, Free Trade, and Naval Strategy, 1840–1860," in Keith Hamilton and Patrick Salmon, eds., *Slavery, Diplomacy and Empire: Britain and the Suppression of the Slave Trade, 1807–1975* (Eastbourne: Sussex Academic Press, 2009), 65–80.

Law, Robin, *Ouidah: The Social History of a West African Slaving 'Port', 1727–1892* (Athens, OH: Ohio University Press, 2004).

——, "Abolition and Imperialism: International Law and the British Suppression of the Atlantic Slave Trade," in Derek Peterson, ed., *Abolitionism and Imperialism in Britain, Africa, and the Atlantic* (Athens, OH: Ohio University Press, 2010), 150–175.

——, "Royal Monopoly and Private Enterprise in the Atlantic Trade: The Case of Dahomey," *Journal of African History* 18:4 (1977): 555–577.

——, ed., *From Slave Trade to "Legitimate" Commerce. The Commercial Transition in Nineteenth-Century West Africa* (Cambridge: Cambridge University Press, 1995).

Leite, Joana Pereira, "Indo-britanniques et indo-portugais: la présence marchand dans le Sud du Mozambique au moment de l'implantation du système colonial portugais," *Revue Française d'Histoire d'Outre-mer* 88:330–331 (2001): 13–37.

Lesger, C. and Noordegraaf, L., eds., *Entrepreneurs and Entrepreneurship in Early Modern Times: Merchants and Industrialists within the Orbit of the Dutch Staple Market* (Den Haag: Stichting Hollandse Historische Reeks, 1995).

Libby, Douglas C., *Transformação e trabalho em uma economia escravista: Minas Gerais no século XIX* (São Paulo: Brasiliense, 1988).

Liesegang, Gerhard, "A First Look at the Import and Export Trade of Mozambique, 1800–1914," in Gerhard Liesegang, Helma Pasch, and Adam Jones, eds., *Figuring African Trade* (Berlin: Dietrich Reimer, 1986).

Liesegang, Gerhard, Pasch, Helma, and Jones, Adam, eds., *Figuring African Trade* (Berlin: Dietrich Reimer, 1986).

Lobato, Alexandre, *Evolução Administrativa e Económica de Moçambique, 1752–1763* (Lisboa: Agência Geral do Ultramar, 1957).

——, *História do Presídio de Lourenço Marques* (Lisboa: Junta de Investigação do Ultramar, 1960).

Lopes, Eduardo Correia, *A Escravatura: subsídios para a sua história* (Lisboa: Agência Geral das Colónias, 1944).

Lopes, Gustavo Acioli, "Negócio da Costa da Mina e Comércio Atlântico. Tabaco, Açúcar, Ouro e Tráfico de Escravos: Capitania de Pernambuco (1654–1760)" (unpublished PhD thesis, Universidade de São Paulo, 2007).

Lopes, Gustavo Acioli, and Menz, Maximiliano M., "Resgate e Mercadorias: uma análise comparada do Tráfico Luso-Brasileiro de Escravos em Angola e na Costa da Mina (século XVIII)," *Afro-Ásia* 36 (2008): 43–73.

Lovejoy, Paul E., *Transformations in Slavery: A History of Slavery in Africa* (Cambridge: Cambridge University Press, 2010).

——, ed., *Identity in the Shadow of Slavery* (New York, NY: Continuum, 2000).

Lovejoy, Paul E. and Richardson, David "Trust, Pawnship, and Atlantic History: The Institutional Foundations of the Old Calabar Slave Trade," *American Historical Review* 104:2 (1999): 333–355.

——, "The Business of Slaving: Pawnship in Western Africa, c. 1600–1810," *Journal of African History* 42:1 (2001): 67–89.

——, "'This Horrid Hole': Royal Authority, Commerce and Credit at Bonny, 1690–1840," *Journal of African History* 45 (2004): 363–392.

——, "African Agency and the Liverpool Trade," in David Richardson, Anthony Tibbles, Suzanne Schwarz, eds., *Liverpool and Transatlantic Slavery* (Liverpool: Liverpool University Press, 2007), 43–65.

Lugar, Catherine, "The Portuguese Tobacco Trade and Tobacco Growers of Bahia in the Late Colonial Period," in Dauril Alden and Warren Dean, eds., *Essays Concerning the Socioeconomic History of Brazil and Portuguese India* (Gainesville, FL: University Press of Florida, 1977), 26–70.

Luna, Francisco V. and Klein, Herbert S., *Slavery and the Economy of São Paulo, 1750–1850* (Stanford, CA: Stanford University Press, 2003). [Portuguese Translation: *Evolução da sociedade e economia escravista de São Paulo, de 1750 a 1850* (São Paulo: Edusp, 2006)].

Luna, Francisco V., Klein, Herbert S., and Costa, Iraci del Nero, "Algumas características do contingente de cativos em Minas Gerais," in Francisco V. Luna, I. del N. Costa and Herbert S. Klein, eds., *Escravismo em São Paulo e Minas Gerais* (São Paulo: Imprensa Oficial, Editora da Universidade de São Paulo, 2009), 17–32.

Manchester, Alan, *British Pre-eminence in Brazil, Its Rise and Decline: A Study in European Expansion* (New York, NY: Octagon Books, 1973a).

——, "The Transfer of the Portuguese Court to Rio de Janeiro," in Dauril Alden, ed., *Conflict and Continuity in Brazilian Society* (Berkeley, LA: University of California Press, 1973b), 148–183.

Mann, Kristin, *Slavery and the Birth of an African City: Lagos, 1760–1900* (Bloomington, IN: Indiana University Press, 2007).

Manning, Patrick, "The Slave Trade in the Bight of Benin, 1640–1890," in Henry A. Gemery and Jan S. Hogendorn, eds., *The Uncommon Market: Essays in the Economic History of Atlantic Slave Trade* (New York, NY: Academic Press, 1979), 107–141.

Marchant, Alexander, *From Barter to Slavery: The Economic Relations of Portuguese and Indians in the Settlement of Brazil, 1500–1580* (Gloucester, MA: P. Smith, 1966).

Marcílio, Maria Luiza, "A população do Brasil colonial," in Leslie Bethell, ed., *História da América Latina* (São Paulo; Brasília, DF: Edusp; FUNAG, 2004), 2: 311–38.

Mark, Peter, *"Portuguese" Style and Luso-African Identity: Precolonial Senegambia, Sixteenth-Nineteenth Centuries* (Bloomington, IN: Indiana University Press, 2002).

Marques, João Pedro, "A Armada Portuguesa no Combate ao Tráfico de Escravos em Angola (1839–1865)," *Anais de História de Além-Mar* 1 (2000): 161–193.

——, *The Sounds of Silence: Nineteenth-Century Portugal and the Abolition of the Slave Trade* (New York, NY: Berghahn Books, 2006).

Marques, José and Barroca, Mário José, eds., *In memoriam de Carlos Alberto Ferreira de Almeida* (Porto: Faculdade de Letras, 1996), 2 vols.

Martin, Phyllis M., *The External Trade of the Loango Coast 1576–1870: The Effects of Changing Commercial Relations on the Vili Kingdom of Loango* (Oxford: Clarendon Press, 1972).

——, "The Cabinda Connection: A Historical Perspective," *African Affairs* 76:302 (1977): 47–59.

——, "The Trade of Loango in the Seventeenth and Eighteenth Centuries," in J.E. Inikori, ed., *Forced Migration: The Impact of the Export Slave Trade on African Societies* (London: Hutchinson, 1982), 202–220.

——, "Family Strategies in Nineteenth-Century Cabinda," *Journal of African History* 28:1 (1987): 65–86.

Martins Filho, Amilcar V. and Martins, Roberto B., "Slavery in a Nonexport Economy: Nineteenth-Century Minas Gerais Revisited," *Hispanic American Historical Review* 63:3 (1983): 537–568.

Marzagalli, Silvia, "Sur les origines de l'Atlantic History': Paradigme interprétatif de l'histoire des espaces atlantique à l'epoque moderne," *Dix-Huitième* 33 (2001): 17–31.

Matos, Artur Teodoro de, *Na Rota da Índia: Estudos de História da Expansão Portuguesa* (Macau: Instituto Cultural, 1994).

Mauro, Frédéric, *Le Portugal et l'Atlantique au XVIIe siècle (1570–1670): étude économique* (Paris: S.E.V.P.E.N., 1960). [Port. Trans. *Portugal, o Brasil e o Atlântico, 1570–1670* (Lisboa: Estampa, 1997)].

Maxwell, Kenneth R., "Pombal and the Nationalization of the Luso-Brazilian Economy,"
    Hispanic American Historical Review 48:4 (1968): 608–631.
McCusker, John J. and Morgan, Kenneth, eds., *The Early Modern Atlantic Economy:
    Essays on Transatlantic Enterprise* (Cambridge: Cambridge University Press, 2000).
McCusker, John J., Morgan, Kenneth, and Menard, Russell R., "The Sugar Industry in
    the Seventeenth Century. A new perspective on the Barbadian 'Sugar Revolution'"
    in Stuart B. Schwartz, ed., *Tropical Babylons: Sugar and the Making of Atlantic
    World, 1450–1680* (Chapel Hill, NC: University of North Carolina Press, 2004),
    289–330.
Mello, Evaldo Cabral de, *Olinda Restaurada: Guerra e açúcar no Nordeste, 1650–1654*
    (Rio de Janeiro: Topbooks, 1998).
Mello e Souza, Marina de, *Reis negros no Brasil escravista: História da festa da coroação
    de Rei Congo* (Belo Horizonte: Editora UFMG, 2002).
Mendes, António de Almeida, "The Foundations of the System: A Reassessment of the
    Slave Trade to the Spanish Americas in the Sixteenth and Seventeenth Centuries," in
    David Elits and David Richardson, eds., *Extending the Frontiers: Essays on the
    New Transatlantic Slave Trade Database* (New Haven, CT: Yale University Press, 2008),
    63–94.
Menz, Maximiliano M., *Entre Impérios: Formação do Rio Grande na crise do sistema
    colonial português* (São Paulo: Alameda, 2009).
——, "As 'Geometrias': o comércio metropolitano e o tráfico de escravos em Angola
    (1796–1807)," *Revista de História*, São Paulo, 116 (2012): 185–222.
Miers, Suzanne and Roberts, Richard, eds., *The End of Slavery in Africa* (Madison, WI:
    Wisconsin University Press, 1988).
Miller, Joseph C., "The Slave Trade in Congo and Angola," in Martin L. Kilson and
    Robert I. Rotberg, eds., *The African Diaspora* (Cambridge, MA: Harvard University
    Press, 1976a), 75–113.
——, *Kings and Kinsmen: Early Mbundu States in Angola* (Oxford: Clarendon Press,
    1976b).
——, "The Significance of Drought, Disease and Famine in the Agriculturally Marginal
    Zones of West-Central Africa," *Journal of African History* 23:1 (1982): 17–61.
——, "The Paradoxes of Impoverishment in the Atlantic Zone," in David Birmingham
    and Phyllis Martin, eds., *History of Central Africa* (London: Longman, 1983), 1:118–159.
——, "Capitalism and Slaving: The Financial and Commercial Organization of the
    Angolan Slave Trade, according to the Accounts of António Coelho Guerreiro
    (1684–1692)," *International Journal of African Historical Studies* 17:1 (1984): 1–56.
——, "Slave Prices in the Portuguese Southern Atlantic, 1600–1830," in Paul E. Lovejoy,
    ed., *Africans in Bondage: Studies in Slavery and the Slave Trade* (Madison, WI:
    University of Wisconsin Press, 1986a), 43–77.

——, "Imports at Luanda, 1785–1823," in Gerhard Liesegang, Helma Pasch, and Adam Jones, eds., *Figuring African Trade* (Berlin: Dietrich Reimer Verlag, 1986b), 165–246.

——, *Way of Death: Merchant Capitalism and the Angolan Slave Trade, 1730–1830* (Madison, WI: University of Wisconsin Press, 1988).

——, "The Numbers, Origins, and Destinations of Slaves in the 18th Century Angolan Slave Trade," in Joseph Inikori and Stanley L. Engerman, eds., *The Atlantic Slave Trade: Effects on Economies, Societies, and People in Africa, the Americas, and Europe* (Durham, NC: Duke University Press, 1992), 77–177.

——, "Angola Central e Sul por Volta de 1840," *Estudos Afro-Asiáticos* 32 (1997): 7–54.

——, "Central Africa during the Era of the Slave Trade, c. 1490s–1850s," in Linda Heywood, ed., *Central Africans and Cultural Transformations in the American Diaspora* (New York, NY: Cambridge University Press, 2001), 21–69.

Morgan, Jennifer L., "'Some Could Suckle over Their Shoulder': Male Travelers, Female Bodies, and the Gendering of Racial Ideology, 1500–1770," *William and Mary Quarterly*, third series, 54:1 (1997): 167–192.

Nardi, Jean-Batiste, *O fumo brasileiro no período colonial: Lavoura, Comércio e Administração* (São Paulo: Brasiliense, 1996).

Newitt, Malyn, "The Comoro Islands in Indian Ocean Trade before the 19th Century," *Cahier des Études Africaines* 23 (1983): 139–165.

——, *A History of Mozambique* (London: Hurst & Company, 1995).

Newson, Linda A. and Minchin, Susie, *From Capture to Sale: The Portuguese Slave Trade to Spanish America in the Early Seventeenth Century* (Leiden: Brill, 2007).

Nirina, Rasoarifreta Bako, "L'esclavage dans le sud-ouest de l'Ocean Indien," Paper presented at the *International Seminar on Slavery in the South-West Indian Ocean* (Mauritius, 26 February–2 March 1985).

Norton, Manuel Artur, *D. Pedro Miguel de Almeida Portugal* (Lisboa: Agência Geral do Ultramar, 1967).

Nunn, Nathan, "Historical Legacies: A Model Linking Africa's Past to Its Current Underdevelopment," *Journal of Development Studies* 83:1 (2007): 157–175.

——, "The Long Term Effects of Africa's Slave Trades," *Quarterly Journal of Economics* 123:1 (2008): 139–176.

Paesie, Ruud, *Lorrendrayen op Africa: de illegale goederen- en slavenhandel op West-Afrika tijdens het achttiende-eeuwse handelsmonopolie van de West-Indische Compagnie, 1700–1734* (Amsterdam: De Bataafsche Leeuw, 2008).

Palacios, Guillermo, *Cultivadores libres, Estado y crisis de la esclavitud en la época de la Revolución Industrial* (México, DF: Colegio de México; Fondo de Cultura, 1998).

Pantoja, Selma, "O Brasil colónia no acervo do Arquivo Histórico Nacional de Angola," *Revista de História* 140 (1999): 123–131.

Parreira, Adriano, *Economia e sociedade no tempo da rainha Njinga* (Lisboa: Editorial Estampa, 1990).

Pearson, Michael N., "Markets and Merchant Communities in the Indian Ocean: Locating the Portuguese," in Francisco Bethencourt and Diogo Ramada Curto, eds., *Portuguese Oceanic Expansion, 1400–1800* (Cambridge: Cambridge University Press, 2007), 88–108.

Peralta Rivera, Germán, *El comercio negrero en América Latina (1595–1640)* (Lima: Editorial Universitaria, 2005).

Pereira, Maria da Conceição Gomes, "As Feiras - Sua importância no contexto comercial de Angola. Sécs XV a XIX," *Africana: Revista da Universidade Portucalense* 6 (1990): 211–233.

Pinto, Virgílio Noya, *O Ouro Brasileiro e o Comércio Anglo-Português* (São Paulo: Companhia Editora Nacional, 1979).

Poortvliet, P.F., *De bemanningen der schepen van de Middelburgsche commercie compagnie 1721–1803* ([Kapelle]: Nederlandse Genealogische Vereniging – Afd., Zeeland, 1995).

Postma, Johannes, *The Dutch in the Atlantic Slave Trade, 1600–1815* (Cambridge: Cambridge University Press, 1990).

——, "A Reassessment of the Dutch Atlantic Slave Trade," in Johannes Postma and Victor Enthoven, eds., *Riches from Atlantic Commerce: Dutch Transatlantic Trade and Shipping, 1584–1817* (Leiden: Brill, 2003), 115–138.

Prado Júnior, Caio, *Formação do Brasil Contemporâneo* (São Paulo: Brasiliense, 1961).

Price, Jacob, *France and the Chesapeake: A History of the French Tobacco Monopoly, 1674–1791* (Ann Arbor, MI: University of Michigan Press, 1973).

Prooijen, Corrie van, "Van goederenhandel naar slavenhandel: de Middelburgse Commercie Compagnie 1720–1755" (unpublished PhD thesis, Leiden University, 2000).

Puntoni, Pedro, *A mísera sorte: a escravidão holandesa no Brasil holandês e as guerras do tráfico no atlântico sul, 1621–1648* (São Paulo: Hucitec, 1999).

Quirk, Joel and Richardson, David, "Europeans, Africans and the Atlantic World, 1450–1850," in Shogo Suzuki, Yongjin Zhang and Joel Quirk, eds., *International Orders in the Early Modern World: Before the Rise of the West* (London: Routledge, 2013), 147–152.

Raposo, Luciano, *Marcas de Escravos. Listas de escravos emancipados vindos a bordo de navios negreiros (1839–1841)* (Rio de Janeiro: Arquivo Nacional, 1990).

Ratelband, Klaas, *Nederlanders in West-Afrika (1600–1650): Angola, Kongo en São Tomé* (Zutphen: Walburg Pers, 2000) [Portuguese Trans. *Os Holandeses no Brasil e na Costa Africana. Angola, Kongo e São Tomé (1600–1650)* (Lisboa: Vega, 2003)].

Rau, Virginia, *Aspectos Étnico-Culturais da Ilha de Moçambique em 1822* (Lisboa: Centro de Estudos Históricos Ultramarinos, 1963). [Offprint: *Studia* 11 (1963): 123–162].

Rawley, James A. and Behrendt, Stephen D., *The Transatlantic Slave Trade: A History* (Lincoln, NE: University of Nebraska Press, 2nd Revised edition, 2005).

Reis, João José, *Slave Rebellion in Brazil: The Muslim Uprising of 1835 in Bahia* (Baltimore, MD: Johns Hopkins University Press, 1995).

Ribeiro, Alexandre Vieira, "The Atlantic Slave Trade to Bahia, 1582–1851," in David Eltis and David Richardson, eds., *Extending the Frontiers: Essays in the New Transatlantic Slave Trade Database* (New Haven, CT: Yale University Press, 2008), 130–154.

Richardson, David, "Cultures of Exchange: Atlantic Africa during the Era of the Slave Trade," *Transactions of the Royal Historical Society*, sixth series, 19 (2009): 151–179.

——, "Involuntary Migration in the Early Modern World, 1500–1800," in David Eltis and Stanley L. Engerman, eds., *The Cambridge World History of Slavery, Volume 3, AD 1420–AD 1804* (Cambridge: Cambridge University Press, 2011), 563–593.

Robertson, Claire C. and Klein, Martin A., eds., *Women and Slavery in Africa* (Portsmouth, NH: Heinemann, 1997).

Robson, Martin, "The Royal Navy and Lisbon, 1807–1808," in Malyn Newitt and Martin Robson, eds., *Lord Beresford e a Intervenção Britânica em Portugal, 1807–1820* (Lisboa: Instituto de Ciências Sociais, 2004), 23–47.

Rodney, Walter, *How Europe Underdeveloped Africa* (Washington, DC: Howard University Press, 1974).

Rodrigues, Jaime, "O Tráfico de Escravos e a Experiência Diplomática Afro-luso-brasileira: Transformações ante a Presença da Corte Portuguesa no Rio de Janeiro," *Anos 90* 15:27 (2008): 112–118.

——, "O Fim do Tráfico Transatlântico de Escravos para o Brasil: Paradigmas em Questão," in Keila Grinberg and Ricardo Salles, eds., *O Brasil Império* (Rio de Janeiro: Civilização Brasileira, 2009), 2: 328.

Romano, Ruggiero, *Conjuncturas Opuestas* (México: Fondo de Cultura, 1993).

——, *Mecanismo y elementos del sistema económico colonial americano. Siglos XVI–XVIII* (México: Colegio de México; Fideicomisso Historia de Las Américas, FCE, 2004).

Russell-Wood, A.J., *The Black Man in Slavery and Freedom in Colonial Brazil* (New York, NY: Macmillan Press, 1982).

Russell-Wood, A.J.R., *The Portuguese Empire, 1415–1808: A World on the Move* (Baltimore, MD: John Hopkins University Press, 1998).

Saldanha, António, *As capitanias do Brasil: antecedentes, desenvolvimento e extinção de um fenômeno atlântico* (Lisboa: Comissão Nacional para as Comemorações dos Descobrimentos Portugueses, 2001).

Salvador, José Gonçalves, *Cristãos-novos e o comércio no Atlântico meridional* (São Paulo: Pioneira, 1978).

Santos, Catarina Madeira, "Luanda: A Colonial City between Africa and the Atlantic, 17th and 18th centuries," in Liam Brockey, ed., *Portuguese Colonial Cities in the Early Modern World* (New York, NY: Ashgate, 2010), 249–272.

Santos, Maria Emília Madeira, *Viagens e Apontamentos de um Portuense em África: Diário de Silva Porto* (Coimbra: Biblioteca Geral de Coimbra, 1986).

Santos Pérez, José Manuel and Souza, George F. Cabral de, eds., *El Desafío Holandés al Dominico Ibérico en Brasil en el Siglo XVII* (Salamanca: Ediciones Universidad de Salamanca, 2006).

Saugera, Éric, *Bordeaux port négrier. Chronologie, économie, idéologie, XVII–XIX siècles* (Paris: Éditions Karthala, 1995).

Scelle, Georges, The Slave-Trade in the Spanish Colonies of America: the *Asiento*," *American Journal of International Law* 4:3 (1910): 612–661.

Schnurmann, Claudia, "Atlantic Trade and Regional Identities: The Creation of Supranational Atlantic Systems in the 17th Century," in Horst Pietschmann, ed., *Atlantic History: History of the Atlantic System: 1580–1830* (Göttingen: Vandenhoeck & Ruprecht, 2002), 179–198.

——, "Representative Atlantic Entrepreneur: Jacob Leisler, 1640–1691," in Johannes Postma and Victor Enthoven, eds., *Riches from the Atlantic Trade: Dutch Transatlantic Trade and Shipping, 1585–1817* (Leiden: Brill, 2003), 259–286.

Schultz, Kirsten, "The Crisis of Empire and the Problem of Slavery: Portugal and Brazil, c. 1700–c. 1820," *Common Knowledge* 11 (2005): 262–282.

——, "The Transfer of the Portuguese Court and Ideas of Empire," *Portuguese Studies Review* 15:1–2 (2007): 367–391.

Schwartz, Stuart, "The Manumission of Slaves in Colonial Brazil: Bahia, 1684–1745," *Hispanic American Historical Review* 54:4 (1974): 603–635.

——, *Sugar Plantations in the Formation of Brazilian Society: Bahia 1550–1835* (Cambridge: Cambridge University Press, 1985).

——, *Segredos Internos: Engenhos e escravos na sociedade colonial* (São Paulo: Companhia das Letras, 1999).

——, "Prata, Açucar e Escravos: de como o império restaurou Portugal," *Tempo* 12:24 (2008): 202–223.

Scully, Pamela, "Malintzin, Pocahontas, and Krotoa: Indigenous Women and Myth Models of the Atlantic World," *Journal of Colonialism and Colonial History* 6:3 (2005).

Searing, James, *West African Slavery and Atlantic Commerce* (New York, NY: Cambridge University Press, 1993).

Sheridan, Richard, *Sugar and Slavery: An Economic History of the British West Indies, 1623–1775* (Barbados: Canoe Press, 1994).

Silva, Alberto da Costa e, *A Manilha e o Libambo. A África e a escravidão, de 1500 a 1700* (Rio de Janeiro: Nova Fronteira, Fundação Biblioteca Nacional, 2002).

Silva, Daniel Domingues da, "The Atlantic Slave Trade to Maranhão, 1680–1846: Volume, Routes and Organization," *Slavery and Abolition* 29:4 (2008): 478–481.

Silva, Daniel D.B. and Eltis, David, "The Slave Trade to Pernambuco, 1561–1851," in David Eltis and David Richardson, eds., *Extending the Frontiers: Essays in the New Transatlantic Slave Trade Database* (New Haven, CT.: Yale University Press, 2008), 95–129.

Silva, Filipa Ribeiro da, "Dutch Vessels in African Waters: Routes, Commercial Strategies, Trading Practices and Intra-continental Trade (c.1590–1674)," *Tijdschrift voor Zeegeschiedenis* 1 (2010): 19–38.

——, "Crossing Empires: Portuguese, Sephardic, and Dutch Business Networks in the Atlantic Slave Trade, 1580–1674," *The Americas* 68:1 (2011a): 125–148.

——, *Dutch and Portuguese in Western Africa: States, Merchants and the Atlantic System, 1580–1674* (Leiden: Brill, 2011b).

——, "Dutch Trade with Senegambia, Guinea and Cape Verde, c.1590–1674," in Toby Green, ed., *Brokers of Change: Atlantic Commerce and Cultures in Pre-colonial "Guinea of Cape Verde"* (Oxford: Oxford University Press, 2012), 125–148.

Silva, Rosa Cruz e, "As Feiras do Ndongo. A Outra Vertente do Comércio no Século XVII," in *Actas do Seminário "Encontro de povos e culturas em Angola," Luanda, 3 a 6 de Abril de 1995* (Lisboa: Comissão para as Comemorações dos Descobrimentos Portugueses, 1997), 405–422.

——, "Saga of Kakonda and Kilengues: Relations between Benguela and Its Interior, 1791–1796," in José C. Curto and Paul E. Lovejoy, eds., *Enslaving Connections: Changing Cultures of Africa and Brazil during the Era of Slavery* (Amherst, NY: Humanity Books, 2003), 245–259.

Simões, Alberto and Toscano, Francisco A., *O Oriente Africano Português* (Lourenço Marques: Minerva Central, 1942).

Simonsen, Roberto C., *História Econômica do Brasil* (São Paulo: Companhia Editora Nacional, 1962).

Soares, José Carlos, *O "povo de Cam" na Capital do Brasil: escravidão urbana no Rio de Janeiro do século XIX* (Rio de Janeiro: FAPERJ & Letras, 2005).

Sommerdyk, Stacey, "Malemba Merchants: A Repositioning of West-Central Africa in the Transatlantic Slave Trade" (Unpublished paper, Stirling, 2009).

——, "Trade and the Merchant Community of the Loango Coast in the Eighteenth Century" (unpublished PhD thesis, University of Hull, UK, 2012).

Sommerdyk, Stacey, and Silva, Filipa Ribeiro da, "Re-examining the Slave Trade in the West-Central African Coast: Looking behind the Numbers," *African Economic History* 38 (2010): 77–106.

Sousa, Laura de Mello e, *Desclassificados do Ouro. A Pobreza Mineira no Século XVIII* (Rio de Janeiro: Graal, 1985).

Spicksley, Judith M., "Pawns on the Gold Coast: The Rise of Asante and Shifts in Security for Debt, 1680–1750," *Journal of African History* 54:2 (2013): 147–175.

Stamm, Anne, "L'Angola a un Tournant de son Histoire, 1838–1848" (unpublished PhD thesis, Université de Paris I, 1971).

Stols, Eddy, "The Expansion of the Sugar Market in Western Europe," in Stuart B. Schwartz, ed., *Tropical Babylons: Sugar and the Making of the Atlantic World, 1450–1680* (Chapel Hill, NC: University of North Carolina Press, 2004), 237–288.

Studnicki-Gizbert, Daviken, "Interdependence and the Collective Pursuit of Profits: Portuguese Commercial Networks in the Early Modern Atlantic," in Diogo Ramada Curto and Anthony Molho, eds., *Commercial Networks in the Early Modern World* (Firenze: European University Institute, 2002), 90–120.

——, "La 'Nation' Portugaise. Réseaux Marchands dans l'espace Atlantique à l'époque Moderne," *Annales* 58.3 (2003). 627 648.

——, *A Nation upon the Ocean Sea. Portugal's Atlantic Diaspora and the Crisis of the Spanish Empire, 1492–1640* (Oxford: Oxford University Press, 2007).

——, "La *Nacion* among the Nations. Portuguese and Other Maritime Trading Diasporas in the Atlantic, Sixteenth to Eighteenth Centuries," in Richard L. Kagan and Philip Morgan, eds., *Atlantic Diasporas. Jews, Conversos, and Crypto-Jews in the Age of Mercantilism, 1500–1800* (Baltimore, MD: Johns Hopkins University Press, 2009), 75–98.

Sweet, James H., *Recreating Africa: Culture, Kinship, and Religion in the African-Portuguese World, 1441–1770* (Chapel Hill, NC: University of North Carolina Press, 2003) [Trad. portuguesa: *Recriar África: cultura, parentesco e religião no mundo afro-português 1441–1770* (Lisboa: Edições 70, 2007)].

Swetschinski, Daniel M., *Reluctant Cosmopolitans. The Portuguese Jews of seventeenth-century Amsterdam* (London: The Littman Library of Jewish Civilisation, 2000).

Tadman, Michael, "The Demographic Cost of Sugar: Debates on Slave Societies and Natural Increase in the Americas," *American Historical Review* 105:5 (2000): 1534–1575.

Tavares, Ana Paula and Santos, Catarina Madeira, "Uma Leitura Africana das Estratégias Políticas e Jurídicas. Textos dos e para os Dembos," in *Africae Monumenta. A Apropriação da Escrita pelos Africanos* (Lisboa: Instituto de Investigação Científica Tropical, 2002), 243–260.

Teixeira, Cândido, "O Movimento Marítimo do Porto de Inhambane no séc. XVIII: a viagem do Batelão S. Ana e S. José, 1753/54," in *Seminário da História de Moçambique* (Maputo: Universidade Eduardo Mundlane, 1996).

Thornton, John K., "Demography and history in the Kingdom of Kongo, 1550–1750," *Journal of African History* 18:4 (1977): 507–530.

——, *The Kingdom of Kongo: Civil War and Transition, 1641–1718* (Madison, WI: University of Wisconsin Press, 1983).

——, *Warfare in Atlantic Africa, 1500–1800* (London: University College of London, 1998).

——, *Africa and Africans in the Making of the Atlantic World, 1400–1650* (Cambridge: Cambridge University Press, 1992) [Portuguese trans.: *África e os africanos na formação do mundo Atlântico: 1400–1800* (Rio de Janeiro: Campus, 2004)].

Thornton, John K., and Heywood, Linda M., *Central Africans, Atlantic Creoles and the Foundation of the Americas, 1585–1660* (Cambridge: Cambridge University Press, 2007).

Toussaint, Auguste, *L'Océan Indien au XVIIIe siècle* (Paris: Flamarion, 1974).

Trivellato, Francesca, "Juifs de Livourne, Italiens de Lisbonne, Hindous de Goa: Réseaux Marchands et échanges interculturels a l'époque moderne," *Annales* 58 (2003): 581–603.

——, *The Familiarity of Strangers. The Sephardic Diaspora, Livorno, and Cross-Cultural Trade in the Early Modern Period* (New Haven, CT: Yale University Press, 2009).

Unger, W.S., "Nieuwe gegevens betreffend het begin der vaart op Guinea, 1561–1601," *Economisch-historisch Jaarboek* 21 (1940): 194–217.

Unger, W.S., *Bijdragen tot de geschiedenis van de Nederlandse slavenhandel II: de slaven-handel der Middelburgsche commercie compagnie 1732–1808* ('s-Gravenhage: Nijhoff, 1961).

Vansina, Jan, "Long-Distance Trade Routes in Central Africa," *Journal of African History* 3 (1962): 375–390.

Vega Franco, Marisa, *El trafico de esclavos con Americas. Asientos de Grillo y Lomelini, 1663–1674* (Sevilla: Escuela de Estudios Hispano-Americanos, 1984).

Verger, Pierre F., *Flux et Reflux de la Traite des Negres entre le Golfe de Benin et Bahia de Todos os Santos du XVIIe au XIX Siecle* (Paris: Mouton & Co, 1968). [Portuguese Translation: *Fluxo e Refluxo do Tráfico de Escravos entre o Golfo de Benin e a Bahia de Todos os Santos: dos séculos XVII a XIX* (Salvador: Corrupio, 1987)].

Viana Filho, Luis, *O Negro na Bahia* (Rio de Janeiro: Nova Fronteira, 1988).

Vieira, Alberto, "Sugar Islands: The Sugar Economy of Madeira and the Canaries, 1450–1650," in Stuart B. Schwartz, ed., *Tropical Babylons: Sugar and the Making of the Atlantic World, 1450–1680* (Chapel Hill, NC: University of North Carolina Press, 2004), 56–61.

Vieira, Alberto, *O público e o privado na história da Madeira* (Funchal: Centro de Estudos de História do Atlântico, 1996).

Vila Vilar, Enriqueta, "La sublevacíon de Portugal y la trata de negros," *Ibero-Americanks Archiv* 2 (1976): 171–192.

——, *Hispano-America y el comercio de esclavos. Los asientos portugueses* (Sevilha: Escuela de Estudios Hispanoamericanos, 1977).

——, "Aspectos maritimos del comercio de escravos con Hispano-America en el siglo XVII," in Klaus Friedland, ed., *Maritime Aspects of Migration* (Köhln: Böhlau, 1989).

Voort, J.P. van de, *Handel en handelsbetrekkingen met West-Indië: wording en bedrijf van de Middelburgsche Commercie Compagnie 1720–1780* (Nijmegen: [s.n.], 1967).

Vos, Jelmer, Eltis, David, and Richardson, David, "The Dutch in the Atlantic World: New Perspectives from the Slave Trade with Particular Reference to the African Origins of the Traffic," in David Eltis and David Richardson, eds., *Extending the Frontiers: Essays in the New Transatlantic Slave Trade Database* (New Haven, CT: Yale University Press, 2008), 228–249.

Wallerstein, Immanuel, *The Modern World System* (New York, NY: Academic Press, 1974), vol. 2.

Wätjen, Hermman, *O Domínio Colonial Holandês no Brasil: Um capítulo da história colonial no século XVII* (São Paulo: Companhia Editora Nacional, 1938).

Wilcken, Patrick, "A Colony of a Colony: The Portuguese Royal Family in Brazil," *Common Knowledge* 11 (2005): 249–261.

Williams, Eric, *Capitalism and Slavery* (Chapel Hill, NC: University of North Carolina Press, 1994).

Wisse, Adriaan, *De Commercie-compagnie te Middelburg van haar oprichting tot het jaar 1754* (Utrecht: Druckkeri, F. Schotanus & Jens, 1933).

Yarak, Larry, "West African Coastal Slavery in the 19th Century: The Case of the Afro-European Slave Owners of Elmina," *Etnohistory* 36:1 (1989): 44–60.

Index